*Part of
my Life*

by the same author

LANGUAGE, TRUTH AND LOGIC
FOUNDATIONS OF EMPIRICAL KNOWLEDGE
PHILOSOPHICAL ESSAYS
THE PROBLEM OF KNOWLEDGE
CONCEPT OF A PERSON
THE ORIGINS OF PRAGMATISM
METAPHYSICS AND COMMON SENSE
RUSSELL AND MOORE: THE ANALYTICAL HERITAGE
PROBABILITY AND EVIDENCE
BERTRAND RUSSELL
THE CENTRAL QUESTIONS OF PHILOSOPHY

Part of my Life

The Memoirs of a Philosopher
by A. J. Ayer

Harcourt Brace Jovanovich
New York and London

Printed in Great Britain

LC 77-73110

ISBN 0-15-170973-4

First American edition

B C D E

To my children

Contents

1	My Family and My Childhood	13
2	Eton	34
3	Holidays	62
4	Oxford	75
5	Marriage and Vienna	115
6	Language, Truth and Logic	139
7	Family Life and Politics	167
8	Friendships and Travel	190
9	Becoming a Soldier	222
10	More Cloak than Dagger	251
11	Return to Philosophy	291
	Index	313

Illustrations

Ayer village   80
My Citroen grandfather and family   80
My mother and father on their wedding day   81
Four generations of the Citroen family   81
My mother in the late 1920s   81
The Citroen grandchildren in 1918   96
The College Wall XI 1928   96
E. E. Cummings's portrait of myself   97
Santander   97
Maurice Bowra with Martin Cooper (*by courtesy of
    Sir Isaiah Berlin*   97
E. E. Cummings   208
Isaiah Berlin as an undergraduate (*by courtesy of
    Sir Isaiah Berlin*)   208
Wittgenstein in the 1930s   208
Gilbert Ryle in the mid 1920s   208
Renee with Nancy Quennell   209
Myself as a lieutenant in the Welsh Guards   209
Myself in the early 1950s   224
My mother and step-father   225
Bertrand Russell and myself   225

Preface

In writing this account of the first thirty-five years of my life, I have had to rely almost entirely upon memory. I did keep a diary during my last year at school but when I re-read it a year or two later I was so embarrassed by its callowness that I threw it away, and except for a travel journal which I have lost, I have never kept another. The few letters that I have preserved all belong to a later period, and such records of my childhood as my mother might have bequeathed to me were destroyed in the war when the warehouse in which she had stored her property was bombed. This partly accounts also for the paucity of illustrations in the book. There would be even fewer of them, were it not for the kindness of Mrs Doris Bamford and Mr Karel Citroen, who provided me with most of the family photographs, Mr John Simopoulos, who sent me a postcard of the village of Ayer, Sir Bernard Burrows, to whom I owe the photograph of the Eton Collegers Wall eleven in which we both appear, Mr William Lakin-Smith, who had kept the snapshot which he took of me in Santander forty-seven years ago, Sir Isaiah Berlin who gave me two photographs, including the one of himself and Mr Peter Quennell, and others to whom I made an acknowledgement where the illustrations occur.

I am indebted besides to Mr Karel Citroen for information about his side of my family, to Sir Isaiah Berlin and Professor Hugh Trevor-Roper for checking my recollection of events in which they played a part, to Mr Peter Carter for consulting the records of Wadham College on my behalf, and to the present Dean of Christ Church, the Very Reverend Henry Chadwick, for information about the terms of my employment there and for supplying me with the details of the abortive attempt to laicize the college.

My thanks are due also to Messrs Faber & Faber Ltd., for giving me permission to quote four poems from the works of E. E. Cummings, to Messrs Routledge and Kegan Paul for permitting me to quote a passage from Cyril Connolly's *The Condemned Playground*, and most of all to Mrs Guida Crowley for the skill and patience she has shown in typing my almost illegible manuscript and for her help in correcting the proofs.

A. J. AYER
10 Regent's Park Terrace,
London N.W.1.
31 July, 1976

My Family and My Childhood

My Jewish grandfather had no liking for Judaism or indeed for any form of religion. He also believed that the Jews, throughout their history, had brought many of their troubles upon themselves by their clannishness and their religious obduracy. He himself had married a Jewess, but he wished that his children, all three of whom were daughters, should marry gentiles. As usually happened in the family, his wishes prevailed. My mother was the eldest daughter and I was her only child.

Neither my mother nor my father was of English descent. My mother's family came from Holland and my father was French-Swiss. There is a village called Ayer, across the border from Chamonix, from which our name may have been derived. My father had a theory that our ancestors were Spanish counts, but if he had any evidence for this he did not pass it on to me. There is indeed a Spanish word *ayer* which means 'yesterday', but I have not heard of its being a Spanish name. The only member of my family of whom I have been able to discover any record in the Swiss biographical dictionary is my grandfather, Nicolas Louis Cyprien Ayer, who was born at Sorens in the canton of Fribourg as long ago as 1825. After a stormy career as schoolmaster, political propagandist and editor of radical journals, he achieved at the age of forty-one what would nowadays be the remarkable feat of being appointed simultaneously to professorships of French, Geography and Economics at the Academy of Neuchâtel. He published a manual of statistical geography, an introduction to the study of Romance dialects, and four books on the French language, of which at least one, his *Grammaire Comparée de la Langue Française*, remained a standard work for many years. He was Rector of the Academy of Neuchâtel from 1873 to 1878 and died in 1884, twenty-six years before I was born.

The Swiss biographical dictionary is silent about my grandfather's private life. All that I know of it is that he married a girl called Sophie Henriette Raetz from the canton of Berne, who was nineteen years younger than he, and that after bearing him two girls and two boys, she left him and came to England, where she earned her living as a governess. I was never told the reason for their separation and never thought to ask any of my family about it.

My father, Jules Louis Cyprien Ayer, was born at Neuchâtel in 1867. When his parents separated, he and, I believe, the other children remained with my grandfather, but on my grandfather's death he joined his mother in England. She had had some Rothschild children among her pupils and made use of this connection to obtain for my father a place as a clerk in a Rothschild bank. My father showed some aptitude for finance and steadily improved his position in the bank. In 1898–9, he published in two parts a set of General and Comparative Tables of the World's Statistics. It makes very dry reading, but contributes to our name's appearing in the catalogue of the British Museum library in three successive generations, a fact of which I am perhaps irrationally proud. He also wrote one or two plays which were never performed or published. The only one of them that I read was a stilted melodrama about the Franco-Prussian war. I doubt whether it would have been any better if he had written it in French. He spoke English very well with hardly any trace of a foreign accent.

At the time when he met my mother, my father had become private secretary to Alfred Rothschild, a man about town and patron of the arts, who belonged to the group of rich men with whom Edward VII liked to be surrounded. In this way my father had gained an entry into Edwardian society, and all his life, remained, with his monocle, something of an Edwardian dandy. He was favoured by his employer and appeared to have very fair prospects. It was indeed partly on the ground of its being a good match that my mother was persuaded to marry a man who was twenty years older than herself.

My mother's maiden name was Reine Citroen. Because her family came from Holland, I had taken it for granted that they were Sephardic Jews, but my cousin, Karel Citroen, who has done some research into our family history, has undeceived me. He is sure that they migrated from Eastern Europe not later than the beginning of the eighteenth century. The earliest member of the family in the male line whom he has identified is a Jacob Moses, an itinerant fruit seller who was born in Amsterdam in 1740 and died in 1814. Towards the end of his life he adopted the surname of Limoenman, which his son, Barend Roelof, changed to Citroen, the Dutch word for lemon, at the request of his wife's parents who were socially superior to him, they being wholesale jewellers and he only a goldsmith, and thought the name Citroen more genteel. Barend Roelof became a retailer of jewellery and, in 1859, his son Roelof Barend founded a jeweller's shop in the fashionable Kalverstraat in Amsterdam. It remained in the possession of the family until the second world war when it was expropriated by the Germans. My cousin Karel's parents, who owned the shop, were deported and murdered, but he, at the age of twenty-one, escaped through France and Spain to England and served in the British Navy. After the war he regained possession of the shop and such of its goods as he could recover, but sold it outside the family a year or two ago, though it still retains the family name.

Barend Roelof Citroen had fourteen children of whom one, Joseph Barend, a wholesale jeweller, was my great-grandfather. Another son emigrated to France and his son, André Citroën, founded the firm of motor-cars which still goes by his name. I met André Citroën once when I was very young and disgraced myself by the child's trick of taking away the chair that he was about to sit on. This is one of the very few incidents of my early childhood that remains in my memory.

My Citroen grandfather was also one of the earliest manufacturers of motor-cars. He was born in Amsterdam in 1860 and given the name Dorus, which he later anglicized to David. He used to speak as if his parents had been poor when he was young, though they afterwards became prosperous. He himself was not at all a penny-pincher, but he always spread his butter thin, because he had been made to do so as a child; his mother told him that it tasted better when it was thinly spread. This could, indeed, be evidence of no more than parsimony. However that may be, he appears to have had to make his own way in the world. He traded in fruit at Antwerp and then prospected for diamonds in South Africa. His wife, Sarah Rozelaar, who was born in London, was the daughter of a diamond-dealer. Having acquired a little capital, he went into partnership with a man called de Jong to found the Minerva motor company. De Jong remained in Belgium and my grandfather took charge of the business in England. The company went out of existence some time between the wars when my grandfather had severed his connection with it, but in the early days of motoring, Minervas were a well-known model, rivalling Daimlers. My grandfather made a lot of money out of them. I do not know the date at which he settled in England, but believe it to have been in the 1890s. My mother was born in Belgium in 1887, but she was brought up and educated in England and spoke English as her native tongue.

My parents were married in 1909. I have a photograph of them, taken at the wedding, my father sporting a large moustache and my mother looking pretty and innocent, as indeed she was; she told my first wife many years later that when she married she was ignorant of the facts of life. They took a flat at Neville Court in the Abbey Road in north-west London, and I was born there on the 29th of October, 1910. The birth was difficult and I believe that my mother was unable to have any more children. I was baptized into the Church of England and christened Alfred Jules, Jules after my father, and Alfred after Alfred Rothschild who consented to be my godfather. As it turned out, this was not a fortunate choice. For reasons which I shall go into presently, my father was dismissed from his employment while I was still a baby, and my godfather took no further interest in us. He gave me a silver christening mug, which I have lost, and a name which I do not like and have never been called by until I became Sir Alfred. To my family and friends I have always been known as Freddie.

Though they had me baptized, my parents were not religious. Officially my father was a Calvinist, but there was nothing Calvinistic in his attitude to life, and while he may have held some vague belief in 'the eternal not ourselves that makes for righteousness', I think it would be accurate to describe him as an agnostic. My mother had stronger religious leanings, but thanks to my grandfather she had been taught little or nothing of the Jewish faith. When she married my father, she became a convert to Christianity, but I doubt if she ever had any very clear idea of the details of Christian theology. My parents never went to church, with or without me, but my mother taught me to say my prayers at night before going to bed, a practice which I continued until about the age of twelve. I had a utilitarian attitude to prayer, and came to doubt its efficacy when it failed to get me into the cricket eleven of my preparatory school. I have a slight recollection also of being once taken to a synagogue, probably to attend the wedding of one of my mother's relations. I remember nothing of the ritual, except that I thought it strange.

When I was about eighteen months old my father went bankrupt. He had been speculating in foreign exchange and in spite of his knowledge of finance was constantly at fault in his predictions. He borrowed from moneylenders to make good his losses, speculated more heavily as his debts increased, and then had to borrow again. It ended with the moneylenders putting bailiffs in our flat. Rothschilds did not like their employees to speculate, even successfully, and my father lost his position and Alfred Rothschild's favour. It fell to my grandfather to rescue us. My grandfather paid his son-in-law's debts but never really forgave him. Like many Jews, he had a very high standard of probity in business, and he regarded bankruptcy as a form of theft. My father's motives in proposing to my mother also became suspect to him. He offered to support my mother and me, if she wanted to separate from her husband, but she said that she did not. This may have been a disappointment to my grandfather, but his sense of responsibility prevailed and he established my father in some business in Brussels, where we went to live. I have no recollection of this period and never learned what my father's business was. It came to an end anyway with the outbreak of the first world war, which sent us back to England. My father, who was a naturalized British citizen, tried to get a commission in the army, but at forty-seven was considered to be too old. When he suggested that even at his age his knowledge of French might be put to some good use, he was told that 'All our officers speak French.' My grandfather then bought him a partnership in a firm of timber merchants. We took a small house in Kilburn, a rather poor quarter of north London. We lived modestly but were not too poor to employ a maid of all work, of whom I was very fond.

My father never recovered from this set-back. He did not like the timber business and I doubt if he was very good at it. His adventurousness alarmed his partner, a Russian Jew called Mr Bick, who feared that my father would ruin him. But by then the adventurousness was more in talk than action and I do not think that Mr Bick came to any serious harm. We used to visit him sometimes on Sundays at his house in Finchley. His grown-up daughters were

usually there with their actual or prospective husbands. I enjoyed
the hot-house domestic Jewish atmosphere and remember once
boring the company by reciting from memory the list of all the
English league football teams in the order in which they then stood.
The Bicks were kind, friendly people, but it was not the sort of
society to which my father had been accustomed. There was a
champagne side to him which languished in a domestic suburban
setting. He had not lost his taste for speculation but, no doubt
fortunately for us, did not have the resources for putting his financial
schemes into practice. The ideas which he had for writing plays
were not developed. He invented an anti-dazzle lamp for motor-cars
but could not get it marketed. In his later years he spent a great
deal of time in solving and composing crossword puzzles and I
remember that we had a great celebration when one of his com-
positions won a prize from some newspaper. He had the reputation
in the family of being a heavy drinker, but I did not learn of this
until after his death. He drank very little at home, and though he
sometimes returned from his office in very high spirits, I put this
down to his natural exuberance. Even as I grew older I did not see
him as an unhappy man, but he must have been more unhappy than
I realized.

The timber business prospered during the first world war and at
the end of it we moved to a better address, a four-storey house in
St John's Wood Park, with a garden large enough for me to practise
cricket in. We still did not consider ourselves rich enough to keep a
motor-car, but we had two servants, a cook and a housemaid, so
that my mother was spared any household drudgery. She had been
an intelligent girl and would have liked to go to a university, but
my grandfather considered this to be a waste of time and money for
girls and sent her instead to an art school for which she had no
aptitude. She used to play the piano, inaccurately but with feeling.
She made some attempt to teach me to play also, but I never got
beyond the scales. Her favourite piece was Coleridge Taylor's
Petite Suite de Concert and I still cannot hear it without nostalgia for
my childhood. My mother was a VAD nurse for some time during
the war and seemed to have enjoyed the experience, though she did
not continue with it afterwards. She was not trained for any other
kind of work, and I think that she suffered from having too little
to do. She was an avid reader, mostly of best-selling novels which
she borrowed from the local library, but she did not maintain the

interest in learning which she had shown as a girl at school. There was a neurotic strain in her which grew stronger as she grew older, and since I was also very highly-strung we were frequently at odds with one another. She would have liked me to be more of what she regarded as a normal boy, and while she was proud of my intelligence, she was also irritated by my display of it. I resented her attempts to impose some sort of discipline on me, was acutely embarrassed by the scenes which she sometimes made in public, and did not show her much respect. She needed more affection than she received from me or, indeed, from my father, who did his best to dissociate himself from our quarrels. Not that we were always bickering. We were happiest when we played games together, tennis and ping-pong, and mah-jong and dominoes and card-games like piquet. I used to go with her when she made the round of the local tradesmen in the mornings and I remember our playing spelling-games and the geography game in which you have to name a town or a country beginning with the letter with which the previous one ended. In many ways, we were more like two excitable and touchy children than like mother and son.

There was very little mixing between the two sides of my family, though each was internally united. My father's mother lived to be nearly eighty and we used to visit her in a small house which she had in Norwood. I was very fond of my grandmother whom I always called *Bonne Maman*. Though she had lived for so many years in England, she had made few concessions to English customs or indeed to the English language, and usually spoke to me in French. The younger of my father's sisters, my aunt Berthe, lived with her. Aunt Berthe was a widow whose husband had been in the Belgian colonial service. Perhaps he had a military post, continuing the tradition of Swiss mercenaries: at least he looked very military in his photograph. They had lived for a long time in the Belgian Congo and my aunt had brought back a pet monkey, a mischievous creature, to be approached with caution. She was a very intelligent woman and I had great affection and respect for her. She disapproved of the way in which my parents were bringing me up, though she did not feel entitled to interfere. She thought that I was nagged too much and also too much cosseted. For instance, I was never given a bicycle, or indeed taught to ride one, because of the danger of riding in the London streets. I cannot, however, claim that I felt this to be a hardship. I was not an adventurous boy, except in thought.

My aunt Berthe was childless, as was my aunt Marie, my father's older sister, who was also my godmother. My aunt Marie lived in Switzerland but she used to come to England regularly and take me out to lunch, always at the Trocadero, which seemed to me very grand, and then to a display of magic at Maskelyne and Devant's theatre. Her husband, my uncle Philippe, had a family connection with the firm of Suchard and had once been rich, but he had gambled his fortune away, setting a bad example to my father who partly blamed him for his own downfall. My father also had a younger brother, my uncle Charles, who was tubercular and lived in the South of France. I met him only once and was struck by his melancholy. He had a daughter whom I did not meet until I was grown up, and a son, Kenneth, who like my father came to England at the age of about sixteen and went to work in a bank. I suppose that he was about eight years older than myself. He was kind to me and used sometimes to take me to football matches. He was a very good-looking boy and had a full sexual life of which I was too young and innocent to be aware.

It was, however, my mother's side of the family of which we saw the most. For some years after I was born, my grandfather had an estate at Essendon in Hertfordshire and I remember a groom's trying to teach me how to ride a pony and my being bad at it and rather frightened. If I ever acquired the skill, I have long forgotten it. When war broke out, my grandfather was suspected of being a German spy, because of his guttural accent; he responded by calling a meeting of his neighbours to vindicate himself, which he did triumphantly. Having worked in the Ministry of Munitions under Winston Churchill, an experience which left him with an abiding contempt for Civil Servants, he was offered a knighthood which my grandmother persuaded him to refuse, on the ground that it would make them look ridiculous. He sold the estate at Essendon and bought a luxurious London house in Hamilton Terrace with a billiard room and a large garden. His second daughter, my aunt Betty, had married a racing driver who was confined to a hospital within a few years of the marriage and she and her two children, my cousins Jack and Doris Holloway, went to live with my grandparents. Jack was two and a half years and Doris five years younger than myself. The third daughter, my aunt Clara, and her husband, Reginald Kingsford, who had an interest in a family business which seemed to leave him a considerable amount of leisure, lived nearby with their two children, Donald, who was about the same age as Doris, and Madge who was two years younger. We all used to come together frequently at Hamilton Terrace and I was more like an elder brother to the others than a cousin. Otherwise I had very few playmates. The only one that I can remember was a girl of about my own age, with whom I used to play ping-pong. She was the daughter of an old schoolfriend of my mother's and her parents sometimes came to the house for dinner and bridge. My parents entertained very little and seemed to have very few friends outside the family. After his bankruptcy, my father's old friends dropped him altogether.

I was a solitary boy but not lonely. I collected stamps, spending many hours identifying them in the catalogue and finding the right places for them in my album and I also collected cigarette cards. I remember having a complete set of Allied generals and of actors and of cards containing tidbits of information such as what was meant by the Plimsoll Line. I had a model railway and a series of Meccano sets which gave me more trouble than pleasure. I tried conscientiously to follow the instructions but found it very difficult. I have never been at all good with my hands and to this day cannot mend a fuse or put up a shelf or master even the simplest piece of machinery. I am slightly ashamed of this incapacity, but perhaps not so much as I should be. I think that I could have made a greater effort to overcome it. To the extent that it leads other people to do things for me, it convicts me of some self-indulgence.

Most of all I enjoyed reading. I had an early enthusiasm for the Brer Rabbit stories by Joel Chandler Harris. Nowadays the old-fashioned Negro dialect in which they are written is thought to make them too difficult for young children, and editions are published which rob them of their flavour. I think this is a pity. I believe that children who have any taste for reading take pleasure in extending their range. I did find *Robinson Crusoe* difficult, attempting it too early, and remember being frightened by an illustration in the second part of a man's having his throat cut. I think that I must have been unusually susceptible to childish terrors, since I also remember being badly scared by a poster on a billboard, presumably a film advertisement, which luridly depicted the railway disaster of the Tay Bridge. This did not prevent me from enjoying the adventure stories of Henty and Major Gilson, and at a slightly older age those of Captain Marryat, especially his *Mr Midshipman Easy*, though some of the incidents in it and still more in his other novels shocked me by their brutality. I was good at memorizing verses and could and all too frequently did recite the whole of the poem about Horatius from Macaulay's *Lays of Ancient Rome*. I am afraid that my parents rather encouraged me to show off in this sort of way, which cannot have been at all good for me. A more personal taste was that which I formed for Barham's *Ingoldsby Legends*, particularly 'The Jackdaw of Rheims', and the one about Lord Tomnoddy and Sir Carnaby Jenks of the Blues.

At the age of eight I was given the first of Kipling's *Jungle Books* as a school prize, and acquired a liking for Kipling's work, both prose and verse, which lasted until I was well into my teens. Though I now find many of his stories rather thin, and think that he showed too much subservience to his 'Gods of the Copy-book Headings', I still greatly admire his skill as a writer. To borrow George Moore's metaphor from his acute appraisal of Kipling in *Avowals*, the splendour of the orchestration makes up for the shoddiness of many of the tunes.

I still possess a handsomely bound book which my grandfather gave me as a reward for winning this school prize. It carries in his clear decisive handwriting the inscription

> To Alfred Jules Ayer
> My dear Freddie
> Your Grandpa is very proud of your
> having gained the first prize at
> your school at the Summer Examination.
> It promises well for your future career.
> I hope you will continue as you have
> begun.
> London, August 1919
> D. Citroen

The rather formal tone, the touch of affection and the wish expressed were characteristic of him and of his attitude towards me. The book was called *Deeds that Won the Empire* and was written by W. H. Fitchett, an author whom I suppose to have gone even further out of fashion than the Major Gilson whom he supplanted in my favour. I must have shown my delight in this present, for a month later my grandfather gave me, in an equally handsome

binding and with a more affectionate inscription, the same author's
Fights for the Flag. I read and re-read both those books until I knew
them almost by heart. Their tone is unashamedly jingoistic and the
style not especially distinguished except in the passages which
Fitchett quotes from Napier's *History of the War in the Peninsula*.
They do, however, remarkably succeed in bringing the land and sea
battles of past centuries to present life. They gave me a taste for
military and thence for political history which I have never lost.

Of course not all my youthful reading was at this level. I think
that I rather quickly put behind me such precursors of present-day
comics as *Puck* and *The Rainbow*, but I was longer in outgrowing
Chums and the *Boy's Own Paper* and the school stories in *Gem* and
The Magnet, made famous by Billy Bunter. There were also novels of
school life, featuring such characters as Teddy Lester and The Bat,
and having such titles as *The Outlaw of the School*, in which the hero
behaved nobly in the face of unjust accusation, and cricket and
rugby football matches were won at the last minute in the fashion
of Newbolt's 'Play up! play up! and play the game!' My addiction to
these stories even survived my actual experience of school.

I was sent to boarding-school when I was seven, which was a
little young even for those days. I was small for my age, so small
indeed that in my first term I was not put into a dormitory but slept
in the same room as the headmaster's wife. Of course it may just
have been that the dormitories were full. I had previously been to
day schools in London but have no recollection of them. The
official reason for my being sent away to school so soon was to
preserve me from the air raids, allowing the headmaster to make a
joke in his speech at the end of term about my having made an
Ayer-raid on the first form; and indeed, one of my few memories
of the first world war is that of being woken during a Zeppelin
raid and carried down to the basement in a blanket. A further
reason, I suspect, for my being sent away was that my mother was
finding it difficult to manage me.

The school to which I was sent was in Eastbourne and was called
Ascham St Vincent's. It was not very different from St Cyprian's,
the preparatory school at Eastbourne which Cyril Connolly has
described in his *Enemies of Promise* and George Orwell much less
favourably in *Such, Such were the Joys*. Perhaps we were a little less
snobbish and not subjected to quite such intensive pressure. We
used to play St Cyprian's at cricket and football. The proprietor

and headmaster was a clergyman called Willis, who for a reason which I never discovered was known to the boys as 'Bug'. Both he and the senior assistant master were former Cambridge soccer blues. There were three or four other assistant masters, a matron, and sixty to seventy boys. We were made to work hard, mainly at mathematics, history and Latin, which I started learning as soon as I went to the school. Some French was taught but I cannot remember learning any science there. We had a school chapel and said prayers there every day, with a longer service on Sundays, though I do not think that our religious instruction was designed to go very deep. The discipline was fairly strict. Only the headmaster caned but the assistant masters and the matron could administer spankings. I received one or two spankings and one caning in my last year there for ragging in the dormitory. I do not remember there being many canings, though when they were given they were quite severe. The victims used to hold court in the lavatories afterwards, displaying the marks on their bottoms which the cane had made.

The school was run on competitive lines. Each boy on arrival was assigned to one of four sections, named after the English admirals, Nelson, Blake, Howe and Collingwood. The sections played one another at cricket and football and were awarded points for victory. Points could also be won individually for the section by doing well at work or games. The progress of the sections was marked on a board with little figures of athletes, or it may have been sailors, running up ladders. I did well at my work and usually came top of my form, not only in the examinations, but also at the weekly mark-reading. This must have been important to me, since I remember that on one occasion when I was listed as coming out third or fourth instead of first, I somehow gained access to the mark-book, found that my marks had been added wrongly, and took the book to the headmaster. I can recall his announcing publicly 'A mistake of a hundred marks' in a very shocked tone. It was clearly only a slip in addition on the part of the form master, though he did happen to be one who disliked me, calling me a little urchin because of my untidy appearance. I do not now think that this story does me very much credit, except as evidence that I had some moral courage. I suppose that I was eight or nine years old at the time.

We had a school uniform of cap and blazer and grey flannels, which we wore every day except on Sundays when we had to dress up in Eton suits and hard collars and were taken for a walk in crocodile along the sea-front. Sometimes we were allowed to ramble over the downs. There were no half-term holidays, but our parents sometimes came down on Sundays and took us out. Mine always took me to the Grand Hotel where I enjoyed listening to the Palm Court orchestra playing sentimental tea-time music. I did not suffer from home-sickness but looked forward to these outings as a break in the school routine.

The worst feature of the school was the bullying. Gangs would turn on one boy and make his life a misery for weeks. Then the pack would select a new victim and the previous victim would join in the hunt. I suffered for one term and used to hide in the lavatories during break to escape my persecutors. There may have been a nationalistic undertone to these persecutions, since a French and an American boy were also among the principal victims of them. The masters can hardly have been unaware of what was going on, but I can remember only two occasions on which they intervened. The persecution of the American boy was brought to an end by an assistant master's arranging a sort of duel. The boy was made to box a couple of rounds with another boy of about his own age who was arbitrarily chosen to represent the rest of the school. On the other occasion, when one of the principal bullies had been receiving an excessive dose of his own medicine, the headmaster read us a homily. The bullying was as much moral as physical. I had incautiously let it be known that I was of Swiss extraction and for a time was greeted regularly with cries of 'Nestlé's little milk-can'. It does not sound very pejorative, but I found it difficult to bear. On the other hand, I do not remember there being any anti-Semitism at this school.

Except for the time when I was being bullied, I got on reasonably well with the other boys. I was befriended by an older boy called Freddie Scott, arousing the jealousy of another boy who asked him what he could see in 'that handkerchief-sucking little thing', and I had a close friend called Nolan, whom I also saw sometimes in the holidays. We lost touch with one another when we subsequently went to different schools and I can remember nothing of him now except that he was thin and dark and good at games. The only contemporaries of mine at Ascham whom I still occasionally see are Robin Brook, now a power in the city and a former director of the Bank of England, who was two years my senior in College at Eton and commanded a cloak-and-dagger section in which I served during the war, and the critic Philip Hope-Wallace, who has a more vivid memory than I have of my being tormented and expresses remorse for his part in it. I remember him rather as a friend.

In my early years at Ascham, I may have overworked, since I came down with what was vaguely described as brain-fever. I walked in my sleep, which I have never done since, and had a series of dreams in which the story, which dimly comes back to me as having been about pirates and more enjoyable than terrifying, was resumed at the point at which it left off the night before. Later on, the work became easier to me, and although I was too competitive ever to be very idle, I did not put more effort into it than was needed to maintain my place in the school and keep myself out of trouble.

My ambition was rather to excel at games. I made no showing at the annual sports, still less at gymnastics, where I had difficulty in springing over the vaulting-horse and never mastered the art of climbing a rope, neither have I ever been able to achieve much more at swimming than to keep myself afloat. I did once reach the semi-finals, at some very light weight, of the boxing competition into which we were annually forced to enter, but that was only through a sort of desperate savagery. I simply covered up when I was then matched against a boy who had some skill. Such prowess as I had was in team-games. The school owned a fairly large playing field in which we played soccer in the winter term, rugby football in the spring and cricket in the summer. I enjoyed all these games, even though my achievement never quite matched my hopes. I showed some promise at cricket as a slow off-break bowler, but after being tried several times for the first eleven, in default of divine assistance I was relegated to twelfth man. I also failed in a trial for the soccer eleven as an inside forward. It was only for rugby football that I succeeded in getting my colours as a wing-forward. I was far too small and light for this position, but I made up for it by my ardour.

My concern with these games was not limited to playing them. It was also strongly vicarious. I took a comparatively slight interest in grown-up rugby football, though I followed the fortunes of the Harlequins and supported Cambridge against Oxford as I did in the Boat Race and in other contests. I had no connection at that time with either University but it was the fashion at Ascham to opt for one or the other. When I actually came to go to Oxford I had no difficulty in switching my loyalty. I supported Middlesex at cricket, since their headquarters at Lord's was close to where I lived, and chose Tottenham Hotspur as my soccer team for no better reason than that they were a London team and I liked the bravado of their name. I began to take an interest in their fortunes in the season of 1919–20 when they won promotion from the second to the first division, and became their devoted adherent in the following season when they won the Football Association Cup. I have remained so ever since.

While I was a schoolboy, my interest in professional football was nourished almost entirely by the reports of matches in the newspapers. I very seldom had a chance to see it played. Perhaps in consequence, I had at that time an even greater love for cricket. Wisden's cricketing annual became almost my favourite reading, and I could have named what I took to be the strongest eleven for every one of the sixteen first class counties. I bought or was given books with illustrations of famous cricketers, and took an interest in the history of the game, making a collection of Wisdens, some of which went back to years before I was born. I had fantasies of playing for England as an all-rounder, which showed a surprising resistance to their manifest improbability. My grandfather indulged them to the extent of paying in two successive years for me to have special coaching at Lord's. He once came to watch me and characteristically took the professional aside to ask him if I was ever likely to be any good at the game. The professional frankly told him that I had no chance at all, but my grandfather was kind enough not to report this to me until I had realized it for myself.

My failure to excel at the game did not at all dampen my enthusiasm for it. On nearly every fine day in the early part of the summer holidays I used to take myself to Lord's, with a packet of sandwiches for my lunch, and watch whatever match was in progress. Usually, at the end of July or in early August, it was a match between schools like Rugby and Marlborough or Clifton and Tonbridge, with none of which had I any reason to identify myself, but that did not matter to me. I made an arbitrary choice between them and became absorbed in the fortunes of whichever one it was. Nor did it matter to me that the cricket was not of the highest standard. There was at least the compensation that the very fallibility of the players made the game more dramatic.

I should indeed have preferred to be watching Middlesex, with Hearne and Hendren making runs for them, but I did not get to see many county matches because of their clashing in August with our family holiday. From the time that I was eight years old, except for one year when I had had whooping cough or some such childhood disease and the bracing air of the east coast of England was thought to be good for me, a change in our usual practice which I much resented, we always took our holidays abroad. Until I was in my teens, when we started going to Switzerland, we invariably went to seaside resorts in Normandy or Brittany, not to the smart places like Deauville or Le Touquet, but to Berneval and Paramé and Etretat, the kind of places that Boudin liked to paint. I think it was at Etretat that I saw Suzanne Lenglen play an exhibition game of tennis and caught a glimpse of the fabulous Lily Elsie who had starred in *The Merry Widow*. We did not do much in the way of tourism, but I remember a visit to St Malo and the Mont St Michel which made a deep impression on me. For years afterwards the omelettes of Mère Poulard to which I was treated at her restaurant in Mont St Michel were my gastronomic touchstone. In general, I was not a greedy boy though I had a particular liking for an anchovy paste known as Gentleman's Relish and also for Brand's A1 Sauce, so-called, according to the legend on the bottle, because George IV, when his chef had served it to him, had said 'Brand, this sauce is A1.' I was sorry to see later that this had been changed to 'Brand, this A1 sauce is excellent', which makes nonsense of the story.

Playing with French children in the hotel or on the beach did more for my French than anything that I learned at school. I saw too little of my grandmother to get much practice at home, though my aunt Berthe, who expected my French to be perfect, encouraged me to speak it when she visited us and went to some trouble to improve my accent. In fact my accent was not so very bad, though in those days I never came near to being bilingual. The first book that I remember reading in French, at about the age of ten, was a novel by Anatole France *Les Dieux ont Soif*, a story of the French Revolution, which my aunt Marie had given me. I managed to get through it but I found it difficult and this may have discouraged me. Starting with *The Three Musketeers*, which was one of my school prizes, I read all the novels of Alexandre Dumas that I could get my hands on, but I read them in English translations.

In the Christmas and Easter holidays we stayed at home and except that I lost interest in my stamp collection, I spent my time very much as I had before I went away to school. I read so much that my mother sometimes tried to stop me, saying half seriously that I would spoil my eyes. Apart from the small collection which I was building up, there were not a great many books in the house and those that we did have were mostly beyond my range, like the works of Voltaire, which I left alone, and the novels of Thackeray which I attempted before I could properly appreciate them. There was, however, also a set of extracts from old volumes of *Punch* which kept me entranced for hours on end. I used to read lying on the floor in front of the gas stove in our dining-room, where my father had hung a picture of a battle scene which he attributed to the Dutch painter, Wouvermans. My grandfather was sceptical and was of course right. It was, as I discovered many years later, a copy of a picture in the principal gallery in Vienna, by some minor German artist whose name I cannot now remember.

If I liked a book I constantly re-read it, so that my own supply kept me sufficiently occupied. I feasted on Sapper's stories of Bulldog Drummond and Jim Maitland, and on Edgar Wallace's *Sanders of the River*. When I discovered P. G. Wodehouse, I succumbed to him entirely, galloping through *Sam the Sudden* and *Jill the Reckless* and *The Girl on the Boat*, which reduced me to helpless laughter, and all the books I could find that featured Psmith. I also made inroads on my mother's reading and took my ideas of adult life from the novels of Ian Hay, condemned by George Orwell as 'an exponent of the "clean-living Englishman" tradition at its silliest', and the arch Denis Mackail and the historical romances of Jeffrey Farnol, with his muscular heroes and proud heroines, and the swash-buckling Rafael Sabatini. I accepted all their values without caring that they bore little relation to anything that I saw around me.

Although I have always prided myself on being a Londoner, and would sooner live there than anywhere else that I know, my knowledge of London as a child was not at all extensive. I was taken on routine visits to St Paul's and Westminster Abbey and the Tower of London, but they did not then capture my imagination. I much preferred going to the Zoo, where I had a particular affection for the sea-lions and the polar bears. My parents were not at all interested in the visual arts and I do not remember ever being taken to the National Gallery or to any of the museums. I liked travelling on the old open-decker buses with tarpaulins that one wore like steamer-rugs to keep out some of the rain, but seldom ventured on any other routes than those of the number 2, which went all the way to

29

Norwood, and the number 13, which took us to the multiple stores with the multiple names, Robinson and Cleaver, and Marshall and Snelgrove, and Debenham and Freebody, where my mother did her West End shopping. Even the name of the agency where we got our theatre tickets was multiple: Webster and Girling, in Baker Street. Just before the bus turned the corner past the park into Baker Street, there was the house where Maltby the tailor murdered his wife, and not knowing how to dispose of the body, left it in the bath until the smell betrayed him. For years afterwards nobody would take the house or the shop and I never passed it without a sense of excitement. That ghost has long since been laid, and though I still sometimes try to identify the place, my memory fails me.

Going to the theatre was our principal family treat. My father liked it less than my mother did and she and I therefore often went to matinées. The shows that I was taken to see were nearly always musical comedies, starting with *Chu Chin Chow* which once held the record for London's longest run. I remember no more of it than the 'Cobbler's Song' and the stately presence of Oscar Ashe. I saw the first London productions of *Rose Marie* and *No No Nanette*, with George Grossmith and Joseph Coyne, and the marvellous series of musical comedies which were put on at the Winter Garden, with Dorothy Dickson as the heroine and Leslie Henson or A. W. Baskcomb as the funny man. I learned the words of many of the songs by heart and sang them enthusiastically off key. I even taught myself to tap-dance and had not very serious visions of my going on the stage. My dancing was strictly a solo performance and on the very rare occasions when I went to children's parties and was cajoled or bullied into taking a partner, I was as awkward as could be. In the Christmas holidays I went at least twice to see *Peter Pan*, resolving not to say Yes when the audience is asked to bring Tinker-Bell back to life by saying that it believes in fairies, and almost certainly failing to keep my resolve; but most of all I enjoyed the old-fashioned Christmas pantomimes, with the masculine dame and the funny broker's men, and a strapping girl as the principal boy. On at least one occasion it ended with a harlequinade. I enjoy them still, though the slapstick has become subdued and the principal boys are not what they were.

My taste in novels and the ease with which I suspended disbelief inside the theatre would have made me a natural customer for films, but it was only much later that I became an addict. Cinema-going did not enter into the pattern of my mother's life, and consequently I went very seldom. The first film that I ever saw, at the age of nine, was an historical melodrama called *The Glorious Adventure* in which Lady Diana Cooper, not usually thought of as an actress, played the heroine. It was about the fire of London and was remotely based on Harrison Ainsworth's *Old Saint Paul's*. Probably my having read the book was the reason for my being taken to it. It gave me nightmares. Otherwise I remember only some spirited performances by Douglas Fairbanks senior, and two of Charlie Chaplin's greatest films, *The Kid* and *The Gold Rush*. The famous scene in *The Gold Rush* in which the little tramp makes elaborate preparations for a New Year's Eve party to which nobody comes moved me literally to tears.

Though I was happier in the holidays, I did not mind going back to Ascham, once I had become accepted by the other boys. I was thought to be scholarship material and at the age of eleven began to be taught Greek by a Mr Foster, a private coach whom the school employed for its scholarship candidates. He had an almost perpetual cold, but he was kind and a good teacher and I enjoyed learning Greek from him. Perhaps on the advice of my headmaster, my parents had put me down for Charterhouse and, knowing nothing about the school except that it figured in the works of Thackeray, I quite looked forward to going there. It happened, however, that another boy called Evans, a year older than I, was going in for a scholarship at Eton, and my headmaster put me in for it too. He did not expect me to be elected but thought that the experience would be good for me. I vaguely remember his coming with us to Eton, like a trainer with his horses, and our staying at a small hotel in Windsor. I was not at all nervous because I did not care about the result. The most that I wanted was not to disappoint my grandmother, then almost on the point of death, who had written in French to my father that while I was not going to be among the first, neither was I going to be among the last. In the event, I came in third, and Evans thirteenth, too low for a place in a year in which only ten scholars were admitted. If I remember rightly, he then got a scholarship to Charterhouse.

I was not at all pleased by my success, thinking of Eton as a snobbish school where the other boys would look down on me, and when my parents came to fetch me by train from Windsor, for the few days' holiday which I was thought to have earned, I spent most of the journey home in tears. They might have been persuaded by me to reject the scholarship, but my grandfather intervened, saying that it would be madness for me to forgo this golden opportunity. My parents not being rich, I could have had my schooling at Eton free, or nearly so, but my grandfather, believing quite wrongly that this might be held against me, insisted on paying the full fees.

I suspect that he also paid the bills at Ascham. He was a generous man and very anxious that his grandsons should make good: the granddaughters would marry and lead domestic lives. He was proud of me and fond of me too, though fonder of my cousin Jack who made up for being much less good at his schoolwork by having much the sweeter nature, but he was always apprehensive that my father's weaknesses would come out in me. I was a little afraid of him but admired and respected him. He did a great deal for me intellectually, presenting me with a fine edition of the works of Shakespeare, and Pepys's and Greville's diaries, and the *Confessions* of Jean-Jacques Rousseau, and Winston Churchill's biography of his father Randolph, surely the best book that he ever wrote, and several of Disraeli's novels. My grandfather had a great regard for Disraeli as a politician, and hoped that I would emulate him, a hope which was shared by my father who frequently reminded himself and me that the younger Pitt had become Prime Minister at the age of twenty-four. Like most men who have made their own fortunes, my grandfather was contemptuous of socialism. His principles were those of a nineteenth-century liberal, but he turned to the Conservatives when he became convinced that the country could no longer afford Free Trade. He had been greatly influenced by the Dutch writer Multatuli, who fostered his strong sense of justice and his religious disbelief. He did not press this disbelief upon me, but was gratified when I came to share it. His mind was practical and he had little taste for abstract speculation. In appearance, he was short and stout and forceful. He spoke French and German fluently as well as English and his native Dutch. Though he collected Chinese pottery, I do not think that he had much aesthetic sense. Like most Jewish people, he kept a good table but himself drank sparingly.

My grandfather was a patriarch, but not a domestic tyrant. My grandmother had a strong character of her own and usually had her own way in the house. There had been a crisis in their marriage when a young girl called Dehra came to Essendon as a companion for their youngest daughter, after the two elder daughters had got married. I think it unlikely that my grandfather had an affair with her, but he paid her such attentions that my grandmother declared that either she or Dehra must leave the house. It was Dehra who left. My grandfather was far too deeply attached to his family kingdom to sacrifice it for love.

He was the strongest influence in my childhood. Except for encouraging my competitiveness, I do not think that my years at Ascham had much effect upon my character. My troubles there had not robbed me of my high spirits or put me out of conceit with myself. I was intellectually precocious but socially immature. It would have been easier for me at Eton, had it been the other way around.

2 *Eton*

I went to Eton in the autumn of 1923, when I was not quite thirteen years old. As a scholar I was put straight into the upper school with boys who were mostly two or three years older than myself. The number of King's Scholars, as we were officially called, because we inherited our status from the foundation of the school in the fourteenth century by King Henry VI, was kept at 70, out of a total, in my time, of about 1100 boys. The scholars were housed together in a mixture of old and relatively new buildings, known in its entirety as College, and were therefore themselves known as Collegers. They were in the charge of a master called the Master in College, and there was also a matron who was supposed to look after their health. The other boys, who were called Oppidans, from the Latin word for 'townsmen', were dispersed in houses within walking distance of the schoolrooms, at an average of something over forty boys to a house. Traditionally, the Oppidans despised the Collegers, who tended to come from a lower social stratum, and spoke of them as Tugs, because they were believed to engage in tugs of war for the few pieces of mutton which was all that they were given to eat. By the time that I went there this prejudice had very largely, if not entirely, disappeared and our diet, if far from luxurious, was anyhow less scanty and more varied; but the nickname remained.

The Collegers who were admitted in a given year were known as an election, the size of an election being determined by the number of places which fell vacant during the year. My own election was unusually small in number. In my first half, as terms are inappropriately called at Eton, there were only five of us. The two above me, who had shared first place in the scholarship examination, were Bernard Burrows and Michael McKenna, a son of Reginald McKenna, a former Chancellor of the Exchequer who was one of the Liberals who had remained loyal to Asquith. Another son, David McKenna, came into College in the following year. The two boys below me were Neil Hogg, whose brother Quintin Hogg, the present Lord Hailsham, was also in College in an election three years senior to ours, and Andrew Carnwath, a quiet self-contained boy whom I found the most sympathetic of the four. Five more boys joined us in the course of the next two halves, but one of them was removed for some delinquency, and after a year or so, Neil Hogg, whose health was not equal to the damp climate of the Thames Valley, was put to school in Switzerland. The remaining eight of us went up in the school order together.

Life at Eton in the nineteen-twenties looked back very much to the previous century, especially in its outward trappings. We still wore black silk top-hats to go to classes and on any walks that took us beyond a particular landmark in the neighbourhood of the school. If you met a master in the course of such a walk you were supposed to touch your hat to him and he was supposed to acknowledge the salute. Collegers wore long black gowns not only in class but at the meals which they took in the ancient college hall. In chapel they wore white surplices. The smaller boys, who had not yet grown to the height of five feet four inches, were dressed in the same sort of outfit as we had worn on Sundays at Ascham. The hard white collars were not very comfortable, especially when the back stud came loose, but one got used to them. I remained in jackets, as it was called, for about three years. Those who had reached the prescribed height wore black suits of morning tails with white shirts, stiff turned-down collars and white ties tucked into them. In winter we wore black overcoats of some regulation pattern. Members of sixth form, which consisted of the first ten Collegers and the first ten Oppidans in the school order, and members of the Eton Society, a small self-perpetuating oligarchy, more familiarly known as Pop, wore stick-up collars and white bow-ties. The members of Pop also had the privileges, denied to other boys, of wearing coloured waistcoats, sponge-bag trousers, braid on their tail-coats, flowers in their button-holes and sealing wax on their top-hats, besides having the exclusive right to carry their umbrellas rolled and walk arm in arm with anyone they chose. The sombre dress of the boys in general was said to be due to the school's having stayed in mourning for the death of George III, unkindly described by Shelley, himself an Etonian, as 'an old, mad, blind, despised and dying king', but one who had taken a particular interest in the school. I can well believe this to be true.

On occasions our dress was less formal. We could walk about the school grounds in what was known as half change, which consisted in the substitution of a cap and tweed coat for the top-hat and tails. How you dressed for games depended in part on your proficiency. Footballers progressed from knickerbockers to shorts; cricketers from dark grey flannels, to light grey to white, the light grey being reserved for the second eleven and the white for the first. Those who had obtained their house or school colours for one sport or another could deck themselves out in a kaleidoscopic assortment of matching caps and blazers and stockings and long woollen scarves. One of the burdens imposed upon new boys was to learn the locations of all the houses, which were named after their housemasters, and the various combinations of colours that were associated with them.

There was also a certain amount of slang to be learned, though little in comparison with the pedantic profusion of Winchester notions. Masters were known as beaks. Oppidans called their housemaster M' Tutor and their matron M' Dame. One referred to one's preparatory school as one's private school and to one's parents as one's people. Food and drink that one bought for oneself was called sock, and to treat someone to something was to sock it to them. Studying was sapping and a hard-working boy was a sap. A boy who had failed to win any colours was a scug and he wore a scug cap. To engage in a rag was to mob and to be birched was to be swiped. In the official language of the school, examinations were trials, classes were divisions and to be in a master's division was to be up to him. Roll-call was absence, and failure to appear at it was shirking, as was missing a class. To be absent on account of illness was to stay out. Boys who were reported to the headmaster for idleness were given white tickets and boys whose work was commended to him were said to be sent up for good. The peculiar brands of football that we were made to play contributed a further score of technical terms.

On their arrival, Collegers were housed in a part of the old buildings called Chamber. Once it had been the Long Chamber and had housed all the Collegers in worse than slum conditions, without even a supply of water until well into the nineteenth century. An earlier request that water be laid on was met with the answer, 'You will be wanting gas and Turkey carpets next.' In the words of Edward Thring, who survived the experience to become a famous headmaster of Uppingham, 'Rough and ready was the life they led. Cruel, at times, the suffering and wrong; wild the profligacy.' No doubt for this reason the Long Chamber had been truncated and what remained of it in my time housed only the fifteen or so most junior boys in narrow cubicles, which were known as stalls. Each cubicle contained, besides a bed and a hard chair, an article of furniture called a burry, which served as a combination of a desk, a bookcase and a chest of drawers. There was also a wash-basin with only a cold water tap. Hot water was fetched in watering-cans from a source outside Chamber, poured into a small tin hip-bath and diluted with cold water which was drawn from the tap by a rubber syphon. The syphon was also used by the Captain of Chamber to beat his juniors for minor transgressions. Our Captain of Chamber was a boy in the election above called James Parr, who was to become a friend of mine at Oxford and like many Collegers returned to Eton as a master. He was a large good-natured boy and did not abuse his privileges.

Our stalls were not heated but a large fire was kept going in winter in the middle of Chamber. The practice of 'roasting' boys in front of this fire had not entirely died out, but it was not carried to any serious lengths. Nobody tried to emulate the Rugbeian brutality of *Tom Brown's Schooldays*. There was a large table beside the fire and one of the mild ordeals to which new boys were subjected was to have to stand on this table and sing a song to an audience of all the Collegers. My musical comedy favourites were not considered suitable and I had to make do with a nervous and squeaky rendering of 'My darling Clementine'. The performance was applauded beyond its merits. At the outset, my being the smallest boy in College procured me some indulgence.

I learned 'My darling Clementine' from a songbook which we used for what was called secular singing. This is one of my more pleasant memories of College, and certainly my most pleasant memory of its master. About twenty of the junior boys used to meet in his rooms and sing traditional songs like the one ending 'Britons never never shall be – married to a mermaid at the bottom of the deep-blue sea'. The one I remember best was an English version of 'The Judgement of Paris' from Offenbach's *La Belle Hélène*:

> Goddesses three to Ida went
> Immortal pains they sufferéd there

with the chorus:

> Evoe, wonderful ways
> Have these Goddesses now and then,
> Evoe, wonderful ways
> For subduing the hearts of men,
> For subdúing the hearts of men.

I still had not learned to sing in tune, but I had a sense of rhythm which carried me along. One of the songs was set to verses which I have always attributed to Kipling, though I cannot now find them in his works. The chorus contained the line 'Hathi, Hathi, Hathi, Hathi, Oont and Buffalo', 'hathi' being an Indian word for elephant and 'oont' an Indian word for camel. It then went on 'Aya, Aya, Aya, Aya . . .' As a result of this I acquired the nickname 'Hathi', which gave me pleasure, not because I particularly liked the name, but because it was bestowed affectionately. To my regret, it did not catch on and I ceased to be called by it after the first year. The more obvious nickname of 'Hot Ayer', which unfriendly Oppidans sometimes gave me, did not please me at all.

During one's first year one had to do a certain amount of fagging for the senior boys. It mainly consisted in being sent on errands, either to buy things in the Eton shops, or to deliver notes to boys in other houses. The sixth-former would station himself at the entrance to Chamber and shout 'Boy' and everyone liable to fagging had to run to his call. Usually the last boy to arrive was chosen for the errand. One also had a personal fag-master for whom one's main duty was to make tea. Sometimes the fag-masters would take an interest in their fags and help them with their work. My fag-master was a boy called Gaspard Willis, who was the son of my old Ascham headmaster. No doubt he chose me for that reason. He was kindly but shy, and I had little contact with him.

After spending a year or so in Chamber, we progressed to rooms of our own, a luxury which Oppidans enjoyed from the start. The rooms were small with beds that folded back into cupboards and what would now be called utility furniture. There was, however, space for an armchair, and having also the occasional use of showers, which had recently been introduced into College, we lived in what we considered to be comfort. I made little effort to embellish my room, being content with some mediocre hunting prints which I bought cheaply from a boy who was leaving the school. I had no interest of any kind in hunting, but thought that I had better have something to put on my walls. I was still very much of a philistine and I remember, to my shame, making fun of a boy in my junior election for his attempts to write poetry. It was not until I was about sixteen that I began to take pleasure in Swinburne and Shelley and Keats, and even later before I developed any interest in visual art.

Having a room of one's own ensured us a degree of privacy which was all the more welcome from our having to do a great deal of work in our own time. School began at 7.30 in the morning. Coffee and biscuits were available beforehand but since one usually had to allow several minutes to get to the schoolroom, and punctuality was insisted on, I seldom got up in time to have them. After early school we had breakfast, and our next duty was to attend chapel for a service which lasted about half an hour. There were two longer services on Sunday, with a sermon, usually by a visiting preacher in the morning and a more racy address by the headmaster at evensong. We also had prayers in College every evening. This was rather an overdose of religion, particularly as we had to study divinity as well, but I enjoyed singing the hymns, especially the rumbustious ones like Bishop Heber's

> What though the spicy breezes
> Blow soft o'er Ceylon's isle;
> Though every prospect pleases,
> And only man is vile:
> In vain with loving kindness
> The gifts of God are strown;
> The heathen in his blindness
> Bows down to wood and stone.

The author had later changed 'Ceylon' to 'Java', presumably to improve the scansion and not as a moral judgement, but we adhered to the earlier version. There was another hymn containing the verse:

> Fading is the world's best pleasure,
> All its boasted pomp and show,
> Solid joy and lasting treasure,
> None but Zion's children know;

and for quite a long time I wondered what the pleasure of fading could possibly be. We had a professional choir to lead the singing, and to perform anthems on their own, and a famous organist called Dr Lee. I did not have the musical taste to appreciate his playing except when he marched us out of chapel to the strains of the trumpet voluntary which we attributed, wrongly, to Purcell.

The two school periods which followed chapel ended at noon and from then on we were free until a quarter to two, when we took our principal meal of the day. This was, however, an interval which we were expected to occupy by working on our own. The junior boys had to do their preparation under supervision in their tutor's pupil-room. My tutor was a Mr Crace who had just become a house-master and married a young wife, having previously been Master in College. He seemed very old to me, but was probably not much above forty. He was a kindly man and a painstaking classical scholar, with a great admiration for the light operas of Gilbert and Sullivan. I remember that when I was in his division he used to set us extracts from Gilbert for translation into Greek or Latin verse. It surprises me now that I was able to do it without very much trouble, but writing Greek and Latin verses, of which little more was demanded than that they scanned correctly and avoided false quantities, was a knack that came fairly easily with practice. It did not require any poetic gift.

On three days in the week there were two periods of school in the afternoon, the second of which ended at 6 p.m. Then we had tea, which we supplemented out of our own pockets, when we could afford it, with cooked food, like sausages and scrambled eggs, which we brought in from a local shop. Later we assembled in one of the old-school rooms for prayers, conducted by the Master in College, and then, after a frugal supper, all but the sixth-formers and the half-dozen boys immediately below them, which constituted a group known as Liberty, went early to bed.

Though we did not spend an excessive amount of time in school, the amount of work that we were expected to do out of school was quite considerable. In the first place, there were Greek and Latin construes to prepare. One had to be able to translate the text and also to comment on any knotty points of grammar that arose. I remember that in my first half we made our way through one of Virgil's *Georgics*, which I did not much care for because it was all about farming, and also, either then or in the next half, one of Aristophanes's plays. We proceeded very slowly and our approach was strictly philological. The masters did not indulge, or encourage us to indulge, in literary criticism. There was also some English history to be learned on our own, and some fairly elementary French, and a set of what seemed to me outrageously difficult mathematical problems of which we had to do as many as we could. I suppose that we also had to do some preparation for our lessons in science, but it cannot have amounted to very much. Neither, indeed, did those lessons themselves. I remember playing about with Bunsen burners and learning some rudimentary biology from a master known as Botany Bill, but that is all. If we were taught any physics, I cannot remember what it was. To this day, indeed, one of my scientific colleagues maintains that Etonian physics is a separate branch of his subject, but I dare say that he exaggerates its idiosyncrasy.

In addition to the work which we had to do in our own time to prepare for our lessons, we had to cope with what were known as Extra Books. This required us to master a book of Homer's *Odyssey* every half. The standard expected of us was such that we came to know the Greek text very nearly by heart. I do not think that any of us ever got the full 100 marks in the examination on it, but several of us came as close as 97 or 98, which I even then felt to be quite a creditable achievement for boys of thirteen or fourteen. Perhaps as a result, I have never cared very much for Homer and have never read his works since I left school.

One subject which we were not regularly taught was English literature. We were made to read some parts of Chaucer for the English paper in the School Certificate examination, but I think nothing else. We did, however, have a holiday task for which we were set a play of Shakespeare's or a novel by Walter Scott, I believe in alternate holidays. I remember reading Scott's *Guy Mannering* in this way and also Shakespeare's *As You Like It*, *The Tempest* and *Macbeth*. I never took greatly to Scott's novels but I was captivated by the Shakespeare plays and worked hard enough at them to win prizes in the examinations which were set on them when we returned to school. We also had 'saying lessons' once a week in which we were required to memorize and recite about twenty lines of verse in any language that we chose. After all these years I can still recite the first few lines of the opening speech of Aeschylus's *Prometheus Desmotes*, though I should be hard put to it to construe any other part of the play. When I chose English poems I took them from *The Oxford Book of English Verse*, selecting them rather for the ease with which they could be memorized than for their literary merits. For instance, one of my standbys was a poem about poets written in the mid-nineteenth century by Arthur O'Shaughnessy, which began:

> We are the music makers,
> And we are the dreamers of dreams,
> Wandering by lone sea-breakers,
> And sitting by desolate streams;
> World-losers and world-forsakers,
> On whom the pale moon gleams:
> Yet we are the movers and shakers
> Of the world for ever, it seems.

The ode takes a turn for the better towards the end, but I am not surprised to find that it has disappeared from the current edition of *The Oxford Book of English Verse*.

Occasionally, also, we were required to write verses of our own composition on any topic that we pleased, subject only to the condition that its name began with a set letter of the alphabet. Having become a great admirer of the works of A. P. Herbert, I tried to write comic verse but was not at all good at it. I remember that on one occasion when the letter 'M' had been set, I indited an ode to mussels which began:

> Oh my mussels, I adore you,
> I prostrate myself before you,

and no doubt continued in the same abysmal fashion. Once when I was in sixth form and confronted with the letter 'J' I wrote a serious sonnet entitled 'Juxtaposition' which greatly impressed Dr Alington, the headmaster. All that I can now remember of it is that it expressed a youthfully cynical attitude to things. I doubt if it had much literary merit. In later life I developed some skill at composing clerihews and acrostics, but my literary bent has always been prosaic.

Apart from the mathematics, for which I was fairly soon moved into a lower set, and the science, such as it was, I found the work relatively easy and did well at it. I seldom came lower than third in the division order, or in trials. On the other hand I never overtook either McKenna or Burrows, though I came within three marks of Burrows in the trials in which our final election order was established. Unfortunately, two boys who had become science specialists and were no longer competing with us had come above me in a previous examination, so that the three marks made a difference of three places. One of these two was a boy called Gregor Grant who, since my relations with Andrew Carnwath had cooled, was the nearest that I had to a friend in my own election. He was a quiet, unassuming boy who had already decided to become a doctor. I took the initiative in our friendship and he bore with my bumptious-ness. We used to go for walks together on Sunday afternoons, almost always to Windsor Castle. We never went inside the castle, which may not at that time have been open to the public, but walked on the terrace around the battlements.

Sunday was the only day on which we had no duty to take exercise. On other days it was compulsory in all seasons except for the most senior boys. I did not object to this because I still enjoyed playing games. In the summer half one could either be a 'wet-bob' and row, or a 'dry-bob' and play cricket: tennis was not much esteemed, but there were a few courts. In the Lent half we had a wider choice. You could play racquets, if you could afford it, or squash or Eton fives, if your hands were hard enough, or soccer or rugger; you could run with the Eton beagles, or if the worst came to the worst, go for a run on your own. In the autumn half there was organized football, which consisted mainly of the Field game. This was a primitive form of soccer, played with a smaller ball and narrower goals. There were scrums, known as bullies, but you could not heel the ball, and nobody could handle it in play. Since passing was not allowed, the game mainly consisted, apart from long kicking by the backs, in a series of mass assaults in which you tried to take the ball on when the man in front of you lost it. Three points were awarded for shooting a goal and one for scoring a 'rouge', for which you had to touch the ball down over the goal-line when it had gone off an opponent or you had kicked it over when in contact with him. After scoring a rouge the attackers could gain an extra point by charging in column and bundling their opponents and the ball into the goal. The column was known as a ram, which was also the name given to the twin columns of Colleger and Oppidan sixth-formers, as they processed into chapel.

I had a great enthusiasm for the game, and played in the College eleven for three years, first getting my colours when I was just sixteen. I played in the position of 'corner' on the edge of the bully, and though I was neither fast nor strong enough to be really good, I was an elusive runner and could control the ball. The College being arbitrarily divided into two sections, A and B, for the purpose of house-matches, I captained College A in my final year. There was, however, never any question of my playing for the school.

There was also the Wall game which was played mainly by Collegers because the wall from which it took its name stood in the College grounds. This must be one of the most boring games to watch that has ever been devised, but it was quite fun to play. It consisted chiefly in a scrummage against the wall with each side trying to gain ground with the ball by pushing the other back. You were not allowed to punch an opponent but you could put your fist in his eye and turn the knuckles. Since, even so, it was difficult to dislodge a player who was kneeling on the ball, the game remained static for quite long periods. When eventually the ball came loose, the aim was to kick it outside a furrow which ran parallel with the wall and a few yards from it. Play was then restarted at the wall at a position opposite to the place where the ball had come to a stop. Towards either end of the wall, chalk lines had been drawn on it, and when the attacking side had succeeded in carrying play beyond one of these lines, it could score a point by a complicated process of hooking the ball back and touching it against the wall. The point was called a 'shy' because it entitled the scorer to shy the ball at the goal, which at one end was a door in a side-wall and at the other a portion of a tree. Since both these targets were small and set at an awkward angle, and since the ball had to attain its mark without touching an opposing player on its way, goals were extremely rare; indeed, whole seasons passed without one's being scored.

One of the events of the school year was the Wall game between the Collegers and the Oppidans on St Andrew's Day. The Oppidans were the better athletes, but the Collegers had had more practice at the game, so that in most years the teams were evenly matched.

I was in the College eleven for two of these games, playing in the position of 'lines' beside the furrow. I forget whether we lost or drew the first of them, but we won the second by three points to nil. Because I was small and slight, it devolved on me to wriggle through to the wall and give the ball its final touch, so that I got to take all three shies. With my last throw I hit the edge of the door, and so narrowly missed securing a place in the annals of Eton, since a goal had not been scored on St Andrew's Day within living memory. After the game the College eleven used to assemble in Hall and drink from a loving cup '*in piam memoriam J.K.S.*' This was J. K. Stephen, a nephew of Leslie Stephen and cousin of Virginia Woolf. He had played Wall for College in the eighteen-eighties or thereabouts and had distinguished himself, if I remember rightly, by kneeling on the ball for a record length of time. He was a good minor poet in a comic and satirical vein, and wrote some very good parodies before he lost his reason.

The Wall game was the only one for which I got my school colours. I played for the school several times at rugby football, in the position of scrum-half, but lost my place after a disastrous visit to Dulwich in which we were defeated by something like forty points to nil. The trouble was that we did not get enough practice to be a match for schools which specialized in the game. There had been a time when Eton excelled at soccer, so much so that the Old Etonians reached the final of the Football Association Cup on six occasions between 1875 and 1883 and twice won the trophy, being the last amateur club ever to do so, but by my day the game had ceased to be taken seriously and no colours were awarded for it. I played at least once for the school as an inside forward and was invited to run the Soccer Club in my last half at Eton, but not having much faith in myself as an organizer and having by then a diminished appetite for playing games, I declined the invitation. I also played twice for College in their match against the Winchester scholars, another annual event. For some reason, which I cannot explain, I remember both games vividly. In the first year, when they visited us, we managed to draw with them after being three goals down: in the following year, on their ground, we won very easily, which rather surprised us, since we were a scratch side and they played regularly. I remember also being struck by the very low standard of comfort which the Winchester scholars appeared to enjoy.

45

I still wanted most to be good at cricket, but here I was disappointed. I had some success with my off-break in junior house-matches, and occasionally made a few runs, but I made no progress at the game and never even got into the College eleven. It is only in the last twelve years or so when I have been playing for the Fellows of New College in their annual match against the choir-school that I have emerged as something of a batsman. At Eton I finally gave up cricket for tennis, at which I was more successful, being in the pair that won the house doubles in my last summer half.

The usual penalty for shirking exercise was to be beaten by the house captain of games. Corporal punishment was mainly entrusted to the senior boys, in accordance with a system which generally prevailed in English public schools, since its introduction at Rugby by the pious Dr Arnold in the early part of the nineteenth century. Authority was exercised in the Oppidan houses by half a dozen boys who were known as the Library, and in College by the members of Sixth Form. The members of Pop also enjoyed special rights in this respect, and indeed made use of a special knotted cane. The procedure in College was for the victim to be summoned after prayers by a fag who went along the passages crying out that so-and-so was wanted. The wanted boy then went down to the room where the sixth-formers had their supper. If he saw a chair put out in the middle of the room he knew that he was for it. Having been told, unnecessarily, that he was going to be beaten, he took off his gown, knelt over the chair and received seven hard strokes, whatever the offence.

The first time that I was threatened with this punishment was at the beginning of my second year. My old Ascham headmaster had come down to Eton on a week-day and taken Robin Brook and me out to tea, causing me to miss a football practice. I either did not know that leave of absence was required in such circumstances or assumed that Robin Brook had obtained it for both of us, so that I was astounded to find the chair put out. I made my halting explanation and was so manifestly innocent of any intention to offend that the captain of College Field, a kindly boy called Richard Lloyd, allowed me to go free. It was the only occasion of this sort on which I did go free. I was beaten five times in all, twice for being generally noisy and obstreperous, a charge against which it was difficult to make any defence, once for being caught mobbing, once for running through a passage through which junior boys were supposed only to walk, and once for reading in bed after lights-out. The beatings, especially when they were performed by hefty athletes, were very painful but one was expected to bear them without crying out or flinching, and to say good-night, when one had resumed one's gown, without a quiver in one's voice. I managed to do this, not because I was particularly courageous, but because of the hatred which I felt for what seemed to me oppression.

One of the boys who beat me was Quintin Hogg, who displayed what seemed to me a more than judicial severity in the performance of the exercise. I have long since ceased to bear him any grudge for this, and though I share neither his political views nor his enthusiasm for the Christian religion, our relations in later life have always been friendly. He was a ferocious player of the Wall game and a brilliant classical scholar both at Eton and at Oxford. Another of my executioners was Freddie Coleridge, not, I now think, an ill-natured boy but an athletic conformist, who honestly believed that bumptious little boys should be forcibly put down. Returning to Eton as a master, he came to be Lower Master and Vice-Provost, and not surprisingly Chairman of the local Conservative party. Another was Anthony Wagner, the present Garter King at Arms in the College of Heralds. He was nothing of an athlete and summoned three of us the following night to apologize for not having beaten us harder. I feared that he was going to try again, but he was content to ask us to take the will for the deed. At that time he was a Jacobite and in some formula involving the royal family, which he had to pronounce as Captain of the School, he once substituted the name 'Rupert' for 'George', Prince Rupert of Bavaria being then the Stuart pretender to the English throne.

The sixth-formers could administer milder punishments, a favourite one being to set the offender a subject for an epigram. I quite enjoyed composing these epigrams, except that it encroached on the time which one needed to do one's ordinary work. The same was true of the punishments imposed by the assistant masters, which nearly always took the form of making one write out lines of Latin verse. If an assistant master wanted a boy to be beaten for idleness or showing disrespect, he had to send him to the headmaster, or to the lower master, in the case of a boy in the lower school. Beatings by the headmaster were ceremonious affairs. They were witnessed by two sixth-formers, called the praepostors, whose duty it also was to go round the divisions and summon offenders for judgement. I suppose that the praepostors were there to prevent the headmaster from carrying the punishment to excess, though I have not found any record of their actually intervening. The culprit was brought in with his trousers lowered and held down over the flogging-block by a porter, who seemed to be specially employed for this purpose. The headmaster then plied the birch, usually administering not less than six strokes. I witnessed one such birching and was glad that I never had to suffer it. Dr Alington was a vigorous man, but, to do him credit, he did not seem to relish the performance. Eton had progressed a little since the days of its most famous headmaster Dr Keate, who once mistook his confirmation class for a batch of offenders and when they protested flogged them all the harder for their impiety. His moral teaching was epitomized in his saying: 'Boys, be pure in heart. If you are not pure in heart, I'll flog you.'

I disapproved of corporal punishment, not only when it was inflicted on me, and when I was in Sixth Form both refused to beat anyone myself and, when others did it, made a rather feeble protest by walking out of the room. I tried to rally a party to help me oppose it more effectively, but met with no success. It was only some years later when I read Cyril Connolly's *Enemies of Promise*, a book which contains a fascinating account of the Eton in which he flourished, that I discovered that beating by sixth-formers had fallen into discredit in College a year or two before I came there, and had for a time been practically abolished. This liberal tradition very largely persisted during my first year when the Captain of the School was a charming and civilized boy called Richard Martineau, to whom I owed a great deal when he returned from Cambridge as our sixth-form master, but it did not take long for barbarity to be restored.

Its restoration was made easier by the personality of the newly-appointed Master in College, a man called H. K. Marsden who was known throughout the school as 'Bloody Bill'. He was a bachelor in his thirties, with a droopy moustache and very long legs which seemed to be always getting in his way. A teacher of mathematics, he had himself been in College shortly before the war, and after taking his degree at Oxford had immediately returned to Eton as a master. The same was true of many of the other masters, but he was exceptional in that his whole mental horizon was bounded by Eton.

This at least led him to take an interest in his boys, which might have borne better fruit had he not been a sadist and a repressed homosexual. He used to prowl about the passages at night and I could not go to the lavatory after lights out without his coming in to my room and asking me where I had been. Being a very innocent boy, I did not realize until long afterwards that he was suspecting me of homosexuality. He was not allowed to beat the boys himself, but he contrived to have them beaten by his sixth-formers, and later when he had an Oppidan house he blackmailed at least one boy, to my knowledge, into letting him beat him. He was much concerned about our masturbating and used on his nightly rounds to question us about our apparent loss of vitality. On one of these occasions I was weak enough to confess to sado-masochistic fantasies. He said little to me at the time, but betrayed my confidence to my grandfather, causing him unnecessary worry. I hated him at school and for some years after, until I saw him drunk at a Christ Church dinner and thought him more pathetic than odious. He was reported to have run his Oppidan house very efficiently and many of his boys were devoted to him, so that I suppose he must have had some better qualities. He was civil to me when I left Eton, saying that he felt that he had never understood me, and he told my grandfather that I should either be a great success or a great failure, which was complimentary in its way. Nevertheless I was angered by the fulsomeness of some of the tributes which were paid to him in *The Times* when he died some years ago.

I was on bad terms also with Miss Oughterson, the matron in College, but here the fault was largely my own. She used to entertain a group of the younger boys in her room when they returned from the holidays and on one such occasion was telling us how an anonymous telephone-caller had repeatedly disturbed her sleep. 'I can't think why anyone would want to do that,' she said. 'Can you?' Even though I could see that the question was rhetorical, I heard my voice saying, 'It depends how much they disliked you, Miss Oughterson,' causing an intake of breath throughout the room. It was a display of gaucherie, not malice – I was simply considering the possibilities – but it was not unnaturally taken as a deliberate insult, which she later returned by remarking of an oriental prince who was reputed, I dare say quite falsely, to think himself debarred by his colour from seeking a place in the school cricket eleven, that it showed the superiority of persons of any colour whose blood was unmixed. Even so, she was kind to me when I came down with mumps at the age of fourteen and swelled up and over like the figure in the advertisement for Michelin tyres. She read me Kipling's 'The Maltese Cat', a story about polo ponies which I still regard as one of his best, in spite of his making the animals speak. She also prayed over me, which I found embarrassing.

By that time I was beginning to have religious doubts, though they were not yet strong enough to prevent me from being con-firmed as a member of the Church of England, after receiving some diffident instruction from the Master in College. I was hesitant about it, but Marsden enlisted the support of my parents, who did not wish me to behave differently from the other boys, and I gave way to them. I went to Communion three or four times, but then decided that I did not believe in Christianity, or even in deism. I became a militant atheist and bored my schoolfellows by haranguing them about the contradictions in the Gospels and the weakness of the arguments for the existence of God. In chapel I used to irritate them further by muttering a running commentary on the fallacies which I thought that I detected in the sermons. It was the practice on Sundays for the boys to write religious essays which were known as Sunday questions, and when I reached sixth form at the age of seventeen, I took advantage of this to expound my anti-religious views. Dr Alington, who set us the questions, was a very liberal cleric and so far from taking offence at my arguments, he helped me to formulate them more effectively and even directed my reading. It was he who put me on to Lecky's *History of European Morals*, which is a storehouse of ammunition against the early and mediaeval Churches. The only thing on which he insisted was that I should continue to go to chapel.

Unlike attendance at chapel, enlisting in the Officers Training Corps was not compulsory. The theory of its being voluntary was, however, interpreted in a somewhat military fashion, and in practice very few boys succeeded in withstanding the pressure that was put upon them to join. The main inducement offered to us was that by obtaining a certificate of military proficiency called Certificate A we should be able to be commissioned straightaway as officers in the next war. It being so short a time since the great war to end war had been waged, I did not think it at all probable that the question of my becoming an officer would ever in fact arise. All the same, I joined the Corps and in due course obtained my Certificate A. I remember nothing of the weekly parades except that the puttees which we wore as part of our uniform were very hard to adjust, and very little of the field days except that they gave some boys an opportunity to smoke, a strictly forbidden act for which they would have been severely punished if they had been caught doing it at school. The officer who commanded the Corps, being a professional soldier and not an Eton master, cared nothing for this rule and contented himself with saying in his upper-class cockney accent, 'Don't loight up down the Hoigh Street.' We used to have to go to camp, with contingents from other schools, for a week or so at the beginning of the summer holidays. I took no pleasure at all in camping, and resented the encroachment on my holidays, but I remember having a feeling of exhilaration when we marched about Salisbury Plain to the strains of 'Bye Bye Blackbird'. I remember also enjoying the camp concerts and finding time to read Michael Arlen's *The Green Hat*. I was not able to identify myself with any of the characters but I took it as a model of sophisticated life.

Not caring much for being drilled, I contrived to have myself appointed to the signal section. I learned the Morse Code, which I almost immediately forgot as soon as I had no further use for it, and spent my time idly flashing lamps and making shutters wink, while chatting to Christopher Hobhouse, a boy in my junior election who became very fashionable at Oxford and wrote a good book about Charles James Fox, before being killed in the war. He shared my taste for the works of Lytton Strachey and the early novels of Aldous Huxley, which the Master in College disapproved of our reading, feeling them to be somehow subversive, without going so far as to confiscate them from us.

Another friend whom I made in the signal section was Randolph Churchill, an Oppidan of my own age who did not appear to have many friends at Eton. It may have been partly that which drew us together. He was a remarkably good-looking boy, who shared my interest in ideas which were not directly related to our work in school. I remember his enthusiasm for Evelyn Waugh's *Decline and Fall*, which I still think a marvellously funny book. He had a great deal of charm and had not then developed the arrogance which made him difficult company in his later years. We remained friends during the brief time that he spent at Oxford but afterwards saw little of each other. On the rare occasions when we did meet, I often found him irritating, especially when he insisted on my having confessed to him to being a member of the Communist party, a proposition which was false on both counts, but I never wholly lost my early affection for him.

After a time, even the delights of the signal section palled on me and I offered my resignation from the Corps. A little to my surprise, it was readily accepted. From then on, while the other boys paraded, I joined in the Greek lessons which the headmaster gave to his two younger daughters. I was a bit intimidated by the Misses Alington, but thought myself very lucky to be included in this aspect of their family life.

It is possible that my knowledge of Greek was more advanced than theirs, since by that time I was doing very little else but Greek and Latin in school. It was the practice at Eton for boys to specialize as soon as they had passed their School Certificate. I took this examination when I was fifteen, obtaining a distinction in Latin, Greek, French, History, English, Divinity and Mathematics, but failing in Higher Mathematics, as I had expected that I might. I thought then of specializing in history, which had remained my favourite subject, but was persuaded, it may have been by Mr Crace, to continue with the classics, on the ground that scholarships in classics were more easily obtainable at Oxford and Cambridge, the only English universities that Eton recognized, than scholarships in history. Before very long, I found myself having to compose in my own time pieces of Greek and Latin prose and sets of Greek and Latin verses every week, besides engaging in a more intensive study of the major classical authors. Our approach to them was still predominantly textual, though I did come to have some appreciation of their literary merits. I read the poems of Catullus for pleasure, and the Greek anthology and several of the plays of Euripides. How narrowly we specialized is shown by the fact that the interest we were expected to take in the ancient Greeks and Romans was very largely confined to their languages and literature. We learned very little about their way of life, not very much about their history, and nothing at all about their art. Other subjects were almost wholly dropped. We had an hour a week of 'extra studies' in which I learned a little more English history and in one half the rudiments of German. If our knowledge of English literature was also broadened it was because of the specimens which we were required to render into Latin and Greek.

I was a proficient classical scholar, but not outstanding. The blue riband for classical scholars at Eton was the annual Newcastle Scholarship, and I never came at all close to winning it in either of the years in which I entered for it. The examination included a paper on divinity, for which a special prize was awarded, and, on the principle of getting to know one's enemy, I worked hardest at the divinity. On the first occasion, the subject for which we had to prepare was the early history of the Christian church, and I became fascinated by the wild abundance of heresies, such as that of the Docetists who believed that Christ's body was a phantom, or the Manichees who thought that the world was delivered over to the devil. I was astonished also by the assurance with which the early fathers booked the front seats in Heaven to enjoy the spectacle of Hell, and the relish with which they looked forward to witnessing the torments of their enemies. My reading did not earn me the divinity prize, nor did it in the following year when we were set the Gospel of St Mark, and came to learn for the first time about the mysterious Q, the lost source on which the writer of Mark, the earliest of the Gospels, was supposed to have relied. One of my examiners in that year was a Mr Jenner from Oriel, whose nicety of scholarship was matched by his Protestant ardour. I took him to be referring to me when he said in his report that if you were as great an evangelist as St Mark or as great a philosopher as Plato you could venture to criticize them, but not otherwise. It struck me even then that life would be made very difficult for aspirants in almost any field of knowledge if this principle were generally applied.

If I disagreed with Plato, it may have been on the question of the immortality of the soul, since I think that we had read the dialogues which relate the trial and death of Socrates. We had also been taken quickly through the pre-Socratics, for once not studying the textual fragments but trying to make sense of a book which summarized their theories. I have to confess that apart from the paradoxes of Zeno, which continue to trouble me, the little knowledge which I have of their work dates principally from that time. On my own account, I had also read at least one book by Bertrand Russell and one by G. E. Moore. I bought Russell's *Sceptical Essays* when it first came out in 1928, and was immediately captivated by the opening sentences:

I wish to propose for the reader's favourable consideration a

doctrine which may, I fear, appear wildly paradoxical and subversive. The doctrine in question is this: that it is undesirable to
believe a proposition when there is no ground whatever for
supposing it true.

Russell went on to say that 'if such an opinion became common
it would completely transform our social life and our political
system', and then and thereafter I was disposed to think him right.

I came to Moore more deviously. Though I still knew very little
about painting, I had become interested in aesthetics and had
bought Clive Bell's book on *Art* in which he defended the now
outmoded theory that the one quality common to all great works
of visual art is their possession of what he and his friend Roger
Fry called 'Significant Form'. A chapter of this book is devoted to
'Art and Ethics', and here Clive Bell followed Moore in taking
'good' to be indefinable and rejecting the hedonist theories which
either identify good with pleasure or at least take pleasure to be the
only thing good in itself. Before drawing on Moore's arguments
for this position, he began by saying:

> I have no mind by attempting to reproduce his dialectic to incur
> the merited ridicule of those familiar with *Principia Ethica* or to
> spoil the pleasure of those who will be wise enough to run out
> this very minute and order a masterpiece with which they happen
> to be unacquainted.

I obeyed this instruction and became an equally ardent convert
to Moore's ethical views. It was not until my second year at Oxford
that I came to doubt whether 'good' was an indefinable non-
natural quality. When I told this story to Clive Bell, some thirty
years later, he was noticeably pleased and repaid the compliment by
writing of me as the leading authority on Wittgenstein. This was
not the less kindly meant for being false.

One of the pleasures in being in the top classical division was
that one came up to Dr Alington. He was not so good a scholar as
Richard Martineau or as Martineau's predecessor Jack McDougall, a
friend of mine in later years, who spent only a brief time at Eton
before deserting us for publishing, but impressed us very much by
the cool, ironic way in which he imparted his considerable learning.
He was not very much older than we were but he seemed to us more
a man of the world than most of the other masters. Dr Alington's

learning was more wide than deep but he displayed it with an enthusiasm that I found infectious. There were those who disliked his style because it infringed the Etonian principle of 'nothing to excess', but I admired the self-confidence which went with his handsome presence and thought that his vitality more than made up for some uncertainty of taste. I was grateful to him also for his readiness to take us outside our narrow curriculum. I remember, for example, a lecture which he gave to the 'first hundred' senior boys on contemporary American politics and the relish with which he quoted the slogan 'Only Al can beat Cal', at a time when it was not yet decided that Al Smith would be the candidate of the Democrats in the presidential election of 1928, and not obvious, at least to us, that he stood no chance against Herbert Hoover, let alone Calvin Coolidge. Though the lecture was mainly designed to make fun of American politics, it left me wanting to know more. I read André Siegfried's *America Comes of Age*, learned all about the Solid South, as it then still was, and became an ardent champion of the Democrats, which I have ever since remained.

I remember also a course of lessons which the headmaster gave us one half on post-classical European history. They were not at all systematic, but conducted with great verve. He used a coded set of mnemonics which I found remarkably effective for memorizing dates. It depended on the choice of certain consonants, occurring as the initial letter of the words, to represent the numbers from o to 9: words which began with other consonants were not used, and words which began with vowels did not count. Thus the sentence 'Depart now or never', with the letter 'd' standing for 6 and 'n' for 2, placed the flight of the prophet Mohammed from Mecca to Medina in A.D. 622. 'The noble Emperor at last succumbs' continues to remind me that Fredericus Secundus, *Stupor Mundi*, died in 1250. For the conflict between the supporters of the Emperor and the Pope in Italy in the eleventh century, I have 'Think of Salerno, Guibert and Guiscard', which places one of the battles in 1077. I cannot explain why I should have found it so much easier to remember these sentences and the code than simply to memorize the dates, but there is no doubt of its being so.

The Provost of Eton in those years was M. R. James, a man of great learning who is now chiefly remembered as a writer of ghost stories. He was one of those people who are reputed to be able to finish *The Times* crossword puzzle while their breakfast egg is boiling. It may even have been true if he liked his egg hard-boiled. He did not do any teaching and for most of the boys remained a distant, if impressive, figure, who read the lessons in chapel. He did, however, run the Shakespeare Society which it was easy for Collegers to join. We used to go to his rooms in the evening and read a few scenes of the play that he had chosen. Assigning the parts beforehand, he sometimes told us to omit certain lines, thereby drawing our attention to obscenities which we might otherwise have missed. The point of them usually escaped me even when my attention had been drawn to them.

I took pleasure also in the meetings of the Essay Society, which was run by Robert Birley, then an assistant master, whom I greatly liked. It gave us an opportunity to try our hands at literary composition. I do not remember what the subjects of my essays were but I know that they were very derivative, being full of quotations from Bernard Shaw and A. P. Herbert and other authors whose wit I then admired. I went in once for the School Essay prize with Money as the set topic. I developed the theme that money is the root of all evil with much moral fervour, but I was outshone by Michael McKenna who, thanks to his father, knew something about economics. I was equally unsuccessful in my attempt to win a prize for declamation with an abstract disquisition on the concept of Power. The prize was awarded to an Oppidan, called Paul Stobart, who made a knowledgeable speech about European politics. The dignitary who was brought in to judge this competition was related in some way to Edward Ford, a self-assured, popular boy in my junior election, who afterwards became one of the present Queen's private secretaries, and I remember making a disgraceful scene with Edward, as if he were responsible for my being robbed of what I quite unjustifiably thought to be my due.

Formal oratory was encouraged at Eton, no doubt in honour of the tradition by which Etonians go into politics. The sixth-formers had to give recitations, known as 'Speeches', every half to an audience of a large section of the upper school. To be different from the others, I sometimes chose to make my recitation in French and I remember giving a histrionic rendering of Victor Hugo's description of a man drowning in a quicksand. My pride in my performance was only slightly diminished by my learning, through the Master in College, that one of the two French masters who actually were French did not think that my pronunciation had been impeccable.

The great day for Speeches was June 4, the day on which we commemorated the founding of the school. It was a whole holiday; even boys who were not in Pop were allowed to wear flowers in their button-holes; one's parents came down for the occasion. Speeches took place in the morning to an audience of masters and boys who had been able to get tickets for themselves and their guests: the performers dressed up in knee breeches. I remember taking the part of the merchant M. Guillaume in *La Farce de l' Avocat Pathelin*, earning praise from the *Eton Chronicle* for my acting and the pace at which I spoke. The *Chronicle*'s critic thought less highly of my delivery of Lord Randolph Churchill's speech about 'Chips' in which he made fun of Mr Gladstone's woodcutting, though my performance was well received and led my friend Randolph, the author's grandson, to share my family's false belief that I was going to follow in the footsteps of Disraeli. After the speeches some boys took their parents to lunch with their housemasters on lobster salad and strawberries; other families brought picnics; the town offered little in the way of restaurants. If the weather was fine, as it nearly always was, the long afternoon was spent in watching the first or second eleven play cricket against teams of Old Etonians. In the evening there was a procession of boats, with the oarsmen dressed like sailors in eighteenth-century prints. At one point each crew had to stand up in the boat, and one hoped, nearly always vainly, that one of them would capsize. A splendid display of fireworks brought the ceremonies to an end.

In spite of its rough justice, there was much to enjoy at Eton. If I was in the main not happy there, except in my first and final years, it was because I got on badly with the other boys in College. This was very largely my own fault. I was too pleased with my own cleverness and I had a sarcastic tongue. As a result, I made enemies without knowing it. I do not think that anti-Semitism had anything to do with it, though one heard reports of its existing in some Oppidan houses. A loutish boy in my election once passed me a note about my tabernacle's being in St John's Wood, but that was an isolated incident, and he had the excuse that I had never been at all nice to him. I wanted to be liked but did not know how to set about it. Finding myself rebuffed, I became pugnacious. As an older boy put it in the report which he wrote about some football match, 'Ayer was continually up in arms over somebody or something.' Later on I learned to bridle my pugnacity, though never wholly to repress it, and took refuge in a forced detachment. The school reports which we were given to take home included a letter from the Master in College. I used to read them on the way and once discovered that Marsden had said of me that I never knew when I wasn't wanted. I suppressed the letter, partly because I was ashamed of what it said and partly because I did not want to worry my family over something that they could do nothing about, but I took the words to heart. My response to them was to assume an affectation of indifference.

I did not maintain it very well. It was the custom for the senior boys to 'mess', that is, take their tea together in small groups in one or other's room. Not finding anyone to mess with, I refused to have a fag. I pretended that it was a question of principle, but in fact I merely wanted to spare myself and some small boy the embarrassment of having him wait on me alone. For a time I joined forces with a boy in my junior election called John Cheetham who was equally at a loose end because his friends in his own election were lower in the school order and had not yet been accorded the right to join a mess. Though we were brought together by the force of circumstance, we got on reasonably well. The son of an ambassador and himself destined for the Foreign Office, he was a cool, well-mannered boy, more worldly than I and in some ways more sophisticated: I remember his being very scornful of my having had even a childish admiration for A. A. Milne's stories of Winnie the Pooh. When his friends were able to join him, he abandoned me for them and I returned to my proud solitude. Some time later this group invited me to mess with them. I believe that they were asked to do so by the Master in College, though I did not know this at the time. Had I known it, I might have refused, but as it was I accepted their invitation with alacrity and very much enjoyed their company.

I had a similar experience with College Pop. Unlike the Eton Society, this had remained a genuine debating club to which Collegers were almost automatically elected when they attained sufficient seniority. The club met in the evening two or three times a half, and when elections had been held, the successful candidates, who had already gone to bed, were usually told of the fact by someone's coming to their rooms. I used to lie awake on those nights, hoping for a knock on my door and suffering when I heard the footsteps pass and the hand knock on another door instead. I had to wait until all the members of my own election and almost all of my junior election had been chosen, before I was allowed to join. Again, my principles should have led me to refuse, but I accepted with tears in my eyes. Once I had been elected, I unintentionally made the members regret their gesture by taking the debates too seriously.

I was not, however, altogether an Ishmael. I got on well enough with most of the boys in a superficial way, and there were two among them with whom my relations were quite close. One of them was a boy called David Hedley, in my junior election, a year or so younger than myself, with whom I made friends very soon after he came to College. He was a fair, sturdy boy, who was good both at work and games. He won the Newcastle Scholarship in my last year, defeating all the classicists in my election as well as his; we played together for College in the Field game, the Wall game and at soccer; he was my tennis partner in the doubles tournament which we won, and he got his school colours for rugby football. After I left, he was elected to Pop, perhaps automatically as Captain of the School, and was reported to enjoy its privileges, though we both had affected to despise such things. No doubt if they had elected me I should have been equally pleased. His father was a prosperous doctor and he had an elder brother in College, also a good athlete though not so good a scholar, who returned to Eton as a master. I once went to lunch with his family in Pont Street, during the holidays, but the occasion was not a success. They clearly thought that I was having a bad influence on their son. It was, indeed, a romantic attachment, though on my side not overtly physical. On the one occasion on which he put his arms around me and said that he loved me I was embarrassed and disengaged myself. After leaving Eton, he went to Cambridge and fell under the influence of Guy Burgess, a contemporary of ours at school whom I did not get to know until some years later. Whether at Guy's instigation or not, he became an ardent communist. On the last occasion that we met, some time in the late nineteen-thirties, I confronted him with a report of the extravagantly fulsome terms in which the speaker at some Russian congress had referred to Stalin. I expected him to agree that they were ridiculous, but he said that they expressed his own feelings. It was not so obvious then, as it has since become, that Stalin was such an unworthy object of them. By then, David was on the point of leaving for

America, having married an American. He ran the Communist party in California and died there in the course of the war. I have heard rumours that he did not die from natural causes but do not know whether they have any foundation. At school we used to read poetry together, and I still possess a beautiful edition of Shakespeare's sonnets which he gave me when I left. It is inscribed very simply:

Freddie, from David, 1924–1929.

My other close friend was Robert Willis, an older boy in my senior election. We became friends only in his last year, when he was Captain of the School. It was a time when I was still suffering from a sense of isolation, and his friendship meant a great deal to me. He was small and dark, as I was, but quiet and self-contained. He took no interest in games, but was a first-rate classical scholar who won all the prizes for classics both at Eton and at Oxford. It was because of him that I tried for a scholarship at Oxford rather than Cambridge and chose Christ Church as my college. I had an unsuccessful trial run on the occasion on which he obtained an open classical scholarship to Christ Church, and the following winter, at the age of eighteen, did better than I expected by gaining the first of the three open scholarships in classics that Christ Church awarded. The second went to John Cheetham and the third to Andrew Wordsworth, a boy from Marlborough, who became my best friend at Oxford. In those days we had to go to Oxford for the examination, but I remember nothing of it except that I profited in the general paper from having read Gilbert Murray's book *The Classical Tradition in Poetry* and that the weather was exceptionally cold. As a reward for my winning the scholarship my grandfather made me a present of £200, with which to buy a motor-car, if I chose. I went so far as to obtain a licence, for which at that time no test was needed, but spent the money on other things. I have never yet bought a car for myself or even learned to drive one.

By then I was much happier at Eton, and though I had declared my intention of leaving at Easter I thought that I might as well complete my six years there by staying on for the summer half. There was no practical purpose to be served by this, as I had already won a leaving scholarship the previous summer by coming second to Fitzroy Maclean, a studious Oppidan and a specialist in modern languages, in an examination called 'The Grand July', but I thought that it might be a pleasant ending to my school career. The reaction of the Master in College was to hint to my family that if they did not persuade me to leave of my own accord the school would insist on their taking me away. This can have been nothing but a piece of bluff, but he still regarded me as a subversive influence and was anxious to be rid of me. Had I known of it at the time I should probably have insisted upon staying, but as it was I yielded to whatever arguments were used and left at Easter as I had originally planned. It was the custom for Collegers when they left to write their own 'obituaries' in the College annals. Not being content just to put down a list of my achievements at Eton, such as they were, and not being able to think of anything witty to write instead, I took the feeble course of leaving my entry blank. I fear that I may have been influenced by my discovery that, many years earlier, Aldous Huxley had done the same.

3 *Holidays*

Except on June 4 and St Andrew's Day, my parents seldom visited me at Eton, but once every half the boys were allowed to go home at a week-end for what was called Long Leave. In the summer I spent two days of it at Lord's, in full morning dress, watching the Eton and Harrow match. My father took little interest in cricket and my mother none at all, but they usually came with me for the social occasion. The match always ended in a draw except in the last of my summer halves when Eton won handsomely, to my great delight. However mixed were my feelings about the school, my identification with its fortunes on the playing field was complete.

This was in addition to my other sporting loyalties, which continued to be fervent. Thus, my chief memory of the period of the General Strike in 1926 is of my celebrating my recovery from an attack of measles by taking myself to an almost deserted Lord's and watching G. T. S. Stevens open the Middlesex innings against Somerset by hitting the first four balls to the boundary. If I thought it a little strange that an amateur should choose to play in a county cricket match at such a time, it was only because I had gained the impression that almost every able-bodied man of his age and class was engaged in driving a bus or something of that sort. I was glad that they were doing so, because it created an atmosphere of gaiety, at least in the quieter London suburbs: I neither shared nor rejected any political views which may have stimulated them. By then we had a wireless set with crystals and earphones, so that I was able to listen to Mr Baldwin's speeches, but I do not recall their making any impression on me except as items of news. It was not until two years later when I read Bernard Shaw's *The Intelligent Woman's Guide to Socialism and Capitalism* that I began to take sides in contemporary politics. The book did not convert me to Shaw's peculiar brand of socialism, but it did instil in me a distrust of the Conservatives which I have never yet found reason to shed.

My long leaves always included a visit to the theatre. Graduating from musical comedy to revue, I developed a strong affection for Jack Smith, the whispering baritone, and for the crooners Layton and Johnson. I was captivated by the whole series of Cochran revues, with Sonny and Binnie Hale and the youthful Jessie Mathews, and took such great pleasure in Noel Coward's *This Year of Grace* that I can still give an imperfect rendering of many of its songs. I have almost as vivid a memory of the first London production of *Showboat* with Cedric Hardwicke as Captain Andy and Paul Robeson singing 'Ole Man River'. This being the level of my musical taste, I was annoyed to discover on one of my long leaves that my parents had taken tickets for a production of Mozart's *Così fan tutte*. As it happened, I enjoyed the opera very much, but I admitted it only as a single exception to our ritual.

I was also a faithful customer for the Aldwych farces, starting with the delicious Yvonne Arnaud and the perennially youthful Ralph Lynn in *Tons of Money* and continuing with the even funnier *It Pays to Advertise*, in which, as in its numerous successors, Ralph Lynn was joined by the raffish Tom Walls and by Robertson Hare, with his bald head and gravelly voice and air of virtuous indignation, who was fated to lose his trousers in almost every play that Ben Travers wrote. The playwright John Van Druten was a distant cousin of my mother's and although we seldom if ever set eyes on him, this may have predisposed me towards his *Young Woodley*, a play in which a schoolboy falls in love with his housemaster's wife. I remember taking the play quite seriously and indeed being greatly moved by it, though this is not something that I should have readily confessed to a few years later. Otherwise, I appear to have made little effort to see more serious plays. I had become a great admirer of Congreve, but as with Shakespeare and Shaw, I read the plays only as literature, without taking advantage of what opportunities there were to see them performed. For some reason I made an exception of Tchekhov, and I have a particularly vivid memory of a remarkable production of *The Three Sisters* which I saw towards the end of my time at Eton. I also once obtained special leave from the headmaster to come up to London to see a performance of Pirandello's *Six Characters in Search of an Author*, on condition that I wrote an essay about it. I had not yet read the play but I had read a review of it and decided that it would interest me. I forget what I put in my essay but think it probable that I linked the play to my fledgling interest in philosophy. As so often in Pirandello's work, the play is concerned with the different interpretations that are given to a series of events by those who participate in them in different ways, and I may well have seen this as putting in question the notion of objective fact.

My preference for comedy extended to the cinema, to which I went a little more often during my adolescence than I had as a child, but not very much. My new favourites were Harold Lloyd, whose films I found funnier than Chaplin's, though they did not compare with them in depth, and Buster Keaton, who combined humour and pathos in a different way from Chaplin but hardly less effectively. I also enjoyed the early silent films of Laurel and Hardy, and in a different vein Cecil B. de Mille's spectacular Western *The Covered Waggon*. But it was not until I went to Oxford that I began to have any serious appreciation of the art of the silent film.

Our social life still revolved mainly around the family. My cousins, Jack and Donald, had followed me to Ascham and it may have been partly for this reason that my grandfather, when he retired from business in the middle nineteen-twenties, disposed of his house in Hamilton Terrace and went to live in Eastbourne, in a house called Trevin Towers which was situated near the school. It was a strange-looking house, in the style of late Victorian architecture with touches of *art nouveau,* but large and comfortable, with a lawn tennis court in the garden, and greenhouses, in which my grandfather grew catleyas and cypripaedia and other varieties of orchid. My aunt Betty did not move with her parents to Eastbourne but took a house near Swiss Cottage in the same road as her younger sister's, so that, apart from the grandparents, the family remained geographically as well as socially united. When he left Ascham, my cousin Jack was sent to Oundle, because it had the reputation of being good for science, which was thought to be his bent. Donald did very well at Ascham, so much so that when my grandfather asked the headmaster whether he was as good at his work as I had been, the headmaster said that I was not in the same street. The unfortunate result was that when Donald duly won a scholarship to Eton, he got little credit for it from my grandfather because he came lower in the list than I had. He arrived in College the half after I left. I remember being asked by Marsden, after he had received a visit from Donald's parents, whether my uncle was an Australian. I chose to take this as a genuine question and simply replied that he was not.

My grandparents' removal to Eastbourne did not very much diminish the part that they played in our lives. The whole family used to assemble at Trevin Towers for Christmas, which we celebrated in a traditionally English way, and I quite often stayed there on my own. I had learned to play bridge, though my game did not meet my grandfather's standards and indeed tried his temper when he had me for a partner, and I became almost his equal at chess and dominoes. As always, I spent much of my time there reading. My grandfather had a magnificent edition, which I now possess, of Boswell's *Life of Johnson*, including the Journal of their tour of the Hebrides, and I became interested enough in Dr Johnson to read the preface to his edition of the works of Shakespeare, in which he brilliantly demolishes the classical theory that the action of a play must be continuous in time and space, and his *Lives of the Poets*, which is probably the best thing that he ever wrote. My grandfather also possessed a complete set of the works of Conan Doyle, and I came to take even more pleasure in the adventures of Brigadier Gerard than in those of Sherlock Holmes.

Trevin Towers was near the Eastbourne golf course and I made an effort to master the game, playing with my father when we were staying at Eastbourne together, and also occasionally elsewhere. My father had taken up bowls in the years when we lived in Kilburn, playing regularly at local clubs, and was also an enthusiastic fisherman, a pursuit in which I sometimes joined him without deriving very much pleasure from it, but he had very little aptitude for golf and I was no better at the game than he. I understood its attraction on the rare occasions when I hit the ball properly, but finding that these occasions did not grow more frequent, I gave the game up, at the age of seventeen or thereabouts, and have never attempted to play it since.

We still went abroad for our summer holidays, exchanging the north-west coast of France for Switzerland. We went once to Lugano, but usually stayed at Thun or at one of the other resorts in the neighbourhood of Interlaken. I did not attempt any serious climbing, having never regarded the existence of a mountain as at all a good reason for exposing oneself to the fatigue, let alone the danger, of struggling to the top, and used to spend the greater part of my time playing tennis. I won a couple of tournaments, including one that was grandiloquently styled the Championship of the Canton of Berne. The tournament did not live up to its title since the entry was pretty well confined to the hotel guests, but it gained me a silver cup which I have long since lost. I was a better than average tennis player, but not more than that. I could place the ball well and was quick about the court, but my service was weak and my strokes did not have enough power to enable me to compete in the highest class. I used to enter for boys' tournaments in England, but seldom got through more than a single round. At one of them, when I was about fourteen, I met Fred Perry and have been guilty of boasting in later life that I played tennis with him, but this is false. I did play against him at ping-pong, at which he was later to become world champion, and may have won a few points. When I was a year or two older I twice entered for the Boys' Tennis Championship which was then held at Queen's Club, but met with no success to speak of. On at least one of these occasions, the championship was won by Geoffrey de Ste Croix, a present colleague of mine at New College, where he is Tutor in Ancient History. There was an annual tennis tournament at Eastbourne, divided into major and minor sections, and I played in the minor events with moderate success. My grandfather had somehow got to know Bunny Austin, who seconded Fred Perry in the victorious British Davis Cup teams, and his wife Phyllis Konstam, an actress who starred in some of Hitchcock's silent films, and had them to stay with him in Eastbourne. In return for my grandfather's hospitality, Bunny Austin once offered to partner me in the local tournament, but I prudently declined the offer, for his sake as much as for my own.

As I grew older, I saw more of my cousin Kenneth, who once came with us to Switzerland, and as much as ever of my favourite aunt Berthe, who continued to live in Norwood after her mother's death. My aunt Marie no longer came to London to take me out, but on the last of our Swiss holidays we visited her and my uncle Philippe at their house at Vevey on the lake of Geneva. My father was in particularly high spirits and I felt closer to him than I had at any time since my early childhood. Less than a year later, he was dead. In the spring of 1928, at the beginning of my school holidays, I was with him one morning in the bathroom of our house in

London when he suddenly collapsed. He proved to have meningitis and lived only a few days longer. During his illness I went to stay with my grandparents in Eastbourne and was recalled to London too late to see my father alive. The funeral was held at the Golders Green Crematorium with hardly anybody but the family present. There was a moment at the end of the service when some machinery was operated to make the coffin slide away, presumably towards the flames, and though I prefer cremation to burial I found this more shocking than the heaping on of earth. Except at that moment, I do not think that I felt the loss of my father very keenly, though later on, when I had come to learn more about his life, I regretted that I had not known him better and that I had not been more of a companion to him.

It had been arranged that I should spend part of the holidays with a family in Auteuil, in the suburbs of Paris, in order to improve my French, and the arrangement was maintained despite my father's death. The place was normally a finishing-school for girls, but it accepted boys in the holidays when most of the girls had gone away. I found another boy there when I arrived and three or four girls who had stayed behind for one reason or another. One of them was a girl called Renée Lees who was eighteen months older than myself. She was the only child of a former colonel in the Royal Marines who had been a member of Shackleton's ill-fated expedition to the South Pole. He was one of the party whom Shackleton left on an ice-floe while he went for help. Captain Lees, as he was then, was not the best of mixers and it has been related that when the party faced the prospect of having to resort to cannibalism, he was chosen as the first to be eaten. Fortunately, Shackleton returned in time to make this unnecessary. After serving in the war, he became a stunt parachutist, performing remarkable feats of daring at a time when the art of parachuting was in its infancy. Having been sent on a military mission to Japan, he decided that he wanted to live there, resigned from the army and supported himself by teaching English at the Peers College in Tokyo. Though the family, the Lees of Blackrock in the neighbourhood of Dublin, belonged to the Irish Protestant ascendency, Colonel Lees was a Roman Catholic and had caused his daughter to be educated in a series of English convents of which she had unhappy memories. She had then spent several years in Japan before her father decided to curtail her freedom by subjecting her to the very light discipline of a finishing-school in France.

Though I did not learn all of this at my first meetings with Renée Lees in Paris, we came very quickly to the point of exchanging confidences. She was a remarkably pretty girl, small and vital, with brown hair, bobbed in the current fashion, a generous mouth and mischievous blue eyes. I was fascinated by her, but being innocent and romantic and unused to the company of girls I made no attempt to make love to her. At that time I think that she was mainly amused by me, interested in my ideas and caught up in my enthusiasm for them. She nicknamed me 'Monk', partly no doubt because of my innocence but also because of my resemblance to the portrait of Père Lacordaire which we saw together in the Louvre. We went about Paris in a group with the other English boy and one or two of the girls from the finishing-school, travelling in buses and on the Métro, talking incessantly, noisy young tourists, indifferent to the impression that we made. We went to the races at Auteuil and Longchamp, dallied in the Tuileries and explored the Bois de Boulogne. It was the first of my many visits to Paris and the most idyllic.

I returned to Eton for what was to be my last summer half and soon afterwards Renée went back to her father in Japan. It was over a year before we met again. We wrote to one another but not very often. I took pleasure in thinking of our time together in Paris but did not yet consider myself to be in love with her.

In the summer I went with my mother to Holland, to visit our relations. It was the first time that I had been there. We went to Amsterdam and The Hague and took a seaside holiday in Scheveningen. My visits to the Louvre in Paris had awakened in me a taste for looking at pictures and I obtained considerable enjoyment from the Rijksmuseum in Amsterdam and still more from the Mauritshuis in The Hague. Vermeer became my favourite artist and I also greatly admired the paintings of courtyards and the interiors of seventeenth-century houses by Metsu and de Hooch. I even liked the genre pictures of artists like Teniers and Jan Steen, though they failed to satisfy the austere criteria by which my reading of Clive Bell had taught me to judge works of art. Otherwise, all that I remember of this visit is the abundance of the hospitality which was offered to us. I came away with the impression that the Dutch ate six large meals a day.

Though my mother was only forty when my father died, her own health was declining. She suffered from sclerosis of the spine, which

did not incapacitate her but made her gait unsteady. My grandfather
had settled enough money on her to maintain her standard of living,
but even with servants to do the housework she was not equipped
either in health or temperament for living alone. So long as I was
at Eton, I was away for the greater part of the year, and when I
went to Oxford, where the holidays were much longer, I did not
spend all of them at home. My mother employed a series of young
women as companions, but either they irritated her or she demanded
too much of them, and none of them stayed for very long. After
about three years she gave up the house in St John's Wood Park and
took a flat not far away in a newly constructed block called Eyre
Court. The building was ugly but the flats were comfortable. My
mother's was large enough for me to have a room there and for her
to continue to employ a maid.

Having left Eton in the spring of 1929, I had to find something
to do in the summer before going up to Oxford. My grandfather
considered that it would be a good opportunity for me to learn
another foreign language and decided that Spanish would be the
most useful, mainly on the ground that the South American
countries were ripe for economic development. He hoped that I
should become a barrister and eventually go into politics, and I was
indeed already entered for the Inner Temple; nevertheless, he
thought it sensible to do something to equip me for a career in
business, and there was also the possibility that a knowledge of
Spanish might be of some advantage to me in the law or in politics. I
had no thought of becoming a business man, but I liked the idea of
learning another language and looked forward to what I foresaw
would be mainly a holiday in Spain. It happened that Professor
Allison Peers of the University of Liverpool ran a summer school
at Santander on the northern Spanish coast, and arrangements were
made for me to attend the course and in the meantime to board with
a family in Santander.

A week or two before I was due to go to Spain, I heard from
Renée that she was back in London. I went to see her at a flat in
Bernard Street where she was staying with some cousins. A year
earlier, on the boat on which she had travelled to Japan, she had
met a major in the Hussars who was sixteen years older than she.
He had fallen in love with her and had continued to pursue her
with the most honourable intentions while they were both in
Tokyo. Though she was not in love with him, she had entered into a

sort of engagement, mainly to please her father who wished to see her settled and thought it a suitable match. The engagement had not been formally announced and she did not seem to take it seriously. I do not think that she had ever written to me about it. There had been nothing in our letters, either, to foreshadow our behaving any differently from the way we had in Paris, but almost as soon as the first moment of shyness had passed we fell into each other's arms. Though we did no more than kiss, it meant a great deal to me, especially as it was an entirely new experience for me. I was going to be away for several months, but I did not fear the consequences for us. I believed that my return would bring us closer, and this sufficiently contented me.

For some reason Renée thought that it would be more adventurous for me to travel to Spain by boat, and though I am a bad sailor and had some qualms about the Bay of Biscay I followed her suggestion. The boat started from Liverpool and stopped for an hour or two at La Rochelle. I remember lying in a park there in the sunshine and having an intense feeling of being in harmony with nature. I wrote a letter to my mother about it in what I am sure was a self-consciously literary style. I had once had a similar experience at Eton when I was walking back alone after playing football and was suddenly seized with an extraordinary elation. These experiences remain in my memory because I have seldom again had anything like them. I am rather the sort of person of whom Wordsworth said:

> A primrose by a river's brim
> A simple primrose was to him . . .

This has not prevented me from admiring Wordsworth's poetry, any more than my lack of a religious sense has prevented me from admiring many works of religious art.

There was an older man on the boat who sought my company and ended by shyly asking me to sleep with him. It was the first time that such a proposal had explicitly been made to me. I was surprised and a little embarrassed but not affronted. I have never thought that the practice of homosexuality was wrong in itself, and the laws which used to discriminate against homosexuals seemed to me unjust. It was for this reason that some years ago I became Chairman of an Association for Homosexual Law Reform, which helped to bring about their amendment. I do not, therefore, think that I should have any qualms about confessing to homosexual practices if I had ever engaged in them; but in fact I never have.

In Santander I lived in the household of Señor Noval y Cagigal, a very small man with a large slatternly wife, a dapper grown-up son who seemed rather to resent the presence of English paying guests, and a plump daughter with dyed hair and a pronounced squint. There was another English boy there, called William Lakin-Smith, of about the same age as myself. The apartment was large enough for us to have separate rooms, and though I was somewhat disconcerted shortly after my arrival to find myself bitten by bed bugs, and though I sometimes wished for a more varied diet than the daily *cocido*, a constant reminder of the song:

> I'm Captain Jenks of the Horse Marines
> And I feed my horse on kidney beans:
> Of course it far exceeds the means
> Of a Captain in the Army

by Etonian standards we lived in reasonable comfort. Señor Noval gave us lessons in Spanish, which I found rather easy, thanks to my knowledge of French and Latin. I did not, however, work hard enough at it to become a fluent speaker. Neither did I make any serious effort to acquaint myself with Spanish literature, though I did acquire a taste for the poetry of José de Esproçeda, who belonged to the romantic movement of the early nineteenth century.

Such work as I did while I was in Santander was mainly on Plato's *Republic*, which I knew that I should have to study when I came to Oxford. I had been given Adam's large edition of the *Republic* as a leaving present by my Eton tutor, Mr Crace, and had brought it with me. I made notes in the margin, among other things pointing out the fallacies in the arguments which Socrates is represented as using in the first book. The fallacies are, indeed, not hard to detect, but looking at my notes dispassionately, at this distance of time, I still think well of them. There is a passage in the second book in which Socrates is made to criticize the poets for implying that the Gods are responsible for evil as well as good, and here I find that I commented:

> The *agathon* of a person can amount to no more than benevolence, and benevolence is not necessarily productive of good. 'Hell is paved with good intentions.' I am assuming that it is possible for a man to be 'good' without possessing discernment. Of course,

if to God's goodness be added omnipotence and omniscient foresight, then from his actions no evil can result. At the same time, since, until mankind becomes a colony of ants, someone's meat will always be someone else's poison, no action can have results wholly evil or wholly good but must be judged by the preponderance of one over the other. Thus if the result of God's action is to be wholly good (not merely good on balance) it follows that he can never interfere on behalf of a single person: and in fact that the act of creation at all is incompatible with causology.

I do not know how I came to think that 'causology' was the proper word for determinism but if one grants the utilitarian assumption that I was tacitly making, the reasoning still seems to me cogent. If I was aware at that time of Leibniz's contention that this is the best of all possible worlds, I probably thought that Voltaire's *Candide* had effectively disposed of it.

Another leaving present which I took with me to Spain was F. L. Lucas's essay on *Tragedy* which had been given to me by Richard Martineau. I thought and still think it a remarkably good book. I was particularly impressed by Lucas's attack on Aristotle's theory that the justification for the portrayal of tragedy on the stage is that it purges the spectators of their pity and terror, as if they normally suffered from a surfeit of these emotions, and I was very much moved by the passages which he quoted from contemporary or near-contemporary dramatists like Maeterlinck and Synge. Though their prose was dangerously poetic, it suited my romantic taste.

The Spanish monarchy was then still in existence, protected by the dictatorship of Primo de Rivera, and for part of the summer the court resided in Santander. One of its main social centres was the tennis club, at which I spent a great deal of my time. I made little contact with what seemed to me a set of rather dilapidated courtiers, but in a handicap tournament I did find myself drawn against the King's younger son, Prince Juan, the father of the present King. He was then a boy of about sixteen. Since I started at minus 40 and he at plus 15, he had little difficulty in beating me. Apart from its being thought desirable that the prince should win, the reason for my being given such an adverse handicap was that I had reached the semi-finals of what was officially described as the Championship of Northern Spain. The competition was not strong and I was very easily defeated by the Spanish Davis Cup player who went on to win the tournament, but it was the nearest that I ever came to playing tennis well.

It must have been at the tennis club that I met a young Englishman whose name was Fonteyn, or something similar to that. He was or had recently been an undergraduate at Cambridge. He took me under his wing and in mockery of my seriousness and innocence nicknamed me 'Clarence'. I tried to disclaim the appellation but he succeeded in giving it currency and I was weak enough to answer to it. He was a frequenter of brothels and on one occasion took me to one, in company with another young man who went around with us. I went reluctantly and when about half a dozen girls were brought into the room where we were and Fonteyn began to fondle one of them I cried out, 'No! No!' and ran from the house, hearing the girls call after me '*Que Loco*' – 'What a madman.' Nor could I be persuaded to repeat the experiment. Fonteyn had asked me to write to him when we got back to England, and I did so, but his answer gave me to understand that while I was a good enough companion for the beaches of Santander, I was not up to his social mark in London. I never saw or heard of him again.

I went to one bull-fight at Santander and had mixed feelings about it. I enjoyed the spectacle and admired the cool arrogance of Felix Rodriguez, the leading matador, and his artistry with the cape. But one of the other performers had difficulty in killing his bull and the sight of the bull with several swords in it, and the matador sweating and the crowd throwing cushions and hurling insults at him was not attractive. The horses wore padding, so that one did not see the wounds inflicted on them, but what I disliked even more than the suffering of the horses was the gradual wearing down of the strength of the bull. A year or so later I contributed a badly written article in defence of bull-fighting to a college magazine, but this was an affectation. I had not become an enthusiast, and never did so, though I was to find great enjoyment in reading Hemingway's *Death in the Afternoon*. When writing to my grandfather about the fight that I had seen I said that such pleasure as it had given me had not been sadistic. In answer he expressed surprise that I knew the word. This was the result of Marsden's betrayal to him of my confidence.

I remember nothing at all about Professor Peers's summer school except that he took us on an excursion to see the prehistoric paintings in the caves at Altamira. I was mildly interested by them but appreciated them very much less than I did the similar paintings at Lascaux which I saw many years later. This was not, I think, because they were any less impressive but because I had not yet developed a taste for primitive art.

One of the first things that I did on my return to England was to go to a performance of Noel Coward's *Private Lives*, with Noel Coward himself and Gertrude Lawrence in the leading parts. This play made a very deep impression on me. For a long time I took Coward's hero as a model of sophistication and made a half-conscious effort to imitate his manner. Happily perhaps, I was not very successful, as the model was not suited either to my ability or my character. Nevertheless, I continue to think it a very good play.

Renée was still in London and, as I had hoped, the effect of my absence was to bring us closer together. It was soon obvious that we were going to be lovers, and before the year was out we spent our first night together at the Royal Hotel in Russell Square. Renée had not entirely thrown off her Catholic upbringing, and her conscience was a little troubled. Mine was not. I was just nineteen and very much in love.

4 *Oxford*

My rooms at Christ Church were in Peckwater Quad, an eighteenth-century addition to the original sixteenth-century College, on the third floor of a corner staircase facing the magnificent college Library. They consisted of quite a large panelled sitting-room, heated by a coal fire, a small and chilly bedroom, and a tiny box-room, which I used only for storage. The college provided work-aday furniture. I covered the sofa and armchairs with flowered cretonnes which Renée helped me to choose. Under her influence also I bought good reproductions of a picture of a railway-cutting by Cézanne and a more famous portrait of a peasant by Van Gogh and hung them on the walls of my sitting-room. At that time the work of the Impressionists was still not very well known in England, and its merit officially contested, so that my choice of these reproductions, even though their originals had been painted in the nineteenth century, was something of a gesture towards modernity.

I resided in these rooms for the three years that I spent as an undergraduate at Oxford. It would have been four years if I had followed the course which was normally taken by classical scholars, but my taste for classical scholarship had waned and I did not relish the prospect of reading for Honour Moderations, which would have meant my spending my first five terms at Oxford doing work of a higher standard but of the same kind as I had done during my last three years at school. I therefore obtained leave from my college to take one of the groups in Pass Moderations at the end of my first term and to devote the next eight terms to Greats, which was primarily a combination of Philosophy and Ancient History. The reading which I was required to do for Pass Moderations amounted only to a book or two of Tacitus's *Annals* and part of Aristotle's

Nicomachean Ethics, and since the examination demanded little more than knowledge of the texts, I was able to pass it without difficulty.

The main method of teaching at Oxford, then as now, was the tutorial system. Throughout the time that I was working for Greats I was given two tutorials a week, one in philosophy and one in ancient history. Like most pupils in those days, I was taken individually, so that I had to write a weekly essay for each of them, on subjects set by the tutors. The essays were read aloud and then discussed for the remainder of the hour. This system was beneficial to the undergraduates, who were forced by it to do a certain amount of reading and also stood to profit from individual attention, but it made heavy demands upon the tutors, not all of whom were equal to them. Some tutors were shy with their pupils; a few were reported even to be inarticulate; some had set pieces which they delivered to each man in turn, no matter what he needed to know or might himself have said; others discouraged their pupils by pouncing too fiercely on what they took to be error: the best of them attended to their pupil's essay, pointed out its mistakes or omissions in a friendly way, argued the controversial issues that it brought up, and guided the pupil forwards, if possible to make his own discoveries. Nearly all of them were conscientious, and the number of their pupils, in addition to the occasional need for preparing lectures and the time unavoidably given to college and university business, left them little leisure for their own research. Fortunately the terms were only eight weeks long and a respectable number of books and articles did somehow get written. The tradition of sloth enshrined in Gibbon's picture of the Magdalen dons as 'decent easy men who supinely enjoyed the gifts of the founder' had stubbornly withstood reform, but a series of commissions had brought it to an end.

My Christ Church tutors in philosophy were Gilbert Ryle and Michael Foster, in Greek history Robin Dundas and in Roman history Bobbie Longden. Of these men by far the most important to me, then and afterwards, was Gilbert Ryle. He was twenty-nine when I first got to know him, a big man with something of a military manner, though he had not been old enough to take part in the first world war. As an Oxford undergraduate he had rowed in trial eights and an oar hung over the mantelpiece in his rooms. A confirmed bachelor, he was, in Dr Johnson's phrase, a very clubbable man and the communal life of the college suited him well. Like many philosophers, he found a pipe an aid to reflection. He had a great admiration, which I came to share, for the novels of Jane Austen. I do not think that he cared very much for twentieth-century literature, though he enjoyed Saki's wit. His own wit was incisive, but free from cruelty.

One of the qualities which most distinguished Ryle as a tutor was the breadth of his philosophical horizon. The dominant tone of Oxford philosophy at that time was surly and unadventurous. The three professors were J. A. Smith, Harold Joachim, and H. A. Prichard, all three approaching the end of their careers. Smith, who occupied the Chair of Metaphysics, was a good comparative philologist and well schooled in the texts of Aristotle; having come across some books by Croce and Gentile when he was at a loss for a theme for his inaugural lecture, he had rallied to their post-Hegelian idealism, for want of any other doctrine to profess. Joachim, who was the Professor of Logic, was a genuine neo-Hegelian, much influenced by Bradley. In 1906 he had published an excellent book on *The Nature of Truth* in which he attacked the correspondence theory of truth and defended a coherence theory. Finding difficulties in this position which he could not resolve, he had turned to the history of philosophy and studied Aristotle and Spinoza. He was a nephew of the violinist, Joseph Joachim, and himself devoted to music. I did not attend his lectures on logic but they were said to be annotated with a musical score, which varied from year to year, while the words remained the same. He was a cultivated man but no longer an active philosophical force. Prichard, the Professor of Moral Philosophy, was the most influential of the three. He had been a disciple of Professor Cook Wilson, the previous holder of the Chair of Logic, a philosopher little known outside Oxford but locally powerful, who was a fervent Aristotelian and had sat like Canute rebuking the advancing tide of mathematical logic. Cook Wilson had been almost morbidly shy of committing his thoughts to print and Prichard, who before his election to the chair had been so conscientious a tutor that his health gave way under the strain, had himself published little more than a short book attacking Kant's theory of knowledge and two or three articles on moral philosophy, in which he credited himself and others with an intuitive knowledge of what they ought to set themselves to do. Prichard was philosophically gifted, but narrow and dogmatic, and like Cook Wilson he disapproved strongly of the new tendencies in philosophy

77

which had been inaugurated at Cambridge by Bertrand Russell and G. E. Moore.

This hostility to the contemporary Cambridge school and in particular to the work of Bertrand Russell was shared by H. W. B. Joseph, the tutor in philosophy at New College, who vied with Prichard for pre-eminence in the lists of Oxford philosophy. Joseph was no less dogmatic than Prichard and hardly less meticulous, but whereas Prichard was hesitant in speech and given to silent disapproval, Joseph was quick and authoritative. He dealt above all in refutation and was ready to take on anything from Marx's economics to the theory of relativity. He was said to be a good tutor to men of ability who were content to follow along the lines that he laid down, but his merits were over-shadowed by the severity with which he lit on any mistake, however trivial, and his intolerance of any approach which differed from his own. The great American pragmatist, William James, hit him off admirably when he wrote, in reply to some published criticism, 'I feel as if Mr Joseph almost pounced on my words singly, without giving the sentences time to get out of my mouth.'

I did not meet Joseph while I was an undergraduate but I attended two courses of his lectures, one on ethics, in which he harked back to Plato, and one on the logic of relations, which was mainly an attack on Russell's views. The lectures were fluent but over-elaborate, and in attacking Russell, Joseph was chiefly concerned with scoring verbal points, without coming to grips with the problems which Russell was trying to solve.

The usual practice in Oxford, especially in the teaching of the school of Philosophy, Politics and Economics, which was starting a run of popularity that would lead to its outstripping Greats, was to concentrate heavily on the history of philosophy. This historical approach, provided that it is combined with criticism, is probably the best way of introducing beginners to philosophy, but a teacher is likely to lose the respect of his pupils if he limits himself to the discussion of what others have said, and they may even lose interest in the subject if it is not presented to them as one to which original contributions can still be made. It was therefore unfortunate that the main body of Oxford philosophers, whether they were tyrannized by Prichard and Joseph, or overwhelmed by their burden of tutoring, appeared to lack the will to develop any views of their own. Two notable exceptions were H. H. Price and R. G. Collingwood, who were to be appointed respectively to the Chairs of Logic and Metaphysics in the course of the nineteen-thirties. Henry Price, whose main interest at that time was in the theory of knowledge, was far from sharing the prevalent hostility to Cambridge. In basing his theory of perception on sense-data, he was both reviving an old philosophical tradition and following the recent example of Russell, Moore, and C. D. Broad. Because of this approach, which has since become suspect, in my view without sufficient reason, his book on *Perception* now seems old-fashioned, but it then opened new horizons to us. I listened as an undergraduate to the lectures on which it was based and was strongly influenced by them. As I put it many years later in the inaugural lecture in which I paid tribute to Price as my predecessor in the Chair of Logic: 'In the sombre philosophical climate of the Oxford of that time, here was a bold attempt to let in air and light: a theory of perception in which the principles of British empiricism were developed with a rigour and attention to detail which they had in that context never yet received.' Whatever the fortunes of sense-data, this still seems to me not to say too much.

My esteem for Collingwood came later. It arose from the books which he published in the nineteen-thirties after I had ceased to be an undergraduate. His view of philosophy as serving only to trace the historical development of the absolute presuppositions of our thought did not convince me, though I now think there is more to it than I then admitted, but I was impressed by the use which he made of it in his book *The Idea of Nature*, and I admired the style of all his books, whether or not I agreed with their contents. As he revealed in his autobiography, he had what seemed a personal as well as an intellectual contempt for the disciples of Cook Wilson and so far as possible avoided contact with them. The result was that he very rarely attended meetings of any of the philosophical societies. I did meet him once at some later time, when he came to dine in Christ Church, but we did not discuss philosophy. I am sorry for this as I think that I should have enjoyed arguing with him and should have profited by it.

Gilbert Ryle resembled Price in his willingness to learn from the Cambridge philosophers, but his interests were different. He had been very strongly influenced by Russell's philosophy of logic and was coming to regard the principal function of philosophy as being that of exhibiting facts in their proper logical form, which was often obscured by the grammatical form of the sentences that were used to state them. The essay 'Systematically Misleading Expressions', which he published in 1931, was his first development of this view in print, and it survives as one of the best examples of a line which others were to follow in the course of the decade. Previously he had been one of the very few British philosophers to take a serious interest in phenomenology, and had surprised his colleagues by putting on a course of lectures on Bolzano, Brentano, Meinong and Husserl. He had even pursued phenomenology into existentialism, at least to the extent of writing a critical but not altogether hostile review of Heidegger's *Sein und Zeit*. But there it stopped. The extravagancies of existentialism were not for him, and he did not trouble his pupils with them. We began in the normal way by studying moral philosophy and I remember writing essays for him on the intuitionism of the Cambridge Platonists and the moral-sense theories of Shaftesbury and Hutcheson, using the selections in Selby-Bigge's *British Moralists* as a text-book. These were not topics on which I had any very original ideas but I must have shown some critical acumen, since it was not long before Ryle gave me to understand that he thought I had the makings of a philosopher.

Though I may in the end have had more tutorials with Ryle than with Michael Foster, I started by going to them in alternate terms. Michael Foster had just arrived at Christ Church, having studied in Germany after going down from Oxford, where he had been a scholar of St John's, and having also put in time as a school-master. He was very different from Ryle, both in character and in his attitude to philosophy. So far from seeing any limitations in the historical approach and seeking to go beyond it, he conceived of philosophy as a purely historical discipline: he thought that it should consist in the critical study of the great philosophical works that had been written in the past. How they could ever have come to be written, if such a view had always prevailed, and why it was not possible that equally great works should be added to them were objections that he did not consider. Even so, he made an able defence of his position in the preface to his book *The Political Philosophy of Plato and Hegel*, a well-written book which was narrower in scope than its title suggested, since it dealt only with Plato's *Republic* and Hegel's *Philosophy of Right*. Foster's scholarship was minute but not extensive, and while he had a thorough knowledge of the *Republic*, he had not had the curiosity to read more than one or two of Plato's other dialogues. I had little liking for the political

The village of Ayer
in Switzerland.

My Citroen grandfather, seated with his arm resting on the table, with his brothers and
sister. About 1895.

My mother and father on their wedding day. London
1909.

Four generations of the Citroen family. My great-
grandmother, my grandfather, my mother and
myself. 1912.

My mother in the late 1920's.

sections of the *Republic*, on which he had most to say, and profited more from the tutorials in which we tried to make sense of the obscurer parts of Kant's *Critique of Pure Reason*, which was another of the works that he had studied. I deliberately provoked him by belittling Kant; otherwise I doubt if I should have got very much from him. He was a buttoned-up man, with an awkward manner and puritanical principles, who had difficulty in making contact with his pupils. In later years he became less interested in philosophy than in religion and was said to have become a Buchmanite. Whatever consolation this brought him, it was insufficient, for he ended by taking his own life.

Robin Dundas, with whom I began my study of Greek history, was among the most senior of the Students, as Christ Church misleadingly calls its Fellows. He had been in the same election as J. M. Keynes at Eton and an undergraduate at New College before the first world war, in which he had fought. A well-to-do Scottish gentleman, he had a soft voice, a quiet manner, a polished style and an astringent wit. He had no thought of making any contribution to his subject, but he read all the relevant literature, and taught his pupils conscientiously, relying on a copious set of notes which he kept up to date: it was a great disaster for him towards the end of his career when he left them in a train. I think that I first caught sight of him in Chapel at Eton, which he used to attend in order to look over the boys who might find their way to Christ Church. He was homosexual in sentiment, though I doubt if he ever practised. For some reason, he conceived it to be his duty to instruct undergraduates in the facts of life, about which some of them may have known more than he did. This was a harmless proceeding, which may in rare instances even have been beneficial, but a few years earlier Wystan Auden, who was then a Christ Church undergraduate, had maliciously pretended to be shocked by it and had complained to Keith Feiling, the Conservative historian, who was a Student of Christ Church before his election to a professorship. Feiling had foolishly taken the matter to the Governing Body and Dundas had been so embarrassed that he had taken a year's sabbatical leave to go round the world. By the time that I came up he was beginning to recover his confidence, though he grew more discriminating in his approach. When I first went to see him, he said that he supposed me to be more mature than most undergraduates. I did not know what he was getting at, or whether to answer 'Yes' or 'No'. I decided arbitrarily to say that I too supposed that I was more mature, and he took this as a sign that I did not need, or anyhow would not welcome, his extra-curricular instruction.

In later years, when I became his colleague, I grew to like Dundas and got to be on quite easy terms with him, but at the outset our relations were frigid. This was my fault. In the syllabus for Greats a choice was given between two periods of Greek history. The first went from early times until the end of the Peloponnesian War, the second from the beginning of the fifth century BC to the death of Alexander the Great. In those days almost everybody did the first period, with the advantage that they got to read Herodotus as well as Thucydides. It was therefore natural for Dundas to say to me, 'I assume that you will be doing the first period.' 'Why,' I said, 'is there an alternative?' He had to admit that there was. 'Which of them contains the least geography?' I asked, adding insufferably, 'Geography bores me.' He said that he thought the second period did. 'Then I'll do the second,' I said, and stuck to my decision though I could see that it displeased him.

The result was more fortunate for me than I deserved. The fourth century was not in Dundas's range, so that for that part of the course he farmed me out to C. E. Stevens, or 'Tom Brown' Stevens as he was more familiarly known. He is said to have acquired the nickname because of the strange old-fashioned clothes in which he first arrived at Winchester. He was later to become a Fellow of Magdalen and to be distinguished, among many other things, for the prodigious amount of teaching which he undertook, but at that time he had not yet obtained a fellowship and I believe that I was his first pupil. He was eccentric in manner, with a high voice which may have been modelled on Collingwood's, Collingwood being an ancient historian as well as a philosopher and admired by Tom Brown for his archeological research into ancient Britain. More importantly, Tom Brown was a man of great learning and a brilliant teacher. He took an immense amount of trouble with me, even going to the length of lending me his own copies of the texts, with the significant passages underlined in red ink. Under his guidance, I developed an interest not only in major events like the rise of Macedon but in questions of detail like the tactics of Chabrias and his mercenaries. From the literary point of view, such writers as Arrian and Diodorus Siculus were no match for Herodotus, but the times about which they wrote seemed to me of much greater historical interest.

I also enjoyed Roman history, though my approach to it was more superficial. In this case, I took the conventional course of studying the period of the early empire, for which the main authority was Tacitus, whom I read with pleasure. Bobbie Longden, who taught me, had been in College at Eton, a year or two before my time there, and a member of Pop. He was good-looking, enthusiastic, boyish in manner and with an air of success about him. He had been a friend of Cyril Connolly's at Eton and it was he who turned me into an admirer of Connolly's writing by getting me to read 'Told in Gath', his parody of Aldous Huxley, which first appeared in a collection called *Parody Party*. I had had a taste for parody since I was a boy, when my grandfather gave me Horace and James Smith's *Rejected Addresses*, and this was a superb example. Bobbie Longden was on easy terms with his pupils and gave parties at which we played charades. I had no pretensions to being an actor, but I remember once scoring a success in the undemanding part of the head of John the Baptist. Though he was well schooled in Roman history, Bobbie was not a scholar by temperament, and it was not a surprise to his friends that he chose to leave Christ Church to become headmaster of Wellington. There was then a fashion for appointing very young headmasters and I believe that he was still in his twenties. He was killed in the war in an air raid, remaining exposed like a good sea-captain, until he had shepherded all the boys into their shelters. Dundas's comment is said to have been, 'Late, as usual.'

Apart from his tutor, the Christ Church dons with whom an undergraduate there was most likely to come into contact were the Dean and the two Censors. Christ Church, commonly referred to as 'The House' because of its Latin title '*Aedes Christi*', is constitutionally attached to the Cathedral of Oxford, which it encloses, and the Dean was the genuine ecclesiastical article. He was head of the college and the Canons who formed his Chapter were members of the Governing Body. They were also professors of theology and amply housed in Tom Quad, the oldest and most splendid part of the college. The Dean, when I came to Christ Church and for some years afterwards, was Dean White, a small birdlike man who had the reputation of being a good scholar and a frank social snob. It was a blow to him that neither of the two dukes who applied for admission to the college during his reign was able to pass the entrance examination. I do not think that he did much entertaining of undergraduates and the only time at which one was sure to meet him was at the end of term, when he sat with the tutors in Hall and delivered to each undergraduate in t᠁n a verdict on his work and conduct. Usually his remarks were brief but he could rise to eloquence, as when he addressed a man with a speech beginning, 'Mr X, you have dragged the name of Christ Church in the mire.' Unfortunately he had mistaken his man, and after the tutor by his side had pulled his sleeve and whispered to him he had to break off and substitute some words of praise. Undaunted, he greeted the next man with 'Mr Y, you have dragged the name of Christ Church in the mire,' and continued with exactly the same speech. A remark of his which I treasure was made when a friend of mine was reported to him as having been caught in bed with a girl, only for the Dean to discover that it had not been a girl but a boy. 'One lesson,' he said, 'which my long experience has taught me is that whenever a case looks black, on inspection it almost invariably turns out to be blacker still.' On another occasion he startled his colleagues by saying of some undergraduate, 'He has offered me the greatest insult that one man can offer another.' The man had got drunk and pissed on the Dean's doorstep.

The Censors, who presumably took their name from Ancient Rome, were the disciplinary officers of the college. They served for five years, following an alternating sequence of two or three years in the Senior Censorship, in order to ensure continuity. Since they had to live in college, they were unmarried and relatively young. Both Gilbert Ryle and Bobbie Longden were Censors in my time, and before them Roy Harrod, who had read Greats at New College and suffered under Joseph, before turning to economics and becoming the first economics tutor to be appointed at Christ Church. I was later to become a friend of Roy's and to owe a great deal to him, but when I first met him he rather intimidated me. Not that he was ever anything but friendly and kind, but perhaps as a result of his association with Keynes, he had acquired something of the Bloomsbury manner, which seemed to demand that one should always be intellectually on one's best behaviour. When I had nothing more to offer than the ordinary small change of conversation, I felt that I was failing to come up to his mark. What I admired in him, especially as I came to know him better, was his rationality. Unlike many professing utilitarians, he really did seem to judge actions by their probable consequences; and he always had the courage to act on his beliefs.

The only other Christ Church don whom I can remember meeting while I was an undergraduate was T. B. L. Webster, a tutor in classics, whose indulgent marking of my papers had helped me to obtain my scholarship. My avoidance of Honour Mods prevented me from becoming his pupil, but I joined a small group which met once a week in his rooms to read and discuss St Augustine's *Civitas Dei.* This was entirely for pleasure, as mediaeval philosophy did not enter into the work that we had to do for Greats, and to this day I am almost entirely ignorant of it. I liked Tom Webster though I occasionally thought him a little querulous. He left Christ Church, while I was still an undergraduate, to become Professor of Greek at Manchester, and I did not see him again until the war brought us together.

Tom Webster's favourite pupil was Robert Willis, who had rooms on the next staircase to mine. Since I had gained four terms on Robert by skipping Honour Mods we were in the same year for Greats. Being a spasmodic worker myself, I was impressed by his regular habits of work. When he had a morning free from tutorials or lectures he used to sit down to his books punctually at nine, with a box of fifty Gold Flake cigarettes, and continue steadily until one. So long as he was studying the classics, his work was a pleasure to him, but his imagination was not fired by ancient history, and since, like many of the best classical scholars, he did not take kindly to philosophy, he failed to share my enthusiasm for Greats. We remained very close friends, though I was not so dependent on him as I had been at Eton. Finding more people who were willing to be friends with me, I became much more of a social figure. I continued on good terms with John Cheetham and also with Randolph Churchill for the short time that he remained at Christ Church, before he was lured away by the discovery that he could make large sums of money by lecturing in the United States. I formed a comfortable friendship with James Parr, who had been a mathematician at Eton but had chosen to read Greats, and improved my acquaintance with former Oppidans, of whom the most remarkable was Lewis Clive, a rowing blue who became a regular officer, resigned his commission when his strong sense of justice led him into politics, and lost his life fighting for the Republicans in Spain. I had no difficulty either in making friends among my fellow-freshmen at Christ Church with those who had come from other schools. David

Stephens, who had the rooms next to mine, was an urbane Wyke-hamist, destined for the Civil Service. I tried unavailingly to disturb his values and was repaid with a protective affection which I welcomed. A still closer friend was Armine Wright, who had been at Sherborne. He was a nephew of Sir Almroth Wright, who had been in some degree the model for the character of Sir Colenso Ridgeon in Shaw's *The Doctor's Dilemma*, and Armine was rightly proud of the connection. Though he was reading history, he was more interested in acquiring a knowledge of anthropology, of which he expected to make practical use in his career as a Colonial administrator. He was large and enthusiastic and entirely free from guile.

Andrew Wordsworth, who soon became my most intimate friend, had been to school at Marlborough, which then had the reputation of being dominated by hearties with a small opposition of rebellious aesthetes. Andrew sided with the aesthetes, but was acceptable to the hearties because of his skill at rugby football. Tall and fast, he was a good enough forward to play in the fresh-men's trial at Oxford, but he lacked the dedication which might have earned him a blue. Like me, he had lost the taste for classical scholarship, and we took the same route to Greats. His appetite for philosophy was not so keen as mine but he was ready to be drawn into discussing it. We also argued not very intensely about religion. He was the youngest of several sons of an Anglican bishop, who had been over seventy when Andrew was born and had died soon after, leaving it to Andrew's mother, a much younger woman of great charm and character, to make sure that the boys grew up as Christians. Andrew was not to be argued out of his faith, but it sat on him lightly and did not interfere with his pursuit of pleasure. He was more worldly than I and much better read, at least in modern literature. He had spent some time in Paris before coming up to Oxford and had discovered the Surrealists of whom I had not previously heard. It was under his influence that I began to read Proust and James Joyce's *Ulysses*, and the works of D. H. Lawrence. Even in those days I did not altogether succumb to the Lawrence cult, disliking the personality which was revealed in his published letters, and finding *Lady Chatterley's Lover* somewhat ridiculous, but I admired *Sons and Lovers* and *Aaron's Rod* and many of the short stories and, apart from their whimsical title, the poems which Lawrence called *Pansies*. It was to Andrew also that I owed my

86

discovery of Peacock, whose novels have never ceased to give me pleasure. *Crotchet Castle*, with its good-humoured ridicule of the early-nineteenth-century march of mind, its satirical portraits of Leigh Hunt, Coleridge and Robert Owen, and its possession, in the character of Dr Folliott, of the best of all Peacock's clerical epicures, has always been my favourite, but I have great affection for the philosophers in *Headlong Hall* and for many of the characters in *Melincourt*, especially Sir Oran Haut-ton, the orang-outang for whom the hero purchases a baronetcy and a seat in Parliament. The rotten boroughs were abolished not very long after the book was written, but the emergence of the party system has allowed the satire to retain its point.

Not all my reading was at this level. I remember being charmed by J. B. Priestley's *The Good Companions* when it first came out, and I had a great affection for Compton Mackenzie's *Vestal Fire*, a novel about the foreign colony in Capri before and during the first world war. One of the characters was modelled on Norman Douglas, whom I admired for the stories told about him and for his attack on D. H. Lawrence, but when I tried to read *South Wind* I found it heavy going. I much preferred Siegfried Sassoon's *Memoirs of a Fox-hunting Man*, little as it had to do with anything in my own experience, and its sequel *Memoirs of an Infantry Officer*, which was one of the many books about the war to appear at that time. Apart from Remarque's *All Quiet on the Western Front*, for which I shared the general enthusiasm, they were mainly autobiographical. The one that I most enjoyed was Robert Graves's *Goodbye to All That* which, like all of my favourite books, I constantly dipped into. Though it is now many years since I last read it, my memory of it is still vivid.

The amount of reading that I did for pleasure did not, I think, detract from my work, nor did it prevent me from leading an active social life. There seemed to be time for everything. One of the apparent differences between the undergraduates of my generation and those of the present day is that, whatever our social backgrounds actually were, we tended to have more of the attitudes of a leisured class. These attitudes were fostered by the material advantages that we enjoyed, not only in the possession of our sets of rooms but also in the service which we could command. Servants at Oxford are known as scouts, and there was in Christ Church at that time a scout and a scout's boy to every staircase. My scout was an elderly man called Milligan, who looked as if he liked to drink but served us with an air of ceremony. We held it for rather than against him that he was believed to reckon among his perquisites a share in our provision of coal. The scout's boy was Fred Wheatley, who was to be my scout at Wadham, when I held a Fellowship there just after the war, and is now the head scout at St Anthony's. I suspect that much of the heavy work, which was mainly that of keeping the fire supplied, was done by Fred, but Milligan called us in the mornings, brought us our hot water for shaving, made at least a show of cleaning, waited at luncheon and dinner parties and brought us most of the other meals that we took in our rooms.

The rules which we were expected to keep, though they preserved a continuity with our schooldays that the modern undergraduate would resent, were not very stringent. The day began with a roll call at 8 a.m. For this you could report to one of the Censors who took his station first in Hall and then in Chapel, but the easiest way, which I always followed, was just to sign one's name in a book at the porter's lodge. In theory, one was supposed to be fully dressed, but it was enough to put on an overcoat and a pair of trousers over one's pyjamas. Oxford colleges were still behindhand in their plumbing, but there was a set of lavatories on one of the staircases in the quad and a set of bathrooms on another. Neither of them was on my own staircase but they were not far away. Breakfast was brought to us in our rooms. The fashion for giving breakfast parties had almost died out, though one or two dons maintained it. Lectures, for which one might have to go to the Examination Schools or to another college, occurred on the hour throughout the morning, from nine o'clock onwards, though not many lecturers chose to begin before ten. There was no obligation to attend them and after my first year I attended hardly any, preferring to get my knowledge from my tutors and from the books and articles that they recommended or that I discovered for myself. The tutors tried to arrange their time-table so as to leave their pupils free to go to the lectures that were thought most useful for them, but clashes could not always be avoided, and when they occurred the tutorial prevailed. It was an offence to miss one's appointment without a reasonable excuse. Gowns had to be worn for both tutorials and lectures. One of the rewards of winning a scholarship was that you wore a longer and more becoming gown. Now that financial grants have rightly been made available to all undergraduates whose parents are not considered rich enough to support them on their own, it is almost the only reward that still remains.

In those days the usual practice was to lunch in one's own rooms and take tea in the Junior Common Room, though the reverse was also possible. Luncheon parties were the main form of social entertainment and often lasted until well into the afternoon. When we were not giving parties or invited to them, Andrew Wordsworth and I made a practice of lunching together, usually on cold meat and bread and cheese, in his rooms or mine. The afternoons were kept free from lectures or tutorials in the interests of those who wanted to play games. I had given up cricket and football and played very little tennis, after entering for the freshmen's tournament and losing in the first round. Mostly I went for walks with one friend or another in the Magdalen or Christ Church meadows. The hours between five and seven were set aside for tutorials and for classes. Among the very few classes that I attended for pleasure was one given by Father d'Arcy. I think that it was nominally about Thomas Aquinas, but it very soon developed into a running argument between him and me about the possibility of proving the existence of God. I do not remember how the audience reacted, though it must have been vexatious for those who wanted to learn something about Aquinas. If it was vexatious for Father d'Arcy he did not show it, and we remained on friendly terms ever since. Many years later I heard that he had described me to his convert Evelyn Waugh as the most dangerous man in Oxford, but if he really held this view he never allowed it to affect our personal relations.

Classes had to be brought to an end by seven o'clock to give the dons time to dress for dinner in Hall, which in Christ Church, as in most other colleges, was at 7.15. The undergraduates did not have to put on evening dress but they were required to wear their gowns. The scholars sat together at a separate table. One was allowed to sign off Hall but was put under some pressure to attend by being charged for at least four dinners in the week, whether one was present or not. For those who preferred to dine out the fashionable restaurant was the George, at the corner of George Street and the Cornmarket. It was notable mainly for the punkahs which served to ventilate it. The food was hardly better than what we were given in Hall and a good deal more expensive. One reason for going there was that one could entertain girls, who were not allowed to dine in Hall in the men's colleges, but the principal motive was just that it was fashionable. We could also obtain leave now and then to give dinner parties in our rooms. On such occasions one was expected to give some small financial compensation to the college chef and to one's scout for the extra trouble to which one was putting them.

One of the advantages of being at the House was that the college stayed open at night until twenty minutes past twelve, while the gates of the other men's colleges were shut at midnight. If you were late like Cinderella, you could still get in by waking the night porter, but the penalty was quite a heavy fine. You could also be punished by being gated, which meant that you had to stay in college throughout the evening. There were ways of climbing into every college, but they were for the most part difficult and dangerous. I never myself attempted it. Male friends could be entertained in college until the closing hour, but women had to be ushered out by ten o'clock. It must have been thought that the probability of their being made love to increased with the lateness of the hour. To be caught making love could get you sent down or rusticated, that is, either expelled from the college or sent away for at least a term. There was, however, an outer door to one's room which could not be opened from the outside without a key. Shutting it was technically known as sporting one's oak. With the oak safely sported you could do what you liked in the privacy of your rooms, so long as you kept to the prescribed hours and did not make a loud disturbance or damage the college property.

Unless one had leave to be away, which was not easily granted, one was supposed to spend every night in college during term. Since the terms were only eight weeks long, this was no great hardship. I was occasionally given leave of absence for the night in order to dine at the Inner Temple. It was necessary to eat a certain number of these dinners in order to be admitted to the Inns of Court, and quite usual to fulfil this requirement before one began any actual study of the law. As it turned out, I never did begin the study of the law, but I ate my Bar dinners conscientiously. They were not at all sumptuous, for which I was grateful in this instance, since I could get through them quickly and so have more time to spend with Renée afterwards. Otherwise I relied on her visiting me in Oxford, which she did quite frequently. In my first year, I seldom came to London in the daytime, though I should not have broken any rule in doing so. There was a train from Paddington, known to undergraduates as the fornicator, which could normally be relied on to reach Oxford in time for everyone to be safely back in college by midnight. The extra twenty minutes which were allowed to us at Christ Church gave one a pleasant feeling of security when the train was late.

The naming of this train is of interest, whether or not it was actually deserved. It showed that those who liked girls were expected to go to London to find them. At that time Oxford society was still almost wholly masculine. Not only did the men very greatly outnumber the women, as indeed they still do, but there was little social contact between them. One or two of the women undergraduates were much sought after, but the majority remained sequestered in the women's colleges. Large parties were given to which no women were invited, and when they were present in any considerable number it was likely that many of them came from outside Oxford. In the performances which were put on by the Oxford University Dramatic Society the female parts were played, not, as they now would be, by women undergraduates but by professional actresses. This disdain for the women undergraduates was due partly to snobbery, since it was still not the custom for upper-class girls to go to the university, and partly to a male dislike for female bluestockings; it being harder for women to get into Oxford, because of the smaller number of places available to them, they had become accustomed to take their work more seriously and did not mind showing it: the men had mostly been trained at their public schools to make a show of indolence, however hard they might actually be working. But the main reason lay in the men's educational upbringing. Having spent so much of their time as boarders in an exclusively masculine atmosphere, they were ill at ease with women. Many fewer of them than would nowadays be the case had had any sexual experience and such experience as they might have had was likely to have been homosexual.

The number of active homosexuals must, indeed, have been relatively small, but they were very much in evidence. The tone was set by three or four celebrated 'Queens', whose flamboyant appearance was joined in artifice by a studied formality of manner. Many of those who paid court to them were not radically homosexual but were merely continuing their schoolboy practice of using boys as substitutes for girls. Others were just subscribing to the current fashion. Its influence was so powerful that one was almost made to feel guilty for not following it. It was a little like being André

Gide's friend of whom he said, '*Bébé est vicieux. Il aime les femmes.*' I was, however, thought to have a sufficient excuse. Renée was so conspicuously attractive that my being seen with her rather increased than diminished my social credit.

I continued to be very much in love with her, more so, I think, than she was at that time with me. She had a young admirer who was addicted to motor-racing and learning about the manufacture of motor-cars in some factory at Basingstoke, and though I had no strong reason to consider him a serious rival, I suffered when she went to see him. I was jealous of her flirting with my friends and could not keep myself from making scenes. I had yet to realize that they are futile, whether one has cause for jealousy or not. But mostly my pleasure and pride in being with her outweighed the pain. It was seldom that many days passed without our meeting and during the intervals we regularly wrote to one another. If I had not heard from her in the morning, I used to wait anxiously for the evening post, going down repeatedly to the foot of my staircase to see if it had yet been delivered. I do not know which was the more acute: my delight when there was a letter from her or my disappointment when there was not. My feelings were genuine but they owed something to the romantic idea of love which I had derived from books; and this was a model which it was difficult to satisfy.

Renée had a strong personality and influenced me in small ways as well as great. For instance, it was mainly due to her that I became something of a dandy. I wore brightly coloured shirts, which was then unusual, and carried a silver-topped walking-stick. When I went about London I frequently wore spats. Renée had given me a Japanese silk dressing-gown which I wore in the evenings in my rooms in place of a jacket, like a character acted by Noel Coward. I used to have flowers in my sitting-room and became skilful at arranging them. I sometimes burned joss sticks to produce a smell of incense. At that time I smoked very little, but the few cigarettes that I did smoke were Turkish or Egyptian: my preference was for Balkan Sobranies, which were expensive but had the advantage of being too strongly flavoured for there to be much inducement to smoke them in quantity. My pretence at sophistication stopped short, however, when it came to drink. I drank sherry but no spirits. I tried but failed to acquire a taste for mulled claret. When I had to choose wine, it was almost invariably white and sweet. I had a great liking for a brand of Sauternes which I bought from a wine-shop in the town. I served it with everything including meat. This must have caused some suffering to my more experienced guests, but they were too well-mannered to complain.

My grandfather made me a small allowance which together with my scholarships brought my income up to £300 a year. In those days, this was quite a handsome sum. It left me enough money, after paying my college bills, to buy all the books and clothes I wanted, to entertain generously if not lavishly, and to have something to spare for holidays. I spent my income but did not run into debt. It helped me that Renée believed in women's independence, and had an allowance from her father. When we went out together, she insisted on paying her share. I told this to my grandfather when he warned me that my resources would not run to much expenditure on girls, but the effect was to alarm him. He was not in this way puritanical, but he did not like the idea of my forming a serious attachment, which might lead to an early marriage. He wanted me first to make my way in the world and then to follow the example of Disraeli by marrying someone who had the money or influence to advance my prospects. When I naïvely repeated this to Renée she was amused but not altogether pleased.

Renée had a Persian cat which she had trained to walk on a lead and used to bring it with her to Oxford, thereby attracting more attention to us when we all went out together. Eddie Playfair, later to become a powerful Civil Servant, who was two years my senior in College at Eton, tells the story of his coming from Cambridge to visit Guy Chilver, an undergraduate and subsequently a don at Queen's, with whom I then had a slight acquaintance. They were standing on the stairs at the George when the door opened to admit first a cat and then a very pretty girl and then me, conspicuous in a green shirt. We swept up the staircase ignoring Guy's diffident attempt to introduce us. Having passed Eddie I turned back and said, 'Don't I know you?', exchanged a word with him and then followed Renée and the cat into the restaurant. Eddie regarded this as so perfect an example of the Oxford manner that he never wanted to visit the place again.

I believe that I met Guy Chilver through the OUDS, which was one of the many societies that I joined. I remember being visited by Valentine Dyall, to see if I was fit for membership, and finding his presence over-awing. I never sought to appear, even as an extra, in any of the OUDS productions, but used its premises as a club. A society in which I was for a time more active was the Oxford Union. I regularly attended its meetings during my first year and made several short speeches from the floor. I thought of myself vaguely as a radical but had no political affiliation. I had formed a friendship with Derek Walker-Smith, who was a year ahead of me at Christ Church, and he and I and a man called Ward-Jackson resolved to constitute a group in emulation of the nineteenth-century 'fourth party', which had helped to make the political fortunes of Lord Randolph Churchill and Arthur Balfour. Lacking their capacity and their intensity of purpose, we achieved very little. Of the three of us, Derek was the most serious politician, as he has later proved, and if I remember rightly he succeeded in attaining office in the Union as a Liberal. I got to be one of the principal speakers in a debate towards the end of my first summer term, having to put on a white tie and tails for the occasion. I forget the subject of the debate or what thesis I was propounding, but I remember that I made a hash of it. I was painfully nervous and gabbled unintelligibly. I have never spoken at the Union since.

It is a proof of my lack of political commitment that I joined the most fashionable Conservative club in Oxford, the Canning Club, and even became its secretary. I read one or two papers to the club and remember not without shame that in one of them I expressed some sympathy for an authoritarian form of government. I suppose that I had been influenced by Plato's arguments against democracy. Many of the other members were former Oppidans whom I had known slightly at Eton. They formed the more intellectual wing of the heartily aristocratic Bullingdon Club, which I neither desired nor was invited to join.

A society of a different complexion was the Poetry Club, to which I was happy to belong though I had no thought of trying to write poetry. At one of the first meetings that I attended I heard Louis MacNeice, then an undergraduate in his final year, deliver a metaphysical address which I found very impressive, though much of it passed my comprehension. It was a salutary shock for me to find someone who was so much more learned than myself and displaying a brilliance which I was sure that I could never match. I took little, if any, part in the discussion and did not get to know MacNeice until many years later. Perhaps my first impression of him never wholly wore off, since, though I liked and admired him, I never found him easy company. A poet with whom I was to form a much closer friendship was Stephen Spender. Like Shelley, whom he rivalled in good looks, Stephen had gone to University College, where he had unsuitably chosen to read Philosophy, Politics and Economics. His philosophy tutor was E. F. Carritt, a kindly man of liberal principles, but philosophically a paler Prichard. He did not succeed in reconciling Stephen to philosophy, though he amused him by saying in the course of one of their tutorials that he was not altogether happy about pleasure. Stephen was a year senior to me and I knew him only slightly as an undergraduate, but well enough to realize that there was a sharp wit and considerable shrewdness behind his air of innocence.

A friend whom I associate with the Poetry Club was Hugh Speaight, a younger brother of the actor Robert Speaight. Like Andrew Wordsworth, Hugh was much better schooled than I in the contemporary arts, and very much more sophisticated. He was amused by my ingenuousness and I was taken with his worldliness. I remember spending a day with him in the holidays at his house in the country and writing a flowery letter of thanks to his mother about the charms of the countryside, which pleased her but embarrassed him. Together with Giles Playfair, then an undergraduate at Merton and an active member of the OUDS, Hugh founded the Balloon Club, in which they enlisted their friends. The idea was to promote the sport of ballooning but I think that only one ascent was actually made, in which only the officers of the club participated. It was preceded by a much publicized luncheon party with Tallulah Bankhead as the guest of honour. As has often been the case where I have been to parties at which celebrities were present, I cannot recall exchanging any words with Miss Bankhead, though I may afterwards have boasted of having met her. Hugh had the character and gifts to become a successful entrepreneur but he died very young.

A more esoteric group of which I later became a member was the White Rose Society, which was nominally a small company of Jacobites. We dined together once a term in full evening dress with white roses in our buttonholes, and drank the health of 'The King over the water'. We possessed a sword, said to have been blessed by the Pope, which our secretary was once reduced to pawning. Eventually we made the mistake of electing a genuine Jacobite, who bored us so much that our meetings were discontinued. I do not know if the society has ever been revived.

The colleges also had their own societies, of varying degrees of smartness and frivolity. Among those to which I belonged at Christ Church was the Essay Society, which demanded a fairly high standard of contributions from its members, and a play-reading society which concentrated on the contemporary theatre. I remember taking part in a reading of Somerset Maugham's *The Circle* and thinking it, as I still do, a remarkably skilful and engaging piece of work. A few colleges had philosophical societies, but the main outlet for fledgling philosophers was the inter-collegiate Jowett Society, named after the famous Master of Balliol who had at one time been a tutor in philosophy, though his contribution to the subject seems to have been limited to a ponderous translation of the works of Plato with introductions to the several dialogues that do little more than summarize their arguments. In recent years the Jowett Society has served mainly as a means for undergraduates to supplement their tutorials by listening to debates between dons, but at that time, though outside speakers were occasionally invited, most of the papers were presented, and the discussions opened, by the junior members themselves. Any undergraduate could become a member, on payment of a small subscription, by attending a meeting as a guest and taking part in the discussion. Once I had been admitted to the society, I attended its meetings regularly and eventually became its secretary.

An outside speaker who offered to address the Society while I was secretary was J. W. Dunne, author of two books, *An Experiment with Time* and *The Serial Universe*, which attracted a great deal of attention in their day. They were responsible, among other things, for the alteration in the ordinary time-sequence of the events in at least one of J. B. Priestley's plays. It was part of Dunne's theory that one could make excursions into the future, and his ground for maintaining this was that it actually happened in dreams. Starting from the premiss that dreams are frequently pre-cognitive, he illogically argued that the events which they foretell must somehow be present to the dreamer. His reason for wishing to address the Jowett Society was not, however, to test the force of his argument but to shore up its premiss. The Society for Psychical Research had supplied him with a group of subjects who recorded their dreams for him, but the result of the experiment had been negative. The dreams could not be plausibly interpreted as foretelling any future events. Mr Dunne was disappointed but not

The Citroen grandchildren in 1918 or thereabouts. From top to bottom, myself, Jack and Doris Holloway, Donald and Madge Kingsford.

The College Wall XI going out to play on St Andrew's Day, 1928. Edward Ford in the middle, David Hadley next but one on his right. Bernard Burrows on his left, and I next to Bernard Burrows.

Photograph of e. e. cummings' portrait of me, painted in 1942. Taken by Marion Morehouse Cummings.

Maurice Bowra in the light suit with Martin Cooper on his left. Photographed in Vienna in 1932 and sent to Isaiah Berlin.

Myself in Santander in 1929.

discouraged. He accounted for the negative result by the fact that the subjects supplied to him had been elderly. 'Age,' he said, 'lives in the past. Youth lives in the future.' And so he turned to Oxford for recruits. I was happy to invite him and organized a meeting at which I alone was present. I had forgotten to send out any notices and he forgot to come. We tried again with better fortune and Mr Dunne explained his theory to a sceptical but friendly audience. He advised us that the best way to recapture our dreams was to keep paper and pencil by our bedsides and start recording them as soon as we awoke, and said that if we followed this method we should soon remember so much that it would take us several hours to write it all down. Since it seemed to me that this would interfere unduly with my work, I declined to join the company of dreamers, but I agreed to collect their reports and inform Mr Dunne if any of the dreams appeared to have been pre-cognitive. In spite of the youth of the dreamers, the experiment again had a negative result. It is true that Andrew Wordsworth dreamed of making love to a girl to whom he subsequently did make love, but this was too much in the natural order of things for anyone to count it as significant.

It was through the Jowett Society that I came to know Isaiah, or as his friends then called him, Shaya Berlin. We already had a slight connection in that his father, who came from Riga, was also in the timber trade and knew both my father and my father's partner Mr Bick, but although we had known of each other through the Bicks, we had never met. Isaiah had gone to school at St Paul's and had come up to Oxford a year ahead of me as a classical scholar at Corpus. Andrew and I called on him in the belief that a meeting of the Jowett Society was being held in his rooms, but either we had been misinformed, or the venue of the meeting had been changed, and we found him alone. Having introduced ourselves, we entered into conversation. It can be said of Isaiah as Dr Johnson said of Burke that he is 'such a man, that if you met him for the first time in the street where you were stopped by a drove of oxen, and you and he stepped aside to take shelter but for five minutes, he'd talk to you in such a manner that when you parted you would say, this is an extraordinary man.' On this occasion, we had hardly begun talking before I said to Andrew, 'Let's not go to the meeting. This man is much more interesting.' Not caring to be treated as if he had been put on show, Isaiah hustled us away to the meeting, but this was the beginning of a friendship that has lasted for over forty years.

One of the things that first brought us together was our common interest in philosophy. This is an interest that we no longer share, since Isaiah was persuaded by the American logician H. M. Sheffer, in the early nineteen-forties, that the subject had developed to a point where it required a mastery of mathematical logic which was not within his grasp: thereafter he chose to cultivate the lusher field of political theory. His approach to philosophy had indeed always been more eclectic than mine and more critical than constructive. In our frequent discussions, his part was usually to find unanswerable objections to the extravagant theories that I advanced. He once described me to a common friend as having a mind like a diamond, and I think it is true that within its narrower range my intellect is the more incisive. On the other hand, he has always had the readier wit, the more fertile imagination and the greater breadth of learning. The difference in the working of our minds is matched by a difference in temperament, which has sometimes put a strain upon our friendship. I am more resilient, more reckless and more intolerant; he is more mature, more expansive and more responsible. At times he has found me too theatrical and been shocked by my sensual self-indulgence. I have sometimes wished that he were more revolutionary in spirit. I credit us both with a strong moral sense, but it expresses itself in rather different ways.

It was a feature of Isaiah's active imagination that he liked to identify his friends with historical personages or characters in fiction. It often seemed to me that he judged them more by the qualities of the counterparts whom he had found for them than by those that they actually displayed. At about the time that I met him I discovered the novels and essays of Stendhal and was so much taken with them that he pretended to believe that I had never read anything else. This helped him to see me as Julien Sorel. If I had to be identified with any of Stendhal's characters, this indeed is the one that I should have chosen, but while I found the comparison flattering in some ways, I thought that it overestimated both the romantic strain in me and the extent of my social ambitions. Though it might have been less plausible, I should have preferred to be identified with Voltaire.

For a long time I believed that I enjoyed the distinction of having been the one to introduce Isaiah Berlin to Maurice Bowra, but I was mistaken. On the occasion of which I was thinking, when they both came to a dinner party in my rooms to which Andrew and I had invited those whom we agreed to be the most brilliant people that we knew, I am assured by Isaiah that they already knew one another. I met Maurice in my first term at Oxford. He had known one of Andrew's elder brothers and came to call on Andrew when I happened to be there. Not long afterwards he asked me to a dinner party in his rooms at Wadham, of which he was then Dean. I was shy and unused to the quantity of drink that he provided, so that I passed most of the evening in a kind of stupor. Not surprisingly, it was some time before I was asked again. Later, when I had acquired more confidence, I was able to contribute enough to the conversation to be fairly welcome to him as a guest. This was not so difficult as it first seemed to me, since his intellectual vitality was infectious. Part of his brilliance as a talker lay in his power to stimulate others to flights of wit and fancy of which they would not ordinarily have been capable.

Maurice was not the only don at that time to cultivate under-graduates but he was by far the most influential. He was just over thirty years of age when I first knew him, short and sturdy, with a massive head, small watchful eyes, and a resonant voice, de-livering words like rapid musketry. At Cheltenham, where he was known as 'Mossy' Bowra, he had earned distinction, not only as a classical scholar, but as a rugby football player, and one could imagine him scrummaging to good effect. His experiences in the war, when he had served for a year in France as an artillery officer, had made a deep impression on him, but he did not care to talk about them. Occasionally he hinted that it was far more awful than we could imagine. As an undergraduate at New College, he had been taught by Joseph, who stifled whatever taste he might have developed for philosophy. His wit was largely of the order of Oscar Wilde's 'Work is the curse of the drinking classes,' an adaptation of clichés and quotations. So, he spoke of someone as the sort of man who would give you a stab in the front and of a girl who was clinging to her lover as a mouse at bay. He described Evelyn Waugh's trilogy of war novels as 'The Waugh to end Waugh' and when E. R. Dodds, who had been a pacifist, was preferred to him for the Regius Professorship of Greek, he responded with 'What did you do in the Great War, Doddy?' The delayed appear-ance of the coffin at the funeral of Humphrey Sumner, who had been Warden of All Souls, elicited from Maurice 'Sumner is icumen in.' I do not know whether he gave any thought to his witticisms but they were always produced with an air of spontaneity and made more effective by his style of utterance and the forceful personality that went with it. He was like Dr Johnson, of whom Boswell's 'noble friend Lord Pembroke' is quoted as remarking that his sayings 'would not appear so extraordinary, were it not for his bow-wow way'. In his love of gossip, Maurice did not spare his friends, but his satire was good-natured so long as he was satisfied of their loyalty. If he thought that they had been disloyal to him, or had behaved in a manner of which he disapproved, he could be very savage and unrelenting. Otherwise he was generous in giving assistance and advice. While he was not a meticulous scholar, the strength of his sympathy for the ancient Greeks relieves the piety with which he wrote about them. He read many languages and had a deep feeling for much of the poetry that was written in them, but for the most part the style of his published criticism is oddly pedestrian. His memoirs are livelier, but unexpectedly benign. He had a great gift for parody, which he exercised in composing lampoons. He was rightly proud of these verses and read them aloud to a chosen few, of whom I was never one. I am judging only by the excerpts which others have quoted.

As this shows, I was never very close to Maurice, though we were always on good terms with one another. He thought of me as gifted, going so far in his memoirs as to refer to me as a 'young genius', but I had the impression that he approved of me more than he liked me. We got on well enough in company but when we were alone together there was a feeling of unease. Behind his bravura there was a sense of insecurity and there were only a few people with whom he wholly relaxed his guard. He had affairs with women, including at least one whom he wished to marry, but he was also homosexual and the homosexual strain in him was the stronger. It may have been partly for this reason that he sought the company of undergraduates, whether or not they shared this sexual taste. Nowadays the younger Oxford dons do not command the service, even if they had the means, to entertain on the scale that Maurice and some others used to do, but this is not the only factor. The Oxford system of education also suffers from the decline in the number of bachelor dons, who take an interest in the undergraduates which extends beyond the supervision of their work. No doubt there was a touch of snobbery in the pride which we took in being favoured by Maurice's notice. In some ways his example was not one that the more conventional among our seniors were happy to see us follow; but he was a strongly civilizing influence even on those who belonged only to the outer circle of his friends.

With all the other demands on my time during my first year at Oxford, I still had enough leisure for frequent visits to the cinema. I joined the Oxford Film Society, which still showed only silent films, and saw for the first time such Russian classics as *Battleship Potemkin*, *Storm over Asia*, *Mother* and *Earth*. I remember being childishly amused by the fact that a film called *Bed and Sofa*, adapting the eternal triangle to the housing shortage in Moscow, had been made by Alexander Room. I took great pleasure also in the German expressionist films such as *Waxworks*, *The Cabinet of Dr Caligari* and *The Student of Prague*, acquiring a lasting admiration for the acting of Conrad Veidt. Later, when he migrated to Hollywood, he tended to be type-cast as a German aristocrat, but however slender the part he always brought distinction to it. Nineteen-thirty was the year in which the talkies, as they were then called, consolidated their victory over the mere movies. One of the first that I saw was the original German version of *The Blue Angel*, with the great Emil Jannings in a part worthy of him, and the young Marlene Dietrich, then a plump siren with only her voice forecasting the sinuous enchantress that Hollywood was to make of her. Though this was a good film by any standards, the earliest talkies for the most part had little but their novelty to recommend them, being either transplanted stage plays, like *The Last of Mrs Cheney*, or unimaginative thrillers, or routine musicals; the flowering of the Hollywood musical began only in 1933, with *42nd Street*, one of those silly stories in which a chorus girl becomes an instant star, but remarkable for its vitality. There was, however, an extraordinary exception in the work of René Clair, who in successive years from 1929 to 1931 brought out *Sous les Toits de Paris*, *Le Million* and *A nous la Liberté*, which I still regard as three of the most charming films that I have ever seen. Renée and I went together to them all and a resemblance which we both thought that we detected between me and the actor René Lefebre, who played a character called Michel in *Le Million*, led her to call me Mickey, a nickname which she continued to use for many years. There may also have been some idea of my resembling Mickey Mouse.

Renée and I faced another separation at the end of my first summer term. She had arranged to return to her father in Tokyo, where her fiancé also awaited her, though she no longer held herself to be engaged to him. He was one man of whom I was not jealous. We celebrated the end of the Oxford year by making up a party for the OUDS ball, a fancy-dress affair to which I went as Puck; this was the last occasion on which I have taken any trouble to appear in fancy dress. The other two members of our party were a girl called Bella Moss, a daughter of the house of Moss Bros., who had been with Renée at her finishing-school in Paris, and a friend of Miss Moss's from Cambridge, a burly young man who sulkily disapproved of what he regarded as a show of Oxford decadence. It annoyed me that Renée appeared to take his side, to the point where I felt that she was dissociating herself from me. I suppose she was anxious that I should make a good impression on her friends and no doubt my appearance as Puck did not display me at my best. The result was that I made a violent scene and we parted in anger. As usual, we were quickly reconciled and I went with her as far as Berlin on the start of a long train journey which would take her to Moscow and then by the trans-Siberian railway to Vladivostok, where she took ship for Japan. We found it very hard to part but were sustained by the thought that she would not remain away for very long.

From Berlin I made my way to Würzburg where I had arranged to meet John Cheetham for a tour of Bavaria. We went to Nuremberg and to Augsburg and to Munich and across the Austrian border to Salzburg, where he stayed on without me. On the whole we had a pleasant time together though it did not deepen our friendship or lead to our seeing more of one another when we were back at Oxford. I had never been to Germany before and knew nothing of baroque architecture which I found unexpectedly attractive. The little amount of German that I had learned at Eton had vanished from my memory, but John, as befitted a future ambassador, spoke the language well enough to make everything go smoothly.

Later in the summer I went to stay with Andrew and his mother in a house which they owned at Lulworth on the Dorset coast. I remember finding this a restful contrast both to the nervous state in which my mother and I still lived together and to the storms and stresses of my life with Renée, though I continued to think myself in love with her and had no eye for any other girl. This was the only occasion in my life on which I have gone out sailing, embarking once or twice with Andrew who had a great enthusiasm for it and owned a small boat. I did not enjoy the experience and to the small extent to which I had to act as crewman, I was more of a hindrance than a help. Altogether the pleasures of 'messing about in boats' are foreign to me and although I just managed to learn to scull and to punt, I did neither with any skill.

By this time Renée was again living in Tokyo and wrote to me regularly. I used to keep most of her letters and had one of them with me when I was visiting my grandparents at Eastbourne. I carelessly left it in the pocket of a coat which was taken to be cleaned and it was returned to my grandmother rather than to me. She read it and showed it to my grandfather, saying that they had lost me. He tried to reassure her by telling her of the excesses of his own youth, of which he had hitherto kept her in ignorance, but admitted to me that he had himself been shocked by the letter which was unusually frank in its expression of physical desire. This was, in fact, quite foreign to Renée's usual style and was the result of her taking D. H. Lawrence as a model. I explained this to my grandfather without convincing him. He drew the old-fashioned middle-class distinction between 'the girls who do' and 'the girls who don't' and believed that the ones who didn't were the ones to marry: one could profit by the existence of the others but it was a mistake to fall in love with them. He continued to have high hopes of me but became increasingly worried about my private life.

I have no doubt that my grandmother would have taken this incident more lightly had she not been ill. She was suffering from cancer, from which she died the following November at the age of sixty-five. Her funeral, like my father's, was held at Golders Green Crematorium. There was no service, but my grandfather, standing by the coffin, made an emotional speech in which he called upon his grandchildren to prove themselves worthy of her. I believe that we were all very fond of her, as she undoubtedly was of us, but the livelier image of my grandfather overshadows her in my memory.

I think it must have been in the Christmas holidays, following my grandmother's death, that my grandfather took me with him on a Mediterranean cruise. The ship called at Gibraltar, Barcelona, Palma, Tunis, Monte Carlo and Naples, all of which I was seeing for the first time. From Palma we drove round the island of Majorca, which was still undeveloped and seemed to me poetic, perhaps because I associated it with Robert Graves. The charm of Naples escaped me, but I responded as a proper tourist to the ruins of Pompeii. At Monte Carlo I was too young to be admitted to the gaming rooms, which I later discovered to be very gloomy, but I was amused by the deference which my grandfather's reply of 'Monsieur Citroën' elicited when the headwaiter at a restaurant to which we had gone to reserve a table asked him for his name. I was enchanted in Barcelona by Gaudi's fantastic church of the Sagrada Familia and nearly delayed the ship by my reluctance to leave a game of pelota, about which I had become an enthusiast since I first saw it played at Santander. I would sooner have spent more time on shore and less time at sea, though I participated readily enough in the organized jollity of shipboard life. Of the other passengers I remember only a man who sang 'Abie, Abie, Abie my boy, what are we waiting for now?' in a mock-Jewish accent, which my grandfather rightly thought it bad taste for me to imitate, and a woman who interested me because she had once earned her living as a relatively passive member of a troupe of acrobats. I went about with her enough to provoke the comment that she was old enough to be my mother, though in fact there was never any question of my making love to her.

Apart from my seeing less of Renée, who did not return to England until February 1931, my second year at Oxford followed the same pattern as the first. I may have worked a little harder and I made a number of new friends. The one of whom I saw most was Martin Cooper, a Wykehamist who, whether for a disciplinary reason or because he had failed in some preliminary examination, had been sent down from his original college and had found refuge on the books of St Edmund's Hall. By the time that I got to know him he was living in lodgings, where I used frequently to visit him. He was reading Modern Languages, having changed from some other subject, possibly PPE, which he had found not to suit him. His main interest was, however, in music and he hoped to become a concert pianist. A son of a Canon of York Minster, he was at that time more irreverent than irreligious: even so, the news of his conversion to Roman Catholicism a decade or so later came to me as a surprise. He was much in the company of Maurice Bowra, who was thought to be in love with him. He was, indeed, very attractive; intelligent, witty, perceptive and full of vitality. He liked my iconoclasm but did not altogether share it. As in Yeats's poem

'Nineteen Hundred and Nineteen' he was willing to mock at the great and the wise and the good but cared more for the sequel:

> Mock mockers after that
> That would not lift a hand maybe
> To help good, wise or great . . .

I quickly came to share his admiration for Yeats's 'The Tower', which contains one of my favourite poems in 'Among School Children' with the marvellous stanza:

> Plato thought nature but a spume that plays
> Upon a ghostly paradigm of things;
> Solider Aristotle played the taws
> Upon the bottom of a king of kings;
> World-famous golden-thighed Pythagoras
> Fingered upon a fiddle-stick or strings
> What a star sang and careless Muses heard;
> Old clothes upon old sticks to scare a bird.

and another in 'Leda and the Swan':

> A sudden blow: the great wings beating still
> Above the staggering girl, her thighs caressed
> By the dark webs, her nape caught in his bill,
> He holds her helpless breast upon his breast.
>
> How can those terrified vague fingers push
> The feathered glory from her loosening thighs?
> And how can body, laid in that white rush,
> But feel the strange heart beating where it lies?
>
> A shudder in the loins engenders there
> The broken wall, the burning roof and tower
> And Agamemnon dead.
>
>   Being so caught up,
> So mastered by the brute blood of the air,
> Did she put on his knowledge with his power
> Before the indifferent beak could let her drop?

It may have been under Martin's influence that I followed my discovery of Proust and Stendhal by turning to French poetry. I remember his amusement when he asked me how I had been spending my time and I said that I had spent it dreaming and reading Racine. In fact I cared less for Racine than for the more romantic Verlaine and Baudelaire. Of the two, I had the greater admiration for Baudelaire but the greater love for Verlaine, knowing several of his poems by heart. I now find them rather sentimental, but their music, like that of Swinburne's poems, still enchants me.

An account of Verlaine is given in *Conversations in Ebury Street*, my favourite among the works of George Moore, whom I also discovered at about that time. I liked the autobiographical books and the books of criticism better than the novels, though I valiantly made my way through the elaborate prose of *Héloïse and Abélard* and *Aphrodite in Aulis* and *The Brook Kerith*, from which I first learned of the theory that Jesus had survived the crucifixion and joined a community of Essenes. I doubt if many people read these novels now, but I should be sorry if the same neglect extended to Moore's *Avowals*, with its fine display of literary prejudice in which Moore's decided preference for Turgenev over Tolstoy is a characteristic feature, or to his *Conversations in Ebury Street*, which is remarkable not only for the mordant literary dialogues but for the portraits of Moore's friends among the leaders of the New English Art Club, most notably Sickert but also Steer and Tonks. It made them so vivid to me that I still welcome any sign that their work is coming back into fashion.

One of Moore's literary heroes was Walter Pater, whose style is so marvellously parodied in W. H. Mallock's *The New Republic*; indeed, this is one of the cases where I think that the parody improves upon the original, which I have always found rather heavy going. The one piece of Pater's writing which strongly appealed to me when I first read it was the famous passage in the conclusion to his essays on *The Renaissance*, written in 1868, which Pater omitted from the second edition of the book, as he 'conceived it might possibly mislead some of those young men into whose hands it might fall'. A fairly long extract is needed to bring out its special flavour:

The service of philosophy, of speculative culture, towards the human spirit is to rouse, to startle it into sharp and eager observation. Every moment some form grows perfect in hand or face; some tone on the hills or the sea is choicer than the rest; some mood of passion or insight or intellectual excitement is irresistibly real and attractive for us, – for that moment only. Not the fruit of experience, but experience itself, is the end. A counted number of pulses only is given to us of a variegated, dramatic life. How may we see in them all that is to be seen in them by the finest senses? How shall we pass most swiftly from point to point, and be present always at the focus where the greatest number of vital forces unite in their purest energy?

To burn always with this hard, gemlike flame, to maintain this ecstasy, is success in life. In a sense it might even be said that our failure is to form habits: for, after all, habit is relative to a stereotyped world, and meantime it is only the roughness of the eye that makes any two persons, things, situations, seem alike. While all melts under our feet, we may well catch at any exquisite passion, or any contribution to knowledge that seems by a lifted horizon to set the spirit free for a moment, or any stirring of the senses, strange dyes, strange colours, and curious odours, or work of the artist's hands, or the face of one's friend. Not to discriminate every moment some passionate attitude in those about us, and in the brilliancy of their gifts some tragic dividing of forces on their ways, is, on this short day of frost and sun, to sleep before evening.

I still admire this passage but do not now think that its precious aestheticism was ever really characteristic of me. Certainly I have never been particularly sensitive to strange dyes or colours, still less to the tones on the hills or the sea. At the best, I can appreciate them when they are pointed out to me, but am mostly too absorbed in my own thoughts to notice them for myself. I cannot claim to be very good at discriminating passionate attitudes, except perhaps when they are directed towards me, nor do I make any serious attempt to avoid forming habits. Indeed, the only way in which I satisfy Pater's model is in having an unusually strong capacity to live intensely in the moment. Nevertheless, there was quite a long period in my youth when I should have said that it represented my attitude to life.

It most decidedly represented the attitude of Goronwy Rees, to whom Martin Cooper introduced me. As Martin reported it to me, Goronwy's first reaction was one of surprise that Martin should make friends with anyone so ugly, but either my looks improved or he became reconciled to them, since he has remained the closest to me of any of the Oxford friends of my youth. He himself had the romantic good looks that one associates with Heathcliff in *Wuthering Heights*, and was full of vitality and charm. He had been brought up at Aberystwyth, where his father, a distinguished theologian, was much in demand as a preacher, and though he had a great affection and respect for his father, he was in moral and intellectual revolt against his Calvinist principles. He had been to school in Cardiff, where he had been conspicuous as an athlete as well as a scholar and had played in a trial as scrum-half for the Welsh schoolboys. Coming up a year ahead of me with a scholarship at New College, he was one of those who prospered under Joseph, and after getting a first in PPE, he was elected to a Fellowship at All Souls. It was said that the All Souls examiners were particularly impressed by an essay which he wrote about the middle class. He already had literary ambitions and his first novel, a love-story with some philosophical overtones, was written while he was still an undergraduate. His critical standards were high and I remember that when I published my affected and ill-written essay about bull-fighting, he advised me quite sharply to stick to philosophy. In fact, I wrote hardly anything as an undergraduate besides my tutorial essays. Apart from the unfortunate essay on bull-fighting, I recall only a review for *Cherwell* of an OUDS production of Flecker's *Hassan*, starring my friend Giles Playfair, in which I was over-indulgent to the play, if not to the players, and an essay on *Cynicism* which I wrote in my first term for a magazine got up by one of my Christ Church friends. The argument of the essay was that love was destructive of pride. I remember only the last sentence, because it impressed Gilbert Ryle: 'The holes in the mantle of Antisthenes have been mended with loving hands.'

Another of the friends that I made in my second year was Gilbert Highet, a classical scholar at Balliol who had already been to Glasgow University, and besides being a year or two older than the rest of us, gave the impression of much greater maturity. He was brought to my rooms by Edward Ford for a meeting of the Canning Club at which I was reading a paper. I forget what the paper was about though I remember that Gilbert described it to me later, when we had become friends, as 'nonsense skilfully arranged'. He deferred to me on questions of philosophy, in which he was not greatly interested, but otherwise I had more to learn from him than he from me. Like Juvenal, of whom he was to publish a study when he became a Professor of Classics, he was inclined to be a stern moralist, and in general he had a predilection for satire, which he later anatomized in another of his books. I remember an epigram on André Gide which he published in *Oxford Outlook*:

> The best known work of André Gide
> Is called 'If perish not the seed'
> And yet his esoteric taste
> Entails the maximum of waste.

Unlike most students of French literature, Gilbert set a high value on the work of Jules Romains, and it was owing to him that I bought all twenty-four volumes of *Les Hommes de Bonne Volonté*. I became surfeited with it before the end but I still think that it has considerable merits as a description of French middle-class society in the early part of the present century. It is a rather more ambitious work than Galsworthy's *The Forsyte Saga*, with which it invites comparison, and at least equally readable.

Gilbert was already engaged to Helen MacInnes, who achieved fame some years after they were married as a writer of thrillers, and he approved of my liaison with Renée, so long as it excluded promiscuity. On one occasion at least, I pretended to be staying with him in Scotland when Renée and I went off together during the vacation, and he went to the trouble of writing me long letters in which he furnished me with a diary of engagements which would have taxed the most conscientious tourist. In this way I came to have an extensive knowledge of Glasgow by description which I have never yet turned into knowledge by acquaintance.

The more peaceful life that I led in Renée's absence would probably not have contented me for long, but I liked it enough at the time to write her a letter in which I said that I did not want our relations to continue. I gave as my reason that I needed to concentrate on my work. I do not know how seriously I meant this, or how seriously she took it, but she had no sooner returned to England than we were back on the old footing. Her method of returning was unusual, and characteristic of her. After sailing from Tokyo to San Francisco, she bought a motor-cycle and rode it across the United States all the way to New York. The publicity which she gained for this exploit enabled her to sell the machine for as much as she had paid for it. She had no trouble on the way, except with the language. Her accent appeared so strange to some farmers who gave her hospitality in Arkansas that they asked her what language people spoke in England.

After she came back we met more frequently in London than in Oxford. She took a room in a house in Limerston Street in Chelsea and I used frequently to spend the day with her there, returning to Oxford by the late train, and sometimes, when I had a tutorial the next day, working on my essay throughout most of the night. One consequence of her having this room was that we no longer went to hotels, except when we travelled abroad together. For some reason, when we had gone to hotels, we had always registered under a false name. We changed it fairly often, which sometimes led to embarrassment as on one occasion when we each wrote a different name in the register. It testifies to the clerk's suspicions that I was not allowed to register for us both. We even carried this custom to France where it could serve no purpose whatsoever. We used to stay at a small hotel in Paris in the neighbourhood of the Gare du Nord, and perhaps inadvertently used a different name on successive visits. The manager recognized me and asked, I think simply as a mark of friendliness, whether I had not already stayed at the hotel. Not stopping to think how unlikely it was that he would have checked my previous or even my present entry in the register, I said that it was not I but a cousin of mine who had been there before. The manager was content to remark drily that my cousin was extraordinarily like me.

In the summer of 1931 we went to St Raphael, which was not then fashionable or expensive, in a small party of Renée's friends. I liked St Raphael, but my relations with Renée became tense, as they usually did when we were in the company of others, especially if they were people that I did not know very well. I was much happier when we went off on our own to visit Arles and Avignon. Though I have never been anything of a Platonic scholar, I had the Loeb text of Plato's *Theaetetus* and *Sophist* with me, and read them with much greater pleasure than the *Republic*. At Arles we stayed in a hotel in the square which contains the statue of the poet, Mistral, and I remember opening the windows of our room in the evening after a shower of rain to savour the romantic atmosphere, and paying for it with a prodigious number of mosquito bites. I remember also my angry embarrassment when I asked some workmen the way to the railway station and failed to make myself understood because I was using the word '*station*' instead of '*gare*'. What I chiefly remember of Avignon is the magnificent discourse, delivered by the guide on the balcony of the Pope's Palace, retailing the glories of Languedoc.

From then on we spent most of my holidays from Oxford together, taking a house at Christmas in a little village in Wiltshire called Anstey Water, and another at Easter on the west coast of Cornwall. By this time it was pretty well settled between us that we were to be married when I came down from Oxford and we paid a more or less official visit to Renée's guardian, a gentlemanly solicitor who lived near Petersfield, not far from Telegraph House, where Bertrand Russell and Dora, his second wife, had set up their progressive school. We drove out to see the school, which seemed to me anarchic, but though I caught a glimpse of Russell I did not then venture to speak to him. Neither Renée's guardian nor his wife thought me at all eligible for her, and I made things very much worse by writing a letter of thanks to my hostess in which I quoted La Rochefoucauld's saying, *Les vieillards aiment à donner de bons préceptes pour se consoler de n'être plus en état de donner de mauvais exemples.* Meaning only to display my erudition, I had contrasted her with those to whom the saying was applicable, nor did I then know that she had been rather wanton in her youth; not unnaturally it was taken as a deliberate insult.

Renée came to grief in her turn when she wrote a letter of thanks to Mrs Wordsworth, with whom we had been staying, in which she spoke of her looking forward to marrying 'little Freddie'. She meant the phrase to be affectionate, but it sounded derogatory and gave the Wordsworths the impression that she was not in love with me. Andrew advised me not to marry her, and I did have some qualms, not so much on account of Renée's attitude towards me as from a half-conscious reluctance to assume the responsibilities of marriage. I did, however, feel myself to be committed and also did not want to separate from her.

In my third and last year as an undergraduate at Oxford, I worked quite steadily but not very much harder than I had before. Isaiah, who had got a first in Greats the previous summer, had stayed on for a fourth year to read PPE, in which he also got a first, and I met him more often to discuss philosophy, using his intelligence as a whetstone. I also profited by having a greater proportion of my tutorials with Gilbert Ryle. The result was that I felt myself to be quite well prepared to face the Greats' examiners. When Derek Walker-Smith, who had gone down the previous summer, rang me up at home at the end of the Easter vacation and asked me whether I was working hard for Schools, I said 'No. I seem to have done it all.' In retailing the story he changed this to 'No. I seem to know it all,' which was more than I should have claimed, but no doubt reflected the impression that I gave.

The prospect of becoming a barrister, in accordance with my grandfather's wishes, was still not distasteful to me, but I thought that I should first like to do some more philosophy, and I was also attracted by the idea of spending at least another year at Oxford. I therefore applied for a Research Lectureship which Christ Church had advertised. As Bobbie Longden had told me that I need not bother about testimonials, I wrote a very short letter of application, saying in two sentences that I was a candidate for the Lectureship and that I understood that in my case no testimonials were necessary. I was told later that this greatly amused the committee, since the numerous other candidates, professing various subjects, had not only supplied testimonials but had given extensive details of their programmes of research. I was appointed, not to the Lectureship for which I had applied, but to one that would normally qualify me for an official Studentship in philosophy. What had happened was that Michael Foster had put in for a professorship at Aberystwyth, and I had been chosen to replace him. The possibility that he might not get the job, among other things not being a Welshman, was strangely left out of account. In fact he did not get it, which was to create a problem both for me and for Christ Church later on. No problem was foreseen at the time because it was assumed that during the three years that the Lectureship could be made to last I should have no difficulty in getting myself elected to a permanent Fellowship at some other college.

Though I had not previously developed any firm intention of pursuing an academic career, I had no hesitation in accepting Christ Church's offer. I was and still am proud of obtaining such an appointment at the age of twenty-one, but a more practical reason was that it made me financially independent. The salary was, indeed, only £350 a year, but Renée had an allowance of £200 a year from her father, which could be expected to continue, and our combined incomes were enough in those days for us to live in comfort, even if I got nothing further from my grandfather. In fact, my grandfather, though he was a little disappointed by my becoming a don, and still thought it a mistake for me to marry so young, was not disposed to quarrel with me. I no longer wanted a regular allowance from him but I knew that if I fell into difficulties I could rely on him for help.

I celebrated my success with a noisy party at the George and for the first and only time in my undergraduate career incurred the displeasure of a proctor, who summoned me to see him the next morning. Being, I suppose, a little the worse for drink, I took this as an affront to my dignity and went on so much about it that Robert Willis, who was one of the party, remarked very truly that there were lacunae in my character. In the end I got Gilbert Ryle to intervene on my behalf, and the proctor was satisfied with a letter of apology.

In the course of congratulating me on my appointment, Dundas remarked characteristically that the last time that Christ Church had elected a philosopher who was still an undergraduate, he had disappointed them, first by getting only second class honours, and then by being such a poor teacher that they did not promote him to a Studentship. He hoped that I would not follow his example. In fact, I did run some risk of following at least the first part of it, since the philosophy examiners in Greats, all three of whom were philosophically conservative, were not very favourably impressed by the papers which I wrote. I did get an alpha mark on my Logic paper, but only beta marks on the Plato and Aristotle, in which I was once again thought to have been too disrespectful to Plato, and on the Morals and Politics paper, where I was so rash as to try to rehabilitate Utilitarianism, which was then considered in Oxford to have been decisively refuted. The story which was later current that I dismissed most of the questions as nonsensical has no foundation at all in fact. I was saved by Tom Brown Stevens, who had coached me so well that I got alpha marks on two of the Ancient History papers. I was also told, I do not know with how much truth, that Wade-Gery, the famous Greek historian, who was one of my examiners, feeling that the philosophers were prejudiced against me, had marked my papers up. The result was that I got a first with only a formal viva, which Wade-Gery conducted. Not realizing that he was championing me, and believing that if I was viva'd on my Greek history it must be because of its deficiencies rather than its merits, I answered his few questions in a cheeky manner, of which I was later ashamed.

Among the messages of congratulation which I received when the result was published was a friendly letter from Marsden, about which I had mixed feelings, and a postcard from Dr Alington just saying 'Clever Mr Ayer'. My grandfather once again hoped that my future career would be equally successful.

5 *Marriage and Vienna*

It was through Gilbert Ryle that I first learned of the work of Ludwig Wittgenstein. Though the English translation of Wittgenstein's *Tractatus Logico-Philosophicus* had been published in 1922, and he himself had been working in Cambridge since 1929, his ideas had hardly penetrated to Oxford. I think it likely that many of the college tutors had not even heard of him. Here too Gilbert was one of the exceptions and he put me on to the *Tractatus* early in my final year.

It made an overwhelming impression on me. I made light of its pictorial theory of language, which even then I can hardly have thought to be defensible in any literal sense, and I disregarded the hint of mysticism which occurs towards the end. Wholeheartedly accepting Wittgenstein's dictum *Wovon man nicht sprechen kann, darüber muss man schweigen* – somewhat archaically rendered in Ogden's translation as 'Whereof one cannot speak, thereof one must be silent' – I ignored Wittgenstein's suggestion that what could not be stated might nevertheless be shown. I had not yet heard of Otto Neurath, but his comment *Man muss ja schweigen, aber nicht über etwas* – 'One must indeed be silent, but not *about* anything' – exactly expressed my attitude. It chimed with the remark of another of my heroes, F. P. Ramsey, the Cambridge philosopher, whose death in 1930 at the age of twenty-six still seems to me to have been a disaster from which British philosophy has never quite recovered: 'What you can't say, you can't say and you can't whistle it either.' Significant propositions, I learned from the *Tractatus*, fell into two classes: either they were tautologies, like the propositions of logic and pure mathematics, or they were empirically verifiable. Everything else, including metaphysics and theology, was literally non-sensical.

As this shows, I took it for granted that the 'atomic propositions', which served in the *Tractatus* to determine the sense of everything that could be said, were propositions which referred to observable states of affairs. This was not made explicit by Wittgenstein himself, and is now thought by some of his disciples not to have been what he intended, but it was an assumption generally made at the time by those who latched on to the *Tractatus*, including philosophers with whom Wittgenstein was personally in contact. If he did not accept it, one wonders why he allowed them to think that he did. Whether he accepted it or not, it was an assumption that suited the positivism which his Viennese followers had inherited and one that also fitted the *Tractatus* into the tradition of British empiricism. Indeed, the two classes of significant propositions which the *Tractatus* admitted, on this interpretation, reproduced in only slightly different terms the division which Hume had made, almost two centuries earlier, between propositions concerning 'relations of ideas' and propositions concerning 'matters of fact', inviting us to ask of any volume 'of divinity or school metaphysics' *'Does it contain any abstract reasoning concerning quantity or number?* No. *Does it contain any experimental reasoning concerning matters of fact and existence?* No. Commit it then to the flames: for it can contain nothing but sophistry and illusion.'

Not only did Hume exclude metaphysics for very much the same reasons as the Viennese positivists were to give, but he can also be seen as having anticipated their famous principle of verifiability, as expressed in their slogan: 'The meaning of a proposition consists in its method of verification.' That Hume implicitly held a view of this sort was something that I came to believe before I knew anything of Wittgenstein or of Viennese positivism. In a comment on Hume's method which I wrote on the fly-leaf of my copy of *A Treatise of Human Nature*, when I first read this work as an undergraduate, I concluded by saying: 'In order to discover what he means, he studies the phenomena by which his proposition is verified.'

I think it unlikely that at that very early date I had already formulated the view that philosophy should consist in nothing more than logical analysis, but it was one that I was already predisposed to accept when Wittgenstein gave me what I saw as the authority for it.

The branch of philosophy which interested me most was the theory of knowledge, and I treated this mainly as the enterprise of finding an analysis of propositions about physical objects which would justify our claim to know them to be true. At that time it was a feature of this approach that one started out with sense-data. This was unorthodox by Oxford standards, but not by those of Cambridge, and with Ryle and Price as my local mentors, I gave my allegiance to the contemporary Cambridge school. Though I had bought a copy of the first volume of Russell's and Whitehead's *Principia Mathematica* and had struggled through the introduction, such understanding as I had of Russell's logical theories was derived from Susan Stebbing's *Modern Introduction to Logic*. I had, however, paid more serious attention to some of Russell's other works, including *Our Knowledge of the External World* and *The Analysis of Mind*, and while I could see that his reduction of the world to the simplest elements of experience had not been wholly carried through, I had no doubt that it was the proper course to follow. This did not preclude my also accepting G. E. Moore's defence of common sense. I got over the apparent inconsistency by relying on Moore's own distinction between knowing the truth of a proposition and knowing its analysis. How much this distinction could be made to bear comes out most amusingly in an early essay of Moore's on 'The Nature and Reality of Objects of Perception', which he reprinted in his *Philosophical Studies*. While he is in no doubt that observation gives us some reason to believe in the truth of the proposition that hens' eggs are generally laid by hens, he is prepared to regard it as an open question whether the facts which make it true are anything like what they are ordinarily thought to be. We could be right in taking the hens and eggs at their face value, but it is also possible that they are really collections of spirits, or configurations of invisible material particles, or sets of sensations, with a very different construe put upon the 'laying' in each case. I suppose that in later years Moore would have drawn the line at collections of spirits, but his attachment to common sense was always much looser than has generally been assumed.

Though I could not accept his causal theory of perception, I also profited by a close reading of C. D. Broad's *Scientific Thought* and *The Mind and its Place in Nature*. Philosophical fashion has not been kind to Broad, and indeed his historical importance is evidently less than that of Russell, Moore or Wittgenstein. Even so, I think that his work is under-rated. He was once described to me by Gilbert Ryle as a philosophical attorney, and though the remark was not intended to be complimentary, it does bring out Broad's virtues. Where he excelled was in drawing up a brief. The subject is discussed from every angle, the various possibilities judiciously set out, the precedents cited, the fallacious arguments exposed: nothing is skimped: looking for reason, we are not fobbed off with rhetoric: there is never a hint of 'something far more deeply interfused'. This is, perhaps, his weakness, that he does not burrow under the surface, but only few can do this with profit, and it is much to have the surface properly scrubbed. His lectures, which I never had the opportunity to attend, were said to be dull, if only because of his habit of reading out each sentence twice, but his books have touches of wit, as when, at the end of his laborious examination of Mc-Taggart's philosophy, covering two vast volumes, he congratulates himself on there being one subject about which he probably knows 'more than anyone in the universe, with the possible exception of God (if he exists) and McTaggart (if he survives)', or when he describes the after-life, on the evidence of spiritualists, as being 'like a perpetual bump-supper at a Welsh university'. Among those who have taken a serious interest in psychical research he was, I believe, unique in the combination of thinking it quite likely that there is an after-life and viewing the prospect with aversion. As he characteristically put it, 'I should be slightly more annoyed than surprised if I found myself in some sense persisting immediately after the death of my present body. One can only wait and see or alternatively (which is no less likely) wait and not see.'

I have already spoken of my debt to F. P. Ramsey. I found the fragmentary essays which were included at the end of his pos-thumously published *Foundations of Mathematics* rather difficult to follow but also very stimulating. Their tendency was pragmatic, and it was this that first made me think that there must be something good in pragmatism, which in spite, or perhaps because, of its having had a passionate local advocate in F. C. S. Schiller, was regarded in Oxford as altogether beyond the pale. It was not until many years later that I read the work of C. S. Peirce, arguably the greatest philosopher of the nineteenth century, but I bought William James's book on *Pragmatism* and found it very enjoyable. I particularly liked his division of philosophers into the tender-minded who were Rationalistic, Intellectualistic, Idealistic, Opti-

mistic, Religious, Free-Willist, Monistic and Dogmatical, and the
tough-minded who were Empiricist, Sensationalistic, Materialistic,
Pessimistic, Irreligious, Fatalistic, Pluralistic and Sceptical. I judged
myself to be predominantly tough-minded.

Philosophy is not one of those matters that they order better in
France, but I discovered two notable exceptions in Henri Poincaré,
whose books *La Science et l'Hypothèse* and *La Science et la Méthode*
first made me aware of the part that convention plays in science, and
Jean Nicod, a philosopher still wholly without honour in his own
country, who had worked with Russell at Cambridge and like
Ramsey had died young. His book, *The Foundations of Geometry and
Induction*, suffered from an exceptionally bad English translation,
but those who were not put off by this were very much rewarded.
The part on induction is ingenious, even if it does follow Keynes in
taking too simple a view of probability as an unanalysable relation,
and the part on geometry most imaginative, especially in its con-
struction of artificial worlds of sense. I referred to Nicod in my
Logic paper in Greats and was told that this caused at least one of
my examiners to read him. Again, this was something that I owed to
Gilbert Ryle.

Among all these influences, that which the *Tractatus* had upon
me was the strongest. I think that it was in my last term as an undergraduate that I read a paper on it to the Jowett Society. I remember
very little of the occasion except that the meeting was held in one
of the Senior Common Rooms at Christ Church and that several
dons were present, including Gilbert Ryle and Roy Harrod, but not
including Joseph or Prichard. Isaiah Berlin replied to the paper and
I gave a dinner party beforehand at which he and Andrew Wordsworth and Gilbert Highet were among the guests. The paper itself
had no great merit, being little more than a résumé of what I took
to be Wittgenstein's opinions, for which reason, indeed, it was
rejected by Moore a few months later when I submitted a more
careful version of it to him for publication in *Mind*. I believe,
however, that I am right in thinking that this was the first occasion
in Oxford on which there had been any public discussion of Wittgenstein's work.

Soon after the examination for Greats was over, Gilbert Ryle
drove me to Cambridge in order to introduce me to Wittgenstein.
They were personal friends though they had their differences, one
of them arising from Gilbert's refusal to admit that it was incon-

ceivable that there should ever be a good British film. Admittedly, Wittgenstein's taste ran to Westerns and to musicals, at which it was not very likely that Elstree would ever rival Hollywood. I do not think that they often discussed philosophy, in which their style was very different although their thoughts were later to run on rather similar lines. Wittgenstein had already moved away from the position which he held in the *Tractatus*, but his current views were imparted only to the narrow circle of his Cambridge pupils. He was at pains to keep any report of them out of general circulation, from a morbid fear of their being misrepresented or plagiarized. It was not until the late nineteen-thirties that one or two copies of notes taken from his lectures, the celebrated Blue and Brown Books, somehow managed to find their way to Oxford. So far as I was concerned, the Wittgenstein whom I was meeting in the summer of 1932 was still the Wittgenstein of the *Tractatus*.

He was then in his early forties but looked younger. He was small, thin and wiry and charged with nervous energy. One could see him as a mountaineer. His face was ascetic and remarkable chiefly for the eyes, which were blue and penetrating. He spoke softly in the manner of one who did not need to raise his voice in order to compel attention. His English was fluent and the Austrian accent not obtrusive. The rooms in which he lived were at the top of a long staircase near the main gate of Trinity. His sitting-room was small and white-washed like a monk's cell. There was hardly any furniture in it, and no apparent provision for receiving guests. However, two deck chairs were brought out of a cupboard and unfolded for us, and a box of biscuits offered to us.

The first question that I can remember Wittgenstein's asking me was what was the last book that I had read. I answered, as it happened truly, that it was Calderón's play *La Vida e Sueño* – 'Life is a dream'. He asked me what I thought of it and I said that I had not understood it very well. This answer obviously pleased him. I am not sure that I had meant much more than that I had found the Spanish difficult, but he took me to mean that there were depths in Calderón's thought which left me puzzled and this was a proof to him that I was serious. I do not remember what else we talked about, but from then on he treated me as a protégé. On the two or three occasions, in the course of the nineteen-thirties, when I visited Cambridge to read a paper to the Moral Science Club, he attended the meeting and took my part, usually finding in my paper more points of interest than I had myself been aware that it contained. I had the impression also that he liked me personally. He is, indeed, reported to have said, 'The trouble with Freddie Ayer is that he is clever all the time,' but I think that if he ever did say anything of this sort, it must have been much later when, as I shall relate, he too readily believed that I had been disloyal to him.

After seeing Wittgenstein, we went next door to King's to call on Richard Braithwaite, of whom I stood in some awe because I knew that he had been very close to Ramsey, both personally and philosophically. He seemed to me very clever, with a command of mathematics and science that was beyond my range, but his enthusiastic manner gave me confidence and I discussed philosophy with him more freely than I should have dared to do with Wittgenstein. The result was that he invited me to read a paper to the Moral Science Club at the beginning of the autumn term. The idea of addressing an audience which might contain Moore and Wittgenstein scared me, but I considered it feeble to give way to my fear and anyhow could think of no good reason to refuse. I was less afraid of Broad since I had heard him read a paper to the Jowett Society on the objects of belief. His theory, which required the admission of possibilities as real entities, seemed to me open to objections which I was at the time too diffident to put, but I had resolved that on any future occasion I should be more courageous.

Since Michael Foster was remaining at Christ Church, there was no immediate need for my teaching, and I was given two terms' leave of absence before taking up my duties as a lecturer. My first inclination was to spend this time in Cambridge, learning all that I could from Wittgenstein, but Gilbert Ryle had what he thought was a better idea. He had met Moritz Schlick, the leader of the Viennese positivists, at an international congress which had been held at Oxford in 1930, and had been very much impressed by him. He had probably also read the early numbers of the journal *Erkenntnis*, which was the official organ of the *Wiener Kreis* – the Vienna Circle, as the group, which Schlick directed, chose to be known. He therefore suggested that I should go to Vienna, enrol myself at the University, and learn as much as I could of the work that the Vienna Circle was doing. As almost nothing was known about them in England, he represented to me that by coming back with a report of their activities I should be not only benefiting myself but performing a public service. I was a little sorry to forgo the opportunity of working under Wittgenstein, but believing, in fact not quite truly, that the members of the Vienna Circle were thinking along the same lines, I reasoned that I should not lose very much by the exchange. Expecting also to be married to Renée by the time I went there, I thought that Vienna would be a more suitable place than Cambridge in which to spend a protracted honeymoon. The main drawback was that I knew very little German, but I was assured by Gilbert that Schlick spoke very good English, and I assumed that once I got to Vienna I should quickly pick up enough German to be able at least to follow the lectures and discussions. I also had time to learn some German before I went there, though I do not remember making much use of it. I intended to try for a Fellowship at All Souls for which the examination was to be held in November, and to go to Vienna only after I knew the result.

As soon as I had had my Greats viva, Renée and I went off together for a holiday in Spain. Partly in order to save money, we went by motor-cycle, with a side-car for me to sit in while Renée drove. We took camping equipment and little other luggage. Passing rapidly through France by the long straight road, mile upon mile of poplars, that goes down to Bordeaux, through Poitiers and Angoulême, we entered Spain at Irun, paused at Burgos to admire the baroque cathedral, and made our way over the mountains to Madrid. At that time not many tourists went to Spain, fewer still rode motor-cycles, and only gypsies camped. Our reversal of the customary roles of driver and passenger also drew attention to us, but the interest which we aroused in the villages where we bought provisions was always friendly. Once, a farmer on whose land we were camping, mistrusting my explanation of our presence or failing to understand my Spanish, summoned the Civil Guard, who brought the priest with him as an interpreter. I showed them my passport which as usual contained the words 'accompanied by his wife', making provision for an entry that was in fact left blank. The priest was able to translate this phrase, and mistaking it for a description, assured the farmer that we were, if eccentric, nevertheless respectable.

In Madrid, which was still a small town for a capital, the chief attraction for us was the Prado, which I remember as one of the best-appointed galleries that I have ever seen. With only a very slight knowledge of Spanish painting, I expected to admire El Greco but was unprepared for the poignancy of Goya or the magnificence of Velazquez. Having found a hotel within our means, we made Madrid the centre for excursions: to the enchanting mediaeval city of Avila, to Segovia with its Roman acqueduct dominating the plain, to the grim fortress of the Escorial and to Toledo where the superb El Greco picture of the burial of the Count of Orgaz, and those of the apostles in the Casa El Greco, confirmed my preference for him.

It was at Toledo that I saw my second bull-fight and Renée her first. This time, it was a *novillada*, at which apprentice bull-fighters try to do well enough to obtain the status of full matadors. But this was no ordinary *novillada*. There was comic relief with a clown in the costume of Charlie Chaplin killing an animal that looked no more dangerous than a calf, and a jazz-band of American negroes performing in the ring, the performance ending to great applause with the efficient dispatch by one of the players of an equally inoffensive bull to the strains of 'Good Night Sweetheart'. Only one spectator booed while the band was playing, provoking my neighbour to remark, '*Que falta de cultura. A el no gusta que los toros* – 'What a lack of culture. He only likes bulls'. Neither Renée nor I felt any desire to go to a bull-fight again.

From Madrid we went south to Andalusia, of which my most vivid memory is the oriental singing of the peasants late in the evening as they slowly rode their donkeys home. Seville was suitably operatic, with its narrow streets filled with the slatternly troops of General Sanjurjo, who failed in his attempted coup against the newly formed Republican government. With the benefit of an amnesty he later betook himself to Portugal, and might have come to power in place of Franco had it not been for his vanity. At the outset of the rebellion in July 1936, a plane was sent to Lisbon to fetch him back to Spain, but the number of full dress uniforms which he insisted on bringing with him made his luggage so heavy that the plane crashed on taking off and he was killed.

In 1932, Seville was the only city in which his rising was temporarily successful. The people seemed apathetic in the clammy August heat, which deprived us also of our energy for sight-seeing. At Granada the heat was less oppressive and we dutifully paid our respects to the Alhambra, which for all its prettiness seemed to me hardly to justify its popular description as one of the wonders of the modern world; no doubt it is part of my general prejudice against the fruits of Islam that I am put off by the fussiness in Moorish art.

Keeping to the mountains, we reached the east coast at Alicante, and then went north again into Catalonia, a Mediterranean province not at all like the rest of Spain. By now we were growing tired of camping and we stayed more often in hotels. Normally we stayed *en pension*, with dinner included in the cost, but once at a small hotel in Murcia, we decided to economize and have an even cheaper dinner at a restaurant in the town. We felt a little guilty about this, especially as we seemed to be almost the only guests in the hotel, and hoped to return to our room unobserved. But the proprietor was looking out for us and as soon as we entered the hotel he sat down at the piano to play us into the dining-room. I muttered something about having dined already, and we went shamefacedly past him up the stairs. I have always regretted that we did not have the grace to force ourselves to eat a second dinner.

I was disappointed by Valencia, which seemed to me ugly and commercial, but not at all by Barcelona, which I liked even better at second sight. I was captivated again by Gaudi's church and more seriously impressed by the monastery at Montserrat, a clerical fortress standing out sharply on a sudden hill. From Barcelona, we took the road to Andorra, a charming little principality, of which the entire population seemed to live by smuggling, entered France again through the Pyrenees, and with our money almost exhausted, went as quickly as possible home. I had hoped to cover our expenses by writing an article about the trip for *The Nineteenth Century and After*, which was then edited by Reggie Harris, a Fellow of All Souls. I had seen him before we left and obtained what I took to be a commission to write the article, but when I submitted it to him, he rejected it. I had written it very quickly, so that he may well have been right in thinking it not worth publication.

I had better fortune with my paper for the Moral Science Club, for which I chose the topic of generalizations of scientific law. Following Ramsey, from whom my paper was mainly derivative, I took the position, which now seems to me mistaken, that they were not propositions but rules. I was criticized by Broad, but not too harshly, and with aid from Wittgenstein and Richard Braithwaite, who seemed conscious of the responsibility of having invited so inexperienced a performer, emerged from the meeting without discredit. I dined with Braithwaite at King's beforehand and was awed to find myself seated opposite to Maynard Keynes; my awe was not diminished by his saying 'How do you do' to me and nothing further. This was also the first occasion on which I set eyes on G. E. Moore. He did not take a leading part in the discussion, but he looked benevolent, and I was very much taken with his puckish charm.

My chances of being elected to All Souls seemed fairly good, as this was a year in which three fellowships were offered instead of the customary two, and it was also the first year in which it was possible to take a paper in philosophy. Previously the examination had been confined to law and history, though the inclusion of general and essay papers had allowed the examiners sometimes to give preference to candidates of general ability over specialized lawyers and historians. The candidates were also invited to dinner, as a test of their manners, and summoned to an interview at which they were required to translate a short passage at sight from Latin or Greek or one of the principal modern languages. Like most others, I chose French and performed reasonably well, though without reaching the heights attained in the previous year by Goronwy Rees, who had greatly impressed the company by seeing that the word '*dragons*', which his nervous competitors translated as 'dragons', must in the context mean 'dragoons'. The subject on which we had to write an essay was that of Originality, which had also been set in the scholarship examination at Christ Church when I made my unsuccessful trial run. This time I approached it more philosophically but to little better effect. In my general paper I was reduced to attempting to answer a question about modern art, and I believe that I made a poor impression at the dinner, where my revival of my father's theory that we were counts of the Holy Roman Empire was not well received. But what was most disastrous for me was the philosophy paper. The first question was to the effect that metaphysics, though violating logic, is demanded by experience and I devoted nearly all the time at my disposal to it, quoting extensively from the *Tractatus* and roundly condemning metaphysics as nonsensical. This was wholly at variance with any philosophy that my examiners had been taught and they were not disposed to be converted. John Sparrow, who was one of them and later to become Warden of the college, is said to have remarked that even if my views were true, I showed a lack of worldly wisdom in the way that I advanced them. I was told that at the meeting at which the examiners' recommendations were discussed, Quintin Hogg made a speech in my favour, but even his advocacy was unavailing. There was never any serious question of my being elected.

I have sometimes regretted this set-back but never thought that it gave me cause for complaint. Isaiah Berlin, who was one of those preferred to me, was, in his greater intellectual maturity, much fitter material for All Souls, and the other two successful candidates both rose to the top of their professions, Sir Patrick Reilly in the diplomatic service, and Lord Wilberforce in the law. I might have taken encouragement from the fact that this was Wilberforce's third attempt, but I was much too well aware of the extent of my failure to have any inducement to try again.

With some idea that All Souls had a prejudice against admitting married men, I had deferred my marriage to Renée until after the examination. This obstacle, if it ever was one, being removed, we saw no reason for any further delay. By this time both our families were reconciled to the match, even if neither was enthusiastic. Renée's guardian and his wife were never going to like me and would in any case have preferred to see her married to someone more aristocratic, but at least they were able to assure her father in Japan that I had been well-educated and had a respectable job. My mother and my grandfather, as soon as they were allowed to meet Renée, liked her very much and did not hold it against her that she was not a wealthy heiress. They only thought the marriage imprudent because I was so young. In the course of giving his consent my grandfather said, 'You've had other girls of course?' and seemed rather dismayed when I told him that I had not.

The question that still remained to be settled was where and how we should be married, and on this we held very different views. I wanted us to be married in a registry office, with an informal party afterwards. Renée was set upon a church wedding, with a formal reception. Not only that, but the church which she had in mind was the Brompton Oratory. She was no longer a practising Catholic, but she wanted to please her family so far as possible, and believed that some of them would be distressed if she were married elsewhere than in a Catholic church. She had a good case on utilitarian grounds and supported it with the argument that it could do me no harm to listen to a rigmarole to which I attached no meaning. The most serious objection was that the priest would not consent to marry us unless I undertook to allow Renée to bring our putative children up as Catholics. After some futile argument with the priest, I signed the undertaking, knowing that it had no legal validity and that Renée would not try to enforce it. Like a child keeping its fingers crossed, I muttered half audibly Euripides's line from the *Hippolytus*: 'ἡ γλῶσσ' ὀμώμοχ', ἡ δὲ φρὴν ἀνώμοτος' – 'the tongue has sworn but the mind has not sworn.' This is an action of which I have always been ashamed. In the event, our two children were not baptized, and have not embraced any form of Christianity, though I never put any obstacle in the way of their learning about its various doctrines.

We were married in the Brompton Oratory on November 25. The ceremony was conducted in a side-aisle and took the shorter form which is prescribed for the case where one of the parties is not a Catholic. I found it less embarrassing than I had feared, though I was disconcerted when the priest suddenly sprinkled us with holy water. A photograph of us emerging from the church appeared the next morning in some newspaper, causing pain, as Isaiah later told me, to the Bicks, whom I had meanly forgotten to invite. The reception took place at a hotel. I had asked David Hedley to be my best man and made him promise that he would not call upon me for a speech. When he broke his promise, I could not think of anything more adequate to say than that I hoped they were all enjoying their champagne. I suppose that my family and most of my Oxford friends were present, but the only other person whose presence I remember at all clearly was Peter Quennell, whom I then hardly knew. He had been in Tokyo, which he much disliked, as a visiting Professor of English Literature at the time when Renée was last there, and she and his pretty wife Nancy had become great friends. Renée had taken me to dine on approval in the Quennells' band-box of a London house, and I had failed to rise to the occasion. The conversation languished to the point where all that Peter could find to say to me was, 'For God's sake, have some more wine.' It was only some years later, when Peter and Nancy had parted, that he and I started to become the friends that we now are.

The day after our wedding, Renée and I left for Vienna. We took a boat from Harwich to Ostend and from there made the long train journey through Germany. Martin Cooper was already in Vienna, studying to become a pianist, and he had found us lodgings at 25 Schönbergstrasse in the 4th Bezirk. We had two rooms in our landlady's flat and the use of the bathroom and kitchen. The rooms were comfortably furnished in a heavy old-fashioned style and heated by a large stove. Our landlady was a Frau Jones, a matronly middle-aged American, who made her living by giving English lessons. She had been so long in Vienna that her English had grown rusty and I was amused when one of her pupils rightly translated '*entweder . . . oder*' as 'either . . . or' to hear her correct it to 'or . . . or'. Frau Jones and Anna, her maid of all work, were both very kind to us, and except for an unhappy fortnight when we thought that it would be nicer to live in the centre of the town and rented a cheerless and rather more expensive set of rooms from a steely Frenchwoman, we remained in those lodgings for the whole of our four months' stay in Vienna.

As soon as we had settled in with Frau Jones, I went to call on Moritz Schlick at his apartment in the neighbouring but rather grander Prinz Eugen Strasse. Schlick was a German by birth and had been a professor at Kiel before he was appointed in 1922 to the Chair of the Philosophy of the Inductive Sciences at the University of Vienna. At the time when I met him he was just fifty years of age, but seemed to me older. He had an American wife of a homely type who looked like a German Hausfrau, whereas he had the suave appearance and manner that I had come through my film-going to associate with an American senator. I had brought with me a letter of introduction from Gilbert Ryle, and after reading the letter and talking to me for about half an hour, Schlick not only made the necessary arrangements for me to attend lectures at the University but invited me to participate in the meetings of the Vienna Circle.

I was pleased and excited by this invitation, but not so surprised as I now think that I should have been. I did not then realize how great a privilege it was. The number of those regularly working in Vienna who had been admitted to membership of the Circle was fewer than twenty, and they were nearly all men of some standing in the academic world; at least seven of them held university chairs. The only person there to whom I came at all near in status was W. V. Quine, who had just obtained his doctorate at Harvard. Although there were several Polish philosophers and logicians, like Ajdukiewicz and Tarski, and a Berlin group, primarily consisting of Reichenbach, von Mises and Hempel, with whom the Circle maintained close relations, I believe that Van Quine and I were the only two visitors ever to become members of it.

The Circle had come into being in the late nineteen-twenties. Its manifesto: *Wissenschaftliche Weltauffassung: Der Wiener Kreis* –

Scientific View of the World: The Vienna Circle – was published in 1929 and it was in 1930 that it took over the journal *Annalen der Philosophie*, in which Wittgenstein's *Tractatus* had first appeared under its German title of *Logisch-philosophische Abhandlung*, and renamed the journal *Erkenntnis*. It was also bringing out a series of pamphlets under the general title of *Einheitswissenschaft* – Unified Science – and a series of books under the general title of *Schriften zur Wissenschaftlichen Weltauffassung*. Though Karl Popper, who was then working as a schoolteacher in Vienna, was not himself a member of the Circle, and has always been at pains to emphasize, indeed to over-emphasize, his differences from it, his celebrated *Logik der Forschung*, translated into English twenty years later as *The Logic of Scientific Discovery*, first appeared in this series in 1935. Later on the Circle made itself responsible for the set of monographs which were eventually published in the United States under the ambitious title of *The Encyclopædia of Unified Science*.

As the repeated references to science indicate, one of the principal aims of the Vienna Circle was to rebuild the bridge between philosophy and science which had been largely broken by the romantic movement and the accompanying rise of idealist metaphysics at the beginning of the nineteenth century. Indeed, its members saw the future of philosophy as consisting, once the fight against metaphysics had been won, in the development of what they called the logic of science. In this, as well as in their tendency to try to reduce the physical world to the elements of sense-experience, they were resuming the Viennese tradition of such men as the physicist Ernst Mach, a previous holder of Schlick's chair, and the philosopher Avenarius, whose attraction for some of Lenin's followers had provoked Lenin into writing his polemical *Materialism and Empirio-Criticism*. It was meant to prevent them from straying from the straight materialist high-road into what Lenin regarded, not wholly without reason, as a form of subjective idealism. Since the position which Lenin takes in this book is hardly distinguishable from that of Locke, it is amusing that it should have become a sacred Marxist text. The members of the Vienna Circle, with the notable exception of Otto Neurath, were not greatly interested in politics, but theirs was also a political movement. The war of ideas which they were waging against the Catholic church had its part in the perennial Viennese conflict between the socialists and the clerical reaction. It was because their forerunners were in this respect his political allies that Lenin, no less intolerant than Marx of any competition, had attacked them so sharply. If the Nazis eventually destroyed the Vienna Circle, it was not because its members were Jewish, which hardly any of them were, but because they were rational.

From its outset, then, the Circle consisted not only of philosophers but also of mathematicians and physicists. Apart from Schlick, its leading philosophical member was Rudolf Carnap. He too was a German who had studied physics at the University of Jena, and had there been one of the few to attend the lectures of the great logician and philosopher of language, Gottlob Frege, who was another of those prophets to be without honour in his own country. Carnap's first major work, *Der logische Aufbau der Welt*, only recently translated into English as *The Logical Structure of the World*, had appeared in 1928. It was an attempt to construct the whole hierarchy of concepts needed for the description of the world with no other materials than the apparatus of modern logic and a primitive relation of similarity, which the subject remembers as holding between two elements of his experience. It was indeed impossible that so very large a rabbit should genuinely emerge from so very small a hat, but like all the best of Carnap's work, the book was remarkable for its technical virtuosity. While writing it, Carnap had been in some contact with Wittgenstein, and duly paid him acknowledgement, but this put an end to their acquaintance. Wittgenstein is reported to have said that he did not mind a small boy's stealing his apples but did mind his saying that the owner had given them to him. If Wittgenstein did say this, it is another piece of evidence against those who now maintain that he never considered himself to be a positivist of the current Viennese type. By the end of 1932, when I arrived in Vienna, Carnap, in company with Philipp Frank, the Circle's leading expert on physics, had left Vienna to take a chair at the German University of Prague, and though I profited a great deal from reading his book and his articles in *Erkenntnis*, I did not meet him at that time.

Throughout most of his career Carnap was strongly subject to other influences, and after Wittgenstein had quarrelled with him, he came under the spell of Otto Neurath, a very different sort of man from Wittgenstein but also one with a very strong personality. It was Neurath who wrongly persuaded Carnap that it was metaphysical to talk of comparing propositions with facts, and so led him for a time to abandon a correspondence theory of truth in favour of a coherence theory, and it was owing to Neurath also that Carnap was drawn into materialism, to the point of maintaining that propositions apparently about mental states were re-expressible in wholly physical terms. Neurath was primarily a sociologist and, as I have said, the only member of the Vienna Circle to take an active interest in politics. He had held an administrative position in the revolutionary Spartacist government in Munich, which briefly held power after the war, and when this government was overthrown with the help of the nationalist Freikorps, he had been chased through the streets with a revolver by Graf von Zeppelin, whose American wife, Amethe Smeaton, subsequently made some amends by translating Carnap's *Logische Syntax der Sprache* into English. Neurath was close to being a Marxist, and consequently set himself to draw Viennese positivism away from the subjectivist standpoint which Lenin had criticized. It was he who took the lead in proclaiming the unity of science, which he understood to imply not only a community of method but also the use of a common language, in the sense that all the sciences, including the social sciences, were ultimately concerned with physical events. Not only that, but he also advanced the view, on which Quine has recently laid so much stress, that our beliefs face the test of experience as a whole, with the result that if it appears that something has gone amiss, we have a choice as to which hypotheses to sacrifice. A simile which Quine has taken from him is that of our being at sea on a ship of which we can repair any part that seems to need it but never the whole of the ship at the same time, since we have to retain some foothold on it.

Neurath was a large man, running to fat in middle-age, with a white puffy skin, reminding me of a marshmallow. He used to sign his letters with the symbol of an elephant. Though his appearance was not prepossessing, he had charm and an attractive vein of humour. When the Germans occupied Austria in 1938 he took refuge in Holland, and when Holland was invaded by them he escaped with his wife to England by rowing across the Channel. With the dissolution of the Circle, his interest in philosophy waned and he made his living in England by running an institute which specialized in the pictorial representation of statistics. I lost touch with him during the war and learned only afterwards from his widow that he had died in 1945.

Next in the philosophical hierarchy, as I saw it, came Friedrich

Waismann, who held a quite junior post in the University as Schlick's assistant. Of all the members of the Circle, he was the one who was most strongly influenced by Wittgenstein. He was writing a book which was listed under the title of *Logik, Sprache, Philosophie* as number one in the series of *Schriften zur Wissenschaftlichen Weltauffassung*. Subsequent volumes in this series appeared in due order, but though it continued to be advertised the first one never did. The reason for this was that Waismann was drawing heavily on the later ideas of Wittgenstein, and every summer when Wittgenstein came from Cambridge to Vienna, Waismann showed him the manuscript and Wittgenstein said that while he could not prevent Waismann from publishing it he thought it would not be fair to him for it to appear in its current state. Waismann made what he hoped were the necessary changes, only for the same procedure to be repeated. The result is that the series of *Schriften zur Wissenschaftlichen Weltauffassung* still starts with number two, though an English translation of Waismann's manuscript was published some years after his death, by which time the publication of Wittgenstein's own posthumous *Philosophical Investigations* had made it largely obsolete. Waismann was, however, permitted to publish an article on probability in *Erkenntnis*, in which he developed a view that Wittgenstein had adumbrated in the *Tractatus*, and a short book, *Einführung in das mathematische Denken* – Introduction to Mathematical Thought – in which the view that the propositions of mathematics are true by convention is subtly and pithily set out.

Waismann was Jewish, and when Vienna fell to the Germans he fled with his family to England. He went to Cambridge, which was willing to accept him, but Wittgenstein did not desire that what he regarded as a deceptive echo of his own thought should be audible in the same university, and therefore announced that anyone who attended Waismann's lectures would not be allowed to come to his. This made Waismann's position in Cambridge impossible, and he moved to Oxford where he was eventually given a Readership in the Philosophy of Mathematics. He came to reject the rigour of his early positivism, finding a contorted merit in metaphysics, but developed a penchant for the branch of linguistic philosophy which consisted in the study of ordinary English usage, undeterred by his own difficulties with the English language. I remember a meeting of the philosophical society at University College, London, in the nineteen-fifties at which he illustrated some subtle point by pronouncing with great emphasis the sentence 'I wear my watch *upon* my pocket.' Though passionate in discussion, he was a shy and lonely man and his loneliness was increased by the suicide of his wife, who was shattered by the discovery that anti-Semitism existed also in England, and later of his much-loved only son. Though he remained at Oxford until his death in 1959, he was always a Viennese who had difficulty in making the adjustment to the English intellectual climate. But he continued working, in his later years not so much straightforwardly at philosophy as at composing philosophical epigrams, of which he once said proudly that he had written over a thousand. I remember only one of them, a pun on the German word *aber*. '*Aberglaube? Aber Glaube!*' – 'Superstition? But belief!'

The principal mathematicians in the Circle at that time were Professors Menge and Hahn, but the one who was to become most famous was Kurt Gödel, then still a young man of twenty-six. He had already published, in 1931, the theorem which proves that any system which has the resources for the expression of arithmetic must contain true propositions which are not decidable within the system, but although it created a difficulty for their conventionalist view of mathematics, the importance of this theorem was not yet fully appreciated by his colleagues: at least I cannot remember there being any discussion of it. I doubt if Gödel himself had very much sympathy for their general position, but he came regularly to the meetings and did not express dissent. I remember him as dark and small and silent and self-contained.

The Circle met once a week in a small room in an Institute outside the university. We sat at a rectangular table with Schlick at the head and Neurath opposite him. Menge and Hahn sat on Schlick's right, and Waismann on his left. The others present, apart from Gödel, were mostly philosophers, of whom I remember Professors Reiniger and Victor Kraft, and among the younger men Bela von Juhos and Edgar Zilsel. The discussion appeared to centre week after week on the topic of what they called *Protokolsätze*, the basic deliverances of perception, with Schlick maintaining that they must be descriptive of sense-experiences, about which the subject could not be mistaken, and Neurath arguing against him that one must start at the level of physical objects, and that no beliefs were sacrosanct. There were, however, occasional diversions. Once, Reichenbach came from Berlin to deliver a long lecture on his

favourite topic of the frequency theory of probability, and Quine
gave us a talk on his current work in logic. Quine has an extraordinary gift for languages and I was very much impressed by his
fluency in German. My own command of the language was still
rudimentary, though I was taking private lessons. I did, however,
learn enough in a few weeks to be able to understand most of what
was being said, though not enough to take any part in the argument.
My sympathies on the principal issue, had I been able to voice
them, lay mainly with Schlick, though I did come to agree with
Neurath that all our beliefs are fallible.

I had more difficulty in understanding Schlick's lectures, which
were the only ones that I attended at the University. He was giving
a course on the philosophy of science, with sufficient scientific
detail for me to be handicapped by my ignorance of the subject-
matter as well as my ignorance of the language. He delivered the
lectures seated, as is the usual practice on the Continent, and spoke
in a monotonous tone without very much exerting himself to
capture the attention of his audience. This was in contrast to his
writing, which was generally sharp and clear. He was not, I think, a
highly original philosopher, though his book on the theory of
knowledge – *Allgemeine Erkenntnis-Lehre* – which was published as
early as 1918, anticipated much of the Circle's programme, but he
had a vigorous intelligence and the Circle, as an organized body,
owed a great deal to his leadership. It never had quite the same
vitality after his murder in 1936. He was shot as he was entering the
university by one of his graduate pupils. The motive for the crime
was thought to have been more personal than political. The man
had been in a mental home: Schlick had rejected his doctoral thesis
on some moral topic: it was rumoured that Schlick, who had an eye
for women, had given the man some cause for jealousy. It is,
however, also possible that the murderer had received some encouragement from Schlick's enemies. The right-wing press did
not go so far as to condone the crime, but there was a suggestion
that if one persisted in teaching them positivism, this was not a
wholly unnatural way for one's pupils to react.

By this time Austria had a right-wing government, headed first
by Dollfuss and then by von Schuschnigg; it had proved its authority
in February 1934 by successfully besieging and partly destroying the
Karl Marx Hof, a big block of workers' flats which had been turned
into a Socialist stronghold. It was, however, vulnerable from

another quarter and in July of the same year Dollfuss himself was murdered by the Nazis. In 1932, the Austrian parliament was almost evenly divided between left and right, though the Socialists were still in command of Vienna itself. The Nazis were not yet very much in evidence, but with Hitler's accession to power in Germany in January 1933, the few that one saw behaved as though the city already belonged to them. They had some support among the students and on several occasions when I went to the University, I found it closed because of rioting.

For the most part, however, the political tensions still lay beneath the surface. No longer the capital of an empire or the seat of a resplendent monarchy, the city appeared a little run to seed, but at the same time it gave the impression of great intellectual vitality. I liked almost everything about it: the heavy baroque architecture of the old imperial buildings: the Kunsthistorisches Museum with its marvellous collection of Breughels and the painting by Tintoretto of *Susannah and the Elders*, for which both Renée and I felt a special affection; the street market where we bought a goose for Christmas; the crowded tramways; the cafés where you could sit indoors for hours over a single cup of coffee reading the newspapers which they provided; the cellars where for very little money you could drink litres of white wine of the newest vintage; the unpretentious night-clubs; the popular dance-halls, where you could ask strangers for a dance. It was at one of these dances that I first realized with a shock of excitement that I might be attractive to other girls besides Renée, and attracted by them. I danced with the girl only once and never saw her again, but the memory stayed with me. She may, indeed, easily have had another motive; as a foreigner I might be supposed to be comparatively rich. In fact, we had little money to spare. On the days when I went to the University, I used to lunch alone at a near-by restaurant, and I seldom could afford anything but boiled beef and noodles, for which I had little liking then and none at all since.

Even so, we did not seriously stint ourselves. We saw a great many German films, in small cinemas, like lecture halls, with rows of wooden seats. The best of them were musical comedies, a little in the style of René Clair, with Willy Fritsch and Willy Forst and Lilian Harvey as the stars. One that I found especially charming was *Die drei von der Tank-Stelle*, of which a French version was made with the characteristically different title of *Le Chemin du Paradis*.

Lilian Harvey appeared in both. She also starred in both the German and English versions of *The Congress Dances*, a very successful film about the Congress of Vienna, with Conrad Veidt playing the part of the romanticized Tsar Nicholas I. The most popular German film actor of the period was the robustly nordic Hans Albers, whom we saw in a number of films of adventure. In one of them we were astonished and delighted to see Goronwy Rees, dressed in a kilt and playing the part of an officer in a Highland regiment. He had gone to Berlin to do research for a book on Lassalle, and had found this way of earning some extra money.

My film-going helped with my German, which I also tried to improve, at my teacher's suggestion, by reading the plays and stories of the Austrian writer Arthur Schnitzler, describing the Vienna of the early part of the century. What began as a chore became a pleasure. I particularly liked the story of Lieutenant Gustl, who allows himself to be snubbed at the theatre by a common baker, spends the remainder of the night trying to nerve himself to commit suicide, learns in the morning that the baker has died of a heart-attack and looks forward with pleasure to the duel which he has fastened on to some inoffensive civilian of his own class. The story, which takes the form of a monologue, ends with his gloating over the prospect of cutting the man to mincemeat. It cost Schnitzler his position as an army doctor, on the ground that it was libellous: a real Austrian lieutenant would have committed suicide anyway. We went once to the Burgtheater, to see a performance of Schnitzler's *Liebelei*, which was later made into a successful film with Paula Wesseley in the leading part, but found the traditional style of the actors excessively melodramatic. It reminded me of Dr Johnson's saying when asked whether he would not start as Garrick did, if he saw a ghost, 'I hope not. If I did I should frighten the ghost.'

My affection for Schnitzler did not lead me further into Austrian or German literature, and I have read very little German since, except for the writings of contemporary German and Austrian philosophers. I share the general admiration for Kafka, and fail to share that for Thomas Mann, but in both cases I have read their works only in translation. I have read some of Heine's work with pleasure but am otherwise almost entirely ignorant of German poetry.

What I did develop in Vienna was a taste for opera, which had lain dormant in me since my parents took me to see *Così fan tutte*, or had anyhow not advanced beyond Gilbert and Sullivan. We were able to get seats in the gallery of the Staatsoper for only a few shillings, and we went as often as we could. This was a season in which they played a great deal of Verdi, of whom I previously knew nothing, and I remember being greatly moved by performances of *Don Carlos* and *La Forza del Destino*, appearing in German as *Die Macht des Schicksals*, and most of all by a fine performance of *Otello*. But, as always in Vienna, the best attention was given to the operas of Mozart, especially to *Don Giovanni* and *Le Nozze di Figaro*. Perhaps they suffered a little from being sung in German; in Leporello's recital of Don Juan's conquests *'tausend und drei'* lacks the gaiety of *'mille e tre'*; even so, they were magnificent. We also saw a splendid production of Richard Strauss's and Hugo von Hofmannsthal's *Der Rosenkavalier*, with Lotte Lehmann as the Marschallin: Baron Ochs's waltz theme has remained one of my favourite operatic pieces. Wagner was not very much on offer, but we went to a performance of *Lohengrin*, with the name-part sung by Leo Slezak, who was famous for saying, on one occasion when the swan failed to appear in time to carry him off the stage, 'When does the next swan leave?' – *'Wann geht der nachste Schwan?'* My appetite for music barely extended to concerts, but I was very much excited by a performance of Stravinsky's *The Rite of Spring*, which I was also hearing for the first time. I remember this concert well for another reason. We had to stand in a packed audience next to a man with exceptionally smelly feet. For a time the competition was close, but the music emerged victorious.

No doubt our receptiveness to music at that time owed something to Martin Cooper, who was very often with us. He had been discouraged by his teacher from attempting to become a concert pianist and was acquiring the knowledge which was to earn him distinction as a music critic. He became as much a friend of Renée's as of mine and the three of us explored Vienna together very happily. We hardly sought for any other company, though we took pleasure in seeing Quine and his handsome wife. The atmosphere of *la vie de Bohème*, which we shared with Martin, was sustained by an attractively feckless English girl, a friend of Renée's, who came out to stay with us, mainly to be with her lover, a pompous young Englishman, who liked us as little as we liked him. She later married into the peerage and he suitably became a Conservative member of Parliament.

After Christmas, while the university was on holiday, Renée and I went off to live alone together in the Wienerwald in a cottage which an American friend of Martin's had lent us. Our hostess had supplied us with the equipment for skiing, and for the first and last time in my life I made an attempt to ski. With no experience and no tuition, the best that I could manage was an ungraceful walk, and that not for very long. Partly because of the cold, and partly to avoid the bother of shaving, I grew a beard which I kept for a while after we returned to Vienna. It made me look like a Rabbi. I shaved it off, not for that reason, but because I decided that it did not suit me.

In the spring we made expeditions to the countryside, nearly always with Martin. One of them was made remarkable by our lunching in an inn which served Arkleitener Bierkäse, the strongest cheese that I have ever tasted: the smell of it hung about me for the day, to the delight of the others who had been more prudent. On two occasions we went further afield. Bernard Burrows arrived in Vienna and took us to Budapest, where we saw a performance of Donizetti's *Don Pasquale*. I enjoyed the opera but found the city less romantic than I had expected. We also made an excursion to Prague, where I thought the old city beautiful, but the people seemed stodgy in comparison with the Viennese.

We left Vienna in March to give ourselves time to get settled in Oxford before the beginning of the summer term. Alan Pryce-Jones, whom I had known slightly at Eton and at Oxford, inherited our lodgings and the motherly affection of Frau Jones. '*Die Ayeren waren so süss,*' she said to him, '*ganz neu verheiratet.*' – 'The Ayers were so sweet! Just married!'

6 *Language, Truth and Logic*

It did not take us long to find somewhere to live in Oxford. We rented a flat on the first floor of a house at the corner of the High Street and Longwall. It contained a sitting-room, a kitchen which served us also as a dining-room, and a bedroom which was separated from the living-room by a narrow passage in which I kept my books. We furnished our living-room in the style of the Second Empire with a sofa and two armchairs, which we bought for a few pounds in a second-hand furniture shop in London. I was so bad at bargaining that I offered the salesman as much for one piece as he was asking for all three: otherwise I could probably have got them even cheaper. Possibly they were genuine. At any rate they looked very elegant, though they were not very comfortable. An American friend of ours in Vienna had painted a modern version of *Susannah and the Elders* for us and we hung it over our bed. It was not a very good picture, but large and spectacular.

We acquired two Siamese cats whose colouring matched that of the furniture. I called one of them Toro, and used the sentence 'Toro is white' to illustrate the distinction between particulars and universals in a paper on Universals which I read to the Aristotelian Society. It appeared in their Proceedings for 1933–4 and was the second philosophical paper that I published, the first being an essay called 'The Case for Behaviourism' which I contributed to *Oxford Outlook*. This was entirely derivative from Carnap and I now think very largely mistaken. The paper on Universals, on the other hand, still seems to me to have some merit.

We hoped that the cats would breed, and so they did, but to little purpose since nearly all the kittens died in infancy. We took them on holiday with us, but even the air of Brighton could not save them, and I walked along the front furtively dropping their bodies, wrapped in newspaper, in a series of litter-baskets. It was at the time when the police were looking for a murderer, who had killed and dismembered his mistress, and I was followed with suspicion.

Our household was completed by a donkey, or more strictly speaking an ass, which Renée had found a carter maltreating in the street and immediately bought from him. We called her Lucia, after Lucius Apuleius, the author of *The Golden Ass*, and paid a small sum to a local farmer to let us keep her in one of his fields. We also bought a cart, with the idea that Renée could drive to do her shopping, but Lucia proved so recalcitrant in harness that we did not pursue the experiment. From then on she lived a life of leisure in the farmer's field until we succeeded in giving her away.

Christ Church allotted me rooms in which to do my teaching, at first in Killcanon, so called because it lay in a windy passage which was thought to be fatal to the canons' fragile health, and later a more handsome set of rooms in Peckwater Quad, immediately below those in which I had lived as an undergraduate. Though my lectureship was mainly designed for me to pursue research, I was allowed to do a small amount of teaching. I took pupils from Christ Church for both Greats and PPE. The fact that they were very nearly of my own age, and in one or two cases actually older than I was, did not embarrass me, though I was disconcerted when one of them turned to me at the end of the tutorial and said, 'What great sad dark brown eyes you have, sir.' All I could find to answer was, 'Er. Do you think so?' I was not very competent at teaching ancient philosophy, but I developed some views about Plato's tripartite division of the Soul and the State, and about Aristotle's account of the different sorts of friendship, which enabled me to get by. I was weak on Leibniz and Spinoza and not very strong on Kant, but more at home with Descartes and the British empiricists. I could cope with moral and political philosophy, and very much enjoyed teaching the philosophy of logic and the theory of knowledge. I did not set out to convert my pupils to Logical Positivism, as the position of the Vienna Circle had come to be called, but I suppose that my enthusiasm for it had an effect upon some of them. One of those most affected by it was an American called Hilary Sumner-Boyd, who was secretary, and for all I could ever discover, the only member of the Oxford Trotskyist party. His extreme gentleness of manner belied the ferocity of his ideas.

I gave my first course of lectures in the autumn of 1933, lecturing once a week on Russell, Wittgenstein and Carnap. Since I had no confidence at all in my ability to improvise I wrote the lectures out beforehand. I did this with nearly all the lectures that I gave in those early years and I sometimes do it still. It has the advantage of making one's discourse more coherent, but the disadvantage of increasing one's distance from the audience: one has to acquire the art of reading without seeming to read. At that time I had not acquired it and since I spoke rather fast, my lectures must have been difficult to follow. Nevertheless, I succeeded in retaining my fairly small audience.

As a lecturer, I was not a member of the Governing Body of Christ Church, but did have all the privileges of the Senior Common Room, so that I now got to know the numerous dons whom I had not previously met, as well as the Canons, who played a relatively small part in the life of the college, apart from their presence on its Governing Body. We met mostly at dinner in Hall, in those days always at least a five-course meal, which we were given free. We had, however, to pay for our drinks and for any guests that we brought in. Women were not admissible as guests, and undergraduates only from other colleges and then only on one day in the week. If one dined in Hall, one was expected to go into Common Room for dessert and more drinks, unless one could give some acceptable excuse, such as having a meeting to attend. The port went round a great many times, and since for reasons of economy I had to limit myself to one glass, I sometimes felt that the proceedings dragged, though quite often the conversation made up for it. The fact that one could not smoke until the coffee was brought in was not then the hardship to me that it would be now. When the formal proceedings were over we continued, in winter, to sit talking around the fire: those who could afford it went on drinking whisky: more often than not there was a table or two of bridge.

The atmosphere of the Christ Church Senior Common Room at that time reminded me of the mess in a smart cavalry regiment, as described in one of Kipling's stories. There was more than an appearance of equality. Except for the nominal commanding officer who was always addressed as Mr Dean, and the Canons, who on the comparatively rare occasions when they dined with us were rather in the position of honoured guests, we were nearly all on Christian name terms. This did not preclude a recognition of differences of rank, but prestige was not a simple function of seniority. It depended on various factors, such as the force that one exercised in college politics, one's social position within the university and more especially in the world outside, the quality of the guests whom one brought in to dinner, one's powers as a conversationalist, even one's skill at playing cards. Academic merit counted for less than might have been expected, except in the case of those who were, or showed promise of becoming, exceptionally eminent. No doubt these factors operate to some extent in all colleges, but I have the impression that in Christ Church, perhaps because of its tradition of nurturing great men, they carried abnormal weight. Thus, Roy Harrod in his fascinating biography of Lord Cherwell found it quite natural to speak of the bulk of his colleagues in the early thirties as 'the riff-raff', not simply voicing his own judgement but using a term that was current at the time. It did not imply that these men were in any way disreputable, either personally or academically, but merely that on the operative scale their rating was not high.

Pride of place was shared between Dundas and J. C. Masterman, whom we addressed respectively as 'D' and 'J.C.'. Dundas was the Senior in appointment and presided in Common Room with quiet authority, but in the internal politics of the college, J.C. was perhaps the more powerful. A tutor in history, he had been educated at the Naval College of Dartmouth and had been an undergraduate at Worcester College before the war, winning a half-blue for the high-jump. Having had the misfortune to be in Germany at the outbreak of war, he was interned and spent the war in captivity. Otherwise, he would undoubtedly have made a first-rate officer. After the war, he developed into a very good all-round athlete and represented England at hockey. He was not married. His attitude to life seemed to me very similar to that which is reflected in the novels of John Buchan, and indeed this comes out to a certain extent in the two novels which he himself published in the 1930's. The weaker of them was very roughly handled in a review by Cyril Connolly, in my view too roughly, just as I think that Dr Leavis has been unfair in his criticism of the more ambitious novels of C. P. Snow. There was thought to be some possibility that J.C. would succeed Alington as headmaster of Eton, but it came to nothing. Instead, he was elected Provost of Worcester, after serving throughout the second world war in Counter-Intelligence, about which he has written an interesting book. In the early thirties there was a sharp difference of opinion among the Governing Body of Christ Church as to the relative importance that the college should attach to the training of undergraduates and the furtherance of research. J.C. led the party of those who gave priority to the training of undergraduates.

His principal opponent was Lord Cherwell, then Professor Lindemann, and generally known as 'The Prof'. The Prof had to operate behind the scenes since his Studentship at Christ Church did not entitle him to membership of the Governing Body. The reason for this was that he was also a Fellow and a member of the Governing Body of Wadham. He preferred, however, to live in Christ Church, and occupied a set of rooms in Meadow Buildings, the nineteenth-century neo-Gothic addition to the College. A man of independent means, he kept a private servant in addition to those that the college provided, and drove a Rolls-Royce car. He too was a bachelor, and perhaps not greatly interested in sex, except in the way of gossip, though he had the habit of telling mildly salacious stories. Being a strict vegetarian, he did not very often dine with us, though he liked to come into Common Room, at the end of the formal proceedings, and take part in the conversation. When he did dine in, he always took the same seat in Common Room, with his back to the fire. He had been a brilliant physicist in his youth, and had distinguished himself in the war by working out a formula for getting aeroplanes out of a spinning nose-dive and taking the risk of testing it himself. Soon after the war, he was appointed to the Oxford Chair of Experimental Philosophy, the old-fashioned denomination for Physics. At that time the natural sciences were not held in very high esteem in Oxford and the Prof was fond of recounting, with more anger than amusement, how the wife of the Warden of All Souls had remarked to him at a dinner party that anyone who had taken a first in Greats could master physics in a fortnight. He had worked energetically to build up his department, but had contributed little more to physics on his own account. One reason for this was the attraction which the great world outside Oxford had for him, and especially the world of politics, into which he had been drawn by his friendship with Winston Churchill and with the first Lord Birkenhead. A frank opponent of equality, he made two unsuccessful attempts to get himself adopted as one of the Conservative candidates for Oxford University, which then had the privilege of sending two members to Parliament; they were elected by a system of proportional representation, in which all those who had taken their Masters degree were entitled to participate, while retaining their right to cast another vote in their residential constituencies. On the second of these occasions, when Sir Farquhar Buzzard, the Regius Professor of Medicine and as such a Student of Christ Church, was preferred to him, he stood as an Independent but was easily defeated.

The Prof was not generally popular. He was thought to be a snob and he did not suffer fools gladly. His wit was caustic, and his tone such that he often seemed to be sneering when he did not mean to be. He was sometimes surprisingly prudish and he nurtured grievances. His political opinions were also widely held against him. On the other hand, he was morally as well as physically courageous, he had a very good brain and high intellectual standards. I did not altogether approve of him but I liked him, partly no doubt because he was very kind to me. He had a contempt for the older Oxford philosophers, dating from a time soon after his arrival when he had clashed in a public debate with J. A. Smith and Joseph over the Theory of Relativity which he understood and they did not, it seeming enough to Joseph to ask the question 'What is Space curved *in*?', and he strongly approved of the campaign which I was starting to wage against them.

It was sometimes alleged, so far as I know on no very good authority, that the Prof was partly Jewish. This would not have been a question of any particular interest, if he had not also been taken for an anti-Semite, like Karl Marx, whom he would not otherwise have wished to resemble. Here again he probably did himself less than justice. He was indeed capable of making anti-Semitic remarks, but I doubt if this was anything more than a trafficking in the common coinage of some of the circles in which he moved. It was not translated into action. On the contrary, at a time when many Conservatives were trying to make excuses for the Nazis, he consistently opposed them, and when Jewish scientists began to be persecuted in Germany, he exerted himself to bring them safely to England and find them academic posts.

His most notable capture was Albert Einstein, for whom he obtained a Research Studentship at Christ Church. Einstein was also made welcome in the United States, but he spent two summers with us before fixing his residence at the Institute of Advanced

Studies in Princeton. I several times sat next to him in Hall and talked to him there and in Common Room, in a mixture of English and German. I was naturally in awe of him, but he very soon put us at our ease. He was in some ways quite a simple man and delighted in telling stories with very little point to them. He had very great charm and genuine modesty. He once said to us, untruly but honestly, that the success which he had attained was not due to his being exceptionally intelligent but to his having made physics his life's work. In his youth he had been influenced by Ernst Mach and he was interested in hearing from me what Mach's successors were doing. He had agreed to give a lecture in Oxford and wanted me to help him translate it into English. He did not remember my name but in asking for me referred to me as 'that clever young man'. Someone understandably thought that he meant Denys Page, who had succeeded Webster as one of the tutors in classics, but he said, 'No. I know Page.' Unfortunately, I had gone to London for the week-end, and since the translation had to be made at once, I missed the opportunity of working with him. It was probably just as well, since I doubt if either my knowledge of German or my knowledge of physics would have been equal to the task. Nevertheless I was very proud of the fact that he had thought of asking me. It has always seemed to me a proof of Einstein's greatness that he talked to young and unknown men, on topics connected with his own subject, as though he could learn something from them.

Two other distinguished members of the Christ Church Senior Common Room at that time were Gilbert Murray, then approaching the end of his long tenure of the Professorship of Greek, and J. D. Beazley, the Professor of Classical Archaeology and a world-famous expert on Greek art. To me they were both remote Olympian figures. I admired Gilbert Murray both as the author of *The Classical Tradition in Poetry* and as the original of Adolphus Cusins in Shaw's *Major Barbara*, but I found him rather frosty. Later I was told that he did not approve of my philosophical outlook. An old-fashioned high-minded agnostic, he considered that Logical Positivists were lacking in reverence. Beazley seemed to me to live in a world of his own. I was aware that Maurice Bowra and other Greek scholars greatly admired him, but beyond that I knew very little about him except that he had once had a pet goose which he used sometimes to bring into college. At that time the senior tutor in classics was a man called S. G. Owen, who was chiefly distinguished for having been mauled by A. E. Housman. The story went that when the goose died and Owen expressed his condolences in a tone of levity, Beazley rebuked him by saying, 'Yes, Owen, Goosey is dead. There are many worse men alive.'

By the time that I joined the Senior Common Room, Owen had retired and spent most of his leisure going on long cruises, but he still favoured us with his company when he was in Oxford. He was known as 'D.T.' Owen because of the amount that he was reputed to drink, and he did indeed look as if he had never found much occasion to stint himself. He died a few years later and his last words were said to have been, 'I must remember to order another bottle of whisky.'

Perhaps the strangest of my colleagues was the law don, Grant-Bailey. He combined teaching with a practice at the Bar and was reported to give his tutorials late at night and sometimes in the train when he could induce his pupils to travel with him. He looked as though he never had time to eat, and he had a slow, melancholy way of speaking. There was a story that he once began a plea with the words 'My Lord, my unfortunate client' and then paused for so long that the Judge said, 'Proceed, Mr Grant-Bailey, so far the Court is with you.' I dare say that this is a legal chestnut which was fastened on to him, but the story sounded credible.

I continued to be on good terms with Gilbert Ryle and Bobbie Longden, though my attitude towards them was still rather that of a favoured pupil, came no nearer to feeling any sympathy for Michael Foster, and overcame my shyness with Roy Harrod. My closest friends among the members of the Governing Body were the two who were nearest to me in age, Denys Page and Patrick Gordon-Walker. Denys, who had overlapped with me as an undergraduate, was already a formidable Greek scholar, a literary stylist, and a man of strong loyalties and no less strong antipathies. I have a volume of Ezra Pound's Cantos, inscribed 'To Aja from the loving twins Denys and Patrick for his fifth birthday, October 29th, 1933,' but this choice of a present was less a mark of their taste than a concession to what they believed to be mine. Patrick, who was a little older than Denys, had been brought back to Christ Church as a history tutor by J. C. Masterman who thought that he would have a good influence over the young men. He disappointed J.C. by developing radical views in politics and getting himself adopted as the Labour candidate for Oxford City. In our different ways we were both rebels, and I liked him for his iconoclasm.

Some of the older men showed me kindness, in particular Nowell Myres, who had worked with Collingwood on Roman Britain and was later to become Bodley's Librarian, Alec Russell, the tutor in Chemistry, who surprised me by taking an interest in my work, and Frank Taylor, the tutor in French, a New Zealander who walked with a limp as the result of being wounded in the war; we were linked by our common admiration for Voltaire.

The Dean did not mingle with us very much and would hardly have been aware of me, had it not been for a ridiculous incident. It fell to me as the Junior Lecturer to deliver an oration, before some ceremonial banquet, on a distinguished former member of the House. I chose John Ruskin, and with the help of a very good book on *The Gothic Revival* which Kenneth Clark had published a few years before, I managed to compose a respectable lecture. I had to put on a white tie and tails for the occasion, and allowed myself what I believed to be ample time to dress and walk the short distance to Christ Church. I had in fact slightly mistaken the time of the meeting but would not have been more than a few minutes late if all had been well. Unhappily, when I started to dress I discovered that my only boiled shirt had been sent to the laundry and had not returned. The result was that when I arrived breathless at the meeting, having somehow procured another shirt, I had kept the company waiting for a full half-hour. Gilbert Ryle loyally put it about that I was locked in the lavatory, but this was not much consolation to the audience, who also foresaw that they would be made late for their dinner. Not realizing quite how late I was, I made a rather perfunctory apology, and then read my lecture at breakneck speed to make up for lost time. The Dean felt that he had been made to look a fool in front of his distinguished guests, and never altogether forgave me.

I still found it hard to think of myself as a senior member of the University, and for such social life as Renée and I enjoyed in Oxford we depended mainly on the new generation of undergraduates. One who became a life-long friend of mine was Bill Deakin, who had been at school at Westminster and had come up to Christ Church to read history. After taking his degree, he became a Fellow of Wadham, and was enlisted by Lindemann to help Churchill with his life of Marlborough. It was not, however, until the war that I got to know him really well. Two other products of Westminster, with whom I also formed lasting friendships were Charles Whitney-Smith, a man of robust vitality and a champion fencer, and Sylvain Mangeot, a son of André Mangeot, the violinist, who played a large role in Christopher Isherwood's autobiographical *Lions and Shadows*. Most of the undergraduates whom we knew well came from Christ Church, but there were some exceptions such as Andrew Graham at Magdalen, a man of great elegance and military bearing who eventually developed into a humorous writer, and Francis Graham-Harrison at Balliol, who had been in College at Eton in an election four years junior to mine and had won the Newcastle at an exceptionally early age. By intelligence and temperament he seemed to me eminently suited to becoming a don, but he chose to enter the Civil Service, where he did what he could to bring some compassion to the Home Office. He shared my liking for the cinema and he and I used often to go to films together. This was the time at which the great series of Hollywood gangster films had started to appear, the best of them, in my view, being *Scarface* with Paul Muni and George Raft, though *City Streets*, starring a youthful Gary Cooper, and James Cagney's performances in a run of films which started with *Public Enemy* gave me almost as much pleasure.

Of my earlier Oxford friends, Andrew Wordsworth had gone to India, where he took a great dislike to most of the representatives of the British Raj, complaining of the airs which they put on without in most cases even being gentlemen. He was married and already had a son. It was not very long before he returned to England and became a master at Westminster. Robert Willis, though he would have preferred to be at the Treasury, appeared to take pleasure in mastering the intricacies of the Inland Revenue. Armine Wright wrote to me from Africa, describing the orgy with which the white colony had greeted his arrival at Nairobi on his way to become a District Commissioner. James Parr had returned to Eton as a master and David Stephens had become a clerk to the House of Lords. Among my contemporaries who had remained at Oxford, I saw most of Isaiah Berlin and Gilbert Highet. Renée and Isaiah did not immediately take to one another, so that I usually visited him at All Souls. Gilbert, by now a Fellow of St John's, had married Helen MacInnes and Renée became a godmother to their son.

At the beginning of the long vacation of 1933, Gilbert Ryle took me to my first Joint Session of the Mind Association and the Aristotelian Society, which took place that year at the University of Birmingham. The meetings, then as now, were held over a weekend and consisted of a Presidential Address, and four symposia, with the slight difference that the number of those who contributed written papers to each symposium was then set at three, as against the two to which it has now been reduced. This was a relic of the Hegelian tradition, the idea being that the first speaker should state a thesis, the second its antithesis, and the third resolve them into a higher synthesis. In fact the pattern of this dialectic was seldom followed, the second speaker not always feeling obliged to contradict the first, and the third speaker usually preferring to advance his own views on the selected topic rather than make any serious attempt to synthesize those of his predecessors. Even so, the proceedings quite often developed into an interesting debate. One reason for this was that the number of those who came to the meetings in those days was reasonably small, so that it was possible to have a general discussion from the floor and, when the chairman knew his business, keep it at least roughly to the point.

Except in the two years in which the meetings were held at Scottish Universities and I was deterred by the expense of travelling so far, I attended these sessions regularly throughout the remainder of the 'thirties. I enjoyed them very much, mainly because of the opportunity which they gave me to discuss philosophy with G. E. Moore. Moore always came to the sessions and on the Sunday afternoon, when there was no official meeting, he used to hold an informal class which about a dozen of us attended. He was then in his sixties but had lost none of the enthusiasm for philosophy or the passion for argument for which he had been celebrated in his youth. He resembled Einstein in his simplicity, his single-mindedness, and his ability to make his juniors feel that they were engaging with him on equal terms. He could become angry when someone persisted in what seemed to him a fallacious course of argument or failed to appreciate an obvious point, and the display of literally open-mouthed astonishment with which he greeted a stupid or pretentious remark could make its perpetrator feel and look a fool: but these were natural reactions, not forensic tricks, and they were directed against the intellectual sin, without animosity towards the sinner. Bertrand Russell, who had a great respect for Moore as a person, but came to disapprove of his philosophical influence, once said to me, 'The trouble with Moore is that he believes everything that his nurse told him.' Though Russell here fell into the prevalent mistake of exaggerating Moore's attachment to common sense, his comment, if unkindly, was not altogether unjust. For all his subtlety and sophistication in argument, Moore always kept some hold of nurse. But though in one way a weakness, this was also part of his strength. His chief service to philosophy was that of the child in Hans Andersen's story: he saw and was not afraid to say that the Emperor had no clothes.

I took an active part in Moore's classes and in the discussion of most of the papers which were produced for the symposia. The first session at which I contributed a paper was the one held at Bedford College, London, in 1935, when I replied to Gilbert Ryle. Moore had agreed to be the third symposiast but I sent him my paper too late for him to get his written in time. The topic was that of Internal Relations, arising from the Idealist theory that every relation in which objects stand to one another affects their identity, with the result that they all become amalgamated in the Absolute, and both Gilbert and I took our departure from a paper, purporting to refute this theory, which Moore had published in the Proceedings of the Aristotelian Society for 1919–20 and reprinted in his *Philosophical Studies*. In his oral reply to us Moore put us at something of a disadvantage by professing not to understand what his own argument had been, but there I think that he was being, if not disingenuous, at least unjust to himself. His paper 'On External and Internal Relations' was not especially difficult, and it did expose the fallacy of which the Idealists had been guilty. What it failed to do was to provide a satisfactory theory of Identity, but that is something for which we have still to seek.

Already at the Birmingham meeting, I had startled the company by the vehemence of my onslaught upon metaphysics. In this way I made some enemies, especially among the older philosophers, who felt that they were being personally attacked. I did not mean to be offensive, but my delight in argument, my conviction of the truth of my opinions, my desire to convert others to them and my impatience with those who refused to see the light were so strong as to obliterate any tact or any respect for persons that I might otherwise have mustered. There were, however, some philosophers near to my own age like John Wisdom, his cousin J. O. Wisdom, Margaret Macdonald, Karl Britton, Max Black, and Austin Duncan-Jones who were thinking along the same lines as myself, and some of our seniors like Richard Braithwaite, Susan Stebbing, by then a Professor at Bedford College, and the philosophical psychologist C. A. Mace were sympathetic to our approach. Most of these philosophers had been trained at Cambridge under Moore and to a large extent drew their inspiration from him.

Having discovered our common interest in the development of analytic philosophy, a group of us who were present at this meeting decided that we needed a journal which would broadly represent our point of view. We did not envisage anything on the scale of *Mind*, but rather a journal devoted to notes and discussions which could be produced and sold cheaply and appear at something like two-monthly intervals. The most appropriate title for it seemed to us to be *Analysis*. We were able to interest Blackwell's in the project and they brought out the first number as early as November 1933. Austin Duncan-Jones, then still doing research at Cambridge, but soon to become a lecturer and later a professor at Birmingham, agreed to be the editor, and there was an editorial board consisting of Susan Stebbing, C. A. Mace and Gilbert Ryle. I published an article in the first number on 'Atomic Propositions', defending the view which I then held that it was possible to be factually mistaken even about the nature of one's present sense-experience, and in a subsequent number in the same volume I engaged in a discussion with Mace about 'The Genesis of Metaphysics', in which I argued that metaphysical nonsense was rather the product of linguistic confusion than an attempt to express poetically what could not literally be said.

In the autumn of 1933, J. L. Austin became a Fellow of All Souls, being the only candidate to be elected in that year. He had come up to Balliol from Shrewsbury as a classical scholar in the same term as I came up to Christ Church, but having read Honour Mods as well as Greats, he had spent a year longer as an undergraduate. Though I may have seen him at the Jowett Society, I do not remember meeting him before his election to All Souls. I used then to see him in Isaiah's company. They shared my admiration for a book called *Mind and the World-Order* by the American logician and pragmatist, C. I. Lewis, and a class which they jointly conducted on this book had a great influence on the new generation of undergraduate philosophers. At that time Austin and I were in much greater philosophical sympathy than his later writings would suggest. His dislike of being labelled may have prevented him from calling himself a Logical Positivist, but he accepted the sense-datum theory, and he was hardly less intransigent than I in his hostility to metaphysics. This may help to explain the fact that when he and I competed that autumn, with four other candidates, for the John Locke Prize in philosophy, which Isaiah had shared two years before with an otherwise unknown philosopher called Budden, the prize was not awarded. The examiners who judged us to be unworthy of it were J. A. Smith, Prichard, Geoffrey Mure, a Fellow and later Warden of Merton, and one of the few remaining Oxford Hegelians, T. D. Weldon, a Fellow of Magdalen, who was later to become an inflexible linguistic philosopher but was then an orthodox Kantian, and Dr Brown, the Reader in Mental Philosophy, who was primarily a psychologist. Dr Brown, being a Student of Christ Church, was questioned by some of my colleagues about my failure, but he could only reply that he had felt bound to defer to the philosophers, who saw no signs of distinction in the work of any of the candidates.

This was undoubtedly an honest judgement, for which I suspect that Prichard was largely responsible. As quite often happens, even with good philosophers, he could see no merit in views that differed radically from his own. Nor did the trenchancy with which I expressed my opinions make them more palatable to him. Not long afterwards, I read a paper to a meeting of the Philosophical Society at which Prichard took a prominent part in the discussion. Our exchanges became so acrimonious that at one point I turned to the company and said, 'Can anybody tell me what he means?', upon which he justifiably muttered, 'Very sharp.' Professor Ernst Cassirer, celebrated as the author of *The Philosophy of Symbolic Forms*, and by then a refugee from Germany, was present at this meeting and privately expressed some astonishment, not at the disrespect which young men in Oxford showed to their elders but at the harshness with which their fledgling offerings were criticized.

He himself was a model of urbanity. Out of respect for his eminence and sympathy with his misfortunes, a number of us attended a weekly class which he gave on Leibniz. He was a learned historian of philosophy, and he spoke English well, but he showed little relish for discussion. When one of us raised a difficulty, he would say, 'That is a very interesting question. That is a question that would have puzzled Leibniz himself,' and pass serenely on to another point. It was not very long before he forsook Oxford for Sweden and then for the United States.

A refugee philosopher whom we took less seriously was Teddy Wiesengrund-Adorno. Later in his career he was to become celebrated as one of the leaders of the Frankfurt School of Neo-Marxists, but at that time he seemed to us a comic figure, with his dandified manner and appearance, and his anxiety to discover whether other refugees had been accorded the privilege, which he had not so far obtained, of dining at High Table. In our philosophical austerity, we were also more amused than impressed by the attention which he was then directing to the philosophy of jazz. It is perhaps not altogether to our credit that we took next to no interest either in aesthetics or in Marxist philosophy, though by the end of the decade Isaiah was to write an excellent introductory book on Marx. There being nothing for him in Oxford, Adorno also found a home in the United States, returning to Germany after the war. He eventually fell a victim to student unrest, suffering a heart attack when some of his female pupils uncovered their breasts and danced around in mockery of him.

One who stayed with us longer was Raymond Klibansky, a gifted linguist and a historian of philosophy with a remarkable range and depth of scholarship. It was only after the war, in which he played a distinguished part in the work of political intelligence, that he left England to become a Professor at McGill University in Montreal. Our common efforts to promote international understanding among philosophers, with the pleasure of travel compensating for the boredom of many international conferences, have cemented a friendship which began with his lending me a copy of Heidegger's preposterous *Was ist Metaphysik?* which I have never yet returned to him. I was initially drawn to him also by learning that he had described me in my appearances at philosophical meetings as being like 'a carp among minnows'. I valued the compliment to my intelligence more than I minded the reflection on my manners.

I must have worked fairly hard in the summer and autumn of 1933, since in addition to the pieces which I wrote for the Aristotelian Society, *Oxford Outlook* and *Analysis*, I also wrote an article ambitiously entitled 'Demonstration of the Impossibility of Metaphysics' which Moore accepted for publication in *Mind*. I had not yet thought of attempting to write a book, but some time during the Christmas holidays when I had been expatiating to Isaiah on some aspect of the Positivistic system, he suggested to me that I should get it all written down before my enthusiasm had been given time to stale. The idea immediately attracted me, but I did not want to go to the labour of starting on a book without the assurance that it would be published. At a dinner party given by Dick Crossman, at that time a recently appointed Fellow of New College, a tutor in ancient philosophy who anticipated Karl Popper in preaching that Plato had anticipated fascism, and the husband of a German woman, soon to leave him, who used to signal her entrance into company by saying 'Little Erica is here', I met a girl who worked in the office of Victor Gollancz, a newly-established and very enterprising publisher. Through her I obtained a letter of introduction to Gollancz, called on him at his office in London, explained my plans for the book, and came out with a contract. Again, this seems more extraordinary to me now than it did at the time. To some extent plagiarizing Waismann, I decided to call the book *Language, Truth and Logic*.

I started at once to write the book and completed it in eighteen months, working at it almost continuously except for the intervals of teaching. I have written all my other books in longhand, but this one I typed, clumsily with two fingers, but in the end producing a serviceable script. Except that the first chapter was adapted ftom my article in *Mind*, I made no preliminary draft, but wrote slowly to avoid the need for corrections. I was satisfied if a day's work yielded me a page of three hundred words. Had I been able to achieve this every day, I should have finished the book in little more than half a year, instead of a year and a half, since it was only sixty thousand words long; but I was frequently held up, not so much by my not knowing what I wanted to say, though this sometimes happened, but by my not being able to decide how most effectively to say it. I was writing with passion, but also taking very great pains to make my meaning clear.

This labour was not wasted. Whatever its demerits, the book did not suffer from obscurity: it can rather be accused of sacrificing depth to clarity. Except in a few details, the thoughts which it expressed were not original. They were a blend of the positivism of the Vienna Circle, which I also ascribed to Wittgenstein, the reductive empiricism which I had taken from Hume and Russell, the analytical approach of Moore and his disciples, with a dash of C. I. Lewis's and Ramsey's pragmatism. I began with a summary trial and execution of metaphysics, using the verification principle

as an axe. Arguing, then, that if philosophy was to make an independent contribution to knowledge, it could consist only in the
practice of analysis, I mistakenly followed Ramsey in representing
analysis as the search for definitions, and the examination of their
consequences. Russell's theory of descriptions supplied me with an
example of analysis at work and I added for my own part a brisk and
indeed perfunctory reduction of statements about physical objects
to statements about sense-contents, a term which I borrowed from
an early paper of Moore's and used in preference to the current
'sense-data'. Turning to the *a priori*, I briefly and vigorously presented the case for holding that all necessity is logical and that all
logically necessary propositions are open or disguised tautologies.
Empirical propositions I construed as hypotheses which were to be
analysed in terms of the experiences which would verify them, and I
continued to follow Neurath in holding that they could never
attain to certainty. Digressing next to ethics, I put forward the view
which had been suggested to me by Duncan-Jones that moral
pronouncements were expressions of emotion rather than statements
of fact, and for good measure I added a short 'Critique of Theology',
in which I maintained that statements purporting to refer to a
transcendent deity were literally nonsensical. This chapter, which
was peripheral to the main tenor of the book, was the one that
aroused the greatest animosity. Philosophically, it was less open to
objection than the ensuing chapter on 'The Self and the Common
World', in which I took what I can now see to be the inconsistent
line of giving a behaviouristic account of the experiences of other
people and a mentalistic account of one's own. Finally, in a chapter
brazenly entitled 'Solutions of Outstanding Philosophical Disputes',
I tried to distil the metaphysical elements from the perennial issues
of Rationalism and Empiricism, Realism and Idealism, and Monism
and Pluralism, and then went on to argue that those of the remaining questions which were not empirical, and so consignable to
science, were easily settled by logical analysis.

Reviewing this work, at a distance of more than forty years, I
have many faults to find with it. Apart from the mistakes that I have
mentioned, the relation between the physical and the sensory levels
of discourse is not so tidy as I made it out to be, the conventionalist
view of logic and mathematics encounters more serious difficulties
than I realized, and my moral theory, though to some extent along
the right lines, was much too crude. Worst of all, the verification

principle, on which so much depended, was far too loosely formulated; and my tendency to analyse propositions in terms of the subject's own possible experiences, with the limitations imposed by his identity and his actual position in space and time, produced some results that were, to say the least of it, implausible. I might have done better, I now think, to appeal to a notional observer, for all the consequent risk of excessive liberality. Even so, I still find myself in sympathy with the spirit of the book, and I still broadly adhere to what may be called the verificatory approach. So indeed does a great deal of subsequent philosophy, though the fact is not often recognized. The verification principle is seldom mentioned and when it is mentioned it is usually scorned; it continues, however, to be put to work. The attitude of many philosophers towards it reminds me of the relation between Pip and Magwitch in Dickens's *Great Expectations*. They have lived on the money, but are ashamed to acknowledge its source.

The rapidity with which the alliance of Logical Positivism with the Cambridge School of Analysis was gaining ground in England is shown by the fact that at the 1934 Joint Session, which was held at Cardiff, it supplied the topics for two of the symposia. Professor Stebbing headed a symposium on the subject of 'Communication and Verification' and Max Black, John Wisdom and Maurice Cornforth debated the question 'Is Analysis a Useful Method in Philosophy?' Max Black surprisingly took the line that while there were possible universes in which analysis could be completely successful, the most it could achieve in the actual world was to throw light on the presuppositions which were made in a given social system. John Wisdom, having defined philosophical analysis as the translation of sentences into sentences of identical meaning with the intention of gaining clearer insight into the structure of the ultimate facts displayed by those sentences, maintained that this just *was* philosophy. Maurice Cornforth, already a combative Marxist, and to this day the only philosopher in England of any standing to have embraced Marxism, maintained on the other hand that philosophical analysis was a device invented by the bourgeoisie for the purpose of reconciling its scientific with its metaphysical ideas. As such he believed it to be useless, harmful and impossible, provoking Moore to remark that it was difficult to see how it could be all three together.

In the autumn of 1934, Rudolf Carnap came to London to give

a series of three lectures at Bedford College. The audience was small and the lectures resolved themselves into informal talks. I went to all three of them, and took part in the discussions that followed. Carnap had just published the original German version of *The Logical Syntax of Language* and after giving us a general conspectus of the position of the Vienna Circle he devoted most of the remainder of his time to explaining his distinction, soon to become celebrated, between the material and the formal modes of speech, the difference being that statements in the formal mode were overtly syntactical, while those in the material mode were syntactical statements, masquerading as statements about non-linguistic objects. For example, the statement that 2 is a number was, in his view, an expression in the material mode of the syntactical statement that '2' is a numeral. This unfortunate substitution of syntax for semantics, which he still proscribed as metaphysical, led him also to maintain that all the genuine questions of philosophy were syntactical questions, and that it was only the habit of expressing them in the material mode that prevented this from being recognized. It took me quite long to see that this could not be true.

Meeting Carnap for the first time, I thought him a little lacking in humour, but I was impressed by his seriousness and the force of his intelligence. He had brought with him his young wife whom he had recently married, after his first wife had left him for a graphologist. She took me down a bit by addressing me as 'one of those young men who revolve around my husband'. The description was, indeed, true but not, I considered, sufficiently particular.

The lectures were sponsored by Susan Stebbing, whom I had grown to like very much. By then in her early fifties, she was still a handsome woman, though careless of her appearance. When she decided that she needed a new hat, she always bought the first one that fitted. She lived with two women friends, who were earning less money than she, but she pooled her salary with theirs, believing that friends should have as much as possible in common. When she came to Oxford to read a paper to the Jowett Society, I invited her to stay with us, though we had no spare bedroom. We pretended that our own bedroom was the spare room and ourselves slept on the sitting-room floor. She was too interested in discussing philosophy with me to notice the deception, or perhaps too tactful to allude to it. Philosophically she was very much a disciple of Moore and she shared his impatience with sloppy or pretentious thinking.

She was quite often brusque but she was never mean. She was one of those persons who make you proud if they think well of you.

It was in 1934 also that Felix and Marian Frankfurter came to Oxford, Felix having accepted an invitation to a visting Professorship. He was still a Professor at the Harvard Law School but he had become one of the most prominent of Roosevelt's New Dealers and was later to be appointed by Roosevelt to the Supreme Court. He had come to America as a child of poor immigrants and had become well known for his defence of Sacco and Vanzetti, the anarchists whose unjust trial and execution for a murder committed in the course of an armed robbery, in which Vanzetti certainly and Sacco quite probably took no part, was one of the political scandals of the nineteen-twenties. Marian belonged to a good New England family and it was her disgust at the part played by the Boston hierarchy in this affair that brought Felix and her together. They were an attractive couple. Felix, small, sharp, extroverted, energetic, Marian, younger but more sedate, sensitive and gracious, and their social success in Oxford was spectacular. A friend who often came over to visit them was Sylvester Gates, who had attended the Harvard Law School after leaving Oxford and was considered by Felix to have been his ablest pupil. Later he was to forsake the law for banking, a move which disturbed Felix less than it did Marian, who liked her friends to be unworldly. At one of their dinner parties we were discussing Wittgenstein's *Tractatus* and Sylvester remarked that the sentence 'Whereof one cannot speak, thereof one must be silent' occurred in it twice. I contradicted him; we made a bet on it; I went home to fetch the book and found that I was wrong. I had forgotten that the sentence occurs in the preface as well as at the end of the book. I put up the feeble argument that the preface to a book is not strictly part of it, but Felix ruled against me and I paid the bet. It was only quite recently that I discovered that I had a stronger defence. The sentence does occur twice in the English translation, but in the original German there is a slight difference, the phrase which Ogden translated on each occasion as 'Whereof one cannot speak' being *Wovon man nicht sprechen kann* in the body of the book and *Wovon man nicht reden kann* in the preface. The difference is of no importance, but in purely legalistic terms it might have enabled me to win my bet.

My position at Christ Church was now coming into question. There was little doubt that my Lectureship would be renewed for a further year, but I hoped for a more permanent post. The Governing Body had decided to appoint another official Student and the choice lay between me and Frank Pakenham, the present Lord Longford, who was a lecturer in politics. Frank had been in the Oppidan Sixth Form at Eton when I first went there and my earliest memory of him is that of watching him defiantly lead his eleven off the pitch, after they had won the final of the House Cup at the Field game, to the accompaniment of boos, because they were thought to have played foully. I first met him at Oxford while I was still an undergraduate. He had gone down some years before and was working for the Conservative Central Office. He was with Elizabeth Harman to whom he had just become engaged. I knew her by repute as having been the most fashionable undergraduate at Oxford among the women of her time. When they were married and Frank and I were lecturers together, they became very good friends of ours. Since there was no tutorial need for a third philosopher, and Christ Church had no official Student in politics, I was not surprised or resentful when the Studentship went to him, though I was disappointed. Frank wrote me a charming note in which he spoke of me as the better man and almost apologized for having been preferred to me.

Renée took this set-back very ill, believing that the decision had not been taken on purely academic grounds. She had not found it easy to settle down in Oxford, where even today, the College system, rooted in a monastic tradition, makes life very much more agreeable for the Fellows and Lecturers than for their wives. We did not lack friends, but this did not prevent her from feeling that she was playing the part of a second-class citizen. The lease of our flat was expiring, and rather than look for another place in Oxford, where she thought it unlikely in any case that we should long be able to remain, she proposed that we should move at once to London. I too preferred living in London, and since the relatively small amount of teaching that I had to do could be compressed into three days in the week, during which I could live comfortably in college, I fell in with her plan.

We had no sooner moved to London than Renée's pessimism about my prospects at Oxford was further confirmed. Collingwood having obtained the Chair of Metaphysics in succession to J. A. Smith, there was a vacancy for a Fellow in philosophy at Pembroke. Tony Andrewes, now Professor of Ancient History and a colleague of mine at New College, was then a Fellow of Pembroke, and wanted me to join him there. I liked Tony Andrewes, whom I had known at the time when we were both undergraduates, and although Pembroke was a poor college and would not at the outset be paying me very much more than I was already earning, I thought it better to have the security of a Fellowship than to wait for a more attractive opportunity. I went to the interview, feeling fairly confident of success, but the Master and some of the Senior Fellows had heard disturbing reports of my philosophical extremism and were afraid that their undergraduates would do badly in their examinations if they were given so unorthodox a teacher. Accordingly, they made the fact that I had gone to live in London an excuse for not appointing me. Instead they elected Donald Macnabb, a rather older man who had been in his last year as a Colleger at Eton when I was in my first. He had read Greats as a pupil of Henry Price, but had not held any academic position since he went down from Oxford.

In this instance, I did feel that I had been unjustly treated, though I had nothing against Macnabb personally or indeed philosophically, since his main interest was in Hume, and readily agreed to his becoming the fourth member of a discussion group which I had formed with Austin and Isaiah. When A. D. Woozley and Stuart Hampshire were elected to All Souls, in 1935 and 1936 respectively, they also joined us and the group was completed a year or two later by the addition of Donald Mackinnon, who became a Fellow of Keble and is now the Professor of the Philosophy of Religion at Cambridge. We met once a week during term after dinner in Isaiah's rooms at All Souls. The discussion was quite informal and meandered on from week to week. It was very seldom, if ever, that anyone produced a written paper. The topics were chiefly those that I had covered in my book. For instance, we devoted a great deal of time to discussing such propositions as 'Green is more like blue than red' which Isaiah firmly held against me to be neither analytic nor empirical. Austin and I still shared much the same general outlook but very often differed on points of detail. His contributions to the discussions were mainly destructive. Isaiah has reminded me that I once said to Austin in exasperation, 'You are like a greyhound that refuses to race but bites the other greyhounds to prevent their racing either.' In later years he was to lead the pack, at measured speed, into the cul-de-sac of the study of ordinary usage, but his teeth never lost their sharpness.

It was characteristic of Austin that he was the only one of us whom the rest never called by his Christian name. He was not unfriendly, but his friendliness was impersonal. With his steely spectacles, his slight taut figure, and the light belted macintosh that he often wore, he made me think of a gunman; not a gangster by any means, but a follower of the Irishman Michael Collins, fighting against the Black and Tans. He had high moral principles and a quiet self-confidence which many people found intimidating. I respected him for his character and his intelligence but never made the effort, which would almost certainly have been fruitless, to get to know him more intimately.

My Lectureship at Christ Church had been renewed for a third year, but there was no possibility of its being extended any further, and as the year 1935 approached, I began to be anxious about my future. I did not fancy the idea of teaching at a redbrick university, even if I could find a post at one of them, which was by no means certain, and I thought that I might after all have to take to the study of the law, even though it would entail there being quite a long period in which I should have to rely on my grandfather to support us. There was, however, a party at Christ Church that did not want to lose me, among them Roy Harrod, who was especially active on my behalf. The Research Studentship which had been created for Einstein had been left vacant since his departure for Princeton, and Roy had the idea of reviving it and getting me appointed to it. In pursuit of this end, he asked G. E. Moore and Henry Price for their opinion of me and received favourable answers from them both. Moore went so far as to describe me as one of the ablest philosophical disputants that he had ever met, though he thought that in my writing, so far as he had seen it, I had not as yet done full justice to the powers that I displayed in oral discussion. Price was kinder about my writing, while agreeing that I was at my best at philosophical meetings. Though he regretted that my clarity and vigour were 'accompanied by a certain narrowness of interest, and a certain indifference or even contempt for some quite reputable but old-fashioned ways of thinking', he judged that my influence in Oxford had on the whole been beneficent. 'A type of theory about which we had only the haziest ideas before has been presented to us so vigorously and incisively, and its consequences, some of them very startling, have been so ruthlessly driven home, that we have been forced to consider it very carefully and to try to make up our minds about it one way or the other. I think that all those who at all sympathize with Mr Ayer's line of approach (as a great many do) would admit that this theory, even if false, is important and instructive, and that he has done us a considerable service in bringing it so forcibly to our notice.'

I had not yet published *Language, Truth and Logic*, but I had written the greater part of it and I gave two of the central chapters in typescript to Roy, who wanted to ask A. N. Whitehead for his opinion of them. After collaborating with Russell on *Principia Mathematica*, Whitehead had increasingly turned from mathematics to metaphysics, and had in his old age accepted a Chair of Philosophy at Harvard. I reproduce his answer to Roy, not only because it flatters my vanity but because of the unexpected light which it throws on Whitehead's attitude to Logical Positivism.

As to your man, A. J. Ayer, since receiving your letter I have discussed him with Felix Frankfurter and with Dr W. Quine, a member of our new society of fellows here. Both of them know him personally. Frankfurter met him in Oxford, and Quine saw a good deal of him in Vienna . . . Both of these men spoke most enthusiastically of their general impressions of Ayer. Of course Frankfurter spoke only as an outsider. But I have plenty of experience of his soundness of judgement. Quine can give an expert opinion.

Also Quine and I have read the literature which you sent. We agree in our high opinion of it. I will develop my opinion more in detail, though without qualification of this summary judgement. Ayer is obviously only a beginner in mathematical logic. As yet he shows no command over its techniques nor does he fully appreciate all the bearings of some of the discussions which have arisen. But he is young, and there is not the slightest doubt that any such slight deficiency will be remedied. [Here I am afraid that Whitehead was too optimistic.]

Also Ayer is an enthusiastic exponent of the more modern movement termed 'Logical Positivism'. Carnap is the leading exponent of this school at present. Ayer shows remarkable ability in expounding this doctrine and discussing its various bearings. There can be no doubt that he is a man of the future. At his age, he reminds me of J. M. Keynes, Bertrand Russell, and others of that type among my old pupils. He has the whole-heartedness of McTaggart at the same stage of development. He is abler than was Barnes, the present bishop of Birmingham, at the same age.

I am not in my own person a Logical Positivist. The claims for it are overstated as is the case in all new movements, e.g. mathematics by the Pythagoreans. But I cannot imagine a greater blessing for English philosophical learning than the rise in Oxford of a vigorous young school of Logical Positivists. The assigning of the proper scope to their method, the discussion of the new problems which it raises or of the new light which it throws on old problems will revivify and reconstruct the presentation of the topics of philosophic thought which the new doctrine fails adequately to deal with. It will rescue the philosophy of the 20th century from repeating its complete failure in the 19th century, when history and science overwhelmed it – even theology deserted it . . . It is a subject on which I feel strongly . . .

These testimonials, coming from such sources, had the desired effect. I was appointed a Research Student for a period of five years and for the first time became a member of the Governing Body of Christ Church. My salary went up to £400 a year and I was allowed to do enough teaching at piece-rates to add about another £100 a year to my income. I had no obligation to lecture and received no extra money for doing so, but having by now got over my initial shyness I found it enjoyable and also found it a useful means of developing my ideas. My main duty, however, was to pursue research, and here I was in some difficulty. I had covered so much ground in *Language, Truth and Logic* and had so narrowly restricted the function of philosophy that it was not very clear what there remained for me to do. Professor Lindemann was anxious that I should branch out into the philosophy of physics, and since I had concluded my book by saying that philosophy had to develop into the logic of science, if it was to make any substantial contribution to the growth of human knowledge, I might very well have thought myself committed to something of that sort. It was even laid down in the terms of my appointment that I was to research into Symbolic Logic and the Philosophy of Science. The difficulty was that I had little skill in mathematics and no scientific training. Austin had gone to some trouble to study mathematics when he was first elected to All Souls and he very kindly gave me a longish list of the books that he had found most useful. I bought one or two of the most elementary ones, but soon became discouraged. I read a fair number of books on the philosophy of physics, but never brought myself to do any of the necessary groundwork, beyond going once to the Clarendon Laboratory to listen to a Geiger counter. I sometimes wish that I had had the force of character to send myself back to school, but I also think it doubtful whether I had the scientific capacity to make the effort worth while. Even without this grounding, I did not entirely relinquish the idea of eventually making some contribution to the philosophy of science, but it began to seem to me that there were still problems in the theory of knowledge that needed further attention: and so I pursued this easier course.

In its endeavours to spread its influence, the Vienna Circle had been organizing international congresses since 1929. Two of them had been held in Prague, one in Königsberg, though Kant did not figure in the Circle's pantheon, and one in Copenhagen. The first one that I attended was held in Paris in the summer of 1935. It was a big affair, with all the affiliates of the Circle strongly represented. Bertrand Russell came and was very much lionized. I remember his winning applause for replying to a French and German speaker successively in their own languages. I was too shy and too respectful of him to introduce myself to him. A philosopher nearer my level, who introduced himself to me, was Karl Popper, at that time a relatively unknown figure, though he had just published his *Logik der Forschung*. I had read and admired the book and was pleased to meet its author, who then had a touch of social diffidence which added to his charm. Though he believed very strongly in the importance of his work, he was still tolerant of criticism, and I found pleasure and profit in his company. My German was then slightly better than his English, and we conversed in German. One of my most pleasant memories of this congress is that of watching Otto Neurath being gallant to Miss Stebbing, speaking to her in English and saying, 'I have always been for the womans.' It was the only occasion on which I saw her at a loss.

Philosophically, the highlight of the congress was the presentation by Tarski of a paper which summarized his semantic theory of truth. It came as a revelation to Carnap, who greatly impressed me by accepting it without demur, although it was almost totally destructive of the claims which he had been making for syntax.

Having been convinced by Tarski that semantics was respectable, he wholeheartedly turned to its pursuit. On this occasion I made a brief plea for Ramsey's theory, which I had espoused in my book, that to predicate truth of a proposition amounted only to asserting it, but this did not give me much of a case against Tarski and I was anyhow too much in awe of the company to press it. My own contribution to the proceedings of the congress was a historical paper on 'The Analytic Movement in Contemporary British Philosophy'. If I had not felt that it would have been carrying coals to Newcastle, I might have extracted a less modest paper from one of the chapters of *Language, Truth and Logic*.

I had completed the book in July, three months before my twenty-fifth birthday. It seemed to me that Victor Gollancz was not entirely happy to receive it. It was not the sort of book that he was used to publishing and he may have wondered how he had been deluded into giving me a contract. However, he produced it very handsomely, in large print with wide spacing, so that the text ran to nearly two hundred and fifty pages. I supplied it with an analytical index and Robert Willis corrected the proofs for me. The book appeared in January 1936, at a price of nine shillings in an edition of five hundred copies. To Gollancz's surprise it sold out very quickly. A second impression of 250 copies came out in April and a third of 250 copies in November. Gollancz still found it hard to believe that a specialized book on philosophy could have the makings of a best-seller and in July 1938, when a new impression was called for, he still printed only 250 copies. By that time, in any case, he was deeply involved in politics, and though he continued to make a success of his business, he was mainly interested in promoting the publications of his Left Book Club. *Language, Truth and Logic* was revolutionary in its way, but it did not point any political moral.

The book was more widely reviewed on its first appearance than I had expected. A reviewer in one of the Sunday papers complained that I had not taken account of Extra Sensory Perception, but was otherwise eulogistic, and Miss Stebbing gave it a long and friendly notice in *Mind*. The only savage review which it received was from E. W. F. Tomlin, who denounced it at great length in the Leavis's magazine *Scrutiny*. He had developed a taste for metaphysics at Oxford and my performances at philosophical meetings had offended him. In later years, when he had gone to work for the British Council, and I lectured under his auspices in Paris, we were to become very good friends.

In Oxford, the book sold well among the undergraduates but was viewed with disfavour by many of their tutors. Long afterwards, Gilbert Ryle told me that on a visit to Blackwell's he had overheard Prichard and Joseph saying that it was scandalous that the book had found a publisher. This does not imply that they had read it. Collingwood, who happened also to be in the shop, turned to them and said, 'Gentlemen, this book will be read when your names are forgotten.' I suspect that this was less a tribute to me than an expression of his contempt for them. He did, however, take the book seriously enough to devote part of his lectures to refuting it. He ended one such lecture by saying, 'If I thought that Mr Ayer was right, I would give up philosophy.' When the audience arrived for the next lecture, they were startled to find that it had been cancelled. The story ends lamely: he had been stricken with influenza.

7 *Family Life and Politics*

By the time that Renée and I went to live in London, both my grandfather and my mother had remarried. My aunt Betty had gone back to take care of my grandfather, after my grandmother's death, but she too had died of cancer towards the end of 1932, her children were almost of age, and my grandfather was not disposed to live alone. His new wife, Dehra Hadfield, was the companion who had put his marriage in brief jeopardy some twenty years before. When she had been forced to leave his house, she had gone to South Africa and got married there. I do not think that my grandfather had seen her since that time, but they had kept in correspondence. She was now widowed with two children, a boy and a girl, aged about ten and twelve. When my grandfather wrote to ask her to marry him, she at once accepted and came to England with her children. The marriage took place early in 1934 and Dehra and her children moved into Trevin Towers. She was quiet, assured, and comfortable and I believe that she made my grandfather happy for the year that he still had to live. He was suffering from shingles and slept badly, so that his temper was more easily tried. Once, when we were staying with them, I was working on my book and failed to attend to something that my grandfather said to me. He became angry and muttered to Dehra, 'They only care about my money.' I was moved when I overheard her saying, 'He, least of any of them.' She was religious and put enough pressure on my grandfather for him to call upon me to support him in his lack of faith.

My mother was lonely after I left home, and it was evident that she would like to marry again. The family was afraid only of her choice. She was not outstandingly rich, but my grandfather had settled enough money on her to tempt an adventurer, and she was not thought to be a very good judge of character. We were therefore a little apprehensive when she announced that she had become engaged to a man whom she had met at a seaside hotel. We soon found that we had no cause for alarm. Richard Vance, whom my mother married in the autumn of 1934, was an Irishman in his sixties who had worked for the firm of Guinness in Dublin as an accountant and had retired on a fairly generous pension. He had not previously been married, and was leading a lonely existence when he met my mother. After their marriage they lived in my mother's flat in Eyre Court. He treated her as the child that she had in many ways remained and I think that she was happier with him than she had been with my father, at any rate in their later years. Richard was a man of equable temper, with a florid, rather ugly face, but considerable charm of manner, to which his slight Irish brogue contributed. I liked him very much, admired the way in which he managed my mother, and enjoyed his company. He shared my pleasure in watching cricket and in the summer holidays we quite often spent the afternoon at Lord's together.

Renée and I had managed to find a house in the centre of London which we were able to rent quite cheaply. It was in a narrow little street called Foubert's Place, a turning at the north end of Regent Street. One of the streets in our immediate neighbourhood was Carnaby Street, which is now a centre of fashion but was then largely occupied by families of journeyman tailors to whom the smarter establishments farmed out their work. Our front door lay between two shops and we had two rooms on each of the two floors above them, with an attic which could be made to serve as a spare room. There was a butcher's shop opposite in which the men seemed always to be singing 'The Melody of Broadway' very loudly in chorus when they came to work early in the morning. One of the shops underneath us was a sweet-shop and tobacconist, where I used to buy my packet of twenty Player's, complete with cigarette card, for elevenpence-halfpenny, or just under five of our miserable new pence. The other shop was later taken by a dealer in wireless sets whose way of attracting customers was to have the wireless going at full blast during nearly all the hours when the shop was open. I am not very sensitive to noise when I am working, but this was too much for me, and I had to resort to banging on his ceiling, which usually won me only a short respite, and then going down to expostulate with him. In the end I harassed him enough to make him play the wireless fairly softly, and then not all day long. He soon went out of business, which made me feel a little guilty, but I soothed my conscience with the thought that even at its noisiest the shop had seldom had any customers in it.

With the increase in my salary, we lived very well. It was still possible to buy an edible four-course meal with wine at a Soho restaurant for three shillings and sixpence, and a presentable suit for fifty shillings, though in practice I paid a few pounds more. We obtained some rather more comfortable furniture and bought a glass dining-table of which we were very proud. Renée did the cooking, but we could afford to employ a cleaning-woman who came in as often as we needed her. Except for a period when we developed a taste for the ballet, which has since deserted me, our chief source of entertainment was the cinema. We went most often in the early afternoon, when the seats were cheaper and more easily available. Emerging into the daylight gave me a feeling of self-indulgence. I still think of the middle and late 'thirties as the golden age of Hollywood, remembering Clark Gable and Claudette Colbert in Capra's *It Happened One Night*, Gary Cooper in his *Mr Deeds Goes to Town*, Marlene Dietrich with Gary Cooper in *Desire*, the title concealing a brilliant Lubitsch comedy, the dancing of Fred Astaire and Ginger Rogers, the inspired clowning of the Marx Brothers, the combined effrontery of Mae West and W. C. Fields, Charlie Chaplin in *Modern Times*, John Wayne in *Stage Coach*, bringing Westerns to a new level, Spencer Tracy in *Fury*, with its terrifying lynch-mob, Claude Rains as the unscrupulous southern politician in *They Won't Forget*, the young Henry Fonda acting with Barbara Stanwyck, Eugene Pallette and William Demerest in the funny and touching *The Lady Eve*, William Powell and Myrna Loy, mingling comedy with detection in *The Thin Man*, the emergence of Cary Grant and James Stewart and Robert Taylor and Jean Arthur and Carole Lombard, and actors like James Cagney and Edward G. Robinson giving striking performances even in routine parts. If I could extend the period into the early 'forties so that it covered Humphrey Bogart, with Peter Lorre and Sydney Greenstreet, in *The Maltese Falcon*, and one or two similar thrillers, it would include nearly all the Hollywood films that have made the most lasting impression on me. I even acquired a great affection for many of the supporting players, like Franklin Pangbourne, Nat Pendleton, Allen

Jenkins, and Edward Everett Horton, and I did not care for them any the less because they constantly re-appeared in similar roles. Alistair Cooke was then the BBC film critic, and I made a point of listening to his broadcasts, enjoying their astringency which was tempered by his affection for the American scene. I got to know him slightly, when he was about to transplant himself to America and wish that I had seen more of him, then and since.

This was also a great period for the French cinema. We now very seldom went to Paris, but most of the good French films came to London and we saw nearly all of them: Jean Renoir's *La Grande Illusion*, one of the best of all war films, with Jean Gabin, Erich von Stroheim and Pierre Fresnay; Jean Gabin and Louis Jouvet in Renoir's *Les Bas Fonds*; Jean Gabin in Renoir's *La Bête Humaine*, a film based on Zola's novel; Pierre Blanchar as Raskolnikov and Harry Baur as the Police Inspector in *Crime et Châtiment*, a faithful version of Dostoyevsky's *Crime and Punishment*; Louis Jouvet, Pierre Blanchar and Marie Bell in the enchanting *Carnet du Bal*; Françoise Rosay and Louis Jouvet in *La Kermesse Héroïque*, making a case for collaboration that seemed innocent in 1935; the comedies of Fernandel; Raimu in *La Femme du Boulanger*; the pathetic *Les Fiançailles de M. Hir*, with an extraordinary performance by Michel Simon; Jean Gabin, Michel Simon, and the beautiful Michele Morgan in Marcel Carné's *Le Quai des Brumes*; Jean Gabin, Jules Berry and Arletty in Carné's *Le Jour se lève*, with the dialogue written by Jacques Prévert. For all the claims that have been made for *la nouvelle vague*, this series of films still seems to me to outdo anything that the French cinema has been able to produce in any subsequent decade.

By comparison, we neglected the theatres, in spite of their mostly being within easy walking distance of our house. I remember seeing John Gielgud give a superb performance of Hamlet, but very little else. By then, the musical comedies had deteriorated, or I had grown tired of them, but we used to go round the corner to the Palladium to watch variety shows, especially if Flanagan and Allen were appearing in them. I liked these two even better on their own than when they joined with Nervo and Knox, and Naughton and Gold, to form the Crazy Gang. I had a gramophone record of their songs and I am still word-perfect in the chorus of 'Underneath the Arches', which is admittedly not very hard to learn. Nostalgically, I try to find room for it when I have to choose records for one of those wireless programmes that constitute a sort of musical auto-biography.

During the summer of 1934, when I was still hard at work on *Language, Truth and Logic,* we stayed with an elderly aunt and uncle of Renée's at their country house in Kent. There was a set of Dickens's novels in the house and for the first time I devoted myself to reading them seriously. I had, as a child, read snippets of *David Copperfield* and *Oliver Twist,* without much caring for them, but now I discovered *Bleak House* and *Little Dorrit* and *Great Expectations* and *Our Mutual Friend* and was wholly captivated by them. These have remained my favourites, but with one or two exceptions, such as *A Tale of Two Cities* and *Barnaby Rudge,* I developed a lasting taste for all of Dickens's works. There are very few of them that I have not re-read many times.

It was then also that I began to form the habit, which is said to be common in academic life, of reading numbers of detective stories. I did not treat them as puzzles, in general preferring not to be able to spot the criminal, but simply allowed myself to be caught up in the action. I found it as easy to suspend disbelief in the achievements of Dorothy Sayers's Lord Peter Wimsey, as in those of Ngaio Marsh's Inspector Alleyn, Marjorie Allingham's Albert Campion or Agatha Christie's Hercule Poirot. The interest of the story mattered to me more than the level of the writing, though I think that some of Dorothy Sayers's early books, like *Murder Must Advertise,* written before she was wholly overcome by her infatuation with her hero, deserved the praise that was accorded them. None of these writers, however, had the vitality, the command of dialogue, and the power to create an atmosphere of villainy that is to be found in the works of the American Dashiell Hammett and the best of his followers, like Raymond Chandler and Ross Macdonald, though this is a style which in the books of its many less gifted exponents too easily degenerates into a dreary catalogue of violence. Nor did they have the psychological insight for which I came to admire Simenon. When André Gide named Simenon as the best of contemporary French writers, it was no doubt a way of putting down his own more obvious competitors, in much the same way as some English writers have over-praised the literary size of P. G. Wodehouse. Even so, Commissaire Maigret is a remarkable creation, for all the slightness of many of the stories in which he figures.

The Christmas of 1934 was the last that the family spent together at Eastbourne. My grandfather's health was failing and on January 25 he died, a little over two months short of his seventy-fifth birthday. In his will, he characteristically directed that his body was to be cremated without any religious ceremony and his ashes dispersed, that 'no flowers or mourning shall be used', and that his funeral should be simple, private and informal. After bequeathing an annuity to his wife and smaller amounts to his two surviving daughters, for whom he had already made sufficient provision, and after making generous bequests to his servants, he divided the residue of his estate equally among his five grandchildren, leaving the capital securely in trust, so that we could not dissipate it. Dehra was allowed the use of the house for six months and it was then to be sold and the proceeds added to the estate. It was typical of my grandfather both that he should have allowed his chauffeur to continue to live in his flat above the garage and earn wages as a caretaker until the house was sold, and that he should have given him a commission of 3% upon the proceeds of the sale 'to ensure him doing his best when an intending purchaser presents himself'. Eventually, the house passed into the possession of the Eastbourne corporation, which has turned it into a home for old people who are no longer capable of fending for themselves.

The net value of my grandfather's estate was estimated for probate at about £150,000. It might have been even larger, or anyhow yielded a larger income, if he had shown the same discernment in placing his investments as he had in the management of his business. Unhappily, when the second Labour Government came to power in 1929, he believed that this heralded the decline of the capitalist system in England, and he therefore disposed of many of his English holdings and invested the proceeds in East European and South American stocks which local politics made almost valueless. Nevertheless, enough remained for us, not indeed to live as rentiers, but to have some sense of financial security. I have sometimes felt doubts of my right to enjoy this extra income, but confess that I have never taken any steps to surrender it, except to members of my family. My moral scruples, such as they were, have grown even weaker, now that the greater part of it is taken from me in tax.

Realizing, perhaps, that my cousins were not altogether happy in the work that he had made them do, my grandfather had empowered the trustees to advance capital to any of his grandsons who wished to buy a partnership in, or qualify for the professions of stockbroker, solicitor, surveyor or chartered or incorporated accountant. They both took advantage of this provision, Jack to leave Ford's and start to become a chartered accountant and Donald to give up stockbroking, of which he morally disapproved, and qualify as a solicitor. My grandfather may also have had some idea of benefiting me, since at the time when he made the will, a month or so before his death, my Lectureship at Christ Church was coming to an end and my election to the Research Studentship was still uncertain.

Before the contents of the house were sold, Dehra was allowed to choose any three articles of furniture or china or ornaments or pictures or silver for herself, my mother and my aunt two apiece, and each of the grandchildren one, choosing in order of seniority. Having been denied my grandfather's books, which the executors reasonably refused to count as a single article of furniture, Renée and I settled for his new radio-gramophone, a choice which was not only lacking in sentiment, but also in practical sense, since he possessed a valuable collection of Chinese pottery, which was sold by auction at Sotheby's. The fact was that we did not admire the pottery and would have thought it wrong not to keep whatever we chose. I must also admit that we had no idea of its value.

I missed my grandfather very much in the years that followed. His dominance of the family could be oppressive, and perhaps he set too high a value on worldly success, but there was a gentler side to him which I came to love as I grew older and met him on more equal terms, and his robust intelligence, his moral courage and his freedom from hypocrisy set me a standard which I wish that I had more fully satisfied. To the extent that I have achieved the success that he set store on, I have always regretted that he was not there to enjoy the pleasure that it would have given him.

In the summer of 1935, my father-in-law came from Japan to stay with us. He did not come alone. Renée's mother had died a year or two previously, leaving him free to re-marry. To Renée's annoyance, he had married his Japanese cook. Her name was Hisako, which was said to mean Tea-Water. The argument which he put to Renée to justify his choice was that what he was in search of was not an attractive younger woman who would expect him to lavish attention on her, but someone who would cause him no anxiety, make few demands on him, and care for all his wants; and these were conditions that he already knew that Hisako satisfied. Here, he miscalculated. No sooner were they married than she developed arthritis, which there appeared to be no means of curing, and he found himself waiting upon her. During the months that they spent with us, she sat like an idol, with her hands half-clenched in front of her, saying very little, but taking notice of everything that went on. It was impossible to tell how much she was suffering, but she did not seem discontented with her lot. She was not at all beautiful but I thought her good-natured and by no means a fool. My father-in-law, whom I was meeting for the first time, appeared to be resigned to the situation and fully equal to it. He had the build of a gymnast and for a man approaching sixty remarkable physical vitality. There was a devil-may-care quality about him, allied to an unexpected prudery, especially in matters of speech. We did not have very much in common, but we were set on seeing the best in one another and on the whole managed very well. His wife called him Orde-Lees San, adding to his surname a Japanese mark of respect, and I was content to follow her example.

My father-in-law had hired a small car and in the long vacation the four of us went on a camping holiday. Renée was over two months pregnant, Hisako was necessarily a complete passenger, I could neither drive nor cook and was in other ways unhandy, so that not only the direction of the party but the bulk of the labour fell upon him. It was something of a military expedition, but very enjoyable. We drove across France into Switzerland and down to north Italy, where I particularly admired the Dolomites, without, however, feeling any urge to climb them. I made some attempt to learn Italian but found, as I still do, that my Spanish got in the way. We returned by the same route, mainly because my father-in-law insisted on our revisiting the lake of Thun in Switzerland, which I remembered with affection from my boyhood and had complained of being hurried past on the outward journey. I kept a journal of this tour which I am sorry to have lost, though I doubt if there was very much in it that a competent guide-book would not say as well.

This was the third of our camping holidays, and the last. In one of the intervening summers we had made another, much shorter, tour of Spain in a car with two of Renée's cousins. The trip was chiefly memorable for our breaking down at Tarbes on the way back and having to spend several days encamped as though we were besieging it, while the car was being mended. I thought that it must have a strong claim to being the dreariest town in France, and wondered why Dumas had chosen it for the birthplace of D'Artagnan. We also visited Lourdes, from which I carried away the memory of the priests intoning *Sainte-Marie, mère de Dieu, priez pour nous, pauvres pécheurs, maintenant et à l'heure de notre mort: ainsi-soit-il. Sainte-Marie, mère de Dieu* . . . over and over again, while the faith of the afflicted shone in their faces, and a brisk trade was plied at the Café du Saint-Esprit.

In the autumn Renée's father and Hisako returned to Japan, and I never saw either of them again. Later, when Japan came into the war, they took refuge in New Zealand. Rumour reached us of his becoming more eccentric and there was a story of his storming into the New Zealand parliament on horseback, as a protest against some measure of which he disapproved. He died in 1958 at the age of eighty-one.

Our first child, a daughter, was born in February 1936. We called her Valerie Jane, having no special reason for the choice of these names, though I dare say that the 'Jane' was the outcome of an aural association with *Jane Eyre*. I was a proud father and even became quite adept at seeing to the baby's comfort. We bought or borrowed books on child psychology and allowed ourselves to be guided by them. In those days the prevailing theory was that babies should be left to cry and not immediately comforted and we did our best to adhere to it, until we were overborne by consideration of our own comfort as well as that of the child. Being persuaded also that she needed more light and air than the house afforded her and having no garden in which to leave her, we had a cage built outside our kitchen window, lined it with blankets and put her out there in a basket when the weather was fine. The cage was large enough for her to stand up in and served as a play-pen when she was a little older. It overlooked the busy street and Valerie became a centre of attraction to the passers-by. I have no reason to think that this did her any harm.

Obedient to our text-books, which enjoined that a child should have the company of other children as early as possible, we sent her to a nursery school before she was three years old. It was within a fairly long walking-distance of our house and we took and fetched her in a push-chair. When I came to fetch her she used to pretend to hide from me, the only trouble being that she never wanted the game to stop. We nearly always started home with her in rigid rebellion in her push-chair, and often in full voice. I used to soothe her by telling her stories which I became quite good at inventing. There was a garden in Hanover Square, ordinarily reserved for residents, to which I managed to obtain access, and we spent many peaceful hours there together, with my keeping one eye on her to see that she did not too greatly torment the gardener or mutilate his flowers, and the other on a book, most probably some newly published work which I was reading partly out of a sense of duty to justify my subscription to *The Times* Lending Library.

Meanwhile, I did not neglect philosophy, although a year or two was to pass before I started to write a second book. In 1936 I published a short article on 'Negation' in *Erkenntnis*, another on 'Truth by Convention' in *Analysis*, and a note in *Mind* in which I tried to resolve the tricky problem of the status of the Verification Principle by treating it as a stipulative definition. I read a paper to the Aristotelian Society on 'Verification and Experience' in which I set out the decisive objections to Carnap's and Neurath's coherence theory of truth, and at the Joint Session of 1937, which was held at the University of Bristol, I engaged in a symposium with Duncan-Jones on the question 'Does Philosophy Analyse Common Sense?' In those days *Mind* used to contain summaries of the contents of other journals and I regularly made fairly long summaries for it of the articles that appeared in each number of *Erkenntnis*, besides writing a review of a German book on logic.

I also at this time made my first incursion into journalism. Goronwy Rees had become assistant literary editor of the *Spectator* and he sent me several books to review, including one on Infant Speech which I tested on Valerie without much result. Another of them was a book on Voltaire by the poet Alfred Noyes, who had become a Catholic and had strangely set himself to bring Voltaire closer to the fold. He therefore stressed his deism, deprived him of all his amours, and denigrated his friends among the *Encyclopédistes*. In the course of my hostile review, I put in a good word for D'Alembert, on the ground that he had made an original contribution to the theory of probability. Since my criticisms of Noyes's conception of Voltaire were not based on any research of my own, his letter of protest might have put me into a difficulty if he had confined it to them, but he rashly accused me of confusing D'Alembert with Condorcet. Though I had in fact been lecturing on probability,

I knew of D'Alembert's work only at second-hand through the references to him in Keynes's Treatise, but a visit to the Reading Room of the British Museum enabled me to vindicate myself with a show of erudition. Noyes wrote a rejoinder which he withdrew before it could be published. I was told that Father d'Arcy had advised him not to pursue the argument, but never found out whether this was true.

It was also in 1936 that I first began to engage seriously in politics, to which I had paid very little attention since I had ceased to frequent the Oxford Union. My sympathies had indeed come to lie vaguely with the left and I remember arguing with my grandfather at the time of the General Election of 1931, when the Labour party was shattered by the defection of Ramsay MacDonald to lead a National Government. My grandfather took my defence of socialism as an attack upon himself, asked what would become of his servants if his money was taken from him, and told me the well-known story of the millionaire who calculated that if his wealth were shared out equally everyone would get a farthing and presented his critic with his share. While I could see that these were not very strong arguments, I was too little concerned with the question to make any serious effort to rebut them, and contented myself with some vague remarks about the re-organization of society. I was in Vienna when the Oxford Union passed its famous resolution against fighting for King and Country, which to the extent that it was serious was a fairly natural consequence of all that my generation had been told about the futility and horror of the first world war. I had, however, voted in the Peace Ballot, organized by the League of Nations Union, the result of which fatally persuaded Baldwin that to pursue a policy of re-armament would cost the Conservatives the 1935 election. Like the majority of those who voted, I took the inconsistent position of opposing re-armament and favouring collective security. Roy Harrod in his book *The Prof* recalls an evening in Christ Church in which he and I argued about this with Lindemann and had the worst of the argument. As a rational man, Roy then started to campaign for re-armament. I am sorry to say that I did not.

What awakened me to politics was not the menace of Hitler or the plight of the unemployed in England, for all that I sympathized with the hunger marchers, but the outbreak of the Spanish Civil War. This was an issue which I saw entirely in black and white.

Franco was a military adventurer employing Moorish, Italian and German troops to massacre his own countrymen in the interest of rapacious landlords allied with a bigoted and reactionary church. The Republican Government against which he was in rebellion was the legitimate government of Spain: its supporters were fighting not only for their freedom but for a new and better social order. The fact that the anarchists, initially much more numerous than the communists, played such a conspicuous part in the Spanish working-class movement increased my sympathy for it. Of course I now know that the facts were not quite so simple. The government had been weak; the anarchists had fomented disorder; there was terrorism on both sides; when the dependence of the Republican cause on the supply of arms from Russia and the help of the International Brigades brought the communists to power, they exercised it ruthlessly. Nevertheless, it remains true that Franco's rule was tyrannical, that he could not have won without foreign help, that the assistance which he received from the Italians and the Germans in men and material came earlier and remained far greater than that which the Government received from Russia, and that the timid and hypocritical policy of non-intervention pursued by the French and British Governments, denying the Spanish Government their right to purchase arms, told heavily in Franco's favour. The hatred which I then felt for Neville Chamberlain and his acolytes, mainly on account of their appeasement of Hitler and Mussolini but also because of their strictly business-like attitude to domestic problems, has never left me, and I still find it difficult to view the Conservative party in any other light.

For all the strength of my feelings about the Spanish Civil War, I never seriously thought of going to fight in Spain. Even if I had had no family ties, I should not have been prepared to resign my Studentship: for I could not have obtained leave of absence for such a purpose. I did, however, feel an obligation at least to take an active part in local politics, and since I was spending the greater part of my time in London, I decided to work for the Labour party there. The street in which we lived was on the fringe of Soho, which came for electoral purposes within the area of Westminster, and Renée and I were immediately accepted as members of the Soho branch of the party in the Westminster Abbey Division.

It was not a flourishing branch. Not only did the constituency invariably return Conservatives to Parliament and to the London

County Council with very comfortable majorities, but the West-minster City Council did not have a single Labour representative among its seventy members. The local Labour party was weak and discouraged; it had no regular agent; such activity as it displayed was concentrated in the more prosperous wards, whose middle-class members looked a little askance at the ragamuffins of Soho. There was so little organization in the Soho wards that I very soon found myself Chairman of the Branch. Since the party had no local office, the ward meetings were held in the members' houses, for the most part in my own.

About half a dozen people attended them regularly. The secretary of the branch was a hairdresser of Polish origin, called Henry Monsash, but known professionally as M. Henri. He was a man of strong character and considerable energy, who saw to it that the chairman did his full share of the work. Another of the faithfuls was Mr Gold, a tailor, who was a man of standing in the local Jewish community. He had two pretty daughters and old-fashioned ideas about their upbringing. They did not give the impression of being much interested in politics but they were enrolled in the League of Youth, which was the liveliest section of the party. There was an upholsterer called Mr Reid, a silent but determined trade-unionist, who took the class struggle seriously and thought it his duty to wage guerrilla warfare against his employers. He and his wife, a comfortable middle-aged woman who also came to the meetings, used to spend their summer holidays in nudist camps. The only orator among them was an Australian journalist called Marshall. His style was flamboyant and he was fond of ending his speeches with a slogan taken from the news-reel: Time Marches On.

When we held public meetings, we hired the use of a room at one of the local schools. We could seldom secure outside speakers and were, indeed, chary of inviting them, since we could not guarantee them a sufficient audience to make them think it worth while to have come. The result was that I nearly always had to speak myself. It was a different style of speaking from that in which I was becoming proficient as a lecturer and I never quite succeeded in mastering it. My nervousness still caused me to speak too fast and I usually tried to cover too much ground instead of dwelling on one or two simple points and making sure of driving them home. There were, however, times when I was able to work myself into a passion which carried my hearers with me. The fact that I was nearly always preaching to the converted and untroubled by hecklers made this easier for me.

What I was worst at was stump oratory. For quite a long period, taking no pleasure in the exercise but regarding it as a duty, I used every Saturday evening to mount a step-ladder at the corner of Broadwick Street and Berwick Market, fix my eyes on two or three passing shoppers, cry out 'Citizens of Westminster', which they quite probably were not, and embark on a political discourse. Since the audience was constantly shifting I found it hard to develop a coherent argument and harder still, as my hearers drifted away from me and others failed to congregate, to continue addressing an almost empty street. I could not bring myself to do it now, and am surprised that I did it then: but the relentless Henry Monsash held me to it.

Another task which I performed conscientiously but with reluctance was that of canvassing. This had to be done nearly all the time; most intensively, indeed, when an election of one sort or another was in prospect, but also in the intervals with the aim of maintaining interest in the party and increasing its local membership. There were numerous blocks of workers' flats in the area which we covered, dark and grimy buildings, put up in the nineteenth century by the charitable Mr Peabody, and it was a wearisome business climbing up and down the iron staircases, calling on families who were indeed seldom hostile but often impatient of one's intrusion upon their leisure. There being no television to distract them, they sometimes liked to talk, at least to the extent of expressing their own views. The tailors in Carnaby Street were more difficult to approach, because they worked late into the night and one felt guilty for interrupting them. They asked me what I got out of doing this sort of thing and I hardly liked to say that my motives were altruistic, although I suppose that it was true. There was also the fact that work of this kind was part of the ritual of politics, like the hours spent folding campaign literature into envelopes, addressing and delivering them by hand. The results of the canvassing bore no proportion to the labour. We unearthed a handful of supporters but made few if any converts to our cause.

It was also part of the ritual that we mustered a small contingent for some of the demonstrations that the Labour party organized in

London. I remember a Sunday afternoon in which we marched, or rather straggled, in a long procession all the way from the Embankment to Hyde Park, calling out slogans of which the most popular was 'Caviare for the upper class, peanuts for the working class'. This was made to sound as though it were something that we were demanding rather than a protest against the differences in the living standards of Disraeli's Two Nations, as they still very largely were.

The main local issue was that of housing. Though Westminster was one of the richer London boroughs, it did not have a good record of slum-clearance. When the council did acquire property, its tendency was to put up office buildings rather than workers' flats. There were financial arguments in favour of this policy, but it bore heavily on the many workers in the distributive and service industries, whose hours of employment and low wages made it a hardship for them to have to travel long distances to and from their work. The accommodation which was available to them locally was of poor quality, increasingly scarce and correspondingly expensive. To be able to speak on the question with more authority, I joined the Westminster Housing Association, a voluntary body, which sought out cases of distress and tried to get something done about them, and very soon had myself appointed to its executive committee. Its most active member was a Mr Pratt, a brother of the actor Boris Karloff, well-known for his playing of such horrific parts as that of Frankenstein's Monster. The physical resemblance between the brothers was detectable even through the actor's heavy make-up, with the result that I found it more difficult to believe in the ogres that he portrayed: for the Mr Pratt that I knew was a model of politeness and humanity.

My service in the Westminster Housing Association provided me with most of the material for a pamphlet which I wrote for use as propaganda in a local election. Entitled 'Your Westminster', it was published in a showy green cover by the divisional Labour party, and probably sold for a shilling or less. I possess no copy of it, and think it most unlikely that any copy of it still exists. So far as I can remember, it sharply contrasted the wealth at the City Council's disposal with the miserable conditions in which many of the citizens were forced to live, and pointed out how much could be achieved by a very small increase in the rates. No doubt it was written in highly emotive language, but I hope that it also contained a measure of solid argument.

The pamphlet, which appeared in 1937, was written partly to serve my interest, since I had myself become a candidate for the Westminster City Council. My residence within the electoral area of Westminster entitled me to stand for any of its wards, but I chose the one in which I lived, largely because it offered the best prospect of success. It was called the Great Marlborough Ward, taking its name from a street adjacent to ours which had the distinction of housing a magistrate's court. The ward returned three members to the council, and the other two Labour candidates were Mr Gold and a man called Lensen, whom we barely knew. I believe that he was insinuated into the list by the local communists who were working for us, more or less under cover. Because of the threat which Hitler's Germany posed to Stalin's Russia, the party line had changed from denouncing the moderate members of the Labour party as social fascists to an attempt to join them in a Popular Front.

Our chances of carrying the Great Marlborough Ward would have been quite good if the voters had consisted of the local residents, but at that time the owners of business premises in the area were also entitled to vote, whether they lived there or not, and most of them could be counted as Conservatives. Our main hope was that not very many of them would bother to go to the poll. My principal opponent was a coal merchant, a man of some local influence who was standing for re-election. It was hinted to me by one or two of the electors that he had promised them a free supply of coal if they voted for him. No doubt this was false, as it would have been a most improper proceeding on his part, and foolish besides, since he would have had no means of telling that they had kept their word: it may even have been a subtle way of soliciting a bribe from me. In any event, I told them that if this were so they would be well advised to vote for the coal merchant. A present of coal was worth having, whereas there was little good that I could do them. Even if two or three Labour members were returned to the City Council, they would be vastly outnumbered by the Conservatives and very unlikely to get any of their measures passed. With some disloyalty to Mr Lensen, I added that since they had three votes, they could give one to the coal merchant and still have two to spare for Mr Gold and me.

On polling day we suffered as usual from a shortage of workers and a lack of motor-cars to take our supporters to the poll, though the lack of motor-cars was less important as the constituency was so very small. Peter Legh, the present Lord Newton, came down from Oxford to help me. He was one of my Christ Church pupils and had developed into an ardent logical positivist. His political sympathies were with the Conservatives, and indeed he was to become a Conservative member of Parliament, an assistant Chief Whip and a Minister of State in Mr Heath's government, but in this instance his personal sympathy outweighed them. I was promised help also by Philip Toynbee, who was not a pupil of mine but my closest personal friend among the Christ Church undergraduates. He said that he would come in a car with several pretty girls to lure the voters. He did indeed start out, but believing that I stood no chance he thought it would do no harm to celebrate on the way and his army never reached the battle-field, like Grouchy's at Waterloo.

In the event, the three Conservative candidates were elected in a very small poll. The coal merchant was quite safe, but with a little under four hundred votes, I was only twenty-four votes behind the third Conservative. Mr Gold with his local following came nearer still and Mr Lensen some way behind me. To tease Philip, I told him that the assistance he was bringing would have put me in, but in fact this was not at all probable. At best, it might have secured the election of Mr Gold.

I should almost certainly have stood again for the Westminster City Council if the war had not intervened. The Great Marlborough Ward continued to return Conservatives, but in one of the neighbouring wards that I had helped to canvas, two communists and a Labour candidate were returned in the first local election to be held there after the war. Though the communists were put out after a single turn of office, it was a remarkable transformation. By then, however, the conditions were so different that I doubt if it bore any relation to the seeds that I had so painstakingly sown. A few years later, when I was again living within the electoral district of Westminster, though not at the same address, I allowed my name to be put on a list of Labour candidates for one of the larger wards, in which there was no serious prospect of success. On this occasion I did no campaigning and I have never since made any attempt to get myself elected to any sort of political office.

My political activity in the years from 1936 to 1939 aroused in me also an interest in political theory. I gave a course of lectures on the subject in Oxford and toyed with the idea of developing them into a book. There had at one moment been a question of my collaborating with Stephen Spender on a book about the decline of Liberalism, which Gollancz would publish in the series of the Left Book Club, but it came to nothing. It is unlikely that our styles would have blended, and Stephen rightly decided that he did not need my help. Nor did I make much progress on my own account. I spent many hours in the Reading Room of the British Museum, delving into works of political theory, but I gained little benefit from them. Part of the trouble was that my philosophical weapons were unsuited to the purpose. Political concepts like those of the social contract, the common good or the general will did not repay minute analysis and I had nothing original to put in their place. The political theory which I had been taught at Oxford consisted mainly in the study of the attempts which various philosophers had made to find a justification for political obedience. One started with Hobbes's ruthless theory of sovereignty, proceeded to Locke's and Rousseau's divergent views of the social contract, and ended in the nineteenth century with Mill's defence of liberty, controlled by representative government, and T. H. Green's pursuit of the common good. Hegel was omitted but his place as champion of the State was taken by the Anglo-Hegelian Bosanquet. In my reading, at least, I ranged a little more widely. I dipped into Marx and Engels and Lenin, went rather more deeply into the works of such anarchist writers as Bakunin and Kropotkin, admiring their brilliant exposures of the abuses of power, but feeling sceptical of the blessings which they thought would follow, when everything was left to the natural goodness of man; was more impressed by the case for Guild Socialism which Russell developed in his *Principles of Social Reconstruction*, and was very much taken by Sorel's *Reflexions sur la Violence*, which Frank Longford remembers my describing to him as devoted to 'the moment of glory and the spanner in the works'. My lectures, however, remained very abstract, to the point of becoming artificial. For instance, in discussing the concept of the common good, I raised the question whether we should confine ourselves to the effects of a course of action upon human beings, or should also take the sensations of other animals into account. This provoked one of the working-class members of my audience, a former miner then at Ruskin College, to complain to Frank: 'That man, Ayer, supposed to be one of your best lecturers. Talks about the sensations of pit-ponies. I'd like to see him ride one.'

In addition to my lectures, I put on a class with Frank on Hegel's *Philosophy of Right*. We had both of us conscientiously read the book, but suffered from our common ignorance of the total Hegelian system into which it fits. The result was that neither of us could find much to say in favour of Hegel's idealization of the contemporary Prussian State. Some of our audience were inclined to be sympathetic to Hegel as a forerunner of Marx, but they tended to be better versed in current communist tactics than in the complexities of Marxist theory. We did, however, have some spirited discussions, even though a genuine follower of Hegel might have thought that they sometimes failed to do him justice.

Frank himself had been moving to the left, and his progress towards becoming an active member of the Labour party was completed by a brush with Sir Oswald Mosley's hooligans at a turbulent meeting which Mosley had organized in Oxford on behalf of his newly-formed British Union of Fascists. Elizabeth was the first of the Pakenhams to become a Labour candidate for Parliament, but Frank caught her up by getting himself adopted for Oxford City, after Patrick Gordon-Walker, who had previously been the Labour candidate there, had reluctantly withdrawn to leave the field clear for A. D. Lindsay, the Master of Balliol. Lindsay, standing as an Independent, came forward as the champion of all those who opposed the Munich settlement, in a bitter election which he lost to Quintin Hogg, who then entered Parliament for the first time as a follower of Neville Chamberlain. Oxford City was then a safe Conservative seat, but it was hoped that Lindsay's prestige and the dislike which many people, including even some Conservatives, had come to feel for the Government's policy of appeasement, would turn the scale. It would have been an illusion, even if the Conservatives had come up with a less eloquent and gifted candidate.

A similar election was held after Munich in the Abbey Division of Westminster. The Liberal and Labour parties having decided not to run candidates of their own but to join in supporting an Independent who would campaign on the issue of appeasement, a committee was set up of which I became honorary treasurer. This meant quite a lot of work as I had not only to keep the accounts but also to send out a great many letters soliciting and acknowledging donations, with no secretarial help and writing everything by hand. Our efforts attracted some attention in the press and I was moderately pleased to find myself described in the *Evening Standard*'s Londoner's Diary as 'a man of diminutive stature but dynamic personality'. I suspect that I owed this to Randolph Churchill who was working on the Diary at the time. The first problem for the committee was to find a candidate. There were several well-known persons who sympathized with our cause, but none of them was willing to go to the trouble of fighting an election which they had next to no chance of winning. In the end we settled on Gabriel Carritt, a son of E. F. Carritt, the Oxford philosopher. Gabriel Carritt who was a few years my senior had overlapped with me as an undergraduate at Christ Church; he had captained the Rugby fifteen at Sedburgh and was a great friend of Wystan Auden who wrote a poem about his footballing prowess. Though he had passed his thirtieth year he was young as politicians go and, taking our cue from the *Daily Mirror*, which came out strongly in his favour, we ran him as the candidate of youth. What we were not told was that he was a member of the Communist party, to whom he preferred to be known as Bill Carritt: he and his wife were, indeed, the two communists who were later to be elected to the Westminster City Council. Had this been known to the committee he would not have been selected, and had it come out during the election he would not have done so well. In England, unlike France and Spain, on the rare occasions when communists were admitted as allies in a popular front, they were expected to keep in the background. As it was, he made quite a respectable showing though his vote fell a long way short of that of the City dignitary who won the seat for the Conservatives. I enjoyed taking part in the campaign and had the satisfaction of raising enough money to cover all our election expenses without running the committee into debt.

Although it had improved its position in the General Election of 1935, the Labour party was still very much of a minority in Parliament, nor did it appear to have the driving force which could restore it to power. As so often, it was divided in its counsels, with the Trade Unions supporting a moderate leadership, and the constituency sections straining towards the left. In spite of its accommodating such firebrands as Aneurin Bevan and Ellen Wilkinson, the general impression which it gave was one of elderly timidity, and it was partly for this reason that many young people, especially at the universities, were attracted to communism. Much of their communism was literary posturing – 'Gain altitude, Auden,

Family Life and Politics

now let the rich beware' – but there was also the genuine feeling that the communists were serious and dedicated in a way that others on the left were not. It was mostly the communists who were risking their lives in Spain in the International Brigade; so Day Lewis could write: 'Why do we all, seeing a Communist, feel small?' This feeling was strong enough in many cases to survive the disquieting reports of Stalin's purges. You had, indeed, to be very deep in the faith to be able to persuade yourself that the confessions made by the old Bolsheviks at the Moscow trials were genuine, but the appalling extent of the Stalinist terror was not known, and it was easier than it would be now to dissociate the principles of communism from what could still be seen as an outbreak of factional warfare among the Soviet hierarchy.

I too felt the prevalent attraction. By 1937 communism had made enough headway among the undergraduates to make it possible for Philip Toynbee, standing as a communist, to become President of the Oxford Union, and he was very insistent that I should join the party. I flirted with the idea for a time and then allowed myself a weekend to come to a decision. Though I was sorry to disappoint Philip, my decision was negative. I declined to join on the ground that I did not believe in dialectical materialism. This seemed frivolous to Philip, whose relatively brief adherence to communism was mainly the outcome of a generous emotion, tinged with a youthful desire to *épater la bourgeoisie*, and he maintained that my real reason for not joining was that I was unwilling to submit to party discipline, which would be exercised over me by undergraduates and, as he had let slip, would extend even to my private life. This may, indeed, have been a factor in my decision, but the reason which I gave him was not a pretext. It did seem to me that if one was to join the Communist party, one ought at least to believe in its underlying theory.

In truth, I was not so much a socialist as a radical. I was morally shocked by the currently gross disparities in wealth and power and wished to see the balance redressed, but I did not believe that a sufficient or even perhaps a necessary condition of a better social order lay in the nationalization of the means of production, distribution and exchange. To the extent that it could be dissociated from the evils of laissez-faire capitalism, I had more sympathy for the outlook of John Stuart Mill than for that of Lenin. This rather uneasy position was characteristic of many of my friends and

187

Part of my Life

acquaintances in Oxford, including the majority of those who regularly attended what was known as the Pink Lunch, a fortnightly occasion at which a modest meal at a local restaurant was followed by the delivery and discussion of a political address. The leading spirit of the group was G. D. H. Cole, the Professor of Social and Political Theory, a left-wing socialist who was so strong a man of principle that he was said to refuse to dance with any woman who held right-wing views, and the membership included, besides such Labour stalwarts as Patrick Gordon-Walker, Frank Pakenham, Douglas Jay and A. L. Rowse, a fair number of the younger dons like Guy Chilver, Tony Andrewes and Isaiah Berlin who, with no very active engagement in politics, were morally drawn towards the left. I remember a meeting at which the group was addressed by John Strachey, who was at that time a communist and had written a successful book for Gollancz on *The Coming Struggle for Power*. A fluent political theorist, he had been led by the labour débâcle of 1931 to join the motley company of Mosley's short-lived New Party, before Mosley deviated into fascism, and reverting from communism was later to become a Labour minister. The argument which he presented to us was that our Fabian approach was bound to be unsuccessful since the members of the ruling class would 'see us coming' and would be able to frustrate any measures of reform that seriously threatened their position. To the objection that they would have the same resources and an even stronger motive for frustrating an attempt to organize a violent revolution, he did not appear to have any adequate reply.

Just as Chamberlain's surrender to Hitler at Munich had strengthened the movement in England for a popular front, so less than a year later the conclusion of the cynical Nazi-Soviet pact immediately dissolved it. Since most of the members of my Soho group were either undercover communists or fellow-travellers, and since their orders to co-operate with the Labour party had been rescinded with the disappearance of their official enmity to fascism, I suddenly found myself a leader with almost no following. Even had this not been so, I doubt if the minutiae of local politics would have kept their attraction for me in the shadow of a coming war. With some naïvety, I had believed almost everything that I read in Claud Cockburn's news-sheet, *The Week*, to which I had long been a faithful subscriber, but his prediction that the Government would contrive a repetition of Munich did not convince me. I hoped only that there would be time for me to finish the book on the theory of knowledge which I had started to write after I had decided that I had nothing of value to bring to the theory of politics. Whatever else I might be doing, my principal concern was still to make some further contribution to philosophy.

8 *Friendships and Travel*

I have always found it easy to move in different worlds, and my life in Oxford in the years preceding the war was very largely independent of that which I led in London. I continued to see a great deal of Isaiah Berlin, first in All Souls and then in New College, of which he became a Fellow in 1938. In the preface to his book on Karl Marx he made almost the same acknowledgement to me as I had made to him in the preface of *Language, Truth and Logic*, but in fact my compliment to him was the more deserved. I may have made one or two literary suggestions, but the subject of his book was not one about which he had anything to learn from me. My part mainly consisted in reassuring him that the book was good.

I also saw something of Maurice Bowra, though less than I had in previous years. After he had become Warden of Wadham in 1938, he used sometimes to send me pupils whom Ian Gallie, the tutor in philosophy at Wadham, did not suit. One of them with whom I formed a lasting friendship was Michael Judd, soon to be a much-decorated fighter pilot, and then to become a Texas oil magnate, while preserving the manner and outlook of an English country gentleman. Michael shared lodgings with Robert Conquest, an agreeable hedonist and a man of great intellectual energy. Like many of those who have been turned into right-wing apologists by their justified hatred of communist tyranny, his youthful leanings were towards the left.

For the most part, however, my Oxford life centred upon Christ Church, and my closest friends in Oxford, apart from Isaiah, were all attached to Christ Church in one way or another. One of the most remarkable of them was Robin Zaehner, later the Professor of Eastern Religions and Ethics at Oxford, and the author of many books on mysticism. Like myself, he was partly of Swiss extraction, though his family came from the German rather than the French part of Switzerland. In the interval between leaving his school at Tonbridge and coming up to Christ Church, he went to Berlin, where Maurice Bowra discovered him. He told me that it was at Maurice's suggestion that he gave up Classics for Oriental Languages. After getting a first in Oriental Languages, he stayed on at Christ Church as a Senior Scholar from 1934 to 1939, when he became a Research Lecturer. It was during this period that I got to know him. He did not live in college but in lodgings in St Giles, with a land-lady who mothered him. He was small, myopic, gossipy, fond of the bottle, and by his own account sexually adventurous though it never seemed that his pursuit of rough trade brought him to any harm. He was an avid reader of the comic stories of Damon Runyon about the sleazier citizens of Broadway, and I came to share his liking for Runyon's style. He too was a cinema-addict, with a great admiration for the actor Mickey Rooney, and an affection for the simpletons among the Disney characters, like Dopey, Pinocchio and Dumbo. He was very learned and, for all his pursuit of pleasure, very hard-working, and he had an extraordinary gift for languages. During the time that he held his Senior Scholarship, he was editing some Zoroastrian texts in Middle Persian, for which he had to compile his own dictionary. He was a very loyal friend, a good listener and a good receiver of confidences if one was in any trouble. He was an Intelligence Officer during the war and while serving in Persia became a convert to Roman Catholicism. Unhappily for me, this put an end to our friendship. He took his religion very seriously, and fearing that I should mock him or even just argue with him about it, he preferred not to see me. We were cordial on the rare occasions that we met, but the old affection had gone. In his last years he appeared increasingly to live in a world of his own into which only those who had pursued a similar course of study could have hoped to follow him.

A friend for whom I felt a stronger intellectual affinity was Hugh Trevor-Roper, who has for long been the Regius Professor of Modern History at Oxford. Three years my junior, he came up to Christ Church as a classical scholar and won all the classical prizes, besides getting a first in Honour Moderations, before turning to History, getting another first in 1936, and obtaining a University

Senior Scholarship. In the following year Patrick Gordon-Walker was away on sabbatical leave and Hugh did his teaching for him, becoming a temporary member of the Senior Common Room. This overlapped with his election to a Research Fellowship at Merton, which he held until the war, returning afterwards to Christ Church as a Student. During the war he was employed in counter-intelligence, an occupation for which he had an exceptional aptitude, as is shown by his remarkable book, *The Last Days of Hitler*. He once spoke of me in print as a convivial soul, a description which I do not disown but one that I think of as applying even more to him. He was as much at home with the young aristocrats of the Bullingdon Club, with whom he shared a common interest in hunting, as in the company of scholars and wits. If he saw himself as an eighteenth-century character, it was not without good reason. Though some might think him lacking in charity, he was a zestful companion and a staunch friend. I admired his intellectual elegance, appreciated his malice, and was delighted to find that he shared my anti-clericalism and my irreverence for authority. I was impressed too by his ability to acquire an extensive knowledge of history without surrendering his mastery of the classics. For some reason it fell to me in 1937 to deliver a Latin speech in the Bodleian on the current state of the Library. As this was a task to which I was quite unequal, I had recourse to Hugh, who composed the speech for me with equal ease and felicity, enabling me to obtain undeserved credit for a fluency in Latin to which, even at the time when I was specializing in the Classics, I could never have laid claim. We divided the fee, which we had a remarkable difficulty in extracting from the Canon who was responsible for paying it.

It was about a year later that Hugh unwittingly embroiled me with Professor Lindemann. He and I and Robin Zaehner had been to some dinner of an undergraduate society at which we had been given a great deal to drink. The party went on until a late hour and after letting Robin out of college by a door known as the bolt-hole for which the members of the Senior Common Room possessed a key, I retired unsteadily to bed. At the same time Hugh and his friend Alastair Buchan were making their way to a garden, reserved for the use of the senior members of the college, to which a similar key gave access. Hugh had by then left Christ Church for Merton but he had kept his key. They were followed at a discreet distance by one of the college porters who in his report to the Censors named me as the only one of the pair whom he could identify. Perhaps he had been drinking too, as I did not in the least resemble either of them. Finding a bicycle in the garden, they disported themselves on it until it broke, and went on their way. The bicycle belonged to Lindemann's servant. He complained to Lindemann and Lindemann complained to the authorities. Having gone home for the weekend, I received a telephone call from Michael Foster, by then the Senior Censor, in which he abruptly asked me whether I had broken Lindemann's servant's bicycle. I replied equally abruptly that I knew nothing whatever about it. When I returned to Christ Church a day or two later, I found that I had been judged guilty not only of a lack of respect for private property but of being a liar, both because of the porter's testimony and because it had been too readily assumed that of the persons present at the dinner only I had the means of access to the garden. Learning of this, I called on Lindemann, found him still in his bed at a late hour in the morning, and rather angrily declared my innocence. I had the impression that he did not really believe me, but he did not try to argue. The Dean at that time was Dean Williams, the future Bishop of Winchester, a pleasant scholarly man, who had succeeded Dean White not long before. He did believe me, but said that he found it regrettable that the names of senior members should appear in the porter's report. Since the only reason for my name's appearing was that the porter had mistaken someone else for me, I thought this a little unfair but did not protest. It was only later, when Michael Foster confronted him in Merton, that Hugh learned of the fuss and of course immediately cleared me. He rightly found the whole thing very funny, though he had to surrender his key.

Apart from this mild contretemps, I continued to be on very good terms with Lindemann and on civil terms at least with all my senior colleagues. Dundas, in particular, became very much more cordial to me, while retaining some doubts as to the extent to which I had become acclimatized. This came out once in an amusing way. In 1937, when the growing Nazi threat to Austria was putting the Viennese Jews in greater jeopardy, Karl Popper was enabled to escape from Vienna by being offered a lectureship at one of the universities in New Zealand. He passed through London on his way to take up this appointment and Renée and I entertained him and his wife. I was pleased to see him again, and sympathized with him on his going into exile. He was putting a brave face on it, but was

clearly a little afraid of what awaited him. Not long afterwards I had
Isaiah Berlin to dine with me in Christ Church and put him next to
Dundas in Common Room. Isaiah and I were talking about Vienna
and I said to him, 'Poor Popper has had to take refuge in New
Zealand.' Dundas leaned across at this and said, 'I never knew your
father was an Austrian.' I found this an enchanting but also a
revealing remark.

When *Language, Truth and Logic* came out, one of those who gave
it a favourable notice was Solly Zuckerman. I had only just got to
know him at that time but in the years that followed I saw a very
great deal of him. He had come to Oxford in 1934 as a Demonstrator
in the Department of Anatomy, two years after he had published his
celebrated book on *The Social Life of Monkeys and Apes*, for which he
had done most of the research by carefully observing the behaviour
of a colony of baboons at the London Zoo. His appointment did
not carry a Fellowship with it but Christ Church eventually made
him a member of the Senior Common Room. He had taken a house
in Museum Road, in the neighbourhood of the Science Museum and
the University Parks, and I frequently visited him there. Solly was
six years older than I and had a very much wider experience of the
world. I admired his sophistication, his scientific attainment and his
intellectual energy, and took considerable pleasure in his company.

Solly's circle of friends intersected the stage and among those
who visited him at Oxford were the actor Charles Laughton and his
wife Elsa Lanchester. Laughton had already branched out into
films and was best known to the cinema public for his playing of the
leading part in Korda's film *The Private Life of Henry VIII*. After
meeting him a couple of times at Solly's house, I invited him to
dine with me in Christ Church, and he seemed pleased to accept.
Though I liked him quite well, I suppose that my reason for inviting
him contained an element of snobbery. I did not tell any of my
colleagues who my guest was to be, and was interested in their
reactions. Dundas, who sat next to him in Hall, turned round and
pointed to a portrait of Henry VIII, the founder of the college, and
murmured, 'That's you, isn't it?' Frank Taylor took me aside in
Common Room and said, 'Have you noticed that your guest is
remarkably like Charles Laughton?' The college servants were the
most impressed. Laughton, for his part, seemed anxious to display
himself as something more than a mere actor, and made knowledgeable remarks about the college silver. I think that he enjoyed his

evening but it did not lead to any further friendship between us. In fact, I do not remember that we ever met again.

It was to Solly also that I owed the beginning of a friendship that came to mean a very great deal to me. He had spent some time in New York and among the many well-known people with whom he had made friends there were the poet E. E. Cummings and his wife Marion Morehouse. Marion, who was strikingly beautiful, had been a show girl in the Ziegfeld Follies and a model; after her marriage to Cummings, she became an expert photographer. Having heard from the Cummingses that they were planning a holiday in Europe, Solly invited them to stay with him in Oxford. Just before they were due to arrive, he found that he had to go abroad to attend a congress, and he asked me to take care of them. It was towards the end of the summer term of 1937. On the afternoon of their arrival, I had been playing tennis in the Parks and I called at Museum Road immediately afterwards, hot and tousled and still carrying my tennis-racket, to find them sitting in Solly's living-room and looking a little bewildered and forlorn. We took to each other at once and I invited them out to dinner. It happened to be an evening on which our philosophical group was due to meet, and not liking either to miss the meeting or to abandon the Cummingses, I brought them with me to Isaiah's rooms. The result, which I should have foreseen, was that instead of our usual philosophical discussion we had a lively party, at which the normally quiet and reserved Macnabb was in particularly high spirits. Mishearing Isaiah's nickname, Cummings referred to him as 'The Shah', which seemed to me quite appropriate. In the day or two that followed before Solly's return I spent nearly all my free time in the Cummingses' company. Among other things, I showed them around Christ Church and translated for their benefit the Latin inscription which ran along the cornice of Peckwater Quad. My assumption that they would not be able to translate it for themselves very much amused Cummings, who had been a classical scholar at Harvard, but he kept quiet about it until long afterwards.

Like D. H. Lawrence, Cummings was almost always addressed simply by his surname. The E. E. stood for Edward Estlin, and he was called Estlin by his family but not by anybody else except for one or two friends of his youth. In his letters and in the books which he inscribed to me he simply signed himself 'Cummings'. In his poems he used capitals only for emphasis, and no doubt it was on the same principle that he chose to have his name and initials appear in lower-case type on the title-page of his books. The exceptional attention that he paid to the typography of his poems may have been linked with the fact that he was also a painter. He had a great admiration for the French Impressionists, especially Renoir, though his own style of painting was more subdued. I have a portrait that he painted of me in the early nineteen-forties when I was staying with him and Marion at their house in New Hampshire. It is gentle and affectionate, and was thought to be a good likeness of me.

In 1937, when I first met them, he was forty-two years of age, and Marion at least ten years younger. With his proud, slightly rugged, questing, humorous face he had the looks, as well as the accent and bearing, of a New Englander of long lineage. Though he was not, in any obvious sense, a puritan, there was something of the best of puritanism in his self-reliance and his independence of spirit. The America in which he believed was the America of Emerson and Thoreau: he was not at home in the 'century of the common man'. He was not in the least a social snob, but he valued people only as individuals and hated anything that in any way savoured of collectivism. His outlook is perfectly expressed in a couplet of William Blake's, which he was fond of quoting:

He who would do good to another must do it in Minute
  Particulars,
General Good is the plea of the scoundrel, hypocrite, and
  flatterer.

If he supported the Republicans against Roosevelt, it was not because he had any sympathy or admiration for big business, but because he associated the Democratic party with corrupt city politics and believed that Roosevelt was arrogating too much power to himself. He had, indeed, a low opinion of politicians in general, as expressed in his poem:

a politician is an arse upon
which everyone has sat except a man.

A radical in his youth, he had visited Russia in 1931 and had been horrified by what he saw there. He expressed his revulsion against the Soviet system and his own individualistic credo in what he later described as 'a mis-called novel' with the title of *Eimi*, the

Greek word for 'I am'. Its appearance at a time when many American intellectuals were at least indulgent to communism and his persistence in maintaining his old-fashioned standards made him rather an isolated figure in the American literary world, so that he even came to suffer from something of a sense of persecution, though his unaffected charm and vitality would always secure him friends. No doubt because he saw it as a statement of faith, *Eimi* was one of Cummings's own favourites among his works, but I have always found it the least readable of them. Its style is so highly expressionistic as to verge on obscurity and its density tends to make it turgid. It does, however, contain some brilliant descriptive passages.

A far better book, in my view, is the other of Cummings's 'mis-called novels', to which he gave the title of *The Enormous Room*. It is an account of his experiences in a detention centre in France during the first world war. He had gone to France as a volunteer in an American ambulance unit, before the United States itself entered the war. His best friend in the unit, a man called Slater Brown, had written letters home which were critical of the French. They were intercepted by the French censors and Brown was accused of being a spy. The head of the section, who disliked Cummings for his indifference to spit and polish and his preference for the company of the French cook and mechanics to that of the more stuffed-shirted Americans, saw this as an opportunity to get rid of him, and therefore suggested to the French authorities that he too was suspect. Cummings came triumphantly through his interrogation and could have gone free if he had been willing to profess a hatred of the Germans, but all that he would say was that he liked the French. So he went, escorted by gendarmes, to a detention centre at the small town of La Ferté Macé, in the department of the Orne, where Brown had preceded him. The enormous room was the home of the male prisoners, Dutchmen, Belgians, Russians, Poles, Frenchmen, Austrians, Spaniards, Turks, Swedes, Norwegians, Arabs, Gypsies, some of them criminals, probably none of them spies. The bulk of the book is a portrait-gallery of villains and heroes, the villains being the prison officials and guards and one or two of the prisoners who are given such names as 'Rockyfeller', 'The Trick Raincoat' and 'The Fighting Sheeny', the heroes and heroines coming from the other prisoners, including some of the prostitutes who were also interned at La Ferté Macé. The principal heroes, 'The Wanderer', 'Zoo-Loo', 'Surplice' and

'Jean le Nègre' are called 'The Delectable Mountains'. Such people seemed to Cummings to have a quality of life in them which he could not define. Feeling that it should be denoted by a verb, rather than a noun or adjective, he called anyone who had it 'an IS'. Throughout his life, the people in whom he thought that he could detect this quality were the only ones that he really cared for. He believed that it gave them a kind of magic armour. That is what I took him to mean when he once wrote to me, 'Nothing bad can happen to good people.'

Cummings spent about three months in the enormous room before the American Embassy in Paris, which had lost all trace of him, discovered where he was, arranged for his release and shipped him back to the United States. The experience did not turn him into a pacifist, or even destroy his liking for France. He loved Paris especially and, like other American writers, spent much of his time there between the wars. He belonged to the same generation as Ernest Hemingway but had little respect either for the man or his work. Among his near contemporaries, the American writers whom he admired were Ezra Pound, Marianne Moore, and the critic Allen Tate. Though he had great personal affection for John Dos Passos, he did not much care for his novels, preferring the less well-known poetry which Dos wrote when he was young.

When I first met Cummings, I had already read *The Enormous Room* but I knew very little of his poetry. Very soon afterwards, I bought his *Collected Poems* and he gave me copies of all his later works. I came to like his poems very much, both on their own merits and because I found so much of him in them. A not altogether friendly critic once described them as 'a combination of sentimental emotion and cynical realism with a technique which depends, to a great degree, on typographical distortion'. I think this is not true of the technique: the distortion hardly appears in the best poems, and only a small proportion of the others depend on it. On the other hand, 'the cynical realism' and 'the sentimental emotion' are indeed there, though not normally in combination. Cummings would probably have accepted the characterization of many of his poems as 'sentimental' but he would not have viewed it as a term of disparagement. I choose one example of each vein, the first pair coming from the early work *Tulips and Chimneys* and the second from *One Times One*, which was published in 1944.

the Cambridge ladies who live in furnished souls
are unbeautiful and have comfortable minds
(also, with the church's protestant blessings
daughters, unscented shapeless spirited)
they believe in Christ and Longfellow, both dead,
are invariably interested in so many things –
at the present writing one still finds
delighted fingers knitting for the is it Poles?
perhaps. While permanent faces coyly bandy
scandal of Mrs. N and Professor D
. . . the Cambridge ladies do not care, above
Cambridge if sometimes in its box of
sky lavender and cornerless, the
moon rattles like a fragment of angry candy.

———

'sweet spring is your
time is my time is our
time for springtime is lovetime
and viva sweet love'

(all the merry little birds are
flying in the floating in the
very spirits singing in
are winging in the blossoming)

lovers go and lovers come
awandering awondering
but any two are perfectly
alone there's nobody else alive

(such a sky and such a sun
i never knew and neither did you
and everybody never breathed
quite so many kinds of yes)

not a tree can count his leaves
each herself by opening
but shining who by thousands mean
only one amazing thing

(secretly adoring shyly
tiny winging darting floating
merry in the blossoming
always joyful selves are singing)

'sweet spring is your
time is my time is our
time for springtime is lovetime
and viva sweet love.'

In a way it is strange that Cummings and I should have become such great friends as we did. The difference in our ages did not matter: his spirit was ageless and even physically he changed very little. I last saw him in 1961, when he had only a year to live, and he seemed very little older than when I first met him, twenty-four years before. Nor did it matter that we disagreed politically, since neither of us took the other's politics very seriously. What might have divided us was a deep-lying difference in our conception of the world, I seeing it prosaically and he poetically, I, though no scientist, a believer in scientific method, he thinking art much the greater source of truth. That he was sensitive to this difference was shown by his saying to my present wife, 'What's a nice girl from New Bedford like you doing, marrying that stainless steel mind?' I also failed to share his feeling for nature and once startled him and Marion by referring to the ground outside their farm-house as 'the floor'. He writes of a similar incident amusingly in one of his published letters:

Well do I remember taking AJ ('Freddy') Ayer – the foremost 'logical positivist' quote – philosopher – unquote extant – for a promenade near Joy Farm; during which stroll, my guest observed (probably anent some entirely spontaneous tribute to Nature which had escaped me) 'you're almost an animist, aren't you'. Quick-as-a-flash – withoutthinkingatall – I deeply surprised myself by replying ' "almost"? I AM an animist' thereby placing our nonhero precisely on a par with the least enlightened of coalblackAfricansavages . . .

He forgave me this and much else because he saw me, if not quite as a Delectable Mountain, at least as someone who was, in his sense, alive.

The Cummingses spent some time in London before they went back to America and I introduced them to Renée who also liked them without being so completely captivated by them as I had been. In general, Renée was socially more reserved than I. She was a good hostess, but lacked my appetite for parties. She was more contented with a purely domestic life. She was strongly attached to her friends but made friends less easily. Her best friend was a girl who had been with her at the finishing-school in Paris. She was called Patricia and was married to a man called Patrick Johnson. The four of us used frequently to dine together, at Foubert's Place or at the Johnsons' house in Hampstead. We were so much at ease with one another that it did not seem impolite on these occasions for me to immerse myself in a book. The Johnsons had a collection of the novels of Dornford Yates and I read them in preference to more serious books, enjoying the pace of the stories and easily digesting the snobbery. Patrick had been in the Air Force, before he became an adviser on patents, and had remained an expert pilot. He gave me my first taste of flying, in a small monoplane, allowing me for a moment to handle the joy-stick. I found it a very exhilarating experience, discovering a sensation of speed which I have never recaptured in all the journeys that I have made as a passenger in modern airlines. I thought of joining the Oxford University Air Squadron and learning to fly, but never did anything about it. If I had, I might have become a pilot in the war and should probably not have survived it.

We continued to be friends with Martin Cooper, though we were never again so close as we had been in Vienna. I used to play tennis in Battersea Park with him and his friend, the novelist Ralph Ricketts, and Goronwy Rees. My relations with Martin became strained as a result of an argument that we had about the impending war. He and Ralph had been to a lecture given by C. E. M. Joad, at which Joad had advanced the view that it was the duty of persons like himself to look out for their own safety, in order that they should survive to make the contribution to civilization that would be needed after the war was over. When they reported to me what Joad had said, I maintained very hotly that this was an insufferably arrogant position to adopt. Since they had in fact been rather impressed by Joad's argument, my contemptuous dismissal of it struck a jarring note. On reflection, I now think that there was more to the argument than I allowed. Cézanne avoided military service in the Franco-Prussian war in order to continue with his painting, and it would be hard to maintain that the world would have been a better place if he had accepted his civic responsibility and had been killed in consequence. At the same time, I think that one has to be very confident of one's genius to be entitled so to make an exception of oneself. It was, in any case, a point that could have been argued coolly, and I suspect that the vehemence of my reaction was due to some inner conflict. I had no desire to run into danger, but I had been saying in my political speeches that we had to resist Hitler, and I felt that this committed me to taking an active part in the war, if it came about. If I had meant that others should resist Hitler, I ought to have said 'You' instead of 'We'.

I think that it was through Goronwy that we met Elizabeth Bowen, one or two of whose novels I had already read and admired. Both Renée and I liked her very much and enjoyed going to her house. She was married to a man called Alan Cameron, who held some administrative post in the field of education. He looked handsome in the photograph which she kept of him as a wartime Highland officer, but he had run to fat and now seemed more cosy than glamorous. Her friends thought him too unimaginative and unintellectual a companion for her, but I think that she depended on his stolidity. She seemed very cool and self-possessed, but she was surprisingly vulnerable, as indeed her novels show. She once told me that she acted out the movements of the characters, which consorts with the precision of their visual detail. In her later works I thought that her writing tended to become over-elaborate, but I retain my admiration for *The House in Paris* and *The Death of the Heart*.

It was at a dinner party of Elizabeth Bowen's that I first met T. S. Eliot. I remember that it was on a Friday, because Eliot alone was eating fish. He had by then become a confirmed Anglo-Catholic. I very greatly admired 'The Waste Land' and others of his early poems, but I found the man very chilly. It was also obvious that he did not take to me. Apart from anything else that might have divided us, including the religious issue, I was philosophically obnoxious to him. He had a great reverence for the philosopher F. H. Bradley, whose disciple he had been, and he found my attack on Bradley's metaphysics harsh and impious. Many years later, when I used to see him in company with our common friend, the critic, John Hayward, a sufferer from a creeping paralysis, of whom Eliot took devoted care, he thawed a little towards me; but our relations never progressed beyond a conscientious civility.

I was very much more drawn to Cyril Connolly, whom I also met at about this time. I already respected him as a parodist and as a trenchant reviewer of novels for the *New Statesman*, to which I had become and have remained a faithful subscriber, and I was further disposed to like him because of the articles which he had written about Spain. For most of his life, he kept aloof from politics but he had visited Spain at the end of 1936 and had been moved into ardent support of the Republican cause. I had also enjoyed his book *Enemies of Promise*, not so much for its literary criticism as for its account of his life as a Colleger at Eton at a time just previous to my own: he had been a great success at Eton, getting himself elected to Pop in spite of having no athletic colours, and he had been one of those who, under the benevolent mastership of Mr Crace, had briefly made College a civilized and happy place to be. Cyril was very much a man of moods, but when he was in good spirits and sure of his company, he was one of the best talkers that I have ever known. He had a curiously soft voice and a slow way of speaking which crystallized his wit. His love of food and drink was already beginning to show in his figure, but he had great vitality and his charm, when he chose to exercise it, was irresistible. Though they were soon to separate, he was then still married to his first wife, Jeannie, an untidy, large, easy-going, hospitable American, with a wit of her own. I thought of their way of living as Bohemian, though they did not suffer the privations of the traditional *vie de Bohème*. The affection which I then had for Cyril and never altogether lost, in spite of our later fallings-out, was related to a different side of him from that which he mainly displayed in his celebrated book *The Unquiet Grave*. It is a beautifully written book, but too mannered for my taste and too repining. I prefer *The Condemned Playground*, a collection of essays in which his high spirits, his flights of fantasy, and his remarkable gift for parody are more in evidence. It contains the brilliant 'Where Engels Fears to Tread', a hilarious squib about a playboy, turned communist, for which the model is said to have been Brian Howard. When the hero is made to discover contemporary left-wing poetry, the target is hit with such fine arrows as

> Come on Percy, my pillion-proud, be camber-conscious
> Cleave to the crown of the road.

'Told in Gath', the parody of the later manner of Aldous Huxley, is rather more serious. Indeed, in such passages as the following it is almost too close to the original:

> Platitudes are eternally fresh, and even the most paradoxical are true; even when we say the days draw in we are literally right – for science has now come largely to the rescue of folk-lore: after the summer and still more after the equinoctial solstice the hours do definitely get shorter. It is this shortness of our northern day that has occasioned the luxuriousness of our literature. Retractile weather – erectile poetry. No one has idealized, in our cold climate, more typically than Shakespeare and Dryden the sub-tropical conditioning. But we can consider Antony and Cleopatra to have been very different from their counterparts in the Elizabethan imagination, for on the Mediterranean they understand summer better and, with summer, sex.
>
> What were they really like, those prototypes of Aryan passion, of brachycephalic amour? Were Cleopatra's breasts such as 'bore through men's eyes' and tormented those early sensualists, Milton, Dante, Coventry Patmore, and St John of the Cross? We shall never know.

The choice of sensualists betrays the parodist but otherwise who could be sure that this was not the master's voice?

By the middle of the 'thirties the Bloomsbury group had dispersed, but some of its members were occasionally to be seen at parties in London. I met Virginia Woolf only once and thought her very handsome and also very formidable. When I was introduced to her, she asked me how I had come to the party and I said that I had come by bus. She asked me then to tell her all about it, expecting me to have noticed or imagined some unusual quality in the conductor or the other passengers. Unhappily, all I could find to say was that it was just an ordinary bus, at which point she understandably lost interest in me.

I had better fortune with Rose Macaulay, whose novels, *Told by an Idiot* and *What Not*, had greatly impressed me when I first read them as a boy. I introduced myself to her on the occasion of some election in Westminster where we were both assisting as spectators at the counting of the votes. My excuse for doing so was that I had undertaken to write an essay for a book to which she had also agreed to contribute. I forget what the central theme of the book was intended to be, though I remember that the project came to nothing. She understood me to say that I was thinking of writing a book and asked me, rather dryly, what was stopping me. After this awkward start, we became friends. She was a gentlewoman of an older generation, formal in her manner, very observant, and with a refreshing sharpness underlying her reserve.

By this time my life with Renée had begun to go awry. Some months before, at the end of a winter term, I was sharing a taxi on the way to Oxford station with a girl whom I knew only slightly when it suddenly became clear that we wanted one another. I immediately told the driver to turn back, took the girl to my rooms and made love to her. I wished it to be something more than a casual affair, but the girl, who was engaged to be married, viewed it differently. I made desperate attempts to see her in London, but on the one or two occasions when I persuaded her to meet me, it was clear that she wished to be rid of me. After that I engaged in a series of affairs which I concealed from Renée, but could not conceal from her that something was amiss. In the summer of 1937, we left Valerie in a Norland nursery and went alone on holiday together, staying in a hotel at Annecy. I was restless and ill-humoured and for the first time in nearly ten years we were not at ease in one another's company. It was distressing to me but also something of a relief to my conscience when Renée, with her deeper nature, became seriously attracted to a friend of mine, a younger man who was very much in love with her. He told me of it but I treated his confession lightly. In the Christmas holidays the three of us went to Paris together, but finding the strain too great, I soon returned alone. I planned to arrive in time for Christmas but there was fog in the Channel and I remember spending Christmas morning on the quayside at Calais, looking disconsolately out to sea and chatting to Carroll Levis, a jovial impresario who had become well-known as a promoter of theatrical discoveries. After some hours the fog lifted and I arrived back in London in time to have a solitary dinner at a Lyons restaurant. For once I felt a little sorry for myself but I soon plunged into a round of parties and was cheerful enough by the time that Renée returned.

We wanted to preserve our marriage, but felt some need of absence to relax the tension, so that when I learned that the Cincinnati branch of the English Speaking Union was offering a scholarship for someone to visit the United States in the Easter holidays I had no hesitation in applying for it. Among the other applicants was Nevill Coghill, later to be a Professor of English Literature at Oxford, and already well-known as a dramatic producer. Since he was a good deal senior to me and had earned a greater reputation, I was not surprised that the scholarship went to him. However, the Cleveland branch of the English Speaking Union, not wishing perhaps to be outdone by Cincinnati, decided to offer a similar scholarship and this time the choice fell on me. Nevill and I travelled out together on the *Queen Mary* in the second class, which was comfortable if not luxurious. Renée came to see me off and writing to me later described the *Queen Mary* as it left port as having the grace of a fat woman dancing. Though he was very prominent in Oxford, I had hardly met Nevill before. I liked him very much, enjoyed travelling with him and was sorry that our paths separated after the first days in New York. It was less of an adventure for him than for me, since he had been to the United States before, but in his sensitive and ironic way, he was indulgent to my enthusiasm.

We arrived at New York early on a fine spring morning. I had got up almost as soon as it was light and as the boat steamed slowly up the Hudson River, past the Statue of Liberty and then the mass of skyscrapers, glittering in the sunshine, I had an extraordinary sense of exhilaration. Apart from the beauty of the city, which I discovered in more detail once we had gone ashore, there was a buoyancy in the air which took possession of me: I felt that I could go for days without having any need of sleep. I must have spent about a week there before setting out on my tour and this excitement never left me. I stayed in some downtown hotel which Nevill recommended to me, and was struck by the handsomeness of the hostesses, who waited on the customers with brisk impersonal friendliness. In writing to Renée about my first impression of New York I used the expression 'bright lights and pretty hostesses' which she remembered for a long time as characteristic of me. Throughout my journey I wrote her a series of very long letters which might have had some interest as a travelogue; but she did not like them because they were too impersonal. Whatever my feelings, I have always found it difficult in writing letters to strike a personal note.

One of my first acts was to call on the Cummingses at their house in Patchin Place, an unexpectedly quiet, leafy little recess on the edge of Greenwich Village. Cummings wrote of the village in one of his poems as 'the little barbarous Greenwich perfumed fake',

but it was his base in New York from which he never liked to move
very far. He would go for walks in Washington Square or venture a
little farther to dine at the Lafayette or the Brevoort, old-fashioned
hostelries, whose disappearance has broken for me a treasured link
with the past. Our boldest expedition was to go to a theatre on
Broadway. The local representative of the English Speaking Union
had offered me tickets for any play that I chose and was visibly
disillusioned when, at Cummings's instigation, I selected a low-class
review. Cummings loved circuses and burlesque shows and this
was the nearest thing to a burlesque show that was then running in
New York. It had the attraction of Gypsy Rose Lee but not being
allowed or no longer wishing to display her skill as a stripper, she
went through her part in an absent-minded, almost condescending
fashion; the burlesque comedian was not so funny as Cummings had
led me to expect, and I thought the show compared badly with the
musical comedies and pantomimes of my boyhood.

I was more interested in seeing a production of *Julius Caesar*
in modern dress, with Orson Welles in one of the leading parts and
the commonly minor episode of the mobbing of Cinna the poet
drawn out into a sinister scene of menace. On this occasion, I went
with Gilbert and Helen Highet, Gilbert having recently left Oxford
to become a Professor of Classics at Columbia University. They
had both adapted themselves quickly and contentedly to the
American scene, though I was a little surprised to find Gilbert
carrying a pair of knuckle-dusters. I do not know whether he ever
had any occasion to use them.

I had met the editor of the American journal, *The Philosophy of
Science*, when he was on a visit to England, and he gave me letters of
introduction to a number of people in New York. For once I was
not too diffident to make use of them. It was in this way that I first
met Meyer Shapiro, with whom I have been friends ever since. An
art historian teaching at Columbia, he is not only immensely learned
in his own subject but has a wider range of knowledge than anyone
that I have ever met, with the possible exception of J. B. S. Haldane.
He is also a spellbinding talker, as good in his different way as
Isaiah Berlin. To go round a picture-gallery with him was a fascinating experience, as he picked out one detail after another, not only
situating them in their aesthetic context but relating them to
scientific theories, theological heresies, literary parallels, and almost
anything else one could imagine that might possibly be relevant. I

am sorry only that not more of his learning has found its way into print, but he is one of those perfectionists who are determined that everything should be exactly right in what they publish and are always finding something to correct or something new to add.

Meyer and his wife Lilian entertained me at their house on West 4th Street, which is one of the few streets in Manhattan that fails to run in a straight line. They also invited Ernest Nagel, a philosopher at Columbia whom I already admired for his work on the philosophy of science. Though very sharp in philosophical controversy and unsparing in his criticism of any lapse in reasoning, or any form of woolly speculation, he is the most gentle and unassuming of men, and we soon added personal friendship to our philosophical sympathy. Ernest had written a text-book on *Logic and Scientific Method* in collaboration with Morris Cohen, a Columbia philosopher of an older generation whom Felix Frankfurter greatly admired. Felix came to New York while I was there and made a point of introducing me to Cohen, whom I remember only for his impressive appearance. He looked as I imagine that Spinoza might have come to look, if Spinoza had lived to be an old man. I do not, however, think that his philosophy was quite up to this standard.

Among my letters of introduction was one to Sidney Hook, who had me to lunch with Dwight Macdonald. At that time they were both involved in left-wing politics, which appeared from their account to be dividing the New York intellectuals into a surprising number of small but bitter factions. If I remember rightly, Macdonald had just about reached the point of breaking with *Partisan Review* in order to found a political journal of his own, while Sidney Hook, who had written a very good book called *From Hegel to Marx*, had not yet developed the profound hostility to communism which has been so conspicuous a feature of his later work. Being again uncertain about my future at Oxford, I discussed with them the possibility of my finding a position in the United States. They were moderately encouraging, but the question was not pursued on either side.

Before setting out on my travels I had a farewell dinner with the Cummingses. Their knowledge of America seemed hardly to extend beyond the north-east coast and, although the tour which had been planned for me took me no further south than Richmond and no further west than Chicago, they treated me as if I were an intrepid explorer. Cummings declared that if my mission was to

e. e. cummings towards the end of his life. Photograph taken by Marion Morehouse Cummings.

Wittgenstein in the 1930's after his return to Cambridge.

Isaiah Berlin as an Oxford undergraduate.

Gilbert Ryle in the mid 1920's. Photograph by courtesy of the Dean, Canons and Students of Christ Church.

Renée, on the left, with Nancy Quennell. Photograph taken in Tokyo in 1930 and supplied by Mr Peter Quennell.

Myself as a lieutenant in the Welsh Guards with Valerie and Julian. Photograph taken in New York in 1943.

spread good-will I ought to try to reach a wider public than the devotees of the English Speaking Union and he advised me to rely on taxi-drivers to lead me to the places of the greatest interest.

From New York I went to Princeton and to Philadelphia. At Princeton I was entertained by Professor W. T. Stace, an Englishman who had studied philosophy while pursuing a career in the Indian Civil Service. By his own account, he had obtained his position at Princeton simply by writing to Princeton to ask for it. In this they showed good sense as he made a serious contribution to the theory of knowledge. At his house I met the celebrated mathematician, von Neumann, a pioneer in the theory of games, who surprised me by advancing as an argument in favour of theism the fact that the actual distribution of atoms in the universe was highly improbable. I was too diffident or too slow-witted to say more at the time than that I did not find the argument convincing; but thinking about it afterwards I saw that the fallacy lay in a misuse of the concept of mathematical probability. Antecedently to experience, we have no more reason to expect an even distribution of atoms than any other. I also took the opportunity to call on Einstein at the Institute of Advanced Studies. He did not greet me by name but when I asked if he remembered me, he replied very graciously, 'How could I forget a face which is associated with one of the happiest periods of my life?'

Philadelphia was a disappointment after New York, though on later visits I have come to recognize that it has a charm of its own. I went to a concert there and wanted to see a celebrated collection of French Impressionist pictures which had been made by Dr Barnes, a local millionaire who had established a Foundation mainly for the benefit of art historians. A few years later, after the disgraceful episode in which Bertrand Russell was judicially pronounced unworthy, on moral grounds, of holding a Professorship at the City College of New York, Dr Barnes was to employ him as a lecturer at the Foundation, quarrel with him, and eventually lose an action which Russell brought against him for wrongful dismissal. I had been warned that Dr Barnes had a miserly attitude towards his pictures, and in fact the English Speaking Union did not have enough influence with him to get me leave to see them.

From Philadelphia I went south to Richmond, the capital of Virginia, where I stayed with one of my former Christ Church pupils. His family lived in a spacious colonial house and proved to me that the legend of southern hospitality still had a solid basis in fact. I found Richmond very attractive and liked the people whom I met there, but was surprised by the extent to which they were still living in the atmosphere of the Civil War. The house was full of books about it; the town was full of monuments to it; one could not be taken on an excursion into the countryside without being shown the local battlefields. Since I was very much interested in the history of the Civil War, I did not mind this at all, but I did think it strange that it should remain so much in the foreground at a distance of over seventy years. When I brought the conversation back to the present and expressed some liberal opinions, I was charged in a friendly way with being a New Dealer. Roosevelt had, indeed, put Virginian conservatives into a difficult position. They were offended and alarmed by the New Deal, but Roosevelt's enemies were Republicans, the political offspring of Abraham Lincoln. It is only in recent years that the allegiance of Southern Conservatives to the Democratic party, which was perpetuated by the Civil War, has come to be shaken.

The American members of the English Speaking Union were mostly people of substance and in Washington, where I next went, the house in which I stayed was evidently a home of wealth and high social station. My hosts, who were total strangers to me, were elderly and formal and we were not at ease with one another. I began badly by allowing my suitcase to scratch the parquet floor of my room and making a vain attempt to cover up the damage. Nor were matters improved when a friend of theirs drove me out to visit George Washington's house at Mount Vernon. Not liking one another's looks, we drove in silence for some miles. He then opened the conversation by saying, 'I have always thought that Sacco and Vanzetti were guilty and rightfully convicted. What is your opinion?' Startled into honesty, I replied, 'Well, I am a great friend of Felix Frankfurter's and he has taught me to think rather differently.' My guide did not pursue the question and we continued in almost total silence for the rest of the expedition. I cannot remember what I thought of Mount Vernon, which I have not revisited. I found much to admire in Washington but thought the city artificial, as if it had been run up by a film producer and might soon be dismantled. Though I have been there several times since, I have never quite lost this impression. It is due not only to the formal layout of the streets, which is true also of New York, but to its containing amongst its inhabitants such a high proportion of officials, who seem to have business in the city but no roots in it. I do not know whether this is a common reaction to Washington, but anyone who has been to Brasilia, the new capital of Brazil, is likely to have had the same feeling.

After my experience in Washington, I was determined to try to avoid staying in any more private houses on my tour, unless they were the houses of friends, and it was therefore a relief to me to discover on arriving in Chicago that I had been booked into a hotel. The local secretary of the English Speaking Union was younger and less solemn than those who had so far taken charge of me and I managed to persuade her that I should contribute more to Anglo-American understanding if I were left so far as possible to my own devices. I went to the University, to which Carnap had succeeded in emigrating from Prague, and attended one of his seminars there. He seemed more relaxed than he had been when he lectured in London and unbent so far as to play ping-pong with me. There was, however, an atmosphere of tension in the department between his adherents and some of the older members who were more inclined towards metaphysics, and as a declared positivist I found myself an unwilling party to it. In particular I thought that the Aristotelian scholar, Richard McKeon, looked upon me with an inauspicious eye, though we have since become good friends. About Chicago itself I had mixed feelings. I greatly admired the waterfront, on Lake Michigan, and was happy to discover a splendid collection of the works of Monet in the Art Institute, but the interior of the city seemed to me ugly and sinister.

Not thinking that it would amuse either Carnap or his pupils, I went alone to a theatre which featured a strip-tease. It was the first that I had seen. The principal performer was neither young nor beautiful but something in her personality and the undisguised sexual hunger of the male audience made the scene erotic, which the few other exhibitions of this sort that I have seen in later years have markedly failed to be. Afterwards, remembering Cummings's advice, I put myself in the hands of a taxi-man, who drove me to a night-club which had nothing remarkable about it except the very high prices that it charged for drinks. In spite of this I returned there on succeeding nights. I formed an innocent friendship with one of the hostesses, a Norwegian from the Bible Belt, who seemed content to listen to me talking, whether or not she understood what

I was saying. On one occasion, when I came to the club, I saw my friend seated at a table some way in front of me with one or two other girls and a company of men, one of whom seemed to be molesting her. As I moved forward to the rescue two enormous bouncers suddenly barred my way. 'Where are you going?' they said. 'I am going to see a friend.' 'You ain't got no friends here, buddy.' I looked at them nervously; they did seem very menacing. 'Er, no,' I said, 'perhaps I haven't,' and returned to my table. Later the girl joined me, and we spent our usual peaceable evening. My pride was slightly consoled by the waiter's remarking that I was a nice fellow and her saying, 'Everybody seems to like you.' At least the management should have been grateful for the amount of money I had spent.

The secretary of the English Speaking Union, of whom I had seen very little, had been receiving a series of anxious letters from a Miss Minna K. Bonham who, as secretary of the Cleveland Branch, was mainly responsible for my tour. We amused ourselves by speculating on what would happen to me in Cleveland and what Miss Minna K. Bonham would be like. When I wrote to her from Cleveland saying, among other things, that Miss Minna K. Bonham was exactly like an old friend Miss Minna K. Bonham, she wrote in reply that I was the worst scholar that the English Speaking Union had ever had in her experience, but the only one who had ever made her laugh.

I made an excursion from Chicago to Urbana, Illinois, where one or other division of the American Philosophical Association was holding its own annual congress. These congresses are seldom very interesting in themselves, serving mainly as market-places for the trade in young lecturers, and so far as I can remember this one was no exception. I was, however, pleased to see Max Black, who had forsaken Cambridge for Urbana, on the way to becoming established at Cornell, and in the course of a drunken evening I made friends with C. H. Langford, who was best known for the pioneering work on modal logic in which he collaborated with C. I. Lewis. He was a Professor at the University of Michigan at Ann Arbor and invited me to give a lecture there after I had fulfilled my obligations in Cleveland. Urbana seemed to me a small town, in the worst sense of the term. I had the impression that as one walked up the main street, the lace curtains on the windows all successively twitched.

Rather to my surprise, since it is not generally thought to have many attractions, I liked Cleveland very much. It was then a growing city, with a large proportion of first generation Americans, and seemed to me full of vitality. I had a number of official duties to perform, including giving a lecture at Western Reserve University, but they left me enough time to amuse myself on my own. I fell in with the Cleveland fast set, for the most part exiles from New York or San Francisco, and again made do with very little sleep, so little indeed that when towards the end of my stay I went to a relatively formal dinner at the home of one of the members of the English Speaking Union, I lost a desperate struggle to prevent myself from falling asleep quite early in the meal. I woke again fairly quickly and my hosts were too polite to make any remark, but I could not wholly persuade myself that my lapse had passed unnoticed.

It was in Cleveland that I saw my first baseball game, having the good fortune to go on a day when the celebrated Bobby Feller was pitching for the Cleveland Indians. I enjoyed the game very much and have been a supporter of the Cleveland Indians ever since. If I remember rightly, they nearly won the Pennant that year and in 1948, when I was again in America, they delighted me by winning the World Series, with the short-stop Lou Boudreau as their player-manager. I have never since had a chance to see them play, but I still follow their fortunes in the newspapers. Unhappily, their performances in recent years have resulted more often in failure than success.

I spent my last evening in Cleveland at a friend's apartment, feverishly working at my lecture for Ann Arbor, and being asked by my friend's maid whether I had 'fixed' it. In the end, I did fix it reasonably well, though I had to finish writing it in the train. It was on the subject of perception and was probably a digest of one of the early chapters of the book that I was writing, on the theory of knowledge. Professor Langford told me that the audience was impressed by the energy which I put into delivering it, but in fact I was literally sweating out the effects of my dissipation.

By this time I needed to relax and I was happy to go to Boston, to stay with the Frankfurters. Patrick Gordon-Walker was spending a semester at Harvard and had come to share my new interest in baseball: we went together to watch the Boston Red Sox. I was pleased to see Quine again and to meet H. M. Sheffer and C. I. Lewis for the first time. Of the two, Sheffer was the more cordial. Lewis's pragmatism was in many ways very close to positivism, but he held strong moral views and disapproved of the ethical theory which I had developed in *Language, Truth and Logic*. Felix Frankfurter made an appointment for me to see Whitehead, but when I arrived at the house Mrs Whitehead, perceiving at once that I had a bad cold, refused to let me in. Her husband was then in his late seventies and she was frightened for his health. Perhaps as the result of her care of him he lived to be eighty-six.

Back in New York, I had time for little more than relating my adventures to the Cummingses, before I took ship again on the *Queen Mary*. They sent me a telegram to the ship saying, 'Hail to thee, blithe spirit.' That they could see me as a skylark pleased me very much.

I think it was shortly before my American trip that Bertrand Russell accepted an invitation to give a course of lectures in Oxford. The lectures were on the subject of Words and Facts and constitute the first draft of the set of William James Lectures which Russell delivered at Harvard in 1940 and published under the title of *An Inquiry into Meaning and Truth*. Apart from publishing *The Analysis of Mind* in 1921 and then *The Analysis of Matter*, resulting from the Tarner Lectures which he gave at Cambridge in 1925, Russell had been mainly occupied since the war in lecturing and writing on more popular topics, engaging in politics, and running his progressive school. It was only in 1936, when the breakdown of his second marriage had led him to sever his connection with the school, that he returned to philosophy with a paper on 'The Limits of Empiricism' which he read to the Aristotelian Society. By the time he came to lecture in Oxford, he was married to his third wife, Peter Spence, and they took a house nearby in the village of Kidlington. Russell complained in his *Autobiography* that hardly anybody called on them, but he was certainly not neglected by the younger philosophers, many of whom attended his lectures and discussed them with him afterwards. It was in this way that I first got to know him, though it was not until the late nineteen-forties that our acquaintance developed into friendship. At the time of these lectures he was in his middle sixties, looking his age, but not betraying it in any lack of physical or intellectual vitality. As a philosopher, he was not at all arrogant; not only did he not talk down to us but he appeared remarkably sensitive to the opinions that we held of his work. This remained true of him also in later years. I did not see very much of him in Oxford out of school, but there were one or two occasions on which I met him and his wife at Solly Zuckerman's house. At least thirty years younger than he, and with very striking looks, she was determined to be seen as a person in her own right. He was obviously proud of her and pleased that attention should be paid to her. The result was that he said less than I had hoped, though his wit, his dry manner of utterance and his astonishing memory for facts and quotations made even his small-talk fascinating. Since his elder brother had died without issue in 1931 he had inherited the earldom which had been bestowed upon his grandfather, but at least at the outset had shown some reluctance to make use of the title. It was therefore not quite clear to us how he wished to be addressed. The point was decided by his saying when Solly had referred to him several times as 'Mr Russell', 'My name is Lord Russell, just as yours is not Lord Zuckerman.' This is a discrepancy that has since been very properly remedied.

In 1938 my Studentship at Christ Church had only two years more to run and it was not at all certain that it would be renewed. I was therefore on the look-out for any other opening in Oxford. I had, however, reason to fear that the success which I had enjoyed with *Language, Truth and Logic* was of a kind to diminish rather than improve my chances. A Fellowship in philosophy had become vacant at Trinity, when Henry Price was appointed to succeed Joachim in the Chair of Logic, but the post went to Anthony Peck, a former Trinity undergraduate, who had been a few years junior to me in College at Eton in the same election as Francis Graham-Harrison. Peck's career as a philosopher was short, since he joined the Civil Service during the war and remained in it afterwards. As the post was not advertised, I had no opportunity to apply for it, but I was told that I had been considered. I heard also that Michael Foster had been consulted and had advised Trinity against appointing me. This made me so angry that I stormed into his rooms and railed at him, saying that it was a monstrous way to treat a colleague and accusing him of being jealous of me. Instead of sending me about my business or even making any attempt to defend himself, he listened to my tirade in pained and embarrassed silence. I think of this episode with shame, as his opinion of me, whether or not it was justified, was undoubtedly honest; and having been asked for his advice, he had every right to give it.

In view of Michael Foster's opposition, it is unlikely that Christ Church would have chosen me to succeed Gilbert Ryle, if Gilbert had been appointed to the Chair of Logic at St Andrews, for which he applied at about this time. Many of us were surprised that he should want to leave Oxford, but having been a college tutor for fifteen years he no doubt felt that he needed more leisure to get on with his own work. We were even more surprised when St Andrews did not appoint him, preferring to promote one of their own lecturers who, though a very charming person, would not himself have claimed to vie with Gilbert as a philosopher. I was very indignant about this on Gilbert's account but glad for my own sake that he had not gone away.

With so many other things to occupy me, I published nothing in 1938 except a short article in *Erkenntnis* 'On the Scope of Empirical Knowledge,' in which I disputed Russell's contention, as set out in his paper on 'The Limits of Empiricism,' that 'experience gives more information than pure empiricism supposes'. Russell had relied among other things upon Isaiah's favourite example of propositions referring to the similarity of colours, and I again tried to show that sentences like 'Blue and green are more similar than blue and yellow' expressed analytic truths on one possible interpretation and doubtful psychological generalizations on another. Russell had also maintained that in giving a description of what one observes, one is directly aware of a causal relation between the object of one's observation and one's verbal utterance, and in disputing this claim I put forward some general arguments against his causal theory of meaning. If he read my article, he was not convinced by it, since he was taking the same line two years later in his *Inquiry into Meaning and Truth*.

In the summer of 1938 the Vienna Circle, which had already been dispersed, held the last of its international congresses. It took place at Girton College, Cambridge, and was described as a congress for the unity of science. Of the original members of the Circle, only Neurath, Waismann, Philipp Frank and Herbert Feigl were present, Neurath coming over from Holland and Frank and Feigl from the United States. The affiliates of the Circle were more strongly represented, including members of the Dutch group who engaged in the pursuit of what they called 'Significs'. I made friends with Carl Hempel, who was then working in Brussels before starting on his very successful career in the United States, and with the Norwegian Arne Naess. Nowadays Naess is more of a metaphysician, but at that time he was best known for his sociological research into what his compatriots understood by 'truth': if I remember rightly, a surprising number of them assented to a coherence theory. Professor Scholz, one of the very few Germans to follow the lead of Frege, was allowed to come from Munster, but he had to ask for a special programme to be printed, with his name in larger letters than the rest, for him to show to Goebbels's Ministry of Propaganda. G. E. Moore gave a short address of welcome and was seconded by Gilbert Ryle, who characteristically queried the point of unifying the language of science; presumably it was not desired that scientists should take to writing in Esperanto. He thought our aim might be to show that conflicting assumptions were made in the different special sciences and to find the best way of removing such contradictions. Otherwise, I remember the congress chiefly for the presence of the aged F. C. S. Schiller who had gone to teach in California after he had retired from his Fellowship at Corpus Christi College. I found him an amiable if rather garrulous old gentleman, and had to make an effort to see in him the fiery pragmatist who had so greatly shocked the Oxford philosophers of thirty years before.

The divisive effect upon the country of the Munich crisis in September 1938 extended to the Christ Church Senior Common Room, the older men, with the notable exceptions of Lindemann and Roy Harrod, being generally in favour of Chamberlain's policy, and the younger men more hostile to it. There was also a division of opinion as to whether a war with Hitler's Germany had been averted or merely postponed. While waiting for an answer to this question, we had our attention diverted to a more domestic issue. Early in 1939 Dean Williams left us for his Bishopric and we had to find a successor to him. The appointment was, indeed, in the hands of the Crown but it was assumed that the King's advisers would take note of our preference. Our trouble was that we had no idea whom to recommend. The Canons had no decided views except for agreeing that it should not be one of themselves. The Students wanted someone who had some academic distinction, but clergymen of the right age and standing who had taken first-class honours appeared to be in short supply. The few that we could discover were thought to be unsuitable on other grounds. There was one more eminent than the rest whom we seriously considered, until Dundas objected that his wife wrote novels in which the characters were taken from life: and this was a risk which we were not prepared to run.

At this point, the suggestion was made, I think originally by Gilbert Ryle, that the college should apply to the Privy Council for permission to change its statutes so as to allow for the possibility of its being governed by a layman. This developed into a choice between two proposals, one being that the college should simply sever its connection with the Dean and Chapter of the Cathedral, the other that the Dean should remain titular head of the college but that the effective head, for all academic purposes, should be a President who would not have to be in holy orders. One of the Canons advanced the constitutional argument that if the more radical proposal were adopted, Christ Church would simply revert to its original composition of the Dean and Chapter. The defectors would belong to a new Foundation, for which 'King's College' might be the most appropriate name. In the event, both proposals were easily defeated. Apart from Gilbert Ryle, those most strongly in favour of one or other of them were Patrick Gordon-Walker, myself and Colin Dillwyn, a young historian of left-wing views, who had replaced Keith Feiling, when Feiling gave up teaching for research. Two or three other members of the Governing Body voted with us, but the remainder, including what may well have been a majority of agnostics, had too strong a respect for tradition for them to be willing to make even the less radical of the changes proposed.

With the defeat of the attempt to laicize the college, we returned to our former predicament. We were still at a loss, when Gilbert suddenly remembered that he had rowed in Trial Eights with a Canadian who was destined for the Church and if Gilbert was not mistaken had got a first. After further reflection, he came up with the name 'John Lowe'. We rushed to the reference books, discovered that Gilbert had not been mistaken and that Dr Lowe was now teaching in some Canadian Seminary. Without further ado, we expressed to the authorities our preference for Dr Lowe: the appointment was offered to him and he accepted it.

When the new Dean arrived, he turned out to be a capable administrator and in due course a conscientious Vice-Chancellor. He was also an enthusiastic bridge-player, with the result that he was more often to be found in Common Room than his predecessors, and the bridge-table became an even more prominent feature of our communal life. Apart from J. C. Masterman, who considered himself to be, and was, too good to play with us, and Gilbert Ryle, for whom cards were a source of philosophical illustrations rather than objects with which one actually played, those of us who took an interest in the game were of much the same moderate standard. Roy Harrod's mastery of the theory of probability could have given him an advantage, but he was no better than I at adapting theory to practice. The Dean was a dashing player, with a tendency to overbid his hand, which corresponded, I thought, to an agreeably impetuous element in his character.

My relations with Renée had not lost their tension, since my visit to America, but with the birth of our son, Julian David, in January 1939, we resolved to make a fesh effort to keep the family together. One consequence was that I began to lead a more domesticated life. When my political activity came to an end, I devoted most of my time to working on my book, which I had decided to call *The Foundations of Empirical Knowledge*. As in the case of *Language, Truth and Logic*, its publication was assured before I wrote it, though not by the same publisher. Gollancz had not demanded an option on my second book, and considering the little faith that he had shown in the prospects of *Language, Truth and Logic*, I did not feel myself committed to him. So when Lovat Dickson called on me in Oxford, in an attempt to secure me for Macmillan, I was ready to accept the slightly better contract that he offered me. I had confidence in Lovat Dickson, whom I found personally sympathetic, and in his successor Rex Allen, and though I never conceded any options to them, I remained a Macmillan author until 1972, by which time they had published eight of my books.

The Foundations of Empirical Knowledge took me longer to write than *Language, Truth and Logic*, but as soon as I settled down to it I made fairly steady progress. My principal concern, as I stated in the preface, was 'to resolve the philosophical problems which are commonly brought under the heading of "our knowledge of the external world",' with the result that I concentrated mainly on the theory of perception. I owed a great deal to Henry Price's book on *Perception*, but whereas he treated the proposition that we directly experience sense-data as if it were a straightforward statement of fact, I regarded it rather as a proposal to adopt a new method of description. Thus I represented the naïve realists who maintained that we directly perceived physical objects, not as making a factual error, but as declining to draw a distinction which could be shown to be philosophically useful. At the same time I argued that, once sense-data had been introduced, we were committed to analysing physical objects in terms of them, and I attempted to give an outline of the way in which this might be done. I think that this outline still has some merit as an account of the ways in which our beliefs about physical objects are based upon our sense-experiences, but I have since come to see that the kind of analysis which it was meant to illustrate is not capable, even in principle, of being carried through.

The chapter which gave me the most trouble was one that I entitled 'The Egocentric Predicament'. The great problem for the theorists of knowledge who think it proper to start with sense-data is that of avoiding imprisonment in a purely private world. There is the difficulty of showing how physical objects can be accorded an independent existence, and the difficulty of finding some good reason to attribute experiences to persons other than oneself. The fashion nowadays is to ignore the first of these obstacles, but even naïve realists are confronted with the second. Re-reading the chapter, I find that I handled the question about physical objects reasonably well, but was markedly less successful with the question of other minds. No longer accepting the behaviourist account which I had given in *Language, Truth and Logic*, I fell back upon the classical argument that the perceptible similarity of other persons to oneself entitled one to credit them with experiences which are analogous to one's own. I failed, however, either to give an adequate answer to the question how one can attach sense to propositions about the experiences of others which one cannot directly verify, or to show how the argument from analogy can be made strong enough to fulfil its function. This is a problem to which I have frequently returned in my later work, but I am still not sure that I have found the right answer to it.

I finished the book by the end of the year and it was published in 1940. Tom Brown Stevens corrected the proofs for me and Francis Graham-Harrison made the index. For the most part it received favourable reviews, though my friend, John Wisdom, said that it showed 'the disastrous effects of qualms upon an iconoclast'. On the other hand, William Empson considered it a much better book than *Language, Truth and Logic*. It was reprinted in 1947 and went into six further impressions before coming out as a paperback in 1968. In the nineteen-fifties Austin made it the principal target of a general attack on the theory of sense-data which he repeatedly delivered in lectures at Oxford: he called the lectures 'Sense and Sensibilia' and they were posthumously published under that title. They are witty and pungent but their arguments are not conclusive, as I have tried to show in a reply to them which I published in a book of my essays called *Metaphysics and Common Sense*.

By the time that *The Foundations of Empirical Knowledge* was ready for publication I was already in the Army, and in signing the preface I gave 'Brigade of Guards Depot, Caterham, Surrey' as my address. I wanted to add 'Sergeant Jackson's Squad', but Sergeant Jackson refused, as he put it, to let me make a fool of him. My plea that he might be rejecting a chance to be immortalized left him unimpressed.

9 *Becoming a Soldier*

It was widely believed in the nineteen-thirties that the outbreak of another European war would quickly lead to the destruction of most of the big cities. Had not Mr Baldwin officially stated that the bomber would always get through? The wailing of the air raid sirens in London a few minutes after the British declaration of war on Germany on September 3 1939, turned out to be a false alarm, but it was thought to presage a real and imminent danger. Nobody had foreseen that the land and air forces of both sides would remain almost wholly inactive throughout the months that separated the fall of Poland in September 1939 from the German invasion of Norway in April 1940. One result was that the Government was given ample time to institute its plans for Civil Defence.

Part of the plan was that young children should be evacuated from London. Valerie being still less than four years old, and Julian a mere eight months, there was no question then of their being separated from their mother, nor had we any friends with country houses in which they and Renée could have gone to live. We were, however, able to surrender the lease of our house in Foubert's Place and rent a small house near Oxford on the outskirts of Headington. It was a modern house of no great architectural distinction, but it was warm and comfortable and set in pleasant surroundings. Having occasion in the last chapter of *The Foundations of Empirical Knowledge* to describe the contents of my visual field, I wrote of my turning to look out of the window and 'perceiving a garden fringed with trees, and beyond the trees the roof of a cottage and in the distance a thickly wooded hill'. A refugee from Germany, called Frau Arendt, came in to help Renée with the housework. It was a come-down for her, but she had a small son to support and was grateful for any form of employment. Not long afterwards, she was able to emigrate with her son to Palestine. We met him once after the war. He had become an officer in the Israeli Air Force, and gave me the impression that his mother had dwelt too much, for his taste, upon the kindness that we had shown to her.

In the second world war, unlike the first, conscription was in force in England from the start. There was, however, a list of reserved occupations, in which university teaching was included. The age of exemption for university teachers was later raised to thirty, but at the beginning it was set as low as twenty-five. Since the vast majority of Oxford dons were over that age and since the call-up of undergraduates proceeded slowly, life at Oxford during that autumn term was not very different from what it had been before. Philosophically the chief event was the presence in Oxford of G. E. Moore, who had retired from his Chair at Cambridge and been succeeded there by Wittgenstein. Moore gave a series of lectures on his favourite subject of Perception and held discussion classes on them. As always, I was impressed and stimulated by the zest with which he engaged in philosophical argument.

I still felt that I ought at least to be preparing myself to take an active part in the war, but my being in a reserved occupation appeared to set a bar to my enlistment. It happened, however, that the Brigade of Guards had been allowed to keep the privilege of choosing its own officers, in a way that made it unnecessary for them to go through the normal process of recruitment. A former Christ Church man called Jock Lewis, who had been a pupil of Gilbert Ryle's and mine and was otherwise distinguished as having been the captain of one of the few Oxford crews to defeat Cambridge in the Boat Race between the wars, had been accepted as an officer by the Welsh Guards. He obtained Gilbert an introduction to the colonel of his regiment, who promised Gilbert a commission, taking no account of the fact that he was not of Welsh descent. When I learned of this, I also sought an introduction to 'Chico' Leatham, as the colonel was called. Being summoned for interview, I procured myself a bowler hat, put on my old Etonian tie, and passed the colonel's brief inspection of me. It then turned out that the time which I had reluctantly spent in the school OTC had not been entirely wasted, since I was able to assure the adjutant that I had obtained my Certificate A. To avoid difficulties with the War Office, I had to make an official pretence of having no profession, describing myself, not altogether falsely, as a man of independent means. I left with the promise of a commission and the assurance that I should be called up in a few months' time.

Gilbert's and my example was followed by Eric Gray, an Australian who had succeeded Bobbie Longden as tutor in Roman History at Christ Church, after Bobbie had left to become head-master of Wellington. Though he was a few months older than I, Eric had been one of the first of my Christ Church pupils. I liked him and was glad at the prospect of having him as a companion in the Welsh Guards. At about the same time Michael Foster, though well into his thirties, contrived to enlist as a private in the Oxford and Buckinghamshire Regiment. Christ Church was, therefore, soon to be bereft of all three of its teachers of philosophy.

I had expected to join my regiment directly as an officer, but not long after my interview with Colonel Leatham, Mr Hore-Belisha, who was Minister of War until his bad relations with the High Command caused Chamberlain to dismiss him, made the sensible ruling that no one under the age of thirty-five was to be given a commission in anything but the Intelligence Corps, unless he had first been through the ranks and then through an Officers Training Unit. This did not affect Gilbert, who would soon be forty, but it meant that Eric and I, at the age of twenty-nine, would be sent to the Guards Depot at Caterham for a two months' stint as Guardsmen recruits, and then, if we had not disgraced ourselves at Caterham, proceed as Officer Cadets to the Royal Military College at Sandhurst, where prospective Guards officers among others received their training. If we did well enough at Sandhurst to satisfy Colonel Leatham, we should be posted as officers to the Welsh Guards training battalion, which was stationed at Esher, occupying the race-course at Sandown Park.

From some source or other, I had learned that cadets at Sandhurst were required in their course of training to do a fair amount of bicycling, and I therefore thought it prudent to teach myself to ride a bicycle. Starting so late in life, I found it unexpectedly difficult, but I acquired enough skill to venture into traffic. I used to enjoy bicycling down the hill from Headington into Oxford, though the return journey was not so pleasurable.

Early in 1940 I received notice that I was to present myself at Caterham in March. I was a little apprehensive of what would await me there and my fears were not diminished by Frank Paken-

Myself in the early 1950's. Photograph taken by Mr Alec Murray.

My mother and step-father.
Photograph taken at a
wedding attended in the late
1930's.

Bertrand Russell and I in
conversation. Photograph
taken at Woburn Abbey in
1962.

ham, who predicted, I thought with some relish, that I should find the experience unendurable. He himself, as part of the process of nursing his constituency, had joined the Territorials before the war and consequently at the outbreak of war had found himself commissioned in the Oxford and Bucks. He had greatly disliked the company of his fellow officers, who were mostly Conservatives of an ungentlemanly sort, had fallen ill and had been discharged from the Army on grounds of health. Shortly before I left Oxford for Caterham, he came to my rooms in Christ Church with a poem which he had written to me. Unhappily neither he nor I have kept a copy of it, but he remembers the last two lines which ran:

> He sneers at duty with indignant voice
> But trembles with a passion for the good.

The implication, which was flattering to me, was that I was too much of an idealist to be able to cope with the harsh realities of life as a Guardsman recruit.

When I arrived at Caterham I found that I had been assigned to a special squad, known as the Brigade Squad, which was reserved for those who had been selected as potential officers by the colonel of one or other of the five Guards regiments. Sergeant Jackson, who was in charge of us, was a regular soldier in the Coldstream Guards, a young man in his middle twenties, smart and efficient but not at all tyrannical, for all his refusal to allow me to mention him in my preface. He was a much bigger factor in our lives than the officers, who regularly inspected us but otherwise took little notice of us beyond coming into the mess-room and asking 'Any complaints?' in a tone which presupposed a negative answer. In fact there was little cause for complaint, as the food, though starchy, was abundant and not badly cooked. It was believed that bromides were put into our tea to dampen our sexual desires, but I do not suppose that this was true.

We had little to do either with Sergeant-Major Moss, a middle-aged man of majestic aspect, whose fierceness of manner was said to overlay a kindly nature. I remember him chiefly for the power of his word of command on the occasions when the whole company paraded. Next to Sergeant Jackson, our chief mentor was a tall young Guardsman who was billeted with us and made responsible for our doing our domestic chores and keeping ourselves, our equipment and the barrack-room in proper condition. We had to address him as 'Trained Soldier', as though this were a mark of rank. He took his position seriously but after lights out he would relax and instruct us in the less formal aspects of a guardsman's life. You could allow yourself to be picked up in Hyde Park and take the money that was offered you, but when the time came for rendering the service you had to display moral indignation, not necessarily stopping short of violence.

There were about sixteen of us in the Brigade Squad. Only one of my companions was previously known to me and he only very slightly, an undergraduate called Willie Bell who was also destined for the Welsh Guards. There was one about the same age as myself, a dark and silent man called Thomas Firbank, who had become a sheep-farmer in North Wales before the war, with no previous experience of farming, and wrote a successful book about it. Otherwise they were all in their early twenties, or even in their teens. Most of them were undergraduates from Oxford or Cambridge. An exception was Bobby de la Tour, who had been on the stage and talked of his success with women. I remember his saying that he always folded his trousers carefully so as to preserve the crease before getting into bed with anyone, which seemed to me to show an excessive detachment. At some stage in the war he volunteered for a parachute regiment and was one of the first casualties of the Normandy landings. A few weeks after our arrival we were joined by Paddy Leigh-Fermor, another future author, who had been wandering around the Balkans and among his many accomplishments, spoke fluent Greek. He had been promised a commission in the Irish Guards, but before completing the course at Caterham was taken away from us by one of the branches of Military Intelligence. A few years later he was to become famous for organizing and helping to effect the capture of a German general in Crete, an exploit which was recorded in a book by one of the other participants and made the subject of a film under the title of *Ill Met by Moonlight*, with Dirk Bogarde playing Paddy's part. I enjoyed Paddy's company, and was happy to meet him again after the war, when our acquaintance quickly developed into a lasting friendship. In fact, I got on very well with nearly all of my companions. It was like being back at school, only this time I knew how to manage. Two of the younger ones whom I have occasionally seen in later years were Hugh Euston, as he then was, and Tom Egerton, neither of them a conspicuously military figure, and both displaying an air of quiet amusement at the circumstances in which they found themselves.

For some reason Eric Gray was not in the Brigade Squad with me but was put into a separate squad of Welsh Guards recruits. This happened also to Richard Powell, another older man whose friendship I enjoyed at Sandhurst and at Esher. Tall, handsome, calm and self-assured, he had an obvious gift for leadership and his exploits in the 1944 campaign were to win him the Military Cross and Bar. His fellow recruits at Caterham were a little in awe of his being a baronet, though pleased to be able to tell him, when George Galitzine joined them, that he had been put in the shade by the arrival of 'a fucking prince'. In this case, the use of their favourite adjective carried no animosity; if it expressed anything, it was the idea of there being something incongruous about the appearance of such a person as a Guardsman recruit: it was a way of saying 'Whatever next?' Quite often the word seemed to be used with no meaning at all, not only with no descriptive meaning but with no emotional force. Its constant repetition could be irritating, just as it is irritating to listen to someone who adds 'you know' to every sentence, or introduces every other word with 'er'. In this sense, the prudish literary custom of replacing the word with a dash or an asterisk was semantically justified.

At this early stage of the war there was no great sense of urgency, and our training cannot have been significantly different from that which guardsmen recruits had been undergoing in peacetime. We spent a great many hours on the barrack square, learning to march in slow and in quick time, to execute left, right and about-turns with the proper stamping of the feet, to salute, to come to attention and to stand at ease, to slope and to present arms, to fix and unfix bayonets. We had bayonet drill in which we gingerly fenced with one another and transfixed men of straw, and we practised shooting at more or less distant targets with our heavy Lee-Enfield rifles. I was a poor shot, snatching at the trigger, failing to keep the rifle steady and not being very good at taking aim, since I had difficulty in shutting one eye without also shutting the other. We were not given much in the way of mental exercise, but we were taught something of the history of our regiments and their peculiarities. Among other things, we learned to distinguish their members by the spacing of the buttons on their tunics. In order of seniority, the Grenadiers wore their buttons singly, the Coldstream wore theirs in pairs, the Scots Guards in threes, the Irish in fours and the

Welsh Guards, the junior regiment which was formed only in 1915, wore theirs in groups of five. This order was observed in the line of march, except that when the Grenadiers were present, the Coldstream brought up the rear, being forbidden to take second place by a literal interpretation of their motto '*Nulli secundus*'. The motto of the Welsh Guards was '*Cymru am byth*', which I knew to mean 'Wales for Ever', though, in my ignorance of the Welsh language, I was never quite sure how it ought to be pronounced.

Great importance was attached to our keeping our persons, our equipment and our barrack-room in proper condition. Before setting out for Caterham, I had taken the precaution of having my hair cut short, but this did not preserve me from the regulation hair-cut which took away most of what was left. I believe that the original intention was to rid the new recruits of lice, but as so often happens the practice had outlived the reason for it. In their subsequent operations, the regimental barbers were less ruthless, at least stopping short of making us look like nineteenth-century convicts. We had to be careful also how we shaved, since any shadow of a beard would bring rebuke. This was not easily avoided in the early morning haste to make ourselves presentable. I used to save a few minutes and gain some needed extra warmth at night by wearing my shirt and socks and underclothes in bed with my pyjamas over them: my trousers went under the mattress to keep them pressed. Much more time was spent in the care of our equipment. Our rifles had to be cleaned and oiled, our belts whitened, our buttons and boots highly polished. The boots were the most troublesome as one had to work them over with a toothbrush before they would take a shine. Since I started with a pair that did not fit me, I had to go through this process twice. Though I never wholly mastered the art of sewing, I could manage to put a button in its place. An hour or so in the early evening was reserved for these daily chores. We were supposed to do them sitting on our beds in silence, though we were allowed to have the wireless on. I came almost to enjoy these sessions, listening to Judy Garland singing 'Somewhere over the rainbow', as I brushed and polished away.

Scrubbing floors was relatively unskilled labour but I found cleaning windows more difficult than I had expected. They seemed to remain misty, however hard I rubbed. On the other hand I became quite efficient at making my bed and I learned to fold my blankets in the morning and lay out my kit on top of them in the ways that were prescribed to us.

The discipline to which we were subject was strict but not oppressive. While no special favours were shown to us, the members of the Brigade Squad may have been treated with some indulgence, especially those like myself who were some years older than the average recruit and departed more obviously from the usual pattern. On rare occasions it worked the other way. For going about the barracks we normally wore fatigue-dress, in which we were not expected to look so smart as in the uniforms that we wore on parade. Since the Guards had not made much provision for men of small physique, my own issue of this clothing was somewhat too large for me and in performing my domestic chores I had allowed it to become rather dirty. Going, so dressed, into the mess-room one day I caught sight of Willie Bell and called out to him, 'Hullo, Willie, shall we sit together?' Though the words were innocent enough, the tone of my voice must have seemed offensively lah-di-dah to a tall Welsh Guards sergeant who was standing nearby, for he rounded on me and started shouting at me, abusing me for my slovenly appearance and pouring scorn on the idea of my becoming an officer. He did not go so far as to strike me, which would indeed have been contrary to the regulations, but under the pretext of doing up a button on the front of my jacket which I had left undone, he shook me to and fro as an angry parent might shake a child. I made no resistance and said nothing, but afterwards I was too upset to eat and when I returned to my barrack-room I continued to tremble in a mixture of shame and anger for quite a long time. I then began to laugh, understanding how a regular sergeant, with an obvious pride in himself and his profession, could find it outrageous that such a travesty of a soldier, as I must have appeared to him to be, should have any chance of becoming his military superior.

I did not come across this sergeant again and met with no similar resentment from any of the other non-commissioned officers with whom we occasionally came into contact. Once one of them asked me what my profession had been before I joined the army. When I told him, he said in quite a friendly way that he had thought that I looked like a bookmaker's clerk. I saw that this was not intended as an insult, but rather as a defence of his authority against any pretensions that I might have carried over from civilian life.

As the weeks passed, we developed into quite a well-drilled squad, even by the exacting standard of the Brigade. The exercises as such were not particularly enjoyable, but I came to take pleasure in our performing them well in unison. With such an expenditure of physical energy, I was mostly too tired to feel the need for any distractions, even if they had been available. At the outset we were confined to barracks, in conformity with the usual regulation for new recruits. When we were thought to have acquired a sufficiently military bearing to be allowed out on our own, we could get a pass out of barracks on Sunday afternoons, with time enough to take a bus to Croydon; but there was nothing to do in Croydon once one got there, except walk up and down its unattractive streets, and I rarely made use of the privilege.

Our training was completed by a spell of guard-duty at an aerodrome. By this time the Germans had occupied Norway and had begun their campaign against France. There was little likelihood of their dropping a force of parachutists into England, while the fighting in France continued, but it was thought advisable to take precautions, if only against saboteurs. In fact, nothing untoward occurred. I found it rather an eerie experience to be left at my post alone at night, and was relieved that I had not been startled into raising any false alarms.

Having conducted ourselves well at Caterham and attained the required standard of proficiency in drill, we were considered fit to proceed to Sandhurst as Officer Cadets. Before leaving, we were each briefly interviewed by a group of officers, including the captain of our company, who said to me that they had all been impressed by the way that I had stuck it. I took this as a compliment but also wondered why they thought that it had been so hard for me. No doubt I seemed to them more of a fish out of water than I actually felt.

Before going to Sandhurst, we were granted a few days' leave. I went back to Headington, to be with Renée and the children, and took the opportunity of displaying myself in Oxford. Though I had nothing smarter to wear than battledress, I was pleased with the figure that I cut. I remember meeting Isaiah and Maurice in the street and causing them to laugh by my reflex action of making a military turn when I said goodbye to them. Frank Pakenham called on me, expecting a tale of horror, and was disconcerted to find me in such rude health. He complained afterwards that I not only did not resent being made to devote my time to spit and polish, but positively enjoyed it. I dined in Christ Church and found Hugh

Trevor-Roper there, already an officer in the employ of one of the departments of Military Intelligence. Professor Dodds, with whom I had formed something of a political alliance in the years before the war, has recently told me that he remembers my sitting next to him in Common Room and saying to him, 'I am going to come back here after the war and I am going to have my revolver with me and I am going to shoot first him and then him and then him,' pointing to three of our senior colleagues. I have no recollection of this incident and think it most unlikely that I really had such murderous feelings towards anybody. If I did, the college was soon to heap coals of fire upon my head, renewing my Research Studentship until a year after demobilization, and making up the difference between my army pay and my salary.

Though it was in some ways even more like being back at school, our promotion to Sandhurst added greatly to our comfort. We had rooms to ourselves and were not put to any menial tasks. The discipline was still quite strict but we were allowed considerably more freedom of movement. The small town of Camberley in which the college lies had not very much to recommend it, but it was an improvement on Croydon and there were two hotels and a cinema which we could frequent in our leisure time. Weekend leave was more generously granted and on Sundays we could go anywhere we pleased provided that we were back in our quarters by the prescribed hour. This occasionally involved us in hitch-hiking of which I had no previous experience. Though it never actually failed us, the uncertainty of it caused me much anxiety. To this day I am almost obsessively punctual and nearly always arrive at a station or an aerodrome far earlier than I need to.

Our course of training at Sandhurst was longer and more varied than that which we had undergone at Caterham. There was much less emphasis on drill and more on the use of weapons. The most modern weapon that we had was the Bren-gun. Owing to the shortage of ammunition we did not often get to fire it, but we became skilled in taking it to pieces and putting it together again. We were taught to read maps and set compasses, and learned something of infantry tactics. The greatest importance was attached to our giving our orders in the proper form. We were given a little practice, by which I did not profit, in the art of driving trucks and were instructed in the workings of the internal combustion engine. We received and sometimes took classes in physical education, went on route-marches and ran over obstacle courses with rifle and bayonet. There were spells of guard duty and occasional practice in night operations. We learned about the properties of poisonous gases and spent uncomfortable periods training in our gas masks. When I complained to our kindly platoon commander, Captain Lonsdale, that mine fitted me so tightly that I could not breathe, he said that I should not have so long a nose; fortunately he was amused by my saying that it might at this stage be simpler to change the mask. The curriculum was, indeed, mainly adapted to the previous war but since we had no tanks or even any armoured cars at our disposal, this was hardly to be avoided.

The prediction that when I got to Sandhurst I should need to be able to ride a bicycle turned out to be correct. What I had not been warned was that we were expected to ride in close formation, to which my lately acquired skill did not prove equal. The same was true of Andrew Cavendish, the present Duke of Devonshire, who had even less knowledge of the art than I had. When we had thrown the company into confusion a couple of times, we were made to follow separately on our own. Though we had little else in common, it gave us a certain fellow-feeling which on my side at least has faintly persisted into later life.

In general I was not a very efficient cadet. I was poor at map-reading, had no eye for country, was slow over the obstacle-courses, an indifferent marksman and awkward in the management of weapons. At the same time, I showed good will, was quite competent at drilling and being drilled, always gave my orders in the proper form and found it easy to memorize and reproduce the substance of the lectures that were given us. Consequently, I was given a higher rating as a prospective Guards officer than I knew that I deserved.

I suspect also that some allowances were made for me. On one occasion I was making an awkward job of getting a Bren-gun into position when a young officer ran up to scold me. I looked up and saw that it was Lord John Hope, who had been one of my friends among my Christ Church pupils. After we had both said 'Sir' to one another in our mutual embarrassment, he went away and left me to it. A result of this encounter was that once, when bad weather had caused some exercise to be cancelled and another use had to be found for the time, John Hope suggested that I be put on to lecture. Not wishing to let him down, or disgrace myself, I thought it best to stick to my own subject, and chose therefore to lecture on Berkeley's Idealism. The view that material objects, including their own bodies and the bullets that might enter them, were nothing but collections of ideas was novel to most of my audience, and even roused one or two of them to indignation, but the lecture was generally well received and at least came as a diversion from our usual routine.

The only other cadet to give a lecture, so far as I can remember, was Philip Toynbee, who had just failed to overlap with me at Caterham and arrived at Sandhurst when I was about half-way through the course. He had paid a brief visit to Madrid during the Spanish Civil War and he gave us a competent lecture on guerrilla warfare, contriving to suggest, without actually stating, that he had had some experience of it. Though he enjoyed this performance, Philip was not happy at Sandhurst, finding the discipline irksome and disliking the public-school atmosphere. He looked to me as an ally, but here I failed him. He has since often told the story how, on the night of his arrival, some popular officer who was leaving Sandhurst was being fêted in the mess. There was a great deal of banging on the table and loud calls for a speech. Alienated by this heartiness, Philip looked around for me, having no doubt that I should obviously share his feeling, and was amazed to see me banging and shouting with the rest. It was not even that I was making an effort to conform. I had adapted myself to this new way of life, got on well with our instructors and with nearly all my fellow-cadets, and was gratified by their liking me.

Our world, like the world of school, was so enclosed that it was easy to forget that we were being trained for actual warfare. Yet the war should not have seemed remote to us. We had not been long at Sandhurst before the French Government sued for an armistice and the greater part of the British Expeditionary Force was evacuated from Dunkirk, with the loss of nearly all its equipment. My young Christ Church colleague, Colin Dillwyn, had been serving as an officer in the Oxford and Bucks and I heard to my sorrow that he had been killed. Later I learned that he had shot himself, rather than become a prisoner-of-war and have afterwards to live with the consequences of what seemed to him certain to be a Nazi victory. In retrospect I find it strange that so few of us in England saw this as anything near a certainty. Of course not many knew how little we possessed in the way of arms, though it was an inference that might easily have been drawn. We listened on the wireless to Churchill's speeches, were moved by his rhetoric, and managed to believe that somehow or other all would still be well.

This feeling of confidence was all the more irrational as we did think it probable that the Germans would invade us. We at Sandhurst prepared to defend our area and set up various entrenchments. One night the alarm was given and the cadets went out cheerfully to man them. I had been unwell and was detained in the infirmary, feeling excited but helpless and listening for the sound of battle. In the morning my companions returned, still showing a spirit of adventure and seeming almost sorry that it had proved a false alarm. Yet it was at least very doubtful whether they had the means to have resisted a serious attack.

At about this time a scheme was set up to send young children with their mothers to the United States, where a number of families had declared their willingness to receive them. It was fostered in Oxford by Kenneth Bell, an energetic Fellow of Balliol, and Renée was urged to take advantage of it. I was in two minds about it, wishing her and the children to be safe, but not liking the idea of their going so far away, and having also begun to doubt whether England would be invaded. In my uncertainty, I left the decision to her and after much hesitation she made up her mind to go. She was influenced by the fact that the children were a quarter Jewish, which she saw as putting them in greater danger in the event of a German victory. As we were still in a state of alert at Sandhurst, I was not able to get leave to say goodbye to them, and I learned of their imminent departure through a telephone call from Renée, which left me in tears, not knowing when I should see any of them again. At the last minute, when they had boarded the ship at Liverpool, Renée decided against going, but it was then too late. They were not allowed to disembark, and the ship sailed with them to America.

When they arrived there, they passed into the charge of a committee which had the delicate task of arranging the temporary adoptions. After considering various offers, including one from the philosopher Charles Stevenson whom I had met and liked, Renée decided in favour of a Mr and Mrs Frederick Godley, who lived at Rye in Westchester County on the outskirts of New York. One of the factors that influenced her was that they were people of very considerable means, so that this addition to their family would not be a financial burden to them. I believe that their money was mostly inherited, though Mr Godley practised as an architect. They were then both probably in their fifties with two grown-up sons and a teenage daughter. Renée liked them personally and was made very welcome by them, but after being with them for a few weeks, she became discontented with her own position. She had not been allowed to take any money to America and did not have a permit to work there, even if there had been any work that she wished to do. It troubled her that she should be living at the Godleys' expense, though she was willing for them to support the children. Accordingly she decided to return to England, leaving the children in the care of the Godleys and of a Finnish nurse whom they had engaged to look after them. It was a difficult decision to reach as Valerie was still only four and a half years old and Julian hardly more than eighteen months. I did not feel entitled to say that it was wrong, though I should have opposed their going in the first place if I had thought that their mother would not be staying with them. Having made her way back to England, Renée joined one of the women's voluntary organizations and served as a dispatch rider in London. This became a hazardous occupation when the Germans started their heavy air raids later in the year, but she escaped without injury.

Meanwhile I was slowly qualifying to become an officer. The examinations with which we were confronted at the end of our four months' course at Sandhurst were not unduly searching. A genuine, if timely, indisposition relieved me from having to answer questions about the internal combustion engine, which might have defeated me, and I coped with the other papers and even with the practical exercises reasonably well. The result was that I was given a report which was good enough to satisfy Colonel Leatham, who came down from London to decide which of his prospective officers he was finally willing to accept. When I went to be interviewed by him, he was reading the report and complimented me on it without looking at me. When he did look up at me he frowned and said, 'Young man, I will not have men in my regiment with dirty upper lips. Grow a moustache.' I came to attention, said 'Sir' very loudly, saluted and marched out. Reasoning that he would be very unlikely to check whether his order had been obeyed, or even to remember having given it, I decided to ignore it but to shave very carefully before any further interview that I might have with him. In fact, this was the last time that I saw him.

So, on September 25 1940, just over a month short of my thirtieth birthday, I was commissioned as a Second Lieutenant in the Welsh Guards and posted to the training battalion at Sandown Park. The uniforms which we had made for us, with five buttons on the front and five on each sleeve, were of a darker shade of khaki than was worn in regiments outside the Brigade and we carried long walking sticks instead of the usual swagger-canes. The traditional bearskins were dispensed with in wartime, but we wore large dark-blue caps with heavily braided peaks, overshadowing the upper part of our faces, and golden leeks embroidered on their fronts. The leek was the regimental emblem and was served in totemistic fashion on St David's Day. It was left to our discretion whether to buy the suits of 'blues', that officers wore as evening dress, and whether to become members of the Guards Club. In both cases I decided against the expense.

At the training battalion I immediately found myself among friends. Eric Gray, George Galitzine, Richard Powell, Bruce Goff and Michael Ling came with me from Sandhurst. Gilbert Ryle was already there, and so was Andrew Graham whom I had continued to see occasionally since he went down from Oxford. Among the officers whom I met for the first time were Richard Llewellyn Lloyd, author of the autobiographical novel *How Green Was My Valley*, which he had published under the name of Richard Llewellyn, and the painters Rex Whistler and Simon Elwes. I was most impressed by Rex Whistler, whose vivid charm was tinged with melancholy. I remember discussing with him whether in the event of our being wounded and disfigured the life of the mind would be sufficient for us. He was to be killed commanding a troop of tanks in Normandy in 1944.

Rex continued to paint portraits, including one of Gilbert Ryle, which admirably brought out the strength of his face. Gilbert was naturally at home in the officers' mess, where he was called the Professor and very much liked and respected. He was not above ragging with his juniors, and I remember thinking on one of our rowdier guest-nights that I could not visualize Immanuel Kant in his position, which was, indeed, more of a reflection upon Kant. After a fairly long stay in the training battalion, Gilbert joined Hugh Trevor-Roper in a counter-espionage unit in which Stuart Hampshire also was employed. He found intellectual refreshment in these breaks in the routine of academic life and it was almost immediately after the war that he began to write his masterpiece, *The Concept of Mind*.

Apart from Gilbert, the one among my fellow officers of whom I have seen most in later life is Martyn Beckett, an architect by profession and a brilliant amateur jazz pianist. My earliest memory of him is of my coming into the mess at Sandown Park and seeing him at the piano, wrapt in his playing, unaware of his audience, translated into a world of his own. I took to him from that moment but he was soon moved to one of the service battalions and our friendship mainly developed after the war. A closer friend of mine at that time was Mickey Renshaw, a man of great elegance who used to take me on Sundays to visit his friends the Portarlingtons, affording me my first experience of the amenities of a large country house. Both were to prove themselves efficient and courageous officers, Mickey becoming a major and being twice mentioned in dispatches, and Martyn, like Richard Powell and Bruce Goff, being awarded the Military Cross.

The training battalion was commanded by Lord Glanusk, a regular soldier who was generously tolerant of the strange medley of wartime officers who had been put under his charge. It was characteristic of him that when two or three of the senior officers complained to him that one of our number was excessively addicted to the use of scent, he sent them about their business, saying that if the man in question smelled badly to them, they probably smelled just as badly to him.

There were enough Old Etonians among us to provide the nucleus of two elevens for the Field game and after a practice match, in which I displayed an unsuspected prowess, I was included in the side to play against one of the other battalions. On this occasion I did less well but still well enough to impress my companions who, like Dr Johnson when he compared a woman's preaching to a dog's walking on its hind legs, were surprised that I could do it at all. We played no other matches and I was content to rest upon my laurels. For all my interest in football, those were the first and last occasions since my schooldays on which I have seriously played any form of it.

The race-course at Sandown served as a training ground, the Grand Stand furnishing the officers' mess, with room for a billiard table as well as a piano. Though we took all our meals in the mess, the officers were billeted in the town of Esher. At first I shared lodgings with Eric Gray but afterwards moved to more comfortable quarters on my own. We now had soldier servants to do our valeting and take care of our equipment for us. We were given command of platoons and made responsible for their training. Since the actual process of training could safely be left to the non-commissioned officers, our duty mainly consisted in saying 'Carry on, Sergeant' and then standing by. Unlike the officers, the men in our charge were almost without exception Welsh, and to this day when I want to recall or try to imitate the lilting Welsh accent, the sentence which comes into my mind is, 'Can't see the fucking target.' We too had some target practice at shooting with revolvers, which I found unexpectedly difficult. Even at very short range I seldom hit the centre of the target and once when I pressed the trigger too soon came very near to shooting myself in the foot.

Except perhaps for a stray bomb or two, there were no air raids in Esher, but we used to hear the aeroplanes passing overhead on their way to attack London, and often in the early morning on our way to breakfast we would see the glow of the fires which the night's bombing had lit. This did not deter us from going up to London, to take part in the night-life which still flourished there. The slight element of danger may even have worked as an added attraction. Sometimes the raids would cause the trains to stop running and once or twice I had to wait until morning for a taxi to get me back to Esher in time to appear on parade. The bombing did not frighten me and when I was sleeping in London I stayed in my room and did not take shelter. This was not just a matter of bravado; it seemed to me, as it did to many others, that the probability that a bomb would fall in my immediate neighbourhood was not high enough to justify the trouble and discomfort to which taking shelter would put me. In fact I did not have even so much as a narrow escape. The only injury that I suffered was on a quiet night when I collided with a lamp-post in the black-out, while running for a bus, and gave myself a stupendous black eye. My true account of the innocent way in which I came by it was not believed in the officers' mess. It must have been at about the time of the Italian invasion of Greece, for I remember giving a lecture on Greek history to my platoon and finding my having to lecture in dark glasses a serious handicap in holding their attention.

During all this time I had seen very little not only of Renée but of the remainder of my family. On my father's side, my aunt Berthe, of whom I had continued to be very fond, had died some time before the war, and I had lost touch with my cousin Kenneth. Of my cousins on my mother's side, the girls were both married and had left London, one to live in the Midlands and the other in South Africa. Jack had become an officer in the Royal Air Force and was not to survive the war, and Donald, after obtaining a commission in the Middlesex Regiment, had got himself transferred to the King's African Rifles and joined them in Africa where he served throughout the war. Having developed a strong interest in African affairs, he applied after the war to join the Colonial Service, but being by that time just over thirty was informed that he was too old to be accepted. I happened to have enough influence to get his case reviewed, but he had also suffered a set-back in his private life, and before the Colonial Office had been able to arrive at a decision, which would probably have been in his favour, he committed suicide. To the extent that this was due to his seeing himself as a failure, he may well have been a victim of the pressure to which we were subjected in our boyhood by my grandfather's desire for our success.

Soon after the outbreak of war, my mother and Richard decided to leave London. They put most of their possessions in store, and after spending some time in Brighton settled down in furnished lodgings at Minehead in Somerset. None of my mother's property survived the air raid upon the London warehouse in which she had stored it. If she had kept any letters or photographs, they also were lost. My mother was proud of my being in the army and when I visited her in Brighton we got on very well. It was the last time that I saw her. The sclerosis from which she suffered had been getting worse and towards the end of 1940 I learned that she was dangerously ill. I obtained compassionate leave to go to Minehead, but by the time I arrived there she was already dead. Aunt Clara had also made the journey and only she and I attended the funeral, since Richard too had fallen ill. He had suffered a heart attack and did not survive my mother by more than a few months. I think that without her he had no very strong will to live. He was sixty-seven when he died, and she only fifty-three. Throughout her troubles and illness, she had retained a youthful zest for life, and it was sad that, having

found happiness in her second marriage, she was given so few years
to enjoy it.

I returned to Esher, but not for very long. From time to time
circulars would arrive from the War Office enquiring into our
special aptitudes and several weeks earlier I had filled in a form
which asked among other things about my command of foreign
languages. This question had already been put to me at Sandhurst
by a visiting officer who had disputed my claim to be fluent in
French on the ground that in conversing with him I made an
improper use of the subjunctive tense. He may well have been right,
though it had seemed to me, judging by his accent, that his own
French was not impeccable. He had also told me, no doubt mistakenly,
that the War Office was disinclined to recruit officers for intelligence
work whose parents were not British-born. Believing therefore that
it did not much matter how I replied to the questionnaire, I got my
landlady's schoolgirl daughter to fill it in for me, and allowed her to
credit me with a good working knowledge of Spanish and German
as well as French. Having sent the form off, I thought no more
about it and was surprised to receive an official note from London
District Headquarters summoning me to Cambridge to attend a
course on the interrogation of German prisoners.

This summons to Cambridge came just in time to prevent me
from learning to drive a car. At Sandhurst I had been taught to ride
a motor-cycle and though I very soon forgot the little that I learned,
I progressed far enough to venture out into the countryside. I
never altogether overcame my fear of the machine, which seemed
to me endowed with a strong will of its own, but I found the
experience quite enjoyable. I was once put at the wheel of a truck,
but having immediately driven it into a ditch, I was subsequently
allowed to leave the driving to the other apprentices, who were
eager to do it, and try to learn what I could from watching them.
When later at Esher the question somehow arose of my being set to
drive an armoured car, I said that I was willing to attempt it, but
that in view of my inability to drive an ordinary car the attempt was
unlikely to be very successful. When I had proved that I wasn't
joking, it was decided that this deficiency should be remedied.
Simon Elwes was the transport officer and was not best pleased
when I brought the car back in a damaged state. He had appointed
a sergeant to instruct me, but after going out with me a couple of
times, the sergeant contrived to find another to replace him. Even

so, I was beginning to master the art when my departure from Esher put an end to the lessons, which I have never resumed.

When I arrived in Cambridge I was pleased to find that Robin Zaehner, by that time an officer in the Intelligence Corps, was also on the course and that one of our instructors was Goronwy Rees. Believing, even more strongly than I had, that war was imminent and that he was committed to taking an active part in it, Goronwy had joined a Territorial Unit early in 1939. His experiences as a private in the Artillery are vividly described in his excellent book *A Bundle of Sensations*. He had been posted to Sandhurst at about the time that I went to Caterham and had emerged as an officer in the Royal Welsh Fusiliers. Being stationed in Liverpool at the end of 1940, he had then met a young girl called Margaret Morris and immediately entered with her into what was to prove a lastingly happy marriage. I had tried to ring Goronwy up in London before meeting him in Cambridge and, getting Margie on the telephone, had spelled my name out to her as 'A for Apple, Y for Youth, E for Excitement and R for Revenge,' these being the first words that occurred to me. In re-telling the story Margie came to substitute 'Arrogance' for 'Apple' and 'Romance' for 'Revenge', but I am very nearly certain that my version is correct. When she came with Goronwy to Cambridge we at once became friends and remained so all her life.

The pupils on the Cambridge course were allowed to make their own living arrangements, and taking advantage of the fact that Trinity and Christ Church are sister colleges, I was able to secure rooms in Trinity and to become a temporary member of the Senior Common Room. One of the pleasures which this brought me was the company of Professor G. H. Hardy, whom I already admired for his book *A Mathematician's Apology*. I was flattered to discover that he had read my book, *The Foundations of Empirical Knowledge*, and was disposed to talk to me about it. Mostly, however, we talked about cricket, for which he had a great enthusiasm. He was a master of cricketing lore and used to stump me with questions like, 'What score did Jack Hobbs most frequently make?' to which the answer was 'o', and, 'Of what county was it said "Where is it now the glory and the dream?"' to which I thought that the most plausible answer was 'Middlesex' though it turned out to be 'Surrey'. Occasionally I got the answers right, which gratified us both. His career as a mathematician brought him to Oxford as well as Cambridge and as a Professorial Fellow of New College he used to captain the Fellows in their cricket matches against the Choir School. I am proud to think that in this respect at least I have followed his example.

While I was staying in Trinity I was honoured by a call from Wittgenstein. Unfortunately I was out, but he left his name with another officer who happened to be there and mistook him for an electrician, whose job, indeed, Wittgenstein was perfectly capable of doing. I did not have the assurance to return his call and did not meet him in Hall or Common Room, since on the occasions on which he dined in College it was always at a sitting at which none of the other Fellows was present. Not long afterwards he left Cambridge to work as a porter in a London hospital, being later persuaded to serve as an assistant to a doctor, who did not identify him but was struck by his manifest intelligence.

I did reasonably well on the course, though my German was not really up to the standard required and I was no good at deciphering the Gothic script in which most German soldiers still wrote their letters. This was reflected in my report, which gave me credit for intelligence and application, but did not rate my command of the German language as being quite sufficient for an interrogator.

When I returned with this report to London District Headquarters, I found that the officer to whom I had to present it was my old friend Tom Webster, who had given me my scholarship to Christ Church. Though, having been born with only one arm, he was physically unfit for military service, he had managed to obtain a commission in the Intelligence Corps and had risen to the rank of captain. He greeted me warmly, congratulated me on the report, and said that if I had no objection he would apply to have me transferred to London District Headquarters as his assistant. I pointed out to him that if my duties would include the interrogation of German prisoners, the report hardly suggested that I was qualified to perform them, but he brushed this aside, saying that I should have other things to do as well, and that whatever my instructors at Cambridge might have thought, he was quite sure that my German was good enough for the purpose or at any rate would soon become so. I was far from sharing his confidence, but I had even less faith in myself as a regimental officer, and therefore accepted his offer, despite an appeal from the adjutant to the Welsh Guards that I should remain with the regiment. I had enjoyed my life at

Sandown, but I was soon due for a transfer to one of the three regular battalions, and I was afraid that their more rigorous standards would show up my deficiencies.

My work at London District Headquarters was not very exacting or indeed of very great interest. I divided my time between an office in a large building in Curzon Street and a house in Kensington, inaccurately described as a cage, in which a few prisoners were kept for a while before being sent to camps in England or in Canada. At that date they were usually members of the German Air Force, though a number of sailors, most often the survivors of submarine crews, also passed through our hands. They had nearly all been interrogated several times before they reached us, so that it did not much matter that my German was not equal to the task. In any case, I made friends with another interrogator there who did speak German fluently, and when we came across a prisoner who seemed to have anything interesting to offer, we interviewed him together. My friend was called Marsden and turned out to be a nephew of my old bugbear, the Master in College. I believe that he too later became a master at Eton. As a rule, the prisoners were quite ready to talk, though I do not recollect their ever giving us information that was of any great significance. On the rare occasions when one of them stood on his rights, and refused to reveal anything but his name, rank and service number, we did not attempt to bully him. They were seldom aggressive, though few of them yet had any doubt that Germany would win the war. It was only in the very rare cases when they revealed themselves as ardent Nazis that I was able to feel any personal hostility towards them.

Apart from conducting these interrogations, my main duty consisted in writing short reports for the news bulletins which we regularly circulated to various units in our area. Since we had no access to secret information, which we should in any case not have been allowed to publish, these reports contained nothing that could not have been discovered from reading the newspapers or listening to the wireless. They may, however, occasionally have been of interest to those who were too busy to do this for themselves. When major events occurred, like the German invasion of Russia, I might be deputed to sketch their historical background. To be engaging in this way in amateur journalism could hardly be viewed as a major contribution to the war effort, but in the summer of 1941, as the Germans penetrated deeper into Russian territory, and the

United States remained neutral, the pursuit of a course of infantry training, which looked to a British re-conquest of Europe, seemed almost equally futile.

Soon after my arrival at London District Headquarters, Tom Webster acquired another assistant in the person of Francis Listowel, whose younger brother, John Hare, had been a contemporary of mine at Eton and one of the Oppidans with whom I had been on friendly terms. Francis, as he then preferred to be called rather than by his family nickname of 'Billy', was one of the very few hereditary peers to support the Labour party. On this account he had quarrelled with his father, who would have liked to disinherit him and did in fact bequeath him as little money as possible. After the war he held various offices in Attlee's Labour Government, among other things presiding as Secretary of State over the grants of independence to India and to Burma. Small, dark and bespectacled, with a quiet manner covering a tenacious strength of will, he was a skilled negotiator. He took an interest in philosophy and had published a historical study of aesthetics. Though I could not pretend to any enthusiasm for aesthetics, I liked him personally and enjoyed his company. When I introduced him to Renée they also became friends.

By this time Renée and I were living apart, though we continued to meet quite often and there was still a strong bond between us. She took a small house in Chelsea and I had the luck to be offered the use of a well-appointed service flat in Pall Mall, at quite a low rent, by the parents of a girl whom I had met in Cambridge. I settled in there contentedly and since we worked no longer hours than those that were worked in offices in peacetime, and I was not disposed to re-engage in philosophy, I began to lead an active social life. At first I did not have many friends in London, but their number soon increased.

For this I was much indebted to Paul Willert, whom I had known slightly at Eton and a little better at Oxford, where he had been an undergraduate at Balliol. After that, he had worked in New York for the Oxford University Press, which had published the American edition of my *Language, Truth and Logic*. Apart from a brief meeting in New York, I had not seen him since he was at Oxford, but now that we met again in London I quickly found myself included in his astonishingly wide circle of friends. He was an admirable host and he and his first wife, Brenda, whom I also liked, were still entertaining on a generous scale. If I remember rightly, he was then employed in some branch of Military Intelligence. Later he joined the Air Force and flew in bombers as a navigator.

It was at the Willerts' house that I first met Arthur Koestler. He had already published *Darkness at Noon* and *Scum of the Earth*, and I had read and admired them both. He had no reason to distinguish me from any other Guards Officer and seemed a little taken aback when we fell into an argument. I was the first to leave, and as I made my way downstairs I heard him ask Paul rather sharply who I was. Since then our relations have been chequered. There have been times when we have been good friends, but longer periods of estrangement in which, on my side, at least, our intellectual differences have been emotionally tinged. This extends to my judgement of him as a writer. I think very highly of his autobiographical books and continue greatly to admire the psychological and political insight of *Darkness at Noon*. At the same time, I cannot help wishing that he would leave philosophy alone.

Among other things, *Darkness at Noon* was the expression of Koestler's own disillusionment with the Communist party. The attraction which Soviet communism held in the middle nineteen-thirties had waned in England as a result of the Moscow trials and the Russian-German pact, but it was renewed with the entry of Russia into the war and increased with the success of Russian arms. A remarkable communist, with whom I made friends at this time, was Wilfred Macartney, the author of a book called *Walls Have Mouths*, which had made a strong impression on me. It was an account of his experiences in prison, where he had served a long sentence for a clumsy attempt at espionage. White-haired and rubicund, with the manner of a hard-drinking journalist, he had a vitality which his years in prison appeared to have done nothing to diminish. He was the most conspicuous example that I have ever come across of those who combine left-wing opinions with an appetite for high-living. I think of him in an expensive hotel suite, which he had the air of having annexed, drinking champagne and surrounded by pretty girls, being still unwilling to deny the possibility that the defendants in the Moscow trials had really been guilty of the charges brought against them. He was not a man whom one could altogether admire but one would have needed to be a greater puritan than I was not to enjoy his company.

I probably met Macartney through a friend of Paul Willert's, a journalist called Kathleen McColgan, who did me a greater service by introducing me to Roland Penrose and to his present wife, Lee Miller. They had a house in Hampstead in which almost every wall was covered with the contents of Roland's magnificent collection of Cubist and Surrealist pictures. Himself a painter, as well as a patron of art, Roland had spent a long time in Paris, where he had become a close personal friend of Picasso and Max Ernst and of the writer Paul Eluard. Though I had been to the Surrealist Exhibition, which had been held in London some ten years before, I knew and understood very little of Surrealist or indeed of Cubist painting, and it was through looking at the pictures in Roland's collection that I first came to appreciate the work of such diverse artists as Braque and Paul Klee and Magritte and Delvaux. Lee too had been in Paris, where she had been painted by Picasso, had played the leading part in Cocteau's film *Le Sang d'un Poète*, and had been encouraged by Man Ray to become a professional photographer. They made an attractive contrast: Roland, reflective, reserved at first acquaintance, essentially an English country gentleman; Lee, an outgoing American, quick in her sympathies, racy in speech, with an infectious zest for life. I became and have remained exceedingly fond of them both.

Though I was enjoying myself in London, I became, as the months went by, increasingly dissatisfied with my work. I had never been able to pretend that it was useful and I had begun to find it boring. Never one to keep quiet about my troubles, I complained of this to my friends, including Robin Zaehner, who was engaged in some form of intelligence work about which he was reticent. He said nothing to me at the time, but not very long afterwards I received an order to report to a room in the War Office. The major who received me said that he had been informed that I was fluent in Spanish. I had good reason to deny this, since I had been tested in Cambridge, at a time when it seemed likely that the Germans would occupy Spain, and had made a poor showing, but I believed that I could recover my knowledge of the language with a little practice, and allowed myself, therefore, to say that I spoke it reasonably well. He then revealed to me that there was an organization called Special Operations Executive which employed agents in South America, among other places. These agents were controlled from New York, and he offered to send me to New York, with the prospect of proceeding as an agent to one of the South American countries. The idea immediately attracted me, but I asked for, and was granted, a short time to consider it.

The reason why I hesitated was that Renée and I had decided to live together again. I was to give up my flat and join her in her house in Chelsea. We were still so much tied to one another that, even in the absence of the children, there seemed little sense in our continuing to live apart. Since we had only just come to this decision, I did not want it to be nullified. On the other hand, going to America would give me the opportunity to see the children, and there was the possibility that if I stayed in New York for any length of time I could arrange for Renée to join me there. If I then went on to South America, I should probably have enough funds to make Renée independent of the Godleys and allow her to remain with the children in the United States. These considerations made it easier for me to yield to my desire to exchange my humdrum job for one that promised to be more exciting. Accordingly, I told the major that I accepted his offer and was thereupon transferred to SOE.

It was arranged that I should go to America by sea, which meant travelling in convoy, and while the convoy was being got together, I had time to say goodbye to some of my friends. Among those whom I made a point of seeing was Philip Toynbee, who had recently got married: I had met his wife, Anne, briefly once at Sandhurst. I arranged to meet the Toynbees, before dinner, at the Café Royal, which in those days still functioned as a café and was still a favourite meeting-place for writers and artists, even if it had lost some of the glory that it had known in the time of Oscar Wilde. When I arrived there I found that Frank Pakenham was with them. The last time that Philip, Frank and I had been together was when Philip had taken us, some years before, to call on a girl whom he wanted to impress: our presence was designed to testify to his respectability. It had not proved a happy idea; the visit was short and embarrassing, and the girl had not been diverted from her preference for a Liberal politician. This time, Frank told us that Cyril Connolly was giving a dinner party at the Ivy Restaurant for the American writer, Thornton Wilder, and that he wanted us all to join it. I was pleased to hear this, since I had seen hardly anything of Cyril since the beginning of the war. He had found a new vocation as editor of the magazine *Horizon*, which he had started with the financial support of his friend Peter Watson. I had read the early numbers and thought them very good. I was also quite pleased with the prospect of meeting Thornton Wilder, whose novel *The Bridge of San Luis Rey* I remembered enjoying when I read it as a boy.

When we got to the Ivy, we found that Frank had been mistaken in saying that Cyril was expecting us to dine with him. His party, which included Stephen Spender among others, and two girls who lovingly gave their services to *Horizon*, was already complete. We managed, however, to secure a neighbouring table and were beckoned over to be presented to Thornton Wilder. Cyril was in an expansive mood and was obviously taking pride and pleasure in being the centre of a literary constellation. We finished our dinner, paid, and left the restaurant first. As soon as we came out into the darkened street, the Toynbees began to discuss Cyril in a mildly critical way. Growing impatient with them, and being in high spirits, I exclaimed in my carrying lecturer's voice, 'How boring you are being. If you want to be malicious about Cyril, the last word was said by Virginia Woolf: "I do not like that smarty-boots Connolly".' From the darkness behind us, a voice, unmistakably Cyril's, said, 'Not so loud, Freddie.' The Toynbees and Frank simply took to their heels. There was no point in my running with them, so I turned and walked slowly back, to confront Cyril and his party. I found them grouped under the dim light of a lamp-post with Stephen Spender looking amused, the girls shocked, and Thornton Wilder bewildered. 'Oh dear,' I said, 'I could cut my tongue out.' 'Pity you didn't,' said Cyril. 'I suppose this is the sort of thing that is never forgiven.' 'No,' he said, 'it never will be.' There seemed to be no answer to that, so I made a vaguely hopeless gesture and walked away. I thought it likely that my companions would have gone back to the Café Royal and I did, indeed, find them there. So far from sympathizing with me, or making any excuse for their desertion, they were concerned only about the possible consequences to themselves. 'Will he remember that I was with you?' said Frank. 'Will he take it out on my next book?' said Philip. Having tried to convince them that they had relatively little cause to worry, I left them and made my way home. I was annoyed with myself and sorry to have hurt and humiliated someone whom I liked.

When I got home, I immediately wrote to Cyril, saying that I was sorry for what had happened but trying to minimize its importance. He must know, I said, how easily one gave rein to malice, and how little it might correspond to one's actual feelings. I concluded by. saying that I hoped he would not allow a few unguarded words to outweigh years of friendship. The letter received no reply. About eighteen months later, I had returned to London and was again in the Café Royal, having a drink with Guy de Rothschild. I could see Cyril sitting at the far end of the room with a group of persons whom I did not know. Philip Toynbee came in, greeted me warmly, and said, 'Come along and talk to Cyril.' I demurred, saying that I did not want there to be a scene, but Philip insisted that it would be all right. As we walked across, I could see that Cyril was undecided how to receive me. At the last moment, he made up his mind, smiled at me, asked me when I had got back and said that it was nice to see me again. I made some suitable answer and soon returned to Guy. This is not quite the end of the story. About two years later still, some months after France had been liberated, I was flying to Paris with Cyril and the painter Bébé Bérard. As we were on our way to the airport, Bérard started talking about *Horizon*. He praised it but added that he thought that it sometimes erred on the side of smartness. 'Yes,' said Cyril. 'One must at all costs avoid being a smartyboots, mustn't one, Freddie?' 'Yes, Cyril,' I said firmly, 'at all costs one must.' Neither of us ever referred to the incident again, at least in one another's presence, but our friendship never really recovered from it. We met fairly often in the years that followed, and were for the most part ostensibly on good terms, but he never wholly trusted me and it was easy for anyone to make mischief between us. On my side, I became more alert to his defects, though I never lost my admiration for him as a writer. Only at our very last meeting, within a year of his death, did something of our original warmth return.

Not long after this unfortunate evening with the Toynbees, towards the end of October 1941, I took ship for America. The convoy moved slowly, going very far to the north to keep out of the way of enemy submarines, and the passage across the Atlantic took us twenty-eight days. I began by finding it exciting, and enjoyed the sight of the convoy keeping in formation, with the destroyers frisking around it like sheep-dogs. We were probably in the greatest danger in the latter part of the journey, when the convoy broke up and the other ships outdistanced us, but we made our way to Halifax without incident and then steamed slowly down the coast to New York. I remember nothing of my fellow-passengers except for a naval officer who astonished me by the quantity of gin that he drank without noticeable effect. He was joining one of the destroyers which the Americans had leased to us. For my part, I was travelling under some civilian cover and wore civilian clothes. I was half glad and half sorry to have left my uniform behind me.

10 *More Cloak than Dagger*

The New York offices of SOE were in Rockefeller Center. It shared them with other Intelligence agencies under the general title of British Security Co-ordination. When I reported there for work, I was delighted to find that the head of my section was Bill Deakin, whom I had not seen since the beginning of the war. Combining authority with tact, he ran the section most efficiently. My first duty was to learn as much as I could about South American politics and the persons and organizations in the various countries who were likely to be German or Italian sympathizers. At the beginning, therefore, my time was mostly spent in mastering the contents of a very large number of files. The countries about which I came to know most were Argentina, Chile, Uruguay and Peru. Much of this knowledge had no very clear relation to the war, but I enjoyed acquiring it and found myself valuing it for its own sake.

My closest colleague was Tony Samuel, with whom I shared an office. The youngest of three brothers, of whom I had known the second slightly at school, he was well provided with money; his grandfather, the first Lord Bearstead, had been one of the founders of the Shell Oil Company. Tony was several years younger than I, but shrewd and worldly wise. He suffered from deafness, which gave him an air and also, I think, a feeling of detachment. Unaffectedly generous, and with a vein of ironic humour, he was an agreeable companion both inside and outside the office. In the fifteen months or more that we worked together, I do not remember that we ever quarrelled.

Among the members of the other sections whom I got to know more or less well, a surprising number had a literary or theatrical background. There was the playwright, Ben Levy, who unlike most of the others was politically conscious and became a Labour member of Parliament for a brief period after the war; his friend, Eric Maschwitz, a composer of lyrics for musical comedies and revues who had written the song 'A Nightingale sang in Berkeley Square'; Montgomery Hyde, the author among many other books of an excellent biography of Oscar Wilde; Christopher Wren, not, I think, himself a writer but the son of the author of *Beau Geste*; and my best friend among them, the elegant and charming Tim Brooke, who had worked in Hollywood. A later recruit from Hollywood was the novelist Noel Langley, who had gone there to make money but complained about its materialist values: he had written among other things the film script for *The Wizard of Oz*. His arrival succeeded that of my old Oxford friend Giles Playfair, an actor turned author, and of Bunty Howard, who was married to the actor Jack Mc-Naughton and herself an actress. They had come from Australia, having escaped from Singapore when it fell to the Japanese.

A more important figure in the office than any of these was an international lawyer called Alexander Halpern, a Russian who had held some position in the Kerensky government. His wife Salome had kept the title of Princess and something of what I took to be the style of the *ancien régime*. They settled in London after the war, and I used often to meet Guy Burgess at their house. They took his discourses on politics more seriously than I did, but I do not believe that they suspected how far his commitment to communism had gone. Another of my colleagues whom I have occasionally seen in later life was Ivar Bryce, who might have served as a model for James Bond, the creation of his friend Ian Fleming, if one could imagine Bond divested of his appetite for violence. Ivar's looks were such that when he walked past our offices, the secretaries, who were massed in the centre, seemed each to give a little sigh. Like my own secretary Margery Cummer, of whom I became very fond, they were nearly all recruited from Canada. One reason for this may have been that the head of the office, William Stephenson, was a Canadian. He is said to have been an impressive person and good at the work, for which he was given a knighthood, but I never rose far enough in the hierarchy to meet him.

Seeing Gilbert Highet again in New York and finding that he had something of a bad conscience about taking no part in the war, I spoke about him to Bill Deakin, who thereupon enlisted him in our section. Gilbert put his considerable energy into the work and did it so well that when Bill left us a few months later to go first to Cairo and then to be parachuted into Jugoslavia, as leader of the first British mission to make contact with Tito, Gilbert was preferred to Tony Samuel and myself as his successor. Being comfortable as we were, neither Tony nor I begrudged him this promotion. It was an embarrassment as well as a source of pride to Gilbert when his wife, Helen MacInnes, published *Above Suspicion*, the first of her long series of spy stories, since he thought that he might be suspected of having broken his oath of secrecy by giving her advice. In fact, I have no doubt that the novel, which was an immediate success, was written entirely without his help. Its villain was modelled on Adam von Trott, who had been a Rhodes Scholar at Balliol when Gilbert was there, and a great social success in Oxford; he had joined the German Foreign Service and was employed in their Embassy in Washington. It turned out later that Helen had done him an injustice. He was indeed a Nationalist but not a Nazi, and his involvement in the unsuccessful plot against Hitler, in 1944, was to bring him torture and death.

Apart from keeping an eye on South America, the main business of our New York office had been to try to counteract the influence of the various groups in the United States that were either hostile to Britain or at any rate determined that their government should maintain a strict neutrality. With the Japanese attack on Pearl Harbor, which occurred about a fortnight after I arrived in the United States, and the American declaration of war on all the Axis powers, our work lost much of its importance. Not only did the American Government assume the chief responsibility for counter-espionage inside its own territory, but, following an old tradition, it regarded the countries of Central and South America as falling within its sphere of influence. At that time its own intelligence services were not very well co-ordinated; it became a joke among us that some South American informants were making a good living out of obtaining doubtful information from one United States agency and selling it to another: nevertheless these agencies saw it as their show and were not disposed to have us meddling in it. This did not mean that we withdrew our agents from the field, but we had to be careful about adding to their number. The result was that, for the time being at least, there was no question of my proceeding to any South American country. Though I found it more interesting, my work was not very different from that which I had been doing in Curzon Street. I collated information and wrote reports which were dispatched to London. I never discovered who read them, but somebody must have, since I occasionally received comments on them. They may have made their way to the Foreign Office, perhaps via the Ministry of Economic Warfare on which SOE was nominally dependent.

I had let the Godleys know that I was coming to America and at the first opportunity I went out to see them, it being only a short train journey from New York to Rye. The children were brought to the station to meet me, but did not recognize me. This surprised me in Valerie's case, since she had been so much in my company before our separation, but eighteen months is a long time in the life of a five-year-old child, and her new environment had made a powerful impression on her. Both children spoke with an American accent, which foolishly disturbed me to the extent of my making a mild effort to correct it. Mrs Godley was amused but also slightly annoyed when, after spending some time with me, Valerie ran across to her and announced, 'I am a little English girl. I don't say "grasse", I say "grarse".' When they returned to England all trace of their American accents was quickly lost. They both seemed happy, though Valerie did not greatly care for the Finnish nurse, who was briskly efficient but unimaginative and did not disguise her preference for Julian. On the other hand, Valerie had taken more readily than Julian to Mrs Godley as a substitute mother. She was an impressive woman, large and handsome, strong-willed but kindly, secure in the possession of money, content with the existing order of things but liberal in her outlook, religious but not puritanical, with an abundance of energy that hardly found sufficient outlet in a purely domestic life. There was no doubt of her being the dominant force in the family. Mr Godley, a tall man whose bluffness had a faint air of unease, was more conventionally conservative. He was a product of Yale, where he had also been Master of one of the colleges, and faithful to its values. Of their children, the eldest, whom I met only later, was in the Diplomatic Service, the second, a friendly good-looking boy, already seeming likely to succeed in business, had just left Yale and was about to join the Navy, and the youngest, a tall girl with a quiet charm that offset her mother's vitality, was studying medicine at Vassar. In relation to the children, she had stepped easily into the part of a much older sister.

My arrival might have made difficulties, but their friendliness and good manners were equal to it. It was arranged that I should spend the weekends with them and I found it easy to fit in with their pleasant way of life. The house at Rye was big and comfortable, with a handsome terrace, a tennis court and a large garden. They had another house at Morris, in the northern part of New York State, to which they went in the summer when the weather in New York City and its neighbourhood became too hot for comfort.

Though it would have been possible for me to commute from Rye, I did not think it right or convenient to quarter myself entirely on the Godleys, even if they had wished it, so that I lived in New York City during the week. I began by taking a room in a mid-town hotel, but managed after a week or two to rent a pleasant ground-floor apartment on 34th Street or thereabouts and Park Avenue. Later I moved to another ground-floor apartment in the fifties nearer to the East River. Its previous owner, who had been conscripted, left me his library which included the Book of Mormon. I tried to read it but the turgid prose of the angel Moroni defeated me. My predecessor was a journalist, and on the ground that he sometimes needed to work at home in peace, had been able to persuade the Telephone Company to fit a device to his telephone which worked in such a way that when the switch was turned off, the instrument remained silent though the caller was greeted with the usual ringing tone. I found this socially very useful, when for one reason or another I wished to convey the impression that I was not at home. My telephone in London sometimes does the same but unfortunately not in a way that I can control.

When it became clear that my work was going to keep me in New York, I enquired whether arrangements could be made for Renée to join me and, finding that they could be, wrote and asked her to come. She replied by telegram, saying that she wanted a divorce. There had been a question of it when things started to go badly between us, but when we decided that we wanted to preserve our marriage, the proceedings had been suspended. They were now renewed and our divorce was made absolute in the course of 1942. It did not destroy our affection for one another and for most of the eighteen years that were to pass before I married again, Renée continued to exert a very strong influence over me. I fear that it did some harm to the children and Valerie, in particular, needed later to be reassured that we were not, as she put it, 'badly' divorced.

Renée's telegram was sent to Rye and arrived there on a weekday, with the unfortunate result that the Godleys opened it, thinking that it might contain some urgent message, which they could transmit to me by telephone. Its contents came as a shock to them, since neither Renée nor I had given them any hint that anything was amiss with our marriage. I had the impression that this made them feel that we had not dealt altogether fairly with them, but it did not noticeably affect their attitude either to the children or to me.

Though I worked rather longer hours in the New York office than I previously had in London, I still had ample leisure for an active social life. I continued my friendship with the Cummingses, staying with them in New Hampshire as well as seeing them often in New York. I introduced Valerie to them and we went together to the circus, where Valerie enchanted Cummings by saying 'Where are you?' to an elephant which she was vainly attempting to feed. He was delighted also with my account of a conversation that I had had with her about the war. She had wanted to know why the Americans and the Japanese were fighting one another and in my attempt to give her a simple answer I had said, among other things, that the Americans wanted to prevent the Japanese from coming to their country and treating them badly. 'Would they hurt me?' she asked. 'No,' I said, 'the Japanese are very kind to children.' Cummings was all the more pleased with my answer, as he had not greatly welcomed America's entry into the war, and particularly disliked the level of the propaganda to which it had given rise.

I was happy also to renew my friendship with Meyer Shapiro. I remember an evening on which I went with him and Ernest Nagel to visit André Breton, the leader of the Surrealist movement, who had escaped from Paris and was very much of an exile in New York. I had been more perplexed than excited by the little that I had read of his prolific writings, but I had heard much about him and was curious to meet him. We went to his apartment, where my eye was caught chiefly by a comic strip posted on a wall with the motto: '*Un bas déchiré accentue le charme.*' Breton was dignified and urbane and received us with formal courtesy. He had not been at any pains to learn English and we spoke in French. There were two women present on our arrival but they very soon vanished. Breton then made a speech saying that he had wanted to see us because of our knowledge of philosophy. As we were doubtless aware, the Surrealist movement took much of its inspiration from the thought of

Hegel. It had therefore been a shock to him to discover, on coming to New York, that the philosophy of Hegel was not taken very seriously there. Could we explain to him why this was so? If the foundations of Surrealism were to be undermined, it would be a very great blow to European culture. It was news to me that the Surrealist movement owed anything to Hegel, who after all proclaimed that the Real was the Rational, but several of its members were also communists and I suppose that the connection was made through Marx. What Breton probably wanted, therefore, was an assurance that Marx was intellectually respectable, but we took him at his word, and did our best to explain to him why the sort of metaphysics which Hegel practised had fallen out of fashion. He received this shock to European culture with surprising equanimity, thanked us for the valuable insights which we had given him, and concluded by saying that we must promise to collaborate in the production of a new quarterly review. One or two numbers of the review did eventually come out, but I did not contribute to them.

It was probably through Jeannie Connolly, who by that time had left Cyril and was living in New York, that I was brought into relation with Tony Bower, who was to become one of my closest American friends. He had been a near contemporary of mine at Oxford and had subsequently lived in London, but our previous acquaintance had been slight. Meeting him again in New York, I was attracted by his wit, his relish for gossip, and his Epicurean attitude to life. He did many things well, though none very earnestly. He was a good dancer and a good skier and a good enough bridge-player to have made a living out of it for a time by playing at London clubs. In New York he was working as a film critic and he was later to become the successful editor of an art magazine. He was reticent about his homosexuality and once made a half-hearted attempt to break away from it. When he had come to accept it, he still kept his social and his private lives apart. He was careless of the dangers to which his private frequentations exposed him, and he paid for them eventually with his life. His murderer has never been caught, or even, I believe, identified.

The circle of Jeannie Connolly's and Tony's friends included Wystan Auden and another English writer, Jimmy Stern, whom I already admired for his short stories but had not previously met. I was equally drawn to him and to his wife Tanya, who conducted a class in gymnastics which Auden attended. I did not see enough of Auden for us to become friends but I liked him better then than I did subsequently when he became a respectable Anglican and disavowed the radicalism of much of his early work. His motive for settling in America had been personal, rather than the simple desire to escape the war, which some of his detractors attributed to him. This did not prevent him from having some sense of guilt, which had the effect of making him more defiantly American. Though Auden himself lived modestly, the contrast between the plenty available to us in America and the privations of wartime England made it easy to feel guilty even for those of us whose presence in America was supposed to be contributing to the prosecution of the war.

One of these was Isaiah Berlin, who was working in New York for the British Information Service. I was very grateful for his company while we were there together, but he was soon transferred to the British Embassy in Washington, where he became deservedly famous for the acuity and wit of his comments on American politics. I only once found occasion to visit Washington, going there by train. When I tipped the Pullman attendant less than he thought was due to him, he tapped me on the shoulder in a way that made me feel that he was putting the evil eye on me. I then found myself sharing a taxi from the station with the film-star Myrna Loy, but I did not have the courage to speak to her. When I saw Isaiah he told me of his meeting with Sheffer and his consequent decision to give up philosophy.

It may have been Isaiah who first introduced me to Raimund von Hofmannsthal. The son of the poet Hugo von Hofmannsthal, Raimund had led a cosmopolitan life before the war, dividing his time between Austria, England and the United States. A resolute anti-Nazi, he ended by becoming an American citizen, though he never lost his affection for the Vienna of his boyhood and many elements in his character were typically Viennese. When I met him he was working for the Time-Life organization, which had offices in one of the other buildings in Rockefeller Center. With his uncommon capacity for seeing the best in anyone he had much to do with, Raimund was one of the few people who actually liked Henry Luce. In later years he was to work only on the business side of the organization, but at that time he was more concerned with its editorial policy. He used to consult me on questions of world politics, characteristically attaching far more importance to my opinions than I can believe that they deserved. One of the qualities which Raimund's many friends most valued in him was his generosity, not only in material ways, but in his being altogether free from any meanness of spirit. He delighted in his friends' accomplishments and was genuinely pleased by their success.

He was nearly thirty-six years old when I first met him, no longer quite the glamour boy that he had been in his youth, but still good-looking with a particularly seductive voice. Though we took to one another straight away, it was some weeks before we met again and then it was by chance, at a night-club called Mabel's, much frequented by my pleasure-loving colleagues, where the main attraction was the singer Jimmy Daniels, specializing in such currently popular songs as 'It was just one of those things'. Raimund was there with his wife, formerly Lady Elizabeth Paget, whom he had married shortly before the war. Tall, dark and graceful, she then had the reputation of being the most beautiful girl in England, and she was and has remained the most beautiful woman that I have ever known. From then on the three of us were often in one another's company and I continued to see a great deal of Raimund after Liz and their baby daughter Arabella had gone back to England. He had many friends in New York, and since he was always anxious that the people whom he liked should know and like one another, we went to many parties together. He also took me to such places as The Stork Club and El Morocco which I should never have thought of visiting on my own, and somehow contrived to transmute the contemporary world of café society into the Vienna of his father's librettos. He had an extraordinary power to make one participate in his romantic view of life, however little relation it may have borne to fact.

In February Tony Bower was drafted into the army and I took his place as film critic for *The Nation*, a radical weekly which devoted more space to politics than to the arts. Since I had no permit to work in the United States, otherwise than for the British Government, I wrote under the pseudonym of P. H. Rye. The choice of this pseudonym may have reflected my addiction to crossword puzzles, since it was derived from the Greek saying '*Panta rei* – Everything flows,' which seemed to me applicable to films. The 'H' was meant to refer to Heraclitus to whom the saying is attributed, and apart from its being a more plausible surname, there was an allusion to the place where my children were living in the substitution of 'Rye' for 'Rei'. I was so unconscientious a reviewer that I wrote only four articles in all, one in February, one in March and two in May, though I believe that I criticized several films in each of them, and probably saw others that I did not think worth writing about. The only one of them that I can remember was a film called *49th Parallel*, about the attempt of some Nazis to escape capture in Canada, the leading Nazi being played by Eric Portman and his most villainous henchman by my friend John Chandos, with Leslie Howard and Raymond Massey playing more virtuous parts. In some ways it was rather crude propaganda, but it held my interest. I might have done more reviewing if I had taken more pleasure in it, but I found that the need for taking a critical attitude interfered with my enjoyment of the kind of films I liked, by making it harder for me to suspend disbelief. I forget how the decision was taken that I should not continue, but it caused me no regret.

Although the chances of our being engaged in any field operations seemed remote, it was thought desirable that at least the younger workers in the New York branch of SOE should receive some instruction in the more active exercise of their profession, and we were accordingly sent, a few of us at a time, to be trained at a battle-school near Toronto. The short course of training mainly consisted in our having to shoot with our revolvers at man-sized dummies which leapt at us unexpectedly out of bushes, and in our learning the rudiments of unarmed combat. What we were taught was a form of karate, which was then not so well known as it has since become. I did not develop into much of a sharp-shooter, but I learned enough karate to know how to disable or even to kill a man with my bare hands, provided that his reactions were slow enough for me to get my blows in first. Since this condition was not very likely to be realized, it was probably fortunate that I was never called upon to try to put my knowledge into practice. The city of Toronto, which we were allowed to visit in our free time, seemed to me unattractive, partly because it still laboured under a form of prohibition, which made it very difficult for the casual visitor to obtain any alcoholic drink. Neither was this the only sense in which it seemed to me to manifest a dryness of spirit. When I visited it again, more than twenty years after the war, I thought that it had changed a good deal for the better, the influx of European immigrants having lessened the force of its Scottish puritanical tradition.

My sense of the remoteness of my work from the realities of war was sharpened by the arrival in New York of my old pupil Michael Judd, wearing his Air Force uniform with enviable decorations. He had been commanding a squadron of fighters in North Africa, and had been sent to the United States on some temporary mission to the American Air Force. At that time I was much in the company of Tony Bower's half-sister, the young and pretty Jean Gordon-Duff, but when I introduced her to Michael they fell in love at first sight and were very soon married. Though the marriage did not last much more than a decade, it was because of her that he decided after the war to seek his fortune in Texas.

A girl whom I should have liked to know better than I did was Betty Bacall, with whom Tim Brooke and Noel Langley had made friends at Mabel's. It was to this meeting that she owed her transformation into the actress Lauren Bacall, since Tim got her a job as a cover-girl on a fashion magazine, and it was for the film *Cover Girl*, in which she was not actually used, that she was originally brought to Hollywood. I took her out several times and once, at a party, we made a record on which she sang 'Chatanooga Choo-Choo' and I recited Marvell's poem 'To his Coy Mistress'. After I left New York, it was more than thirty years before I saw her again, to discover, not surprisingly, that she had only a very vague recollection of our having met before. I did not have the opportunity to ask her whether she had kept the record, but think it very improbable.

My friendship with Guy de Rothschild began in the office, to which he was recruited in the latter part of 1942. He was then in his early thirties and up till the war had combined an active engagement in the family business of banking with a fashionable social life. Among other things, he had been a good enough amateur golfer to represent France. Having served as an officer in the French Army, and distinguished himself in battle, he had remained in France after the armistice until the worsening position of Jews, not only in the occupied sector of France but also under the Vichy régime, made him think it advisable to take his family out of the country. While he had never sought to disown his responsibilities as one of the most prominent members of the Jewish community, his wealth and his social position had sheltered him before the war from any unpleasant exposure to anti-Semitism. It, therefore, came as a great shock to him to discover that the mere fact of being a Jew could make him vulnerable. One result of this was that his political sympathies took a leftward turn, and he treated me as something of a political mentor. Later, when he joined the Free French forces in England, he came even more under the influence of Arthur Koestler, who could in those days still be counted as a man of the left, though he was already tending to judge political issues predominantly in the light of his own break with the Communist party. Guy talked of giving up banking after the war, engaging in politics and founding a left-wing journal. He was undoubtedly sincere, but the family tradition proved too strong for him and after the war he resumed his heritage without very much of a struggle. Though our friendship has not endured, I remember him with affection as he then was: physically small and taut, good-looking, generous, very attractive to women, intellectually eager and receptive.

Early in 1943 our superiors decided that SOE needed to add to the number of its agents in Buenos Aires, and it was proposed that Guy and I should be sent there to work together. The idea appealed to us both, but for some reason which was not explained to us it was not put into effect. By that time each of us had come to the conclusion that the work which we were doing in New York was not of sufficient importance to justify our remaining there, so when the Buenos Aires project came to nothing, he resigned from SOE and I asked for and obtained permission to return to England. Since there had been no serious air raids on London for over a year, I decided to take the children with me. The Godleys were sorry to see them go, but they agreed with me that it was time that they were reunited with their mother. I had had little news of Renée since she had asked for a divorce, but I knew that she had moved to a different address in Chelsea, that she was no longer doing any war-work, and that she would be glad to have the children back. For some reason I had got her to send me out my uniform and I wore it on the voyage. By this time I had risen to the rank of first lieutenant, merely as the result of my having held a commission for more than eighteen months.

The only reason for which I might have hesitated to take the children with me was the danger of the crossing. As it happened, the convoy previous to ours, in which Guy de Rothschild was travelling, was attacked, his ship was torpedoed and he spent some time in the water before he was rescued. Fortunately for my peace of mind on the journey, I learnt this only after I saw him again in

London. Not that his misfortune made any difference to the risks that we were running, since the submarine campaign had long been in operation, but the knowledge of it would have brought them more forcibly home to me. In fact, our crossing, which on this occasion was comparatively rapid, was almost wholly uneventful. Once, during the daytime, when I was playing chess in the state-room with one of the other passengers, the children rushed in excitedly to tell me that a submarine had been sighted, but it was probably a false alarm. In any case, the convoy was not attacked. When we arrived in Liverpool, I telephoned to Renée to say that we were safe, and brought the children to London on the following day. After nearly three years' separation they did not recognize their mother, but it did not take them long to make the adjustment, though Valerie, who had grown very fond of Mrs Godley, never altogether ceased to miss her. One thing which struck them both was the inevitable decline in their standard of living. At the first Christmas which they spent at home, we did our best, with help from Francis Listowel, to secure an adequate supply of food and presents, but the four-year-old Julian's face still fell as he complained, 'There isn't any much.' By that time Renée had established herself and the children in a pretty house in Hampstead, and when I was in London I visited them regularly at the weekends.

When I reported to the headquarters of SOE in Baker Street, I discovered that no provision had been made for my return. The first suggestion that was put to me by the officer who received me was that I should take at least a month's leave, but I pointed out to him that it was not any want of leisure, but rather the feeling that I ought to be more seriously involved in the war, that had caused me to give up my position in New York. He then proposed that I should rejoin my regiment; but I did not care for this suggestion either, since I was no longer fit to be posted to a service battalion and would therefore have to start all over again at Esher with a group of much younger officers whom I did not know. In the end, I consented to take a short spell of leave, while they tried to find something suitable for me. When I went back, I was told that there was a vacancy in their establishment at Accra, in what is now Ghana but was then still known as the Gold Coast, and that this was all that they could offer me. Though I found it difficult to see how such a remote African colony could be much involved in the war, I was attracted by the prospect of visiting a part of the world where I had never yet been, and against my better judgement accepted the offer. I had myself inoculated against typhoid, tetanus and yellow fever, started taking medicine to ward off malaria, acquired a solar topee and other articles of tropical clothing, packed a sufficient supply of books and embarked, again as a civilian, on a Dutch ship which made its way slowly past Cape Finisterre and the Canary Islands, down the west coast of Africa to Freetown in Sierra Leone, and then to Takoradi which was the port for Accra.

Since the ship was travelling on its own, it was thought to be especially vulnerable to submarines, and the passengers were asked to help the crew in keeping watch. Taking my turn with the others, I was once reprimanded by the captain for having only one eye on the ocean and the other on a book. In fact, our only moment of danger came from the air. One day a solitary aeroplane appeared out of a clear sky and attempted to drop bombs on us. Standing by our anti-aircraft gun, as it fired back at the plane, I had a strange feeling of detachment as though the action did not concern me. It was quickly over without any damage to either side, the aeroplane flew away, and for the rest of the journey we were left in peace.

The books that I had brought with me were mainly works of philosophy, to which I had paid almost no attention for over three years, since I left Oxford to become a Guardsman recruit. Among them was Kant's *Critique of Pure Reason* which I had never fully understood, though I had been obliged to make some attempt to teach it and had referred to parts of it in my writings. Re-reading it on the boat, I had got as far as the Transcendental Deduction of the Categories, one of the most important sections in the book, but also one of the most obscure, when I had a sudden flash of illumination. It was as if I had entered into Kant's mind and was at last able to appreciate the full force of his argument. Unfortunately I did not make a note of what I thought that I had discovered. Later in the day I came down with sunstroke and was in a high fever for the next twenty-four hours. By the time the fever left me, I had lost my insight into Kant and have never since recaptured it.

I took advantage of this fever to obtain a certificate from the ship's doctor to the effect that my health might not be suited to a tropical climate. With more time for reflection, I had come to consider it more improbable than ever that there would be any work of interest for me to do in Accra, and I thought that if I wanted to get away quickly the certificate might help me. Perhaps I was unconsciously ashamed of this manoeuvre, for when I disembarked at Takoradi I found that I had left the certificate behind on the boat.

On the short drive from Takoradi to Accra, I discovered with pleasure that the scenery of the Gold Coast bore a striking resemblance to the jungle pictures of the *douanier* Rousseau. I am sure that he had never seen it, or possibly anything like it, but he had remarkably captured it in his imagination. It was indeed very much the sort of jungle, complete with monkeys, though not tigers, that a child or a primitive painter would be likely to imagine. Accra itself was a great deal less impressive. Apart from one or two government buildings of no artistic merit, it seemed to consist of a random set of one-storey bungalows, erected on stilts as a precaution against snakes or termites, and principally equipped with mosquito nets and wicker furniture. Its most attractive feature was the local population, dressed in the bright cottons that had brought fortune to Lancashire. The white colony at that time kept mostly to itself, but it employed numerous native servants to whom one was expected to speak in Pidgin English. Apart from such oddities as the use of the expression 'chop chop' for 'quickly', this differed from ordinary English in having a much poorer vocabulary and a minimum of grammar. It could make do with so little because it was employed almost exclusively for the purpose of giving simple orders. I found its use embarrassing and not, in fact, necessary in order to be understood.

My fears that there would be no work of any importance for me to do in Accra proved only too well founded. The original reason for SOE's presence there had been the supposed need for surveillance of the neighbouring French colonies, of which the governors had stayed loyal to Vichy. They were never much of a threat and had ceased to be even a potential source of trouble when the Vichy administration lost its hold on North Africa. Thus, by the time of my arrival, there was not enough work in the office to keep even one person occupied, let alone the half-dozen that we mustered. The colonel who commanded the unit had had a distinguished record in the first world war. It was said that at one stage in his military career he had kept pace with Montgomery. It was therefore particularly hard for him to admit even to himself that the post which he held was one of no importance. When I presented myself to him, he told me that he proposed to make me transport officer. I said that I was possibly not the best choice for this, as I had not learned to drive. 'All the better cover,' he said. 'Cover for what, sir?' I asked, and was told that some other officer would explain that to me.

Nothing more was said about my being transport officer, and I spent the next week in idleness. The conditions were quite agreeable. I liked the other members of the section and found them easy to get on with. One of them was the anthropologist, Meyer Fortes, whom I had known slightly at Oxford. He was probably the happiest among them, in having a field for the pursuit of his professional interests, but the others seemed quite contented with their leisurely way of life. The climate may have been partly responsible for this, since it fostered a feeling of lassitude, though the heat was less great than I had expected. The main social event of the week, at which there was some mingling of the races, was a dance at the King George V Memorial Hall. The most popular dance was the High Life, which may have had a tribal origin. It had all the gusto of the Charleston, and I danced it with enthusiasm, if not with accuracy.

Having brought the books with me, I could have profited by my leisure to resume work on philosophy, but a mixture of pride and guilt prevented me. On the assumption, which I still held, that I ought not to accept detachment from the war, I felt that some better use could be made of my abilities. I therefore went to the colonel and said that since there seemed to be nothing for me to do in Accra, I should be grateful if he would arrange to send me home as soon as possible. He agreed to my request, having indeed already sent a message to London to say that he was not finding me co-operative. Fearing, however, that my example would breed disaffection if I remained any longer with his other officers, he interned me in a neighbouring camp of gold-miners, to wait for the next ship. He also had decided, or been instructed, to return to London, probably to discuss his own position, but he travelled by air. I forget whether the aeroplane met with an accident or was brought down by enemy action, but in either event he was killed.

In the few days that I spent at the gold-miners' camp, I passed much of the time playing poker and vingt-et-un. I am not at all good at either of these games, but the mining engineers showed so little regard for the calculus of probability that even without being particularly favoured by the cards I won a considerable amount of money from them. By the time that the ship came to take me away, they were looking at me a little bit askance. It happened, however, that most of the other players were themselves going back on leave and in the course of the voyage, which was otherwise uneventful, I managed through a combination of bad hands and reckless bidding to return most of the money to them.

When I reported back to Baker Street, I was mildly reproached for my behaviour in Accra and told that I had been posted to one of the French sections, which were under the overall command of my old schoolfellow Robin Brook. There were, in fact, two principal French sections, one headed by Colonel Buckmaster, which was chiefly concerned with training and dispatching British agents to organize resistance groups in France, and the other headed by Colonel Hutchison, which maintained what were sometimes stormy relations with its Gaullist counterpart in London, and helped to serve the needs of the indigenous forces of resistance. I was put to work in Colonel Hutchison's section under the immediate authority of Major Dismore, a journalist who had worked before the war as sub-editor on the Paris *Daily Mail*. He was calm, conscientious, and unobstrusively efficient. I shared an office with the novelist Bruce Marshall, who was old enough to have fought in the first world war, in which he had lost a leg. A Scottish puritan, he was inclined to disapprove of what he regarded as my hedonism, but otherwise we got on pretty well. The only one of his novels that I can remember reading was a hair-raising account of what I took to be his own experiences at a tough public-school in Scotland in the early part of the century. Later he was to write a successful book called *The White Rabbit* about the exploits of Wing-Commander Yeo-Thomas, a director of the fashion house of Molyneux before the war, who was one of the most resourceful and courageous agents that we sent to France. It was Yeo-Thomas who received me when I first reported to the section. Though we normally wore uniform in the office, I was then in plain clothes and not having been advised of my arrival he was suspicious of me. He pretended to be a Frenchman and, thinking that my French was being tested, I did the same, until the misunderstanding was cleared up. I never got to know him very well, but I shared Bruce Marshall's admiration for him.

My duties mainly consisted in reading and analysing the wireless messages, reports and other documents that were constantly reaching us from France. I learned to distinguish the seven or eight principal resistance movements, with their different political affiliations and their respective areas of influence. The fact that they had to work in secret kept their numbers relatively small, though they had gained strength through the recruitment of the many young men who went into hiding rather than be drafted to work in Germany. The word *maquis*, which originally referred to the Corsican brushwood, was applied first to the hilly parts of the country in which these men took refuge and then collectively to the men themselves. Its incorrect use, in the English press, to refer to the whole of the resistance, reflected the publicity which the *maquis* received, in contrast to other groups which were better organized for gathering intelligence or carrying out sabotage. Not that these other groups were always sufficiently clandestine. The serious losses which they suffered were due not only to the risks which were inseparable from their activities, but also to an insufficient regard for security. Here an exception should be made for the communists, who joined the resistance in force after the German invasion of Russia. Their method of operating in small cells, with the contacts required for the transmission of orders reduced to a minimum, ensured that if a unit was penetrated or betrayed, or one of its members gave way under torture, there was relatively little information that the enemy could gain. The groups which were organized by agents sent from England were also more vulnerable, in that they needed to keep in touch with London by wireless to arrange among other things for the delivery by parachute of arms and supplies, and their wireless operators ran a considerable risk of being detected. The communist groups themselves came to depend on these deliveries, in addition to what they could capture from the Germans, but they obtained them indirectly.

In the autumn of 1943 the allegiance of the forces of resistance within France was not yet fully accorded to de Gaulle, but he was in the process of acquiring it, just as he succeeded in defeating General Giraud in the contest for the leadership of the French forces in North Africa, in spite of Giraud's having strong American support. Earlier in the year the attempt to unify the internal resistance under de Gaulle's titular leadership had met with a set-back when Jean Moulin, who was both de Gaulle's chief delegate in France and the head of the *Conseil National de la Résistance*, was captured at a meeting of the *Conseil* in the suburbs of Lyons. Jean Moulin died under torture without revealing any secrets, but his loss and that of the other resistance leaders who were captured with him brought about a temporary crisis. New delegates were sent out by de Gaulle, but they no longer formed part of the *Conseil National de la Résistance*, which was reconstituted, with representatives from all the main resistance groups, under the chairmanship of Georges Bidault, a member of the Catholic *Mouvement Républicain Populaire* and subsequently Foreign Minister in de Gaulle's first post-war government. The new national *Conseil* held only one formal meeting before the Liberation, but there was some communication between its members, and though it acted autonomously, its acceptance of de Gaulle as the overall leader of the resistance very much strengthened his position.

While it was increasingly probable that de Gaulle would be at the head of the first régime in France to result from the country's recovery of its independence, it was much harder to predict what political form the régime would take. This question was of growing interest to the internal resistance movements and a considerable quantity of the material that reached me related to it. There was a widespread agreement that there should not be a simple return to the institutions of the Third Republic, but no very clear idea what should replace them. Since most of the old political parties were thought to have been discredited by the conduct of many of their representatives both before and during the war, there was a hope in various quarters that the resistance movements would survive as political organizations and that some coalition of them would assume the government of France. In fact, this hope was very largely vain. One of the most remarkable features of post-war French politics was the rapidity with which the old political parties recovered their position, appearing, like the Bourbons, to have learned and forgotten nothing, and when a Gaullist party eventually came into being, it was far from reflecting the whole spectrum of the resistance.

Though I occupied too humble a position in the office to have any say in the policy of SOE, and though I had nothing to do with the dispatching of its agents to France, or their maintenance in the field, I found my work interesting and did it diligently enough to earn a somewhat belated promotion to the rank of captain in September 1943, almost three years to the day since I had first been commissioned. The problem of finding somewhere to live in London was solved for me by Kathleen McColgan, who had once served as a secretary to Wilfrid Roberts, a Liberal member of Parliament. He lived in a flat in the neighbourhood of the House of Commons, and she persuaded him to accept me as a lodger. I had not met him before but was already disposed to like him because of his active opposition to the policy of the Chamberlain Government during the Spanish Civil War. He represented a constituency in Cumberland with which he had family connections, and when he lost his parliamentary seat in the election of 1950 he devoted himself to the management of his property. He was ten years older than I, very tall, unmistakably English, quiet, with an undercurrent of strong feeling, cultivated and philanthropic. He accepted my presence with good grace, and since I was at work during the day and often out in the evenings, I did not intrude too much upon him. With a housekeeper to take care of us, we got on very well.

Except for my pieces of film criticism, I had published nothing in the last three years, but after I had settled down to my work in Baker Street, I found time to write an article on 'The Concept of Political Freedom', which Cyril Connolly accepted for *Horizon*. In spite of its title, it was not concerned with matters of self-government so much as with the possibility of measuring freedom in terms of the proportion of one's desires that one was able to satisfy. I think that it had some merit, though there were many questions that it left unanswered. I was anyhow pleased to discover that I had not entirely lost my capacity for abstract thought.

Early in 1944 I volunteered for a mission which would have meant my being parachuted into France. I was provisionally accepted, but before I even started my course of training, the project was cancelled, not altogether to my regret. I was not so much afraid of being killed as of being captured and tortured. One was provided with a pill of cyanide, but this in itself presented a problem. It would be cowardly and foolish to take it if there was any likelihood of one's not being gravely suspect, or thought to possess information of any serious importance, but if one was thoroughly searched, and the pill found in one's possession, it would be evidence that one had something to tell. Worries of this sort would probably have made me an unsatisfactory agent, and I dare say that I should have shown myself in training to be unsuitable in other ways. I was, however, sorry not to have been given at least the opportunity to learn to parachute. If I had needed consolation for being deprived of this adventure, it came in March 1944 in the much less dramatic form of a mission to Algiers. The reason for my going there was that I was thought to have become an expert on French politics and

Algiers, which then counted as a part of France, had become de Gaulle's headquarters. He was still not recognized by the Allied powers as the head of the French Government, but this had not prevented him from setting up an administration with an Assembly which to some extent functioned as a Parliament. My duties were to be substantially those of a political correspondent. To improve my standing with the French politicians and officials whom I should need to meet, I was given the rank of local major.

SOE maintained a station, just outside Algiers, under the command of Colonel Douglas Dodds-Parker, a Guards Officer who had been in the Colonial service before the war and was later to become a Conservative member of Parliament. He was in England on leave when I arrived, and I reported to Brooks Richards, a young naval officer who was responsible for the dispatch of agents from Algiers into the southern parts of France, having previously himself been engaged in the hazardous work of transporting them by sea. I quickly made friends with Brooks and with his assistant Barley Alison, a small, dark, intelligent, vivacious girl, who like the other women working in this branch of SOE was misleadingly enrolled in the First Aid Nursing Yeomanry. My reception from Dodds-Parker when he returned from England was not so cordial. He may have held it against me that I had been sent out to do a job which he regarded as unnecessary, in so far as it was not already being done by himself and his staff, and he also did not care for my looks, partly, as Barley told me, because my military bearing had by this time ceased to have very much resemblance to that of a typical officer in the Brigade of Guards. This was not a charge that could be brought against him, and I judged from his manner that there were very few subjects on which our opinions were not likely to be at variance. We were, therefore, both content to see as little as possible of one another.

This was made easier by the fact that I lived in the centre of Algiers itself, in an apartment on which SOE had taken a lease. At the beginning I shared it with a young psychoanalyst, who was employed to determine whether prospective agents were psychologically suited to the work. We used to have breakfast together and I noticed that he displayed some excitement when I nibbled the ends of the long French rolls which were supplied to us. When I remarked on this, he asked me whether I realized that I had a castration complex. He may have been right, but I thought that he was judging on rather slender evidence. I felt more at ease when his work took him away and I had the apartment to myself.

I spent two months in Algiers and enjoyed them very much. The situation of the town was beautiful, though I did not think that the best had been made of it. The Arab population seemed withdrawn and listless, by contrast with the bustle of the French. De Gaulle was in the process of coming to terms with the communists, and the debates in the Assembly and the intrigues that went on outside it were fascinating to follow. I did not get to meet any of the leading politicians but I frequented several of the second rank and obtained some useful information from them. As so often in the war, I also found myself among old friends. One of them was Bill Deakin, who had risen to the rank of colonel and been awarded the DSO for his exploits in Jugoslavia, having shared the bad and good fortunes of Tito's partisans. He had been brought out to make way for Fitzroy Maclean's mission, which included Evelyn Waugh and Randolph Churchill. I had lost contact with Randolph since we were undergraduates and enjoyed seeing him again in Algiers, though he was inclined to be scornful of me as a warrior. Two Welsh Guards Officers whom I was also pleased to find there were Richard Llewellyn Lloyd, whom I had not seen since I left the Training Battalion, and John Follett, a coolly elegant figure and a bridge-player of international standing, who had been with me at London District Headquarters and was also attached to SOE. I remember an evening which he, Bill Deakin and I proposed to round off by visiting the Kasbah, the Arab quarter of Algiers, which was technically out of bounds to us, when we were foiled by an air-raid warning which plunged the whole town dramatically into darkness. I had a romantic view of the Kasbah, derived from films like *Pépé le Moko*, which probably would not have survived an actual visit. I was also with Bill and Richard Lloyd, having drinks on the terrace of a café, when Marlene Dietrich made a sudden appearance, posing for photographers not many yards away from us. I remembered that she knew the Hofmannsthals and had the idea of claiming to have met her with them and inviting her to join us, but my courage failed me. Richard Lloyd was more impressed by Bill, not previously having met him and finding it extraordinary that a decorated colonel should look so young.

It was in Algiers that I first met Malcolm Muggeridge, who was serving in one of the other branches of intelligence. Our acquaintance then was slight but it later developed into something approaching friendship. I came to like him for his moral courage, his kindness in private and his acerbity in print. Unhappily, his transformation into a religious zealot has put an end to any show of friendliness between us. In personal relations, I have usually found religion to be less divisive than politics, but for all my dislike of the party which he led, I have never lost my respect for Harold Macmillan or failed to find pleasure in his company. He was Minister-Resident in Algiers for the British Government and I renewed an acquaintance with him which I originally owed to his having become my publisher. Even politically, I was disposed to think well of him, as he had been one of the few Conservatives to show dislike not only for the feebleness of the Baldwin and Chamberlain Governments' foreign policy, but also for their domestic harshness and philistinism.

I travelled back from Algiers with the members of an ENSA company, which included Hermione Baddeley and Robert Harris, both of whom I came to like in the short time that we spent together. Our aeroplane was grounded for several days at Rabat, where I thought the French colonial city, with its gleaming white buildings, a great improvement on its old Moroccan neighbour. This impression was confirmed when I returned to Rabat to lecture many years later. A point which struck me then was the extent to which the French had imposed their culture upon the educated Moroccans, unlike the British in Africa who behaved like the masters at a public school, keeping strict order but otherwise leaving their charges to their own devices.

When I got back to London, thereby reverting to the rank of captain, I resumed my work in the office which grew in interest as the forces of the French Resistance made their preparations for D-day. Their military commander, whom I knew only by the pseudonym of Arc, was Chaban-Delmas, later to be Prime Minister under Pompidou and to be robbed of the succession by the more bureaucratic Giscard d'Estaing. How much the resistance contributed to the success of the Allied campaign in Normandy is difficult to assess. It was probably not an essential factor, but by sabotaging communications and drawing off German forces, it did help the Allies to achieve their victories more quickly and at a smaller cost.

In the weeks following the Normandy landings, some of the senior members of the French sections in Baker Street themselves went to France: those of us who were left behind in the office found little work to do. There was a possibility of my being attached to General Patton's army as a liaison officer with the French. When this came to nothing, I managed to persuade my superiors to let me return to Algiers. Restored to the rank of local major, I arrived there in the middle of July. At that time preparations were being made for the landing on the Riviera, mainly by French and American troops, which took place on August 15th. With Paris about to be liberated and Patton's army advancing towards Germany, it is arguable that there was no military necessity for this second invasion of France, but it was important for the morale of the French that the army which they had assembled in North Africa should be allowed to take part in the liberation of their country. The German hold upon the south of France was relatively weak and was made weaker still by the activity of the French internal resistance. The result was that within a few days of its landing the Allied army had advanced a considerable distance up the valley of the Rhône.

SOE played its part in this operation by sending in parachutists before the landing. Two of them whom I encountered in Algiers were Xan Fielding, a friend of Paddy Leigh-Fermor's, who also won the DSO and later developed into a writer, and Julian, better known to his friends as 'Lizzie', Lezard. I met them both again some years after the war and Lizzie Lezard soon became one of my closest friends. A South African by birth, he had been a tennis blue at Cambridge and I remembered having seen him play in the tennis tournaments at Eastbourne. Primarily a doubles player, he used to partner an American called Van Allen, and I believe that they once reached the final, or at least the semi-final, of the Wimbledon championship. Lizzie was heavily built for a tennis player but strong and agile, though in later years he ran to fat. He must have been well into his thirties when I first met him. He was an inveterate gambler and was for this strange reason parachuted into the neighbourhood of Monte Carlo. He broke his leg on landing but fell into friendly hands and escaped capture. After the war he continued to be known as Captain Lezard. He had been married, and was very attractive to women, but when I knew him he lived alone. He had just enough money not to have to work and led a strenuous social life, showing great attachment to his numerous friends whom he used to telephone at all hours of the day just for the pleasure of conversing with them. He was shrewd, perceptive, generous and vulnerable, and I can think of very few people who did not take pleasure in his company. He shared my interest in games and we used often to go to cricket and football matches together. It is now nearly twenty years since he died from the shock of an operation, which was not expected to be serious, and I still miss him very much.

One person who was not at all pleased to find me back in Algiers was Colonel Dodds-Parker. He allowed me the use of the same apartment but made it clear that he saw less reason than ever for my being there. He was not altogether wrong about this, since the political situation had grown more stable and apart from military matters, which were not my concern, there was little for me to report. I continued to cultivate the French, but this time less for business than for pleasure. Most of my friends in SOE were scheduled to go to France shortly after the first landings, but to my regret there was no question of my going with them. Instead, Dodds-Parker took me with him on a flight to Italy, drove with me from Naples to Ravello, a pretty holiday town overlooking the gulf of Salerno, installed me in a handsome villa, which its absent English owners had left at the disposition of officers on leave, and drove away again, saying that so far as he was concerned I was welcome to stay in Ravello until the end of the war.

The villa was well-appointed. There were two other officers there to keep me company and servants to take care of us. There was even a good supply of books, including Whitehead's *Process and Reality*, which I then read for the first time, finding it obscure but having enough respect for Whitehead to think there was probably more to it than I understood. Altogether it was a very comfortable place in which to be marooned. In time, my superiors in London, with whom I had no means of communicating, might start to wonder what had become of me, but my disappearance would be covered by Dodds-Parker's action. Indeed, it was arguably my duty to remain in Ravello until further orders.

In fact, I never had any serious intention of doing so. Ravello might be a more agreeable place than Accra in which to opt out of the war, but to remain there indefinitely would be not only ignoble but ridiculous. I did stay in the villa for about a week, but then I walked out and managed to hitch-hike back to Naples, where I persuaded some military authority to put me on the first plane to Algiers. The proper course then would have been for me to return to London, since my mission to Algiers had evidently been completed, but my escape from Ravello had unleashed my spirit of adventure, and coming across a friendly major who had been left behind at SOE headquarters, I got him to give me a movement order which empowered me to go to France. There was still the problem of getting there, since seats on military aeroplanes were then not easily available, but I was able to convince some transport officer that my presence in France was urgently needed, and very soon afterwards was flown into St Tropez. At that time, St Tropez was still a small town, attracting relatively few tourists in the years before the war. I had visited it thirteen years earlier, when Renée and I were staying in St Raphael, and I spent the evening of my arrival wandering alone along the almost deserted waterfront, thinking nostalgically of the past.

The next day I got a lift in a truck which was going up towards the front. By this time the fighting had reached the outskirts of Lyons and at General Headquarters, some way behind the field of battle, I located the representatives of SOE. Fortunately, Colonel Dodds-Parker was not with them. Reporting to Brooks Richards, I obtained his sanction to remain in France and was given a roving commission to tour the liberated areas with the principal object of making an assessment of the political situation. This would involve my trying to determine how far the local prefects whom de Gaulle had appointed were succeeding in establishing their authority, what were the political attitudes of the different resistance groups, what was the extent of the reprisals that were being taken against former collaborators with the Germans, and in general how the transition was being made to a new civil order. With another SOE officer, who was responsible for seeing what had happened to our agents, and an officer from the French Intelligence Services, with whom I had made friends in Algiers, I immediately set off for Marseilles.

Having quite recently been liberated, Marseilles was in a state of effervescence. There was still some sporadic shooting in the streets, but it seemed to be due more to the enthusiasm of the members of the French Forces of the Interior, who had joined in large numbers after the Allied landing, than to any attempt on the part of German sympathizers to make a final stand. There were no signs that de Gaulle's representatives would have much difficulty in assuming control. After spending a few days in Marseilles, we journeyed westwards to Toulouse, stopping at a number of small towns on the way. In some places we were the first British officers that the inhabitants had seen since the first year of the war and the warmth of their welcome, which was expressed mainly in the form of offering us food and drink, was made only slightly less enjoyable by our being conscious that we had done little to deserve it.

The resistance forces in the area of Toulouse, which had helped to speed the German withdrawal, were led by men of strong personality, including the writer André Malraux, who had served in the Republican Air Force in the Spanish Civil War, and had in other ways shown his political sympathy with the left, though he was later to become one of the most fervent supporters of de Gaulle. Their overall command had been rather surprisingly entrusted to an Englishman, Colonel George Starr, a Buckmaster agent previously known to me by his pseudonym of Hilaire, who had spent over two years in the region, courageously and efficiently building up his resistance organization, and had acquired a devoted local following. He had received the command from the French General Koenig who, while still in North Africa, had been put in titular authority over the French Forces of the Interior. The civilian prefect, appointed by de Gaulle, was Pierre Bertaux, who had been in Toulouse before the war as a Professor of German at the University. He was a capable administrator and for a period shortly after the war enjoyed a stormy career as head of the Paris Sûreté, with responsibility for the police, before returning to his academic pursuits.

When I arrived in Toulouse at the beginning of September the town was quiet, though Starr regarded himself as responsible to General Koenig and the Allied High Command rather than to Bertaux, and the members of the principal resistance groups showed greater loyalty to their own leaders than to any central authority. They also seemed reluctant to return to the comparatively humdrum routine of an ordered civilian life. Some of them were revolutionary in spirit, but did not appear to be making any plans for concerted political action. I called on Pierre Bertaux, with whom I subsequently became friends, and gained the impression that while he was aware of the factors that might make for local disorder, he did not see them as posing a serious threat to his position.

I was in Toulouse on September 16 when de Gaulle arrived to receive the homage of the city. Accompanied by André Diethelm, whom he had appointed Minister for War, he was making a tour of the principal French cities, as a means of solidifying his authority. A lunch was arranged in his honour to which George Starr among others was invited. However, when Pierre Bertaux, not finding the General easy to converse with, told him what he meant to be no more than a mildly amusing story of Starr's disposition to stand on his dignity as local military commander, de Gaulle flew into a rage, cancelled Starr's invitation to the lunch, summoned him into his presence and gave him forty-eight hours to leave the country. When Starr replied that he took his orders not from de Gaulle but from the Allied High Command, he was threatened with arrest. The fulfilment of this threat would not have added to de Gaulle's popularity in Toulouse, even if he had been in a position to execute it, and the interview ended with the two men shaking hands. Even so, it was thought advisable that Starr should return to England, though he allowed himself to exceed de Gaulle's time-limit by a week. Some amends were later made to him by his being awarded the Légion d'Honneur and the Croix de Guerre, in addition to his English decorations of the DSO and the MC. What made de Gaulle so angry, as he relates in his memoirs, was the fact that a British officer should still be exercising direct command over French troops.

A similar incident occurred the next day in Bordeaux, when Roger Landes, whom I knew as Aristide, was given only two hours to leave the country, and two of his principal French lieutenants were threatened with arrest. The news of this actually provoked a demonstration against de Gaulle, and Landes, who did leave Bordeaux but remained in the neighbourhood for another three weeks, considered leading his men against the city. When I arrived there a day or two later, one of the two Frenchmen whom de Gaulle had threatened came to me in distress and anger and I had to persuade him of the folly of Landes's plan. It was perhaps understandable that de Gaulle should see the influence which some British agents had acquired in their districts as a threat to his authority, though they had certainly not been sent out with any such political motives, but he might have behaved more graciously to men who had risked torture and death in what was effectively his cause. I did not meet him on either occasion, though on Starr's instructions I took part in his victory parade in Toulouse.

By this time I had detached myself from the SOE officer with whom I started on my travels and joined forces with a captain from another intelligence unit whom I had first met in Algiers. When he left the region, I inherited from him a large Bugatti, together with its chauffeur, Aristier, a burly taciturn peasant of middle age, who seemed anxious to prolong his absence from his family. On my own account, I recruited a bodyguard and a wireless operator. I did not have any obvious need for either of them, but thought it just possible that they might be useful. From time to time one or two other persons attached themselves to me for one reason or another. We went up to La Rochelle, which was the only city in the west of France that the Germans still occupied. A detachment of the FFI was besieging them but lacked the materials to storm their strong position. I believe that the garrison held out until the final German surrender.

Oscillating between Toulouse and Bordeaux, I also toured the Pyrenees. There was a rumour that German sympathizers were taking refuge in Andorra, and with another SOE officer who had remained in Toulouse, I went there to investigate. We did not go so far as to adopt false identities, but travelled in plain clothes. We called on the Mayor, from whom we learned nothing of interest, but had the pleasure of presiding with him at a local football match. While we were in Andorra one of our retinue disappeared and I had the uneasy feeling that I might actually have helped a collaborator to escape. The reprisals taken against the collaborators in the south-west did not appear so savage or extensive as they were said to be in some other parts of France, though one saw a few women, who had been denounced for being too friendly with the Germans, going about with shaven heads.

Quite a large part in the local resistance had been played by Spaniards, who had taken refuge in France when the Republican cause was lost in the Civil War. They understandably hoped that the overthrow of Hitler and Mussolini would be followed by that of Franco and looked to the Allies for some assistance. I was naturally sympathetic to their aims but was not sure how far my superiors would approve of my becoming involved in their plans. I therefore made use of my wireless operator to send a message to Baker Street, asking for instructions. It was the first indication that I had given the head office of my whereabouts since I had left for Algiers more than two months earlier. The response was a message sent to SOE officers in the region, ordering them to detain Major Ayer and dispatch him back to London. I learned of this through a friend, who was willing to forget that he had seen me, but strongly advised me at least to go to Paris, if only to protect Brooks Richards who had taken the responsibility for my being in France. By that time Brooks, who was to join the Foreign Office, was working under Duff Cooper at the Paris Embassy. Accordingly, I disbanded my troupe and having discovered that some friends of mine in the French Intelligence Service were going to Paris, I travelled up with them.

When I reported to Brooks, he said that he could not cover me any longer and that I would have to fly back to London within two days. Not knowing whether I was in serious trouble, I thought it prudent to take out some insurance, and on my last night in Paris, after going out on the town with some of my friends from Toulouse, I stayed up till morning writing my report, which I handed in at the Embassy before I left. In my attempt to make it interesting, I somewhat over-dramatized the activities of the rival factions in Gascony, and thereby misled Duff Cooper into thinking that I believed them to be of greater political significance than I actually did.

My report, to which Brooks Richards added some comments of his own, was sent to London in the first week of October and apparently remains in the Foreign Office archives. It is briefly referred to by Mr M. R. D. Foot in his admirable history of *S.O.E. in France*. Mr Foot also mentions his discovery of a Foreign Office file of about this date with the title 'No job for Freddie Ayer'. Since he says that this was not a declaration of policy, I think that it may have been a comment on the position which I held in SOE. This is borne out by the fact that when I presented myself at Baker Street, to receive a mild rebuke for leaving them so long without news of me, I was told that they had designated me for a job in France, which would have brought me a step in rank, but had been over-ridden by the Foreign Office, which had claimed me for one of its own Intelligence Departments. This department cared nothing for military distinctions, so that, having automatically ceased to be a local major, I changed my rank only for the worse. For all practical purposes I reverted to being a civilian, and most often wore civilian clothes. I spent two months doing office work under the tutelage of Nigel Clive, whom I had already known and liked when he was an undergraduate at Oxford just before the war, and then in January 1945 returned to Paris as an attaché at the British Embassy.

In the meantime, my academic future had been made secure by my election to a tutorial Fellowship at Wadham. Ian Gallie's health had declined to the point of his having to resign his Fellowship and I was chosen to replace him. I heard later that Professor Lindemann had expressed some qualms, not about my ability to teach philosophy but about my holding left-wing views in politics, and that Maurice Bowra had reassured him by saying, not altogether truly, that I had very largely outgrown them.

I was already disposed to resume work on philosophy and had found time in London to write a fairly long article on 'The Terminology of Sense-data' which Moore accepted for *Mind* and published in the autumn issue of 1945. The article mainly arose out of my reading of Moore's own reply to his critics in the volume on *The Philosophy of G. E. Moore* which had appeared in the series of *Library of Living Philosophers* in 1942. I tried to show that the question, which continued to puzzle Moore, whether sense-data could ever be identical with parts of the surfaces of physical objects, could be settled only by fixing the usage of the technical term 'sense-datum'; that Moore himself had not sufficiently explained his usage of the term, but that from such explanations as he had given it clearly followed that the identification was not logically possible. The view that I took of the status of sense-data was one that I had already advanced in *The Foundations of Empirical Knowledge*. In the course of his friendly appraisal of the book in *Mind*, Henry Price had raised some objections to my proposal that sense-data should not be credited with having any properties that they did not appear to have, and I concluded my article with an attempt to answer him. The article might now be thought to suffer from its unquestioning acceptance of the role of sense-data in the theory of perception, but I still think that it contained some good argument.

I had been continuing to see Guy de Rothschild in London, and when he heard that I was going to work in Paris, he offered me the use of his house in the Avenue Foch. With servants to take care of me, I lived there very comfortably for two or three months, staying on for a short time after Guy's own return to Paris. I then moved into a room in the Hotel Castiglione, which the British Embassy had commandeered for its staff. I did quite a lot of entertaining while I was living in the Avenue Foch, and I also made considerable use of Maxim's, which had been turned into a club for British officers. There were still some food shortages in Paris, and the restaurant had not yet recovered its luxurious standard, but we were very well supplied with wines and liqueurs at controlled prices which were almost ridiculously low. I developed a taste for Verveine, which, like my undergraduate enthusiasm for Sauternes, I have never since been able to recapture.

I worked, with a secretary, in a room of my own in a remote corner of the Embassy. There was not a great deal for me to do. I compiled a card index of the leading characters in French official life, bequeathing it to the Embassy when I left. I heard later that it was thought to be inaccurate. I wrote a report on the current state of French politics, in which I compared de Gaulle to Pétain, and annoyed Duff Cooper by sending it straight to London instead of showing it first to him. I attended the weekly meetings which Duff Cooper held with his staff but seldom contributed much to the discussion. Though my relations with him were distant, I rather liked Duff Cooper. He had a violent temper and could be very rude when he was angry, but he was intelligent and courageous and there was nothing of the outlook of the petty shop-keeper in his old-fashioned Conservatism. It was some time before Lady Diana was aware of my presence in the Embassy, but I then took a modest place in her social circle. If I was a little lax in my attendance at Embassy parties, it was not that I did not enjoy them, but that I often had other engagements. In the earlier part of my stay in Paris I spent most of my time with a French girl of Turkish origin whom I had got to know in Algiers. She was employed by one of the French Intelligence Services, but when we were together we put our work aside.

I had many friends in the Embassy itself. Barley Alison was there as well as Brooks Richards. Charles Whitney-Smith was working in the Press Department and outdid me, if not in the pursuit of pleasure, at least in the capacity to dispense with sleep. The head of Chancery was Patrick Reilly, whose mastery of his profession made me think it understandable that All Souls had preferred him to me. Paul Willert was the air attaché. He had an attractive apartment in the Place Dauphine, which he had acquired before the war, and his remarkable gifts as a host were displayed there as fully as they had been in London. I am sufficiently stage-struck still to remember one of his parties as the occasion of my only meeting with Noel Coward. The enchanting Yvonne Printemps was there as well, with her husband Pierre Fresnay, whose career was temporarily threatened because of his acting in a film, made under the Occupation, which was thought to have shown his countrymen in an unfavourable light. A similar cloud hung over Jean Cocteau, who was reproached for admitting Germans to his friendship. No action was taken against him, but it took a little time for him to recover his prestige. On the evening when I saw him at the Embassy, he seemed unsure of himself and did not sparkle. I was more impressed by Louis Jouvet, who was the lion of one of the *salons* that were again becoming a feature of Parisian society. With his sonorous voice and measured gestures, he carried into private life the atmosphere of the Comédie Française. I felt in his presence as though I were playing the part of an extra in one of the many films in which I had seen him. Though I was fascinated by his performance, I preferred the company of Gabrielle D'Orziat, an actress of an older generation, who was almost equally prominent in the French theatre of the time. She was witty and wise and differed from nearly all the theatrical people that I have known by her readiness to converse on subjects other than the stage.

It was through Paul Willert that I met Francette Drin and her older sister, Nicole Bouchet de Fareins, who together with their brother Jean Joba have been my friends ever since. They had been active in the resistance, which had cost Francette's husband his life when the Germans captured him. Paul brought them to lunch with me in the Avenue Foch, and from then on I was often in their company. Besides seeing them in Paris, I used to stay in Normandy in a house belonging to Nicole. Part of my book *The Problem of Knowledge* was written there ten years later. I used to work on it out of doors, alarming the gardener who thought I must be mad, as he watched me walking up and down, juggling a watch-chain and talking to myself.

I wanted to meet André Malraux, whose novel *La Condition Humaine* had made a strong impression on me, and Francette arranged a dinner party for the purpose to which she also invited Camus, whose work I had just discovered, and Solly Zuckerman, who was then passing through Paris. Solly had played an important part in the war mainly as a scientific expert on the effects of bombing and had been given some high rank in the Air Force. The party was not a success because we were all three of us intimidated by Malraux. I do not suppose that he meant to be disdainful, but he had a habit of sniffing which produced this effect. He also gave the impression of having little regard for anyone who had not been an active combatant in the war. It was only after his early departure that our tongues were loosened, and we then vied with one another in a display of intelligence which we were ashamed of not having shown to him. I happened to see him the next day at a party of Paul Willert's, but while the amount that he had had to drink made him more approachable, it also prevented me from trying to develop our acquaintance.

Although Francette's party failed in its main object, it did have the happy result for me of my making friends with Camus. As is obvious from his writing, he was a man of great integrity and moral courage, with a keen intelligence, allied to good looks, modesty and charm. I shared the general enthusiasm for his novel *L'Etranger*, which was translated into English as *The Outsider*, and admired the intellectual content of his plays, *Le Malentendu* and *Caligula*. Not long after meeting him, I saw *Caligula* performed in Paris, with Gérard Philippe in the leading part. I was greatly impressed by Gérard Philippe's acting but a little disappointed in the play, which had seemed to me better when I read it. From a dramatic point of view, I thought it inferior to Sartre's *Huis Clos*, which I also saw during this period in Paris. On the other hand, I greatly preferred Camus's semi-philosophical essay *Le Mythe de Sisyphe* to Sartre's very much longer and more pretentious metaphysical treatise *L'Être et le Néant*. This came out in the articles on Sartre and Camus which I contributed to *Horizon*, in the course of the year, the one on Sartre appearing in two parts. Though I was critical of some of the philosophical implications of *Le Mythe de Sisyphe*, my treatment of Camus's work was generally sympathetic, whereas I dealt very harshly with Sartre's metaphysics, finding nothing to praise in *L'Être et le Néant* except a few psychological insights and concluding that Existentialism, on this evidence, was principally an exercise in the art of misusing the verb 'to be'. My articles were read by both their subjects, with the result that Camus demurred only to my having described him as a teacher of philosophy in his youth in Algiers, when he had in fact been a professional footballer, while Sartre was greatly offended, complaining, not wholly without reason, that my attack on him was unfair since *'je ne me place pas au point de vue de la logique.'* Olivier Todd, who had read philosophy at Cambridge, tried to bring us together but Sartre refused to meet me, saying that in his opinion, *'Ayer n'est pas très fort.'* Nor was he conciliated by the reply that I took the same view of him. In saying this, Olivier went rather too far, since there was much that I admired in Sartre's writing, as distinct from his philosophy, but even if this had been told to Sartre, I think it unlikely that he would have been mollified.

I did, however, make friends with Maurice Merleau-Ponty, who at that time stood very close to Sartre. They were both inclined to ally themselves with the communists on the dubious *a priori* ground that whatever their actual policies might be, the Communist parties represented the interests of the working class, and were consequently on the side of history. It was largely in this spirit that they conducted their new left-wing review *Les Temps Modernes*. Philosophically, Merleau-Ponty was more of a Phenomenologist than an Existentialist and his book *La Phénoménologie de la Perception*, which I later arranged to be translated into English for a series which I edited, has always struck me as one of the best productions of this school. The German philosopher Edward Husserl was the originator of it, just as Husserl's pupil and supplanter Martin Heidegger was the immediate source of French Existentialism, many passages of Sartre's *L'Être et le Néant* being little more than transcriptions of passages of Heidegger's *Sein und Zeit*. Its continual subservience to German masters is indeed the most striking feature of contemporary French philosophy. Existentialism has now gone out of fashion but a revival in interest in the philosophy of Hegel has very largely taken its place.

Though it is often conducted in terms of which it is difficult to make much sense, the investigation of concepts by Husserl and his followers bears some affinity to the sort of conceptual analysis that G. E. Moore engaged in, and it might therefore have been expected that Merleau-Ponty and I should find some common ground for philosophical discussion. We did indeed attempt it on several occasions, but we never got very far before we began to wrangle over some point of principle, on which neither of us would yield. Since these arguments tended to become acrimonious, we tacitly agreed to drop them and meet on a purely social level, which still left us quite enough to talk about. Under any conditions, his vitality and the breadth of his intellectual interests made him stimulating company. In later years, when he had achieved the honour of becoming a Professor at the Collège de France, I think that his work may have suffered from too little local criticism, but his relatively early death was still a serious loss to French philosophy.

Paris in 1945 attracted many English visitors on one pretext or another. Mr Attlee came to the Embassy, some time before the General Election brought him to power, but had little to say to the Duff Coopers or indeed to anyone else. Laurence Olivier, who came with a theatrical company and enjoyed a great success with his Parisian audience, showed a similar modesty at the party which was given for him. I was struck by this as I had been prepared for another Louis Jouvet. Among my own friends, Tony Bower appeared as an American soldier, Lee Miller as a photographer in the uniform of a war correspondent, and Philip Toynbee as an Officer in the Intelligence Corps.

Philip had reached Paris soon after the Liberation and at once made for the Café des Deux Magots, knowing instinctively that St Germain des Près was going to replace Montmartre. Stephen Spender, who had done his war service in the London Fire Brigade, also came over on some literary mission. It was through Stephen that I met Jacques Legris, who soon became one of my closest friends. He was a few years younger than I, had served in the Free French forces and was employed in some department of the Radio-diffusion Française. At our first meeting, he mistook me for a Frenchman and when he heard me converse with Stephen was surprised at my command of English. He reminded me a little of David Hedley, though he was more interested in women, more worldly wise and less intense.

Another new friend that I made at this time in Paris was George Orwell, who was then a foreign correspondent for the *Observer*. He had been in College at Eton in the same election as Cyril Connolly, but had left before I came there. I first heard of him in 1937 when he published *The Road to Wigan Pier* for Gollancz's Left Book Club. By the time that I met him in Paris, I had also read two of his other autobiographical books, *Homage to Catalonia* and *Down and Out in Paris and London*, and greatly admired them both. Though I came to know him well enough for him to describe me as a great friend of his in a letter written to one of our former Eton masters in April 1946, he was not very communicative to me about himself. For instance, he never spoke to me about his wife, Eileen O'Shaughnessy, whose death in March 1945 left him in charge of their adopted son, who was still under a year old. I had assumed that it was simply through poverty that he had acquired the material for his book *Down and Out in Paris and London* by working as a dish-washer in

Paris restaurants and living as a tramp in England, before he
escaped into private tutoring, but I came to understand that it was
also an act of expiation for his having served the cause of British
colonialism by spending five years in Burma as an officer of the
Imperial Police. Not that he was wholly without respect for the
tradition of the British Empire. In the revealing and perceptive
essay on Rudyard Kipling, which is reproduced in his book of
Critical Essays, he criticizes Kipling for his failure to see 'that the
map is painted red chiefly in order that the coolie may be exploited,'
but he goes on to make the point that 'the nineteenth century
Anglo-Indians ... were at any rate people who did things,' and from
his talk as well as his writings I gained the impression that for all
their philistinism he preferred the administrators and soldiers whom
Kipling idealized to the ineffectual hypocrites of what he sometimes
called 'the pansy left'.

Though he held no religious belief, there was something of a
religious element in George's socialism. It owed nothing to Marxist
theory and much to the tradition of English Nonconformity. He
saw it primarily as an instrument of justice. What he hated in
contemporary politics, almost as much as the abuse of power, was
the dishonesty and cynicism which allowed its evils to be veiled.
When I first got to know him, he had written but not yet published
Animal Farm, and while he believed that the book was good he did
not foresee its great success. He was to be rather dismayed by the
pleasure that it gave to the enemies of any form of socialism, but
with the defeat of fascism in Germany and Italy he saw the Russian
model of dictatorship as the most serious threat to the realization of
his hopes for a better world. He was not yet so pessimistic as he had
become by the time of his writing *1984*. His moral integrity made
him hard upon himself and sometimes harsh in his judgement of
other people, but he was no enemy to pleasure. He appreciated good
food and drink, enjoyed gossip, and when not oppressed by ill-
health was very good company. He was another of those whose
liking for me made me think better of myself.

Prominent among those who held court in Paris in the months
following the Liberation were Gertrude Stein and her companion
Alice B. Toklas. They were a special attraction for American soldiers,
and Miss Stein appeared to welcome the homage paid to her by her
countrymen, even though few of them were likely to have read her
work. I did not much care for what I knew of her writing but I too

was anxious to see her, especially as I had missed the famous meeting of the Poetry Society at Oxford at which she had more than held her own against the undergraduates who had hoped to make fun of her. It was indeed just a question of seeing her, as she was not disposed to enter into conversation at least with the crowd of casual visitors. Her appearance was remarkable for the masculine strength of her face and still more for her seeming almost as broad as she was tall. Miss Toklas was even shorter, dark with hunched shoulders, looking much like a child s conception of a witch. In conjunction, I found them rather alarming though I had no reason to regard them as in any way malevolent.

In my last month in Paris I was much in the company of Isabel Delmer, who was married to the journalist Sefton Delmer but separated from him. Later she was to marry Constant Lambert and, after Constant Lambert's death, another composer, Alan Rawsthorne. She herself was a painter and had studied painting in Paris before the war. Except that she did not appear so fragile, her looks reminded me of the girls in Marie Laurencin's pictures. She shared my taste for the French cinema, with a predilection for the films of Marcel Carné, especially when their scripts were written by Jacques Prévert. We once went as far as Pantin for a showing of Carné's little-known *Le Crime de Monsieur Lange*, with my old favourite René Lefèbre as the hero, and Jules Berry giving one of his marvellous performances in the part of a crook masquerading as a priest. I still possess a book which she gave me about one of the earliest and most imaginative film-makers, Georges Méliès. Little of his work survives as it was mostly destroyed to make heel pieces for the French Army in the first world war.

Isabel had many friends in Paris and introduced me to them. It was through her that I met the writer Georges Bataille, whom I vainly tried to persuade that time was not merely a human invention, the poet and anthropologist, Michel Leiris, Tristan Tzara, the inventor of Dadaism, from which Surrealism followed, the sculptor Alberto Giacometti, the atonalist composer René Leibowitz and his attractive wife Françoise. Until I met René Leibowitz I knew nothing about the theory of atonal music, though I must have listened to a good deal of it without identifying it as such. I was a little disappointed in Tzara who had abandoned his youthful extravagances to become an orthodox communist, but charmed by Giacometti, of whom I had not previously heard, and fascinated by his work. I thought, however, that he indulged his fantasy too much when he destroyed his little statues on the ground that they were too delicate to live for more than a few hours.

I was once having drinks with him and Isabel at Le Sphinx, a well-known brothel which functioned also as a café, when a young man, who was making a disturbance by the doorway, started brandishing a revolver. For no reason that I can think of, except that his conduct annoyed me, I went over to disarm him. My companions were then alarmed to see him catch me by my tie and yank me out of the room. Forgetful of my training in unarmed combat, I remonstrated with him quietly, and he put the gun away. I returned to our table, feeling rather pleased with myself, but found that I had gained no credit with Giacometti, who saw nothing in my behaviour but a foolish act of bravado. I advanced some general argument about the merit of not giving way to violence, but in this particular instance I think that he was right.

I did not have many occasions to leave Paris though I once went down to St Jean de Luz, mainly to see a girl with whom I had made friends in the previous year, enjoyed a short holiday with Isabel in Blois, from where we conscientiously toured the châteaux of the Loire, and, putting on uniform for the occasion, gave a not very successful lecture in Rennes on the contemporary state of Britain. In July at the time of the General Election I was back in England on leave. I had had some vague thought of offering myself as a Labour candidate, but had decided that I should prefer to return to academic life. If I had been a candidate, I might well have been assigned a constituency for which I should have been elected but I do not regret the lost opportunity. I do not think that I should have enjoyed the life of a professional politician or that I should have been very successful at it. At the most I might have obtained some minor office. The Labour victory took me by surprise, as it did almost everyone that I knew, and gave me very great pleasure. Nor did the consequences disappoint me. Though the Attlee government ended by losing its inspiration and self-confidence, its achievements during its first period of office were remarkably great. We are now so accustomed to the Welfare State and so alive to its shortcomings that we tend to underestimate both the extent and the value of the social changes which it brought about.

My being in England at that time gave me the opportunity to settle a question which had arisen about my future. Collingwood had died in 1943 and Gilbert Ryle had been appointed to succeed him in the Chair of Metaphysics. There was therefore a vacancy for a philosophy tutor at Christ Church and Maurice Bowra, thinking that I might prefer to remain at my old college, very generously offered to release me from my engagement to Wadham, if Christ Church wanted to retain me. At that time I should have preferred to remain at Christ Church and I accordingly called on Dean Lowe to ask him what my chances were. He could not say more than that there would be less opposition to me than there had previously been. I said that this seemed to me strange, since I had done hardly any philosophy during the war, but he replied that this was not the point. Presumably what he had in mind was that my war service had made me more acceptable to some of the senior Students. When I pressed him for a more definite answer, on the ground that I could not decently keep Wadham waiting, he called in Dundas and Masterman. Dundas was non-committal but Masterman strongly advised me to close with Wadham. He said that while I should evidently be considered for the position of Gilbert's successor, the Governing Body would feel bound to advertise it and there would then be the risk of some other candidate's proving successful. I reported this to Maurice and told him that it left me with no doubt that I wanted to come to Wadham. Some time later, Christ Church made the excellent choice of Jim Urmson as Gilbert's successor, without advertisement.

University teachers were high in the queue for release from the Armed Forces and I was back in Oxford for the autumn term of 1945. It was not until November 1, just after my thirty-fifth birthday, that I was officially demobilized. I went for the purpose to Chelsea Barracks, where, in exchange for my revolver, I was given an issue of civilian clothes. It included a flannel suit, with a rather too noticeable stripe, which proved unexpectedly hard-wearing. After nearly six years in the army, I retired with the honorary rank of captain. My conduct and services were said to have been satisfactory.

11 *Return to Philosophy*

At the end of the war Wadham was still a small college. Whereas there are now thirty-eight Fellows, in addition to the Warden, there were then no more than nine, of whom only six were engaged in the routine of college teaching. Apart from myself the only one of them to live in college was T. C. Keeley, the tutor in physics, who had already been a Fellow for many years. The Warden and some of the other Fellows usually joined us for dinner, but sometimes we found ourselves alone together at High Table and proceeded to Common Room to pass the port to one another. He was kindly and wise, with a vein of shrewd humour, and I very much enjoyed our quiet companionship.

Because of the shortage of unmarried Fellows, I was immediately appointed Dean of the college, with responsibility for maintaining discipline. This was an office which Maurice Bowra had held before he was elected Warden. It brought my salary up to the modest figure of £500 a year. In real terms this came to a good deal more, since I paid nothing for my rooms or my dinner in Hall or the services which the college afforded, but with the need to provide for Renée and the children, I should have had little to spare for any self-indulgence, if it had not been for my grandfather's legacy. As it was, I lived very comfortably. I had an attractive set of rooms in the north-east corner of the quad with a view over the college garden, which is one of Wadham's most agreeable features. Fred Wheatley, who had resumed his old occupation after campaigning as an infantryman, had also moved from Christ Church to Wadham. He was the scout on my staircase and took very good care of me.

My duties as Dean were not onerous. Most of the undergraduates had served in the war and were consequently more mature than their predecessors who had come to Oxford straight from school. They were disposed to take their work seriously and saw no point in breaking the college rules. I think I had only once to take disciplinary action, and then it was a matter of imposing a small fine on two men who had engaged in a relatively harmless drunken frolic. The college ran smoothly under Maurice Bowra's direction, and both on the Wednesday mornings when he and the tutors met at breakfast and at the less frequent formal college meetings, the business was quickly and effectively dispatched. Though I remained on good terms with Maurice, I did not see very much of him in private. He was heavily engaged in university as well as college administration, and still found the time to produce a considerable amount of work. When one walked through the college at night past the Warden's Lodgings, one could hear the rattle of his type-writer, as the muster of modern poets, whether they wrote in English, French, Spanish, Russian or Modern Greek, was sub-jected to brisk review.

Bill Deakin was still a Fellow of Wadham but he remained for some time after the war at the British Embassy in Jugoslavia and when he did return to Oxford he soon left Wadham to become the first Warden of St Anthony's. He had got married during the war to a Roumanian girl whom he met in Cairo, where she was working for British Intelligence. When I first met Pussy Deakin in Oxford, she seemed a little discouraged by the provincialism of academic life, but her vivid personality enabled her to draw the best out of it, and her position at St Anthony's gave her occasion to exercise her remarkable gift for hospitality. I liked her very much from the outset, and my affection for Bill very soon developed into an equally strong affection for them both.

Apart from Bill, I had no very intimate friend among my col-leagues at Wadham, until the arrival of John Bamborough whom we elected as a Fellow in English. He and his wife Anna were parti-cularly kind to Valerie, when she was sent to boarding-school in Oxford a year or two later. By that time I was working in London but I used frequently to return to Wadham at the weekend, in order to take Valerie out. She remembers my reading the novels of Jane Austen to her, sitting under the large copper-beech in the college garden. It was at the Bamboroughs' house, where I used to take Valerie to tea, that I first met Merlin Thomas, soon to be elected to a Fellowship in French at New College, and one of my best friends among my present colleagues, and the gifted theatrical producer Frank Hauser. Merlin shared Frank's interest in the theatre and it was owing to them that many years afterwards I became an honorary director of Meadow Players, which was the company responsible for running the Oxford Playhouse. My duties, however, went little further than countersigning cheques and I can claim no credit for the many excellent productions that Frank and his collaborators staged. It was not their fault that even with an Arts Council subsidy the theatre could not pay its way.

Of my friends elsewhere in Oxford, Solly Zuckerman had returned to his house in Museum Road but fairly soon left to become Professor of Anatomy at Birmingham University. He had married Lady Joan Isaacs just before the war and in their case also my friendship with him was quickly transformed into a friendship with them both. Gilbert Ryle's professorship had taken him to Magdalen and Hugh Trevor-Roper, after completing his investigation into the death of Hitler, settled down as a tutor in history at Christ Church. Adhering to his resolution to give up philosophy, Isaiah Berlin spent only a few years more at New College before returning to All Souls, where he remained after his election to the Chair of Social and Political Theory. Robin Zaehner was also to find his way to All Souls as Professor of Eastern Religions and Ethics, but with the diminution of our friendship we saw little of one another. Among the new friends that I made at this time were Hans and Aline Halban. An Austrian, who had worked before the war in France, Hans was a very good experimental physicist and had played an important part in the development of the atom bomb. He had no academic position in Oxford when he came to live there, though he maintained some association with the Clarendon Laboratory and later became a Fellow of St Anthony's. There were times when he seemed to care more for his own comfort and his social position than for the advancement of physics, but I found him good company and respected his intelligence. Aline was related to the French Rothschilds and I had met her with Guy in New York before she married Hans. It was not, however, until she came to Oxford that we became friends. It is a friendship that has been cemented in later years by her subsequent marriage to Isaiah Berlin.

Being the only philosophy tutor at Wadham, I had to teach all the branches of the subject that were required both for Greats and for

PPE. After nearly six years during which I had only occasionally thought about philosophy, I had to refresh my memory of the standard authors, especially Plato and Aristotle, of whom my knowledge had never been very deep, but the need to take trouble over my tutorials made them more interesting to me, and I do not think that my pupils suffered from my ignorance. I tried to vary my comments to suit the different interests and abilities of the men who came to me, so that even when the mismanagement of my programme resulted in my having to listen to three very similar essays on the same topic in three successive hours, I did not often succumb to boredom or relapse into a set speech. I found that I enjoyed teaching, even more than I had before the war, and I hope that I succeeded in communicating some of my enthusiasm to those whom I taught. At any rate, when they came to be examined, they mostly achieved good results.

Besides doing a full stint of tutoring, I gave a course of lectures on Perception, in which I defended very much the same position as I had set out in *The Foundations of Empirical Knowledge*, and in another term held a class, perhaps on the philosophy of logic, which was attended by Ernest Gellner and by Peter Medawar. It may be partly as a result of this that Gellner has always dealt kindly with me in his attacks on Positivism. Peter Medawar was already a Fellow of Magdalen and was soon to join Solly in Birmingham as a Professor of Zoology, before accepting a Chair at University College, London, and among other things winning a Nobel Prize. He had never formally studied philosophy but he had read a great deal of logic on his own and was keenly interested in the problems of scientific method. With his adherence to the views of Karl Popper, I do not think that he learned very much from me, but it was the beginning of a friendship that has lasted ever since. His writings on the philosophy of science have mostly been critical, but I have enjoyed their tough-mindedness and their spirited resistance to any attempt to enlist biology in the cause of contemporary unreason.

Though next to no philosophy had come out of Oxford during the war, the few philosophers who remained there being wholly occupied in teaching, the philosophical climate had undergone a drastic change. It was not just that the older men had died or retired; their outlook had vanished with them. My own views, which had been thought so revolutionary before the war, were now regarded not merely as orthodox but even as old-fashioned. I had mysteriously passed from being a young Turk to being, at the age of thirty-five, almost an elder statesman, without ever having known the plenitude of office.

A hint of what was to come was given at the Joint Session of the Mind Association and the Aristotelian Society which was held at Manchester in the summer of 1946. One of the symposia was devoted to the problem of our knowledge of other minds, and the main participants were John Wisdom, John Austin and myself. Neither John Wisdom, who opened the discussion, nor I, who spoke third, found anything much to add to what we had already written on this topic, but Austin, while largely ignoring the main question at issue, made some interesting and original remarks on the subject of knowledge. In the course of developing what is in fact a rather weak analogy between the use of the expression 'I know' and the use of expressions like 'I promise', he drew attention to the existence of what he called 'performative statements'; that is, statements of which the function is not to assert a fact but to commit the speaker in some way or other, or play a part in bringing something about. For example, when a judge says to a defendant 'You will go to prison for six months,' he is not making a prediction. If the defendant immediately succumbs to a heart-attack, the judge's sentence is nullified but not rendered false. Austin's expression of interest in statements of this sort was the beginning of the general concern with so-called speech-acts that he did so much to foster. He had had a successful career at the War Office, rising to the rank of colonel and becoming an expert on the battle-order of the German Army, and he had there acquired the belief that the division of labour, which served in the obtaining of military intelligence, could usefully be applied to philosophical research. Proceeding on this principle, he was able to organize a group of his younger colleagues into a kind of general staff and set them to work on various aspects of English verbal usage. Their efforts helped to constitute the linguistic philosophy with which Oxford came to be principally associated. In the form in which Austin and his followers practised it, linguistic philosophy has gone almost entirely out of fashion, but in its heyday it aroused very strong feelings both among its practitioners and among those, like myself, who were sceptical of its importance.

The height of Austin's power was not, however, reached until the nineteen-fifties. In the years immediately following the war the strongest philosophical influence in Oxford was undoubtedly that of Gilbert Ryle. His major work, *The Concept of Mind*, was not published until 1949, but he had hit upon its central doctrines several years before. They were already formulated in an un-published paper called 'The Mind is its own Place', which he sent me as early as 1946. His attack on the traditional view of the relation between mind and body, depicted in his famous phrase as the idea of 'the ghost in the machine', won him many adherents among young philosophers who were favourably disposed towards materialism. For all its brilliance, I do not myself think that *The Concept of Mind* was wholly successful in its principal aim; apart from the criticisms that can be made of some of its arguments, there are passages in it which show that the ghost has not been entirely laid to rest. Even so, it remains a seminal work, and anyone who is inclined, as I still am, to try to preserve something of the classical distinction between mental and physical events requires to reckon with it.

Independently of the attractiveness of his theories, Ryle's rule in Oxford was beneficent, in a large measure because it was not tyrannical. Unlike some other contemporary philosophers, he was not interested in recruiting a set of faithful disciples. It was less important to him that young people should accept his views than that they should learn to think philosophically for themselves. He was also to render a great service to Oxford philosophy by pro-moting the introduction of a new form of higher degree, which attracted philosophical graduates to Oxford in large numbers from universities throughout the English-speaking world. Though it has now reached the point where the supply threatens to outrun the demand, this helped to ensure that the rapidly growing need for teachers of philosophy in the years following the war was adequately met.

While the analytic movement, in one form or another, took increasing control of the English philosophical scene, there were some pockets of resistance to it. One of those who fought a rear-guard action against it in Oxford was the English scholar C. S. Lewis, who had once had the ambition to become a tutor in philo-sophy and still took a lively interest in the subject. He presided over the Socratic Club, which then drew a large audience to meetings at which the principal speakers usually struck a religious note. At one of these meetings, not long after my return to Oxford, I under-took to reply to a paper by Michael Foster, who had spent part of the war as an officer in Northern Ireland and had come back strengthened in his puritanism. I dealt with his paper rather harshly, and when he made little effort to defend it, C. S. Lewis took over from him. Lewis and I then engaged in a flashy debate, which entertained the audience but did neither of us much credit, while Foster sat by, suffering in silence. Lewis was at that time still a Fellow of Magdalen and when he next saw Gilbert Ryle in Common Room, he said to him, 'I met your man Freddie Ayer at the Socratic Club. He is not at all what I expected.' 'What did you expect?' said Gilbert. 'I had pictured a sort of dour Scotsman.' 'No, he is not like that,' said Gilbert, 'how would you describe him?' 'I think you would have to go to the animal kingdom,' said Lewis, 'a cross between a rodent and a firefly.' When Gilbert reported this conversation to me, I did not feel altogether flattered, but I had some idea what Lewis meant.

The paper available to publishers was in short supply during the war and when their stocks of *Language, Truth and Logic* ran out, Gollancz did not reprint it. There was a clause in my contract which restored the rights in the book to me if the publisher failed to keep it in print, and on my return to Oxford I wrote to Gollancz to say that if he was no longer interested in the book, I should wish to take advantage of this clause. I had no assurance that any other publisher would want to take the book over, but I thought it at least worth trying to find one. Gollancz made this unnecessary by saying that he would himself bring out the book in a new edition, provided that I wrote a second introduction to it. I accepted this condition and at once set to work, with the result that the book was republished in 1946. As a piece of book production, the second edition was very inferior to the first. To save paper, the 237 pages of the original text were compressed into 123, and the paper itself was of much less good quality. I foolishly allowed the new index to be compiled by a professional indexer, who instead of merely altering the pagination of the items in my analytical index, made nonsense of it by re-arranging them in alphabetical order. It was also a pity that the new 36-page introduction was set at the beginning of the book. Since it took the form of a commentary on the main theses of the first edition, it would have made more sense to the reader if it had been printed as an appendix.

Reviewing my work in this introduction after an interval of ten years, I began by acknowledging that the principle of verifiability, on which so much depended, had not been properly formulated. I made a rather elaborate attempt to reformulate it in such a way as to remove the weakness of the former version, but my precautions were insufficient, as was shown by the American logician, Alonso Church, in a review of the second edition which he contributed to the *Journal of Symbolic Logic*. Some critics of the book had raised queries about the status of the principle of verifiability itself, and I tried to answer them by declaring it to be a stipulative definition. Seeing that this laid me open to the objection that its adoption then became a matter of choice, I could do no more than claim that the principle gave a satisfactory account of the way in which common sense and scientific statements were ordinarily understood, and that if anyone wanted to attach sense to statements of a different character from these, the onus lay on him to specify the conditions for their acceptance. I made a slight attempt to clarify the view, to which I still adhered, that the propositions of logic and pure mathematics were true by convention and I also stood by my old account of moral judgements, while admitting that it had been stated too summarily. On the other hand, I let common sense prevail over my earlier views that ascriptions of mental states to others were to be treated behaviouristically and that statements about the past were to be analysed in terms of present and future evidence. Finally, I recognized that my description of philosophical analysis, as consisting in the provision of definitions, had been too narrow, and gave rather a vague indication of the ways in which I thought that it should be enlarged.

The general effect of this new introduction was to water down the destructive content of the book, but this did not appear to diminish its effect. Gollancz still found it hard to believe that many people could want to read it, but this time he went so far as to print an edition of 1000 copies. His economies in the use of paper made it possible for him not to increase the price. The book sold well enough in this second format for a new impression to come out on the average annually throughout the next fourteen years. In the United States, where the book had not sold particularly well in the edition originally published by the Oxford University Press, the concession of the paperback rights of the second edition to Dover Publications led to sales which have by now amounted to over 270,000 copies, but so long as he lived, Victor Gollancz refused to allow any English publisher to bring the book out in paperback. This was in my financial interest as well as his, since the royalty which he was paying me had risen from ten to twenty per cent, and it was not probable that the extra number of copies which the book might be expected to sell in paperback would compensate for my receiving a much smaller royalty on a lower price. Nevertheless, I was anxious that the work should reach a wider public, even at the cost of some financial sacrifice, so that when, after Gollancz's death, the firm was willing to accept an offer from Penguin for the paperback rights, I readily consented to their doing so. The Penguin edition first came out in 1971, and has already sold 46,000 copies compared with the 43,000-odd which the Gollancz editions have sold in their twenty-one impressions. The book was translated into Spanish and Hungarian before the war and subsequently into Swedish, Japanese, French, Italian, Italian Braille, Argentine Spanish, Catalan, German, Dutch, Korean, Hindi and Mahrathi. So far as I know, the Japanese translation, which has reached its eighteenth impression, has been the most successful and the French translation probably the least, even though the translator sought to make the book more palatable to his countrymen by adding notes in which he animadverted on what he took to be the author's mistakes. One of Descartes's least happy legacies to France has been the belief that empirical questions can be decided *a priori*, and one of these *a priori* judgements is that among foreign philosophers only the Germans need be taken seriously.

Language, Truth and Logic made my name as a philosopher and I am gratified by its continued success. What sometimes annoys me is to find it still rated above all my later work. I should prefer to think that I had made some progress in the course of the past forty years. This is not, however, for me alone to judge and, at the worst, I still count it better fortune to have gained a reputation by a youthful performance than never to have gained one at all.

It may have been through my friendship with George Orwell that I came to join the Editorial Board of a new magazine called *Polemic*, of which the first number appeared in October 1945. The magazine was financed by a rich young Australian called Rodney Phillips and edited by Humphrey Slater, with whom I also very soon made friends. A few years older than I, Humphrey, who was then known as Hugh Slater, had been an art student at the Slade in the early nineteen-thirties and a member of the Communist party. Having gone to Spain as a political journalist, he joined the International Brigade in 1936 and showed such military skill that he became its Chief of Operations. By the time that he left Spain in 1938, his experiences there had turned him against the communists, so that his political position was similar to that of George Orwell. He had, however, developed a greater interest in philosophy than in politics and sought to make *Polemic* as much a philosophical as a political or literary magazine. Thus, in his first editorial, he listed 'the four aspects of contemporary life with which we are especially concerned' as '(1) The discovery of the Unconscious, (2) The evolution of the problem of verbal meaning, (3) The success of Marxism, (4) The fundamental significance of the arts.' The contributors to the first number, which was sold out within two days of publication, were Bertrand Russell, George Orwell, Stephen Spender, the psychologist Edward Glover, the American writer Henry Miller, C. E. M. Joad, Rupert Crawshay-Williams and myself. Russell supplied a critical but mainly friendly account of Logical Positivism, George Orwell a longer essay called 'Notes on Nationalism', taking 'nationalism' in a broad sense in which it covered uncritical devotion to any sort of creed, Joad attacked the view, which he attributed to scientists like Julian Huxley and C. H. Waddington, that ethics depends on the direction of evolution, and I contributed an essay on 'Deistic Fallacies', in which I tried to bring out some of the logical difficulties which confront the belief that the world is a divine creation. I ended by drawing the conclusion that our lives can have no other meaning or purpose than those that we choose to give them.

Though I did not see so much of Russell at this time as I did a few years later, we were already on the way to becoming friends. He talked to me more freely than he had when I first met him, and I became even more impressed by his vitality, the breadth of his learning, and his extraordinary feats of memory. The basis of our friendship was also partly philosophical. Though there were many crucial points on which I disagreed with him, my approach to the subject and my general standpoint were similar to his own; and his recognition of this, and of the respect in which I held him, was important to him at a time when he felt that his work was being undervalued by most of the younger English philosophers, as compared with that of Wittgenstein and Moore. His resentment of this injustice gave a personal edge to his disapproval of current fashion; in allowing his hostility to the idiom of linguistic philosophy to extend to nearly all its content, he was sometimes unjust in his turn. Even so, I think that his view of the philosophical limitations of the study of ordinary usage, as it came to be practised, was substantially right.

We also sometimes talked about politics, in which he retained a strong interest, though he was not yet so absorbed in it as he became in the last decade of his life. He had long held the view that the only remedy for the evils of nationalism lay in the establishment of a world government and he then believed that the only practical way in which this could come about was through the hegemony of the United States. Though there was much that he disliked in its political and social climate, he still preferred it to that of Soviet Russia; but this counted with him for less than the fact that the Americans possessed the atomic bomb, while the Russians did not. He was convinced that it would be enough for the Americans to threaten the Russians with the bomb, without actually using it. This did not, however, absolve him from holding the view that in the last resort its use would be justified. In later years, when he was leading the campaign for nuclear disarmament, he forgot that he had ever taken this view and admitted that he had done so only when it was shown that he had expressed it in print. His critics naturally accused him of inconsistency, but they could have been wrong. Taking, as he did, a predominantly utilitarian view of politics, he could have argued that so long as only one power possessed this superior weapon, the evil resulting from its limited employment, though very great, would be outweighed by the probable longer-term good; when two rival powers possessed it, the harm done by their each employing it would almost certainly be greater than any good that could be expected to result. But while Russell might have accepted this argument theoretically, I doubt if he would have been ready to see it put into effect. His reason was often in conflict with his emotions, and this is most probably an instance in which his emotions would have prevailed. If it had come to an issue, I think that he would have recoiled from the infliction of so great an immediate evil, even with the prospect of its leading to a greater good. It was because I believed this at the time that I did not on this point take him wholly seriously.

Russell had a very low opinion of Cyril Joad, whose name he sometimes deliberately mispronounced, referring to him as 'Joad'. Apart from disliking his manner and appearance, he also accused him of plagiarism. There is a story that when asked to review one of Joad's books, he wrote in refusal: 'Modesty forbids'. Joad had become famous as a broadcaster, appearing regularly with Julian Huxley and Commander Campbell, a breezy ex-naval officer, on a programme called *The Brains Trust*: it was originally a wireless programme, though later transferred to television. Joad did this very well, though he may have slightly misled the public by giving the impression that philosophers typically begin their answers to every question by saying, 'It depends on what you mean by . . .' He taught philosophy at Birkbeck College, London, where they refused to make him a professor, though he allowed himself to be called so on *The Brains Trust*. His talent for popularization came out also in his writing, and the introductory books on philosophy which he wrote before the war performed a useful service, perhaps all the more for what they owed to Russell. He held progressive views on most topics, including the view that one should not take too many baths, on the ground that they robbed the body of its natural oils. I rather liked him for his animal spirits, though I did not respect him. I remember meeting him by accident towards the end of the war and being told, when I asked him what he was working on, that he was writing a book in favour of religion. When I showed some surprise, he said quite seriously that I did not seem to understand that after the war religion would be coming back into fashion. Many years later he underwent what was, to all appearances, a genuine religious conversion.

Rupert Crawshay-Williams was another of the friends that I made through *Polemic*. He too was on its Editorial Board and he contributed to three of its eight numbers. We had been neighbours in St John's Wood Park, but though I used sometimes to play tennis with his sister Jill, who was later to marry Anthony Greenwood, he was sufficiently older than I for us then to know each other only by sight. He had been a schoolmaster during the war and afterwards settled down with his wife, Elizabeth, in a small house at Portmeirion, in North Wales, supplementing his private income principally by reviewing gramophone records. It was then that he began to develop a strong interest in philosophy, which may have been fostered by his having Russell for a neighbour. In the second number of *Polemic* they engaged in a debate on the subject of Universals. Both he and his wife became very much attached to Russell, and the short account which he has given of their friendship in his book

Russell Remembered shows a remarkable insight into Russell's character. At the time when I met him over *Polemic*, Rupert was at work on a book called *The Comforts of Unreason*, which was published in 1947. Subtitled 'A Study of the Motives behind Irrational Thought', it reminded me of Susan Stebbing's *Thinking to Some Purpose* in its felicitous choice of examples. Since his approach to philosophy was wholly pragmatic, a position for which I already had some sympathy, though not so much as I have since developed, and his attitude to politics consistently radical, my personal liking for him has been sustained by a community of interest. His passion for fast cars is one of the few tastes that we do not share.

Though it was originally intended that *Polemic* should be a monthly magazine, in fact it came nearer to being a quarterly, its eight numbers appearing at irregular intervals over a period of about twenty months. Like all such magazines it ran at a loss, even without being particularly generous to its contributors, whom it paid at the rate of five guineas per thousand words, and it came to an end when Rodney Phillips decided that he would prefer to lose his money in the theatre and Humphrey Slater was unable to find another backer. Humphrey published two novels of which one, called *The Heretics*, was partly historical, on the theme of the massacre of the Albigenses. He sold the film rights to it for quite a large sum of money, which he ran through very quickly. After that he spent most of his time playing an ingenious race-game of his own invention which he never succeeded in marketing. He was also a keen chess player and we used often to play together, though I was hardly a match for him. I still possess the handsome set of chess-men which he left in my keeping before going to Spain on a visit, during which he fell ill and died. His health had been bad for some time and he did little to take care of it. He was a generous man, with a wide range of talents and considerable charm, but there was a vein of self-destruction in him. Perhaps he never wholly recovered from the loss of his political faith.

For the second number of *Polemic* I wrote a review of *Secret Session*, the English translation of Sartre's *Huis Clos*, praising the play but also raising some objections to it as an illustration of Sartre's philosophy. My other contributions, appearing in later numbers, were an essay on 'Freedom and Necessity', in which I attempted, not, as I now think, very successfully, to reconcile free will with determinism, and one called 'The Claims of Philosophy', in which I divided contemporary philosophers into the classes of 'pontiffs' and 'journeymen', associating myself with the journeymen, but arguing also that they should aim at the reunion of philosophy with science if they wished to put an end to what I called 'the unfortunate disparity between the richness of their technique and the increasing poverty of the material on which they are able to exercise it'. This is a moral that I have frequently drawn in my writings, though I cannot claim that I have myself done much to act upon it.

My essay on 'The Claims of Philosophy' was based on a talk on Contemporary British Philosophy which I broadcast and had published in *The Listener* some time in 1946. To the best of my recollection, this was my first appearance as a broadcaster. I was nervous and read my script too fast. Though I have had considerable experience of broadcasting since, I still do not find it easy to read from a script. I do not have the same difficulty in lecturing from a prepared text, but there the presence of an audience makes a great difference: half-consciously one adjusts one's manner of speaking to its response. Faced only with a microphone, I feel the want of this control, and allow my natural disposition to speak fast to get the better of me. For this reason, I much prefer to take part in a discussion, whether on the wireless or on television. It still does not prevent me from speaking very fast when I am caught up in the argument, but this matters less in the course of a discussion, where the context and the response of the other speakers can help to make one's meaning clear.

Having undertaken to give this broadcast, I was uncertain what to do about Wittgenstein. It seemed ridiculous not to refer to him in giving even a superficial account of contemporary British philosophy, yet I knew from the experiences of others that one had to be very careful in what one said about him if he was not to take offence. In particular, he had displayed a tendency to denounce any reference to his current views either as plagiarism or as mis-representation. I knew something about the development of his thought in the nineteen-thirties through the copies of the notes taken from his lectures which had found their way to Oxford, but I did not think that this was a sufficient basis for me to risk making any detailed comment on work he had not yet brought himself to publish. I therefore decided to quote only from the *Tractatus* and to content myself with just a vague reference to Wittgenstein's later teaching. Unfortunately, my comment on the *Tractatus* was not entirely respectful. Having quoted one of its concluding sentences:

> The right method of philosophy would be this: to say nothing except what can be said, i.e. the propositions of natural science, i.e. something that has nothing to do with philosophy: and then always, when someone else wished to say something metaphysical, to demonstrate to him that he had given no meaning to certain signs in his propositions. This method would be unsatisfying to the other – he would not have the feeling that we were teaching him philosophy – but it would be the only strictly correct method . . .

I remarked, rather facetiously, that the philosopher was thereby 'reduced, or elevated, to the position of a park keeper whose business it is to see that no one commits an intellectual nuisance: the nuisance in question being that of lapsing into metaphysics.' I then went on to say that I did not know whether Wittgenstein was still of this opinion, though if he were I thought that he would express it rather differently, but that what I did know was 'that the effect on his more articulate disciples has been that they tend to treat philosophy as a department of psychoanalysis'. I had in mind principally John Wisdom, whose work I described as 'of fascinating subtlety', while again expressing a doubt whether the curing of intellectual cramps was all that the philosopher was fitted to achieve.

In the ordinary way, my broadcast and the *Polemic* essay which grew out of it would have escaped Wittgenstein's notice, but one of his pupils drew his attention to them. He was extremely vexed, not so much, as I learned long afterwards, because of my comment on the conclusion of the *Tractatus*, as because of my suggestion that John Wisdom's view of philosophy could be taken as a pointer to his own. In particular, he did not admit any kinship between the practice of psychoanalysis and his own method of dealing with philosophical confusions. He made an attempt to get one or other of his pupils to publish a reply to me but none of them would undertake it. No doubt they distrusted their ability to do him justice. The result was that he himself sent me a letter of rebuke, by registered post. It began with his saying that he had every reason to believe that I was not so ignorant of his recent work as I had pretended to be in my broadcast and in my article in *Polemic*, and ended by asking me whether, if I was ashamed to acknowledge that I had received many valuable ideas from him, it would not be more in accordance with elementary decency to refrain from mentioning him than to spread misleading insinuations about his teaching.

I was upset by this letter, both because I was sorry to have offended Wittgenstein, and because I did not believe that I had done anything to deserve so sharp a rebuke. I wrote what I hoped was a dignified reply, explaining why I had thought it right in the circumstances to refer only to his published work and adding that so far from being anxious to conceal the debt that I owed to his *Tractatus*, I had frequently proclaimed it. He answered briefly, saying that he accepted my apology but that if one really wanted to be fair to a man one would avoid even the appearance of unfairness. Though my intention had been rather to justify myself than to apologize, I received this answer with relief.

This was not quite the end of the story. Wittgenstein had resumed his professorship at Cambridge and I was due to go there in the following week to read a paper to the Moral Science Club. I seem to remember that it was on the topic of Perception. Though I had spoken there several times, I had always found it something of an ordeal, and this time I had the additional worry of not knowing what Wittgenstein would do. If he really had forgiven me, he would come to the meeting and treat me with his usual indulgence, but that seemed too much to hope for. I had some fear that he would come and demolish me, but thought it more likely that he would stay away. In fact, I had not considered all the possibilities. He came to the meeting, listened to my paper, made some remarks to John Wisdom, who had opened the discussion, and then left rather noisily, without having said anything to me. I took this as measuring the extent to which I had lost his favour. It was the last time that I ever saw him. He had been more of a patron to me than a friend, but I was sorry that our acquaintance ended in this fashion.

Most of the practical work in editing *Polemic* was done by two girls who were Humphrey Slater's editorial assistants. One of them was Moira Sutherland, whom Humphrey married, and the other was Celia Kirwan, who before her marriage to a journalist had been called Celia Paget. Her twin sister Mamaine was soon to marry Arthur Koestler. Celia's marriage had broken down and we soon became very much attached to one another. She and Mamaine were identical twins, both small and slender, exceptionally pretty, staunch and vulnerable. They had an almost telepathic understanding of each other's thoughts and feelings. Through being with Celia I came to see more of Arthur Koestler and liked him better than I had before. We went to stay with him and Mamaine in a house which they had taken in North Wales, in the neighbourhood of the Russells and the Crawshay-Williamses. Russell and Koestler got on well together, finding a bond at that time in their common hostility to Russia. My own position, which the Crawshay-Williamses shared, was rather that of an 'anti-anti communist'. I still think that we were right in wishing to diminish rather than increase the temperature of the cold war, but I must also admit that we underrated both the extent and the ruthlessness of Stalin's tyranny.

Since the breakdown of my marriage I had made no attempt to resist the attraction which women had for me. In the Easter vacation of 1946 I returned to Paris to see my friends there and conceived a sudden and violent passion for an English girl whom I had met once before in Oxford and had not especially planned to see again. She was married, already had a child, and was carrying another, but she nevertheless agreed to leave her husband and join me in the summer. I found a place for her to live in London, until she could get a divorce. I had previously started an affair in Oxford with a friend of hers, a younger girl with whom I did not wholly succeed in breaking, though I told her what had happened. This friend went to stay with her in Paris, a few days before she was due to join me in London. When they had compared notes, she sent me a telegram to say that she was not coming. I did not reply to the telegram, or ask for any explanation. My feelings were a mixture of regret and relief. I did not pretend to myself that I had come at all well out of it, but I already knew that I was not yet emotionally equipped for the responsibility that I had undertaken.

By contrast, the summer brought a change in my professional life. University College, London, had been without a Professor of Philosophy since 1944, when John Macmurray, who had held the Chair for sixteen years, abandoned it to become a professor at Edinburgh. When the College at last decided to fill the vacancy, the Provost, Dr Pye, invited me to come and see him. He made it clear that he was not offering the position to me; he and his colleagues were not entirely sure that they wanted me, as they had, for example, been sure that they wanted Roy Harrod for their professorship of economics, which Roy refused: nevertheless, they were sufficiently interested in me to wish me to be a candidate. I believe that a similar approach was made to John Austin, who turned it down. After thinking it over for some time, I decided to apply. Though I was quite happy at Wadham, I liked the idea of becoming a professor, and I thought that I should prefer living in London to living in Oxford. At the same time I was not going to feel unduly disappointed, or humiliated, if my application failed.

I do not know how many philosophers, apart from John Austin, were similarly approached, but when I presented myself at University College for the interview, I found that I had only one competitor, an older man called Louis Arnaud Reid who was already a professor at Newcastle. I had seen him one or twice before the war at philosophical meetings and I had written a brief and hostile review of a book which he had published on aesthetics. His style of philosophy was so different from mine that I was surprised that the issue should have come to rest between us.

The committee with which the decision lay was mainly composed of representatives of University College. The only one of them that I already knew was J. Z. Young, the Professor of Anatomy, whom I had met in Oxford: we were later to become good friends. None of them was a professional philosopher, though J. B. S. Haldane, Cyril Burt, the Professor of Psychology, and John Young himself all took an interest in the subject. There were, however, two expert assessors, acting for London University, which held what was in effect a power of veto over professorial appointments at its constituent colleges. These experts were H. F. Hallett, the Professor of Philosophy at King's College London, and Sir David Ross, the Provost of Oriel. Hallett was best known for having written a very large book in which he claimed to be following in the footsteps of Spinoza; I had seen him once at a Joint Session, when he had engaged in an acrimonious discussion with Susan Stebbing. A stickler for his rights, he was said to have refused to displace himself with the other members of King's College, when it was evacuated during the war, on the ground that his contract obliged him only to lecture in London. Ross, a distinguished Aristotelian scholar, was the author of two books on moral philosophy, in which he took a position similar to that of Prichard. A pious Scotsman, he had helped to turn the Oriel Senior Common Room into a stronghold of puritanism. Neither he nor Professor Hallett was disposed to think well of my philosophical principles, but the questions which they put to me were not unfriendly. I readily conceded that there was more to be said about ethics than I had found to say in *Language*,

Truth and Logic, and when Ross asked me whether I was prepared for less intelligent pupils, I countered by asking whether he thought that all our Oxford pupils were of first-class quality. Professor Haldane, who had himself fought with conspicuous bravery as an Infantry Officer in the first world war, appeared to count it in my favour that I had been in the Welsh Guards, even though I had seen no active service with them. John Young put some questions to me which were calculated to make me show to advantage, and their colleagues gave me a general impression of benevolence. I was told some time later that Ross and Hallett had advised the committee that Louis Arnaud Reid was the better philosopher, but that I had appeared to be the livelier man. In any case, I was informed a few weeks later that I had gained the appointment.

The Chair to which I had been elected was the Grote Professorship of the Philosophy of Mind and Logic. It had been named after the historian George Grote, the friend of John Stuart Mill, and one of those responsible, together with Brougham and other disciples of Jeremy Bentham in the late eighteen-twenties, for founding University College. A product of the march of mind which Peacock satirized, and for the same reason contemptuously referred to by Thomas Creevey as 'Stinkomiles College at the end of Gower Street', University College was founded partly for the benefit of those whose inability to adhere to the doctrines of the Church of England denied them admission to Oxford or Cambridge. In consequence, the college has never yet had a department of theology. When, during my time there, a sum of money was offered to us for a course of lectures on the Bible, it was decided after a lengthy and spirited debate, that the subject was admissible as Jewish history, but the condition imposed by the prospective donor that the Dean of St Paul's should have a say in the choice of the lecturer was found unacceptable, and the offer was withdrawn. The college had indeed been tolerant enough to permit the first holder of my Chair to be a Unitarian clergyman. Though he retained the position for a great many years, I cannot discover that he made any contribution to the subject. Among the more distinguished of his successors was Croom Robertson, the first editor of *Mind*. Later the Chair became a Chair of Psychology and was held by Professor Spearman, a great promoter of intelligence tests, who invented the concept 'G' as a means of legitimizing the factor of general intelligence which the tests were supposed to measure. When an official Chair of Psychology was created for him, the Grote Chair reverted to philosophy.

The college's debt to Jeremy Bentham was marked by its possession of his auto-eikon. He had not held any belief in personal survival, but wishing to have some semblance of an after-life, he had made arrangements in his will for his body to be mummified in a seated position, and expressed the hope that it should sometimes be admitted to the company of his friends. There is a legend that one of these friends, having fallen on hard times, was transporting this relic of Bentham to the pawnshop when the cab was waylaid by members of University College and the effigy taken into their custody. Whether it was acquired in this way or not, it has remained in the college ever since. Unfortunately, the mummification had not been altogether successful and in the course of time the head grew so unsightly that it was thought more seemly to sever it from the body and replace it with a wax head, made by the Department of Egyptology. The result, since the body is fully clothed, is that, apart from having a slight odour, the exhibit does not sensibly differ from those that are to be seen at Madame Tussaud's. I believe, however, that the original head is still available and may even be shown to those who have sufficient curiosity to want to see it.

I had applied for the Professorship knowing hardly anything about University College and nothing at all about its Department of Philosophy. When I heard that I had been elected, I thought that it might be as well to pay the department a discreet visit. The result was to make me wonder whether my decision to go there had not been an act of folly. The college had suffered from bombing during the war, and though its fine main portico was still intact, there was a ramshackle air about the place as a whole. When I enquired for the Department of Philosophy, I found that its premises consisted of two tiny rooms in one of the outlying and more dilapidated parts of the college. In one of these rooms I came upon two or three disconsolate undergraduates, who brightened up a little when I introduced myself to them as their new professor. They told me that there were three or four other undergraduates in the department besides themselves, no graduates, and just two teachers, one a senior lecturer and the other a temporary assistant. The temporary assistant was a Greek lady who had been Macmurray's secretary. I suppose that she had some other professional qualification but I do not remember what it was. Her transfer to the staff had left the department without a secretary; indeed, its prestige in the college was so low that it did not even possess a telephone.

Dr Keeling, the senior lecturer, had been in the department for a number of years. A good philosophical scholar, he was best known for a book which he had published on Descartes. He must have had hopes of succeeding to the Chair, and it was insensitive of the college authorities to allow him to learn of my appointment from its announcement in a newspaper. The shock to him must have been the greater for my being much younger than he and holding philosophical views of which he disapproved. Nevertheless, from the very start he behaved to me with unfailing courtesy. An ardent Francophil, with a special dislike for the English climate and for English cooking, he contrived, with his small pointed beard, wide-awake hat, stick and cloak, to give the appearance of a stage French-man in the comedies of my childhood. Even his oratorical manner of reading out his lectures was French. Making no concessions at all to current fashion, he served the department loyally for several more years, but it was clearly a relief to him when he was able to retire and settle for good in his beloved France.

Finding the department so run-down had the advantage at least that I could hardly do other than improve it. The business of acquiring a telephone for it assumed a symbolic importance. Like many other things at that time, the instruments were in short supply, and the college administration would or could do nothing to procure one. Happily, my friend Francis Listowel had obtained the office of Postmaster General, and by appealing to him I had a telephone installed. From then on everything went well. I replaced the Greek lady by the much better qualified Stuart Hampshire, who was to succeed me in the Chair. Richard Wollheim, its present holder, joined us a few years later. My pupils made up in enthusiasm and often in ability for their shortage in number. When their number increased, I was able to appoint more lecturers. In time the department acquired its own secretary, the devoted and efficient Miss Lindsay Darling. Its territory expanded until it came to occupy a house in Gordon Square. Altogether I count the thirteen years that I was to spend at University College as a most happy period in my professional life.

My appointment there started in the autumn of 1946, just before my thirty-sixth birthday. I had resigned my Fellowship at Wadham but because my successor, Ian Crombie, was not immediately free to come, I taught there for another term besides doing some teaching in London. Though I had spent only a short time in the college, I was very sorry to leave it. When the Senior Common Room servant, the imposing Mr Minns, asked me why I was going, I said that it was to take a better job. 'What could be better,' he said, 'than being Dean of Wadham?' – a reproach to which I found no answer. I felt it as a return of good for evil when some years later the college made me an Honorary Fellow.

When he learned that I was leaving Oxford for London, Hugh Trevor-Roper, fearing, as it proved correctly, that I should succumb to the pleasures of London life, wrote me a charming letter in which he said that whereas he had no chance of becoming a second Gibbon, I should not too lightly sacrifice my own prospect of emulating Hume. So high a comparison pleased and flattered me, but I already knew that I did not deserve it. I was old enough to realize that philosophically I was 'not Prince Hamlet nor was meant to be', though I still had pretensions to being something more than 'an attendant lord'. What I have achieved since is for others to estimate, but if I could be thought even to have played Horatio to Russell's Hamlet, I should consider it glory enough.

Index

Accra 265-6
Algiers 270-3, 274-5
Alington, Dr C. A. 42, 48, 50, 54-5, 114
Alison, Barley 271, 282
Allen, Rex 219
All Souls, Fellowship of 122, 125
Altamira 74
America 206-14, 249-63
Analysis 151
'Analytic Movement in Contemporary British Philosophy, The' (A.J.A.) 165
Andrewes, Antony 159-60, 188
Arendt, Frau 222-3
Ascham St Vincent's School 23-5, 26, 31
Association for Homosexual Law Reform 70
'Atomic Propositions' (A.J.A.) 151
Attlee, Clement 286
Auden, Wystan H. 81, 186, 257, 258
Austin, Bunny 66
Austin, J. L. 151-2, 160-1, 163-4, 220-1, 295, 307
Ayer (Switzerland) 13
Ayer, Charles (uncle) 20
Ayer, Jules Louis Cyprien (father) 13, 14, 16, 17, 18, 65, 66-7
Ayer, Julian David (son) 219, 222, 235, 254, 263
Ayer, Kenneth (cousin) 20, 66, 239
Ayer, Nicolas Louis Cyprien (grandfather) 13-14
Ayer, Reine (*née* Citroën, later Vance) (mother) 13, 14, 16, 17, 18-19, 30, 68-9, 167-8, 239
Ayer, Renée (*née* Lees) 67-8, 69-70, 74, 90, 92, 93, 101-2, 103, 109-11, 122, 123, 126-7, 137, 138, 140, 148, 159, 168, 174, 178, 201, 205, 206, 219, 222, 234-5, 244, 247, 255, 262, 263
Ayer, Sophie Henriette (*née* Raetz) (grandmother) 14, 19, 31

Ayer, Valerie Jane (daughter) 175-6, 222, 235, 254, 255, 256, 292

Bacall, Lauren 261
Bamborough, John 292
Bankhead, Tallulah 95
Barnes, Dr 209
Bataille, Georges 288
Beazley, J. D. 145-6
Beckett, Sir Martyn 237
Bell, Clive 54
Bell, Willie 226
Bentham, Jeremy 310
Bérard, Bébé 249
Berlin, Isaiah 97-9, 111, 119, 126, 148, 153-4, 160, 188, 190, 194, 230, 258, 293
Bertaux, Pierre 277, 278
Berthe (aunt) 19-20, 28, 66, 239
Bick, Mr 17, 97
Bidault, Georges 269
Birley, Robert 56
Black, Max 150, 156, 212
Bouchet de Fareins, Nicole 283
Bowen, Elizabeth 202
Bower, Tony 257, 259, 286
Bowra, Maurice 98-101, 104, 190, 191, 281, 290, 291, 292
Bradley, F. H. 202
Brains Trust, The 302
Braithwaite, Richard 121, 124, 150
Breton, André 256-7
British Security Co-ordination 251
Britton, Karl 150
Broad, C. D. 79, 117-18, 121, 124
Broadcasting 304
Brook, Robin 25, 46, 267
Brooke, Tim 252, 261
Brown, Dr 152
Bryce, Ivar 252
Buchan, Alastair 192
Buckmaster, Colonel 267

Index

Bull-fighting 73, 108, 123
Burgess, Guy 59, 252
Burrows, Bernard 35, 138

Calderón, Pedro 120
Cambridge 241-2
Cambridge School of Analysis 117, 150-1, 156
Cameron, Alan 202
Camus, Albert 284
Canning Club 94, 108
Carnap, Rudolf 130-1, 156-7, 162, 164, 211
Carnwath, Andrew 35, 43
Carritt, E. F. 95, 186
Carritt, Gabriel 186
'Case for Behaviourism, The' (A.J.A.) 139
Cassirer, Ernst 152
Caterham 225-30
Cavendish, Andrew, 11th Duke of Devonshire 232
Chaban-Delmas, J. M. P. 273
Cheetham, John 58, 60, 85, 102
Cherwell, 1st Viscount see Lindemann, F. A.
Chicago 211
Chilver, Guy 93, 188
Christ Church, Oxford 75, 83, 87-90, 140, 141-2, 158, 161, 217-18, 231
Churchill, Randolph 51-2, 57, 85, 186, 272
Citroën, André 15
Citroën, Barend Roelof 15
Citroën, David (formerly Dorus) (grandfather) 13, 15-16, 17, 18, 20, 22, 27, 32-3, 64, 65, 69, 103-4, 112, 114, 126, 167, 172-3
Citroën, Joseph Barend 15
Citroën, Karel (cousin) 14, 15
Citroën, Reine see Ayer, Reine
Citroën, Roelof Barend 15
Citroën, Sarah (née Rozelaar) (grandmother) 15, 103
'Claims of Philosophy, The' (A.J.A.) 303-4
Cleveland, Ohio 213
Clive, Lewis 85
Clive, Nigel 280
Cocteau, Jean 283
Coghill, Nevill 206
Cohen, Morris 208
Cole, G. D. H. 188
Collingwood, R. G. 78-9, 82, 159, 166, 289
Communism 186-7, 245, 268, 285
Concept of Mind, The (Ryle) 296
Condemned Playground, The (Connolly) 203-4
Connolly, Cyril 23, 48, 83, 142, 203, 247-9, 270

Connolly, Jeannie 203, 257
Conquest, Robert 190
Conseil National de la Résistance 268, 269
Cooke, Alistair 170
Cooper, Lady Diana 31, 282
Cooper, Duff, 1st Viscount Norwich 280, 282
Cooper, Martin 104-6, 107, 127, 137, 138, 201
Cornforth, Maurice 156
Crawshay-Williams, Rupert 300, 302-3, 307
Critique of Pure Reason (Kant) 81, 264
Crossman, Richard 154
Cummer, Margery 252
Cummings, E. E. 195-201, 206-7, 208-9, 214, 256
Cummings, Marion (née Morehouse) 195, 196

D'Alembert, Jean 176
D'Arcy, Fr M. C. 89, 177
Darkness at Noon (Koestler) 245
Darling, Lindsay 311
Deakin, William 147, 251, 252-3, 272, 292
De Gaulle, General Charles 268-9, 271, 277-8
De la Tour, Bobby 226
Delmer, Isabel 288, 289
Dickson, Lovat 219
Dietrich, Marlene 101, 272
Dillwyn, Colin 218, 233
Dismore, Major 267
Dodds, E. R. 99, 231
Dodds-Parker, Col Douglas 271, 275
D'Orziat, Gabrielle 283
Douglas, Norman 87
Drin, Francette 283
Duncan-Jones, Austin 150, 151, 155
Dundas, Robin 76, 81-2, 83, 113, 142, 193, 194, 290
Dunne, J. W. 96-7
Dyall, Valentine 93

Egerton, Tom 226
Eimi (Cummings) 196-7
Einstein, Albert 144-5, 209
Eliot, T. S. 202-3
Elwes, Simon 236, 240
Empson, William 220
Encyclopaedia of Unified Science, The 129
Enemies of Promise (Connolly) 23, 48, 20
Enormous Room, The (Cummings) 197-8
Eton College 31-2, 34-61
Euston, Hugh 226
Existentialism 80, 284, 285

Feigh, Herbert 216

314

Feiling, Keith 81, 218
Fielding, Xan 274
Films 101, 135, 148, 169-70, 226, 260, 288
Firbank, Thomas 226
Follett, John 272
Foot, M. R. D. 280
Fortes, Meyer 266
Foster, Michael 76, 80-1, 112, 121, 146, 193, 215, 224, 296-7
Foundations of Empirical Knowledge, The (A.J.A.) 219-21, 222
France 28, 67, 110, 175, 276-89
Franco, Francisco 178
Frank, Philipp 216
Frankfurter, Felix 158, 162, 208, 210, 214
'Freedom and Necessity' (A.J.A.) 303
Fresnay, Pierre 282

Galitzine, Prince George 227, 236
Gallie, Ian 190, 280-1
Gates, Sylvester 158
Gellner, Ernest 294
George III 36
Giacometti, Alberto 288
Glanusk, Wilfred Bailey, 3rd Baron 237
Gödel, Kurt 133
Godley, Mr and Mrs F. 234-5, 254-6, 262, 263
Goff, Bruce 236, 237
Gold, Mr 179, 182, 183
Gollancz, Victor 154, 165, 219, 297, 298
Goodbye to All That (Graves) 87
Gordon-Duff, Jean 261
Gordon-Walker, Patrick 146-7, 185, 188, 192, 213, 218
Grace, Mr 40
Graham, Andrew 148, 236
Graham-Harrison, Francis 148, 215, 220
Grammaire Comparée de la Langue Française (N.L.C. Ayer) 13-14
Grant, Gregor 43
Grant-Bailey, Mr 146
Gray, Eric 224, 227, 236, 238
Guards, regiments of 227-8

Hadfield, Dehra (later Ayer) 32, 167, 172
Halban, Aline (later Berlin) 293
Halban, Hans 293
Haldane, J. B. S. 308, 309
Hallett, H. F. 308
Halpern, Alexander 252
Halpern, Salome 252
Hampshire, Stuart 160, 236, 311
Hardy, G. H. 241-2
Harris, C. R. S. (Reggie) 124
Harrod, Roy 84, 119, 142, 146, 161, 177, 217, 219, 307
Hauser, Frank 293

Hayward, John 202
Hedley, David 59-60, 127
Hegel, G. W. F. 257
Heidegger, Martin 285
Hempel, Carl 216
Highet, Gilbert 108-9, 119, 148, 207, 252-3
Hobhouse, Christopher 51
Hofmannsthal, Elizabeth von (*née* Paget) 259
Hofmannsthal, Raimund von 258-9
Hogg, Neil 35
Hogg, Quintin (Baron Hailsham) 35, 47, 125, 185
Holland, 68
Holloway, Betty (*née* Ayer) (aunt) 20, 64, 167
Holloway, Doris (cousin) 20
Holloway, Jack (cousin) 20, 32, 64, 173, 239
Hook, Sidney 208
Hope, Lord John 232
Hope-Wallace, Philip 25-6
Howard, Bunty 252
Hume, D. 116
Husserl, Edward 285
Hutchison, Colonel 267
Hyde, Montgomery 252

Intelligent Woman's Guide to Socialism and Capitalism, The (Shaw) 62-3

Jackson, Sergeant 221, 225
James, M. R. 55-6
James, William 78, 118
Jay, Douglas 188
Joachim, Harold 77, 215
Joad, C. E. M. 201, 300, 301-2
Joba, Jean 283
Johnson, Patricia 201
Johnson, Patrick 201
Johnson, Dr Samuel 65, 100, 136, 237
Jones, Frau 127-8, 138
Joseph, H. W. B. 78, 99, 144
Jouvet, Louis 283
Jowett Society 96, 119
Juan, Prince 72
Judd, Michael 190, 261
Juhos, Bela von 133

Kant, Immanuel 81, 264
Karloff, Boris 181
Keeley, T. C. 291
Keeling, S. V. 311
Keynes, J. Maynard 81, 124
Kingsford, Clara (*née* Ayer) (aunt) 20, 239
Kingsford, Donald (cousin) 21, 64, 173, 239
Kingsford, Madge (cousin) 21

Index

Kingsford, Reginald 20
Kirwan, Celia (*née* Paget) 306
Klibansky, Raymond 153
Koestler, Arthur 245, 262, 307
Koestler, Mamaine 306, 307
Kraft, Victor 133

Lakin-Smith, William 71
Landes, Roger 278
Langford, C. H. 212, 213
Langley, Noel 252
Language, Truth and Logic (A.J.A.) 154-6,
   162, 165, 215, 244, 297-9
Laughton, Charles 194-5
Lawrence, D. H. 86
Leatham, Colonel 'Chico' 223, 235
Lees, Colonel 67, 173-4, 175
Lees, Hisako 173-4, 175
Lees, Renée *see* Ayer, Renée
Legris, Jacques 286
Leibowitz, Rene 288
Leigh, Peter, 4th Baron Newton 183
Leigh-Fermor, Patrick 226
Lenin, V. I. 129, 130
Levy, Ben 252
Lewis, C. I. 212, 213
Lewis, C. S. 296-7
Lewis, Jock 223
Lezard, Julian ('Lizzie') 274-5
Limoenman, Jacob Moses 15
Lindemann, F. A. (later 1st Viscount
   Cherwell) ('The Prof') 142, 143-4, 147,
   163, 177, 193, 217, 281
Lindsay, A. D. 185
Ling, Michael 236
Linguistic philosophy 132, 295
Listowel, Francis Hare, 5th Earl of 244,
   263, 311
Llewellyn, Richard (R. Ll. Lloyd) 236,
   272
Logical Structure of the World, The (Carnap)
   130
Longden, Robert P. 76, 83, 84, 146,
   224
Lourdes 175
Lowe, John 218-19, 290
Loy, Myrna 258

Macartney, Wilfred 245
Macaulay, Rose 204-5
McColgan, Kathleen 246, 269
MacDonald, Dwight 208
Macdonald, Margaret 150
Mcdougall, Jack 54
Mace, C. A. 151
MacInnes, Helen 109, 148, 253
McKenna, David 35
McKenna, Michael 35, 56

McKeon, Richard 211
Mackinnon, Donald 160
Maclean, Fitzroy 60
Macmillan, Harold 273
Macmurray, John 307
Macnabb, Donald 160, 195
MacNeice, Louis 94
Malraux, André 277, 283-4
Mangeot, Sylvain 148
Marie (aunt) 20, 66
Marsden, H. K. 48-9, 50, 58, 114
Marshall, Bruce 267
Martineau, Richard 48, 54
Maschwitz, Eric 252
Masterman, J. C. 142-3, 146, 218, 290
Maxim's 281
Meadow Players 293
Medawar, Peter 294
Merleau-Ponty, Maurice 285
Metaphysics and Common Sense (A.J.A.) 221
Miller, Lee 246, 286
Milligan (scout) 88
Mind and the World-Order (Lewis) 151
Monsash, Henry 179, 180
Moore, G. E. 54, 117, 119, 125, 149-50,
   157, 161, 217, 223, 281
Moore, George 106
Moral Science Club, Cambridge 120, 121,
   124, 306
Morehouse, Marion 195, 196
Moss, Bella 102
Moss, Sergt-Major 225
Mosley, Sir Oswald 185, 188
Moulin, Jean 268
Muggeridge, Malcolm 272-3
Mure, Geoffrey 152
Murray, Gilbert 145
Myres, J. N. L. 147

Naess, Arne 216
Nagel, Ernest 208, 256
Nation, The 259, 260
Neumann, John von 209
Neurath, Otto 115, 129, 130-1, 133, 134,
   164, 216
New York 206-8, 251-62
Nicod, Jean 119
Noval y Cagigal, Señor 71
Noyes, Alfred 176-7

Officers Training Corps, Eton 50-2
Olivier, Laurence 286
'On the Scope of Empirical Knowledge'
   (A.J.A.) 216
Orwell, George 286-7, 300
Oughterson, Miss 49-50
Owen, S. G. 145-6
Oxford 75-101, 104-13, 139-63, 166

Page, Denys 145, 146
Pakenham, Elizabeth, Countess of Longford (*née* Harman) 159, 185
Pakenham, Frank, 7th Earl of Longford 159, 184, 185, 188, 224-5, 230, 247-8
Paris 67, 68, 280, 281-9
Parr, James 37, 85, 148
Pater, Walter 106-7
Peace Ballot 177
Peacock, T. L. 87
Peck, Anthony 215
Peers, Allison 69, 73
Peirce, C. S. 118
Penrose, Roland 246
Perry, Fred 66
Phenomenology 80, 285
Philippe, Gérard 284
Phillips, Rodney 299, 303
Pirandello, Luigi 64
Playfair, Edward 93
Playfair, Giles 95, 108, 252
Poincaré, Henri 119
Polemic 299-300, 302, 303, 306
Popper, Karl 129, 154, 164, 193
Positivism, Logical 116, 121, 131, 134, 140, 156, 163
Powell, Richard 227, 236, 237
Pragmatism 118
Price, H. H. 78-9, 161, 215, 219, 281
Prichard, H. A. 77-8, 152, 166
Private Lives (Coward) 74
Problem of Knowledge, The (A.J.A.) 283
Pryce-Jones, Alan 138

Quennell, Peter 127
Quine, W. V. 128, 131, 134, 137, 162, 213

Rabat 273
Ramsey, F. P. 115, 118, 165
Ravello 275
Rees, Goronwy 107, 125, 136, 176, 201, 241
Rees, Margaret (*née* Morris) 241
Reid, Louis Arnaud 308, 309
Reid, Mr 179
Reilly, Patrick 282
Reiniger, Professor 133
Renshaw, Mickey 237
Republic (Plato) 71, 80-1
Resistance movements, French 267-8, 273, 277
Richards, Brooks 271, 276, 279-80, 282
Richmond, Va. 209-10
Roberts, Wilfrid 269-70
Romains, Jules 109
Ross, Sir David 308
Rothschild, Alfred 14, 16, 17
Rothschild, Guy de 261-2, 281

Rowse, A. L. 188
Russell, Bertrand, 3rd Earl 53-4, 111, 117, 149, 164, 184, 209, 214-15, 216, 300-2, 307
Russell, Dora 111
Russell, Eric 147
Russell, Peter (*née* Spence) 214, 215
Ryle, Gilbert 76-7, 79-80, 84, 111, 115, 118, 119-20, 121, 146, 147, 148, 150, 151, 166, 215-16, 217, 218, 223, 236, 290, 293, 296, 297

St Croix, Geoffrey de 66
Samuel, Tony 251, 253
Sandhurst 230-6
Sandown Park 236-40
Sanjurjo, General 123
Sartre, Jean-Paul 284, 303
Sceptical Essays (Russell) 53-4
Schiller, F. C. S. 118, 217
Schlick, Moritz 121, 122, 128, 133, 134
Schnitzler, Arthur 136
Scholz, Professor 217
Schriften zur wissenschaftliche Weltauffassung 132
Sense-data 117, 151, 155, 220, 281
Shackleton, Sir Ernest 67
Shapiro, Meyer 207-8, 256
Sheffer, H. M. 98, 213
Simenon, Georges 171
Six Characters in Search of an Author (Pirandello) 63-4
Slater, Humphrey (Hugh) 299-300, 303
Slezak, Leo 137
Smeaton, Amethe 131
Smith, J. A. 77, 144, 152
Spain 69, 71-3, 104, 122-4
Spanish Civil War 177-8
Sparrow, John 125
Speaight, Hugh 95
Spearman, Professor 309
Special Operations Executive (SOE) 246, 251, 253-4, 260, 262
Spender, Stephen 95, 184, 248, 286
Stace, W. T. 209
Starr, Colonel George 277, 278
Stebbing, Susan 117, 150-1, 156, 157-8, 164, 165
Stein, Gertrude 287-8
Stephen, J. K. 45
Stephens, David 86, 148
Stephenson, William 252
Stern, Jimmy 257
Stern, Tanya 257-8
Stevens, C. E. ('Tom Brown') 82, 113, 220
Strachey, John 188
Sumner-Boyd, Hilary 140-1

Index

Sutherland, Moira 306

Tarbes 174-5
Tarski 164-5
Taylor, Frank 147, 194
'Terminology of Sense-data, The' (A.J.A.) 281
Thomas, Merlin 292-3
Thring, Edward 37
Todd, Olivier 284
Toklas, Alice B. 287, 288
Tomlin, E. W. F. 165
Toronto 260
Tottenham Hotspur F.C. 26-7
Toynbee, Anne 247-8
Toynbee, Philip 183, 187, 233, 247-8, 249, 286
Tractatus Logico-Philosophicus (Wittgenstein) 115, 119, 129, 158, 304-5
Tragedy (Lucas) 72
Trevin Towers, Eastbourne 64, 65
Trevor-Roper, Hugh 191-3, 231, 236, 293, 312
Trott, Adam von 253
Tzara, Michel L. T. 288

University College, London 307-12
Urmson, James O. 290

Van Druten, John 63
Vance, Richard 168, 239
Veidt, Conrad 101, 136
Verifiability, principle of 116, 156, 297-8
'Verification and Experience' (A.J.A.) 176
Vienna 127-8
Vienna Circle (Wiener Kreis) 121-2, 128-34, 140, 157, 164, 216-17

Wade-Gery, H. T. 113
Wadham College, Oxford 280, 291, 311-12
Wagner, Anthony 47
Waismann, Friedrich 132-3, 216
Walker-Smith, Derek 94, 112
Wall game 44-5

Walls Have Mouths (Macartney) 245
Washington, D.C. 210-11
Waugh, Evelyn 89, 99, 272
Webster, T. B. L. 85, 242
Weldon, T. D. 152
Westminster City Council 182, 183
Westminster Housing Association 181
Wheatley, Fred 88, 291
Whistler, Rex 236
White, H. J. 83-4, 193
White Rose Society 95
Whitehead, A. N. 162-3, 214, 275
Whitney-Smith, Charles 148, 282
Wiener Kreis see Vienna Circle
Wiesengrund-Adorno, Teddy 153
Wilder, Thornton 248
Willert, Paul 244-5, 283
Williams, A. T. P. 193, 217
Willis, Gaspard 38
Willis, Robert 60, 85, 113, 148, 165
Wilson, John Cook 77
Wisdom, J. O. 150
Wisdom, John 150, 156, 220, 295, 305, 306
Wittgenstein, Ludwig 115-16, 119-21, 124, 130, 132, 223, 242, 304-6
Wollheim, Richard 311
Woolf, Virginia 204, 248
Woozley, A. D. 160
Wordsworth, Andrew 60, 86, 89, 97, 99, 102, 111, 119, 148
Wren, Christopher 252
Wright, Sir Almroth 86
Wright, Armine 86, 148

Yeats, W. B. 105
Yeo-Thomas, Wing-Comdr F. E. 267
Young, J. Z. 308, 309
Young Woodley (Van Druten) 63
'Your Westminster' (A.J.A.) 181-2

Zaehner, Robin 190-1, 192, 241, 246, 293
Zilsel, Edgar 133
Zuckerman, Solly 194, 195, 215, 283, 293